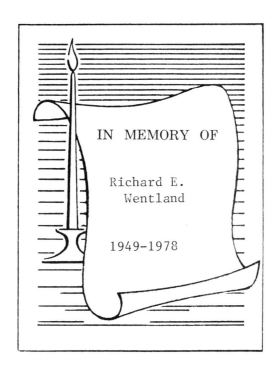

IN MEMORY OF

Richard E.
Wentland

1949-1978

History and Will

This volume is sponsored by the
CENTER FOR CHINESE STUDIES
University of California, Berkeley

HISTORY and WILL

Philosophical Perspectives of Mao Tse-tung's Thought

FREDERIC WAKEMAN, JR.

University of California Press
Berkeley, Los Angeles, London

University of California Press
Berkeley and Los Angeles, California
University of California Press, Ltd.
London, England

Copyright © 1973, by
The Regents of the University of California
Paperback Edition 1975
ISBN 0-520-02907-0
Library of Congress Catalog Card Number: 75-170722

Printed in the United States of America
Designed by Jean Peters

This book is dedicated to the three men
whose influence shaped it most:

my father, Frederic Wakeman
my teacher, Joseph R. Levenson
my friend, Irwin Scheiner

Acknowledgments

This book was written while I received sabbatical and research funds from the Center for Chinese Studies of the University of California, Berkeley and from the American Council of Learned Societies. My research assistants, Jonathan Grant and Edward Hammond, provided me with both materials and an opportunity to discuss some of the issues dealt with here. Carolyn Grant, who edited the original versions of the manuscript with such a keen eye, comes close to deserving a collaborator's place on the title page, because so many of her thematic suggestions are reflected in the contents. My colleague, John Starr, generously offered invaluable documentary help with many of the Mao papers. I am also very grateful to those members of the Chinese history colloquia at Stanford University, of the Institute of International Affairs at the University of Washington, and of the Research Scholars Group at Berkeley who read and discussed portions of the manuscript. Finally, I owe particular thanks to those fellow scholars who so helpfully scrutinized the first draft: Ch'en Shih-hsiang, Jack Dull, David Keightley, Angus McDonald, Nicholas Riasanovsky, Moss Roberts, Irwin Scheiner, Tu Wei-ming, Jonathan Unger, Frederic Wakeman, Sr., and Judith Whitbeck.

Preface

Like most foreign students of China, I was astounded when the Great Proletarian Cultural Revolution erupted in 1966. As reports filtered through to outsiders, as *Asahi Shimbun* correspondents began reprinting big-character posters, as trussed corpses floated down the Pearl River to Hong Kong, it seemed as though the People's Republic had completely lost its political bearings. Partly a failure of communication, partly a failure of vision, our perceptions were as confused as the events we dimly witnessed. Then, as consistency slowly emerged, it became clear that Mao Tse-tung had both discovered and declared class war within his own Communist Party. Go to Peking University and face the Cultural Revolution in person, he ordered his party secretaries in July of 1966. "Students will surround you. Let them. You will be surrounded as soon as you begin to talk to them. More than a hundred people have been beaten up at the school of broadcasting. This is the beauty of our age. . . ." * Some of the very same cadres who had marched alongside Mao from Kiangsi to Yenan in 1935 were now told that adolescents, born long after the Civil War, made more effective revolutionaries. "Trouble making," Mao declared, "is revolution." †

To me at least, such statements were a staggering revelation. How

* Mao Tse-tung, "Talk at the Reception of Secretaries of Big Regions and Members of the Central Cultural Revolution Team—Notes for Circulation" (July 22, 1966), in Jerome Ch'en, ed., *Mao Papers: Anthology and Bibliography* (London: Oxford University Press, 1970), pp. 26–30.

† Mao Tse-tung, "Talk at the Reception of Secretaries, Second Version" (July 21, 1966), in Ch'en, *Mao Papers*, p. 33.

could any Marxist–Leninist so laconically abandon his own party, vanguard of the proletariat and bearer of the socialist consciousness? Where did Mao himself derive the certainty that his conception of ongoing revolution was correct?

Perhaps because I knew so little then of the sources of Mao's thought, I found it very difficult to reconcile this visionary with the pragmatic revolutionary of the 1930s. To be sure, other scholars like Stuart R. Schram, Jerome Ch'en, Maurice Meisner, and Benjamin I. Schwartz had already carefully analyzed the "Prometheanism," "voluntarism," "populism," and "Jacobinism" of Mao Tse-tung's thought. But all those "isms," however admirable the research and thought that detailed them, left me dissatisfied. Stuart Schram, for instance, had shown precisely how Mao's view of Communist society ("something which does not necessarily represent the ultimate destiny of humanity") was the product of a certain "dialectical bent" in his thought. Yet how was the bent determined in the first place? Like Schram, I felt that, "The quest for the antecedents of the dialectical bent of Mao's thought is a fascinating —though perhaps insoluble—problem in intellectual history." *

True, it was possible to create a consistent political portrayal of Mao Tse-tung in strategic revolutionary terms alone. But such a depiction remained hazy when it came to explaining the buttresses of Mao's theory of permanent revolution. Was he an existentialist, stepping boldly off into the void? Was he a Marxist romantic, resolving theory with a mystique of praxis? Or was he even—as some have gingerly suggested —a Taoist dialectician, replacing *yin* and *yang* with antagonistic contradictions?

I found it impossible to answer these questions directly. One could, of course, refuse to take Maoism seriously. Why—just because Mao Tse-tung led the Communist Party to victory in 1949—ascribe theoretical wisdom to a revolutionary pragmatist? Why confuse successful strategy with intellectual subtlety by believing that his famous essays, "On Practice" and "On Contradiction," were anything more than an emulation of Stalin's theoretical pretensions? Why complicate the simple by transforming Mao Tse-tung into a Marxist philosopher? After all, Mao was first and foremost a revolutionary who had discovered a mission even before he possessed the socialist vocabulary for it. But, gladly conceding that "the battlefield was [Mao's] school," I also assumed that conscious revolutionary action is informed by theory. That

---

* Stuart R. Schram, "Mao Tse-tung and the Theory of the Permanent Revolution," *China Quarterly*, 46:225–226.

ideology, in turn, is supported by a scaffold of assumptions of which the actor himself is often barely aware. The genesis of those assumptions can sometimes be directly traced, especially when the person in question is intellectually introspective. Mao was usually not.

Consequently, I found myself facing a problem in modern Chinese intellectual history which transcended Mao Tse-tung. Because his most significant problematic was the contradiction between objective history and subjective will, I would have to fathom the fundamental assumptions about man and nature which he shared with many of his contemporaries. These assumptions—which constituted the uniqueness of the Marxist revolution in China—remained inarticulable unless they were placed in historical perspective. Nevertheless, simple contrast was fatuous. Sweeping generalizations ("Eastern man accommodates himself to nature; western man strives against it") attributed timeless, and therefore historically meaningless, characteristics to particular cultures. They also relied on universal qualities when there existed no concretely universal language to bridge the gap between those cultures.

To be sure, any specific national language was, in Antonio Gramsci's words, a "continuous process of metaphors." As he once wrote, "Language is at the same time a living thing and a museum of the fossils of life and civilization." * Therefore, the one language which Mao knew carried both the immanent ideas of his Chinese past and the neologisms of his Marxist present. If we read that language from both perspectives, we can begin to understand some of Maoism's basic assumptions. We can also better comprehend the way in which foreign and native ideas melded in the thought of twentieth-century Chinese revolutionaries, because Marxism was not only historically important for them; it is heuristically instructive for us. By its own pretension a universal truth, Marxism takes national forms, so that it combines universality and particularity in such a way as to permit the kind of analysis which many other "languages" deny. In fact, as "Maoism," Marxism became a hybrid language of its own in modern China.

In order to expose that hybrid quality, the first section of this book consists of montages. A few concern Mao alone: his fear of revolutionary retrogression, his personal cult, his attitudes toward intellectuals, and so forth. But most of the synchronic montages pose Mao and his policies alongside other political examples, often by way of disanalogy. Some of these are historically concrete, like the Ch'ing village covenant

* Antonio Gramsci, *The Modern Prince and Other Writings* (New York: International Publishers, 1957), pp. 110–111.

system which may even have inspired similar institutions in modern China. Others are conceptually abstract, like Rousseau's Great Legislator, or even metaphorical, like Gramsci's myth–prince. The montages are therefore imagistic: first, by looking through the guises of Mao as though he were a transparent overlay to the theory of government as such; and second, by evaluating Mao's own political symbols which frequently correspond to the popular Chinese imagery of revolution. For, Mao is as much myth-maker as politician, expressing through allegory and symbol the yearnings of his people.

The montages are designed to suggest the two languages of Western and Chinese Marxism. To elucidate their differences I have employed a philosophical vocabulary—not because I regard it as a transcendental language of its own, but because it affords a more articulate mode of contrast. The next several sections of the book therefore present a logically coherent exposition of the philosophical foundations of Sino–Western thought. A reader solely interested in political Maoism may find these distracting. Why, after all, delineate the evolution of K'ang Yu-wei's theories when Mao and his contemporaries so misjudged them? Here, I contend that the history of ideas is illuminating as such. Although the intricacies of K'ang Yu-wei's thought were not known to Mao, K'ang's monistic concept of *jen* (humaneness) and his theory of the three stages of human history permeated the thinking of Mao Tse-tung's entire generation, breaking the tyranny of Confucian relationships to prepare the way for even more radical forms of social criticism. It is partly in this spirit of K'ang's pervasive importance, then, that I devote so much space to him.

But why also fully explicate the philosophy of Immanuel Kant just because Mao Tse-tung considered himself a "Kantian Idealist" as a youth? Mao, in fact, did not even know the works of Kant firsthand. Instead, he learned about that philosophy from a book by Friedrich Paulsen—a secondary Neo-Kantian who chose to emphasize only some strains of the original philosophy. Were we solely interested in the quality of Mao's early idealism, surely a study of Paulsen's transmission alone would suffice. Why return to the original source? The most obvious answer is the simplest: ideas have to be defined in context. Here, Mao Tse-tung's intellectual environment is the object of study, but its components are more significant for us when we see them move from their primary setting (which must be understood for itself) to the new context. Not only does this tell us a great deal about the force of the *blosse Idee;* it also—to use a physical image—establishes the fields in which the particles move. One of the primary assertions of *History and Will,* for example, is that Mao Tse-tung's dialectic was not truly Marxian because Chinese metaphysical constructions did not possess the universal ontological categories of European rationalism. The bare statement of such a proposition hardly demonstrates its truth. To render the meaning intelligible, therefore, I have imposed upon the reader my understanding of the nature of those categories by retracing the development of transcendental logic. Consequently, the exposition of Kant's thought in this book is designed to show just how adamantine are the categories behind Western Marxism, whereas Maoism employs the identical integers with more resilience and flexibility because of a different intellectual context. Much of *History and Will,* therefore, tries to demonstrate the primary qualities of Western and Chinese thought about man and nature by taking the reader through segments of each world of ideas rather than simply by declaring that the differences exist.

In the end, I depend heavily upon the reader to draw these intellectual segments together for himself. Every author hopes that his audience will help construct the final synthesis of his work by retaining the accumulated levels of an argument until the structure is completed. But *History and Will* presumes more because it is not built up in this manner. Rather, it is a series of essays which are thematically cohesive but not discursively sequential. Having finished one segment, the reader is asked to hold on to the image of that argument until it can be placed alongside another. That is, the book tries to present a group of reflections as in a hall of mirrors. Each of these is different, but they finally converge in the single focus of the Cultural Revolution. At that moment, when history (bureaucratic routinization) and will (Mao's permanent revolution) conflicted so dramatically, the reflections were united at last.

F.W.
Berkeley, 1972

Contents

PART ONE

Montages

The east is red
The sun is rising
In China appears Mao Tse-tung

Tung-fang hung

1

The Revolutionary Founder

Mao Tse-tung's singular prominence within the Chinese Communist Party was not quickly won. His share of leadership was secured during the famous Tsun-yi conference of January 1935; but it was not until 1942, after seven years of ideological compromise and political maneuvering, that he and his thought dominated the party alone.[1] However, the image which his hagiographers project has been far more dramatic: a prescient revolutionary whose unwavering vision of the sole path to victory carried him to a stunning triumph over far lesser rivals. Lenin may be extolled for his ability to compromise and to adjust personal beliefs as the situation demanded. Mao is praised for his unswerving commitment to an individual and constant perception of the dynamics of modern Chinese history.

One reason for this particular image of stubborn integrity was Mao's initial pragmatism. The strategies he claimed—reliance upon peasant radicalism in 1927, guerrilla warfare during 1933, and the decision to head north to fight the Japanese (*pei-shang k'ang-jih*) in 1935— usually conflicted with orthodox Marxism–Leninism as well as with Comintern instructions. Mao never adhered to these doctrines exclusively nor did he develop them singlehandedly, but he did realize sooner than any other Chinese Communist leader that revolution would be launched from the countryside by a Red Army devoted as much to mobilizing the peasantry as to waging warfare.

The history of the Chinese revolution then becomes the struggle of

Mao to emerge from the wilderness—from doctrinal isolation within his own party, and from geographical exile in the loess hills of Yenan. Cast as a prophet whose message was heeded too late for earlier victory, Mao thus appeared to carve out revolution alone, so that Communist victory became his personal triumph and twentieth-century Chinese history his story. More so even than Nikolai Lenin, Mao Tse-tung embodied—*possessed*—the revolution. Its destiny was his fate; its fulfillment, his self-realization. All of us become our own figments as we slip into the roles we project. What distinguished Mao from most was the identification of that image, that story, with history itself. It was not just because of his own mortality that Mao feared civil routinization and was obsessed by retrogression after victory. Rather, he believed that he could not make his revolutionary story permanent unless history were so, unless revolution itself became permanent.

Mao became concerned about the defeat of his revolution when the civil war was on the way to being won. On the eve of victory in 1949, he detected the likelihood of power corrupting the revolutionary purity of his comrades.

With victory certain moods may grow within the party—arrogance, the airs of a self-styled hero, inertia and unwillingness to make progress, love of pleasure and distaste for continued hard living. The flattery of the bourgeoisie may conquer the weak willed in our ranks. There may be some communists, who were not conquered by enemies with guns and were worthy of the name of heroes for standing up to these enemies, but who cannot withstand sugar-coated bullets.[2]

Victory would bring a generation of revolutionaries out of rural China and into the bourgeois metropolis; it would distance the cadres from the masses as fighters became bureaucrats. "A dangerous tendency has shown itself of late among many of our personnel—an unwillingness to share the joys and hardships of the masses, a concern for personal fame and gain."[3] Victory would also lull the Communists into believing that their struggle had finally ended with the nationwide seizure of power and the defeat of their military enemies, even though—Mao insisted—there was still a principal internal contradiction between the working class and the bourgeoisie. "After the enemies with guns have been wiped out there will still be enemies without guns; they are bound to struggle desperately against us, and we must never regard these enemies lightly. If we do not now raise and understand the problem in this way we shall commit the gravest mistake."[4]

The Korean War and its accompanying mobilization campaigns within China generated enough mass enthusiasm and party zeal to alleviate Mao's retrogression anxieties temporarily. But they returned all the more sharply after Khrushchev denounced Stalin in February of 1956. On April 5, 1956, an editorial, "On the Historical Experience of the Dictatorship of the Proletariat," appeared in *People's Daily*. Probably written by Mao himself, it warned that "if we want to avoid falling into such a [Stalinist] quagmire we must pay fullest attention to the use of the mass line method of leadership, not permitting the slightest negligence." [5] Once again, then, Mao was to underscore the uncertainty of absolute victory and the necessity of continuing class struggle. In February of 1957, he announced that there were still "remnants of the overthrown landlord and comprador classes" in China. "The class struggle is by no means over. . . . The proletariat seeks to transform the world according to its own world outlook, and so does the bourgeoisie. In this respect, the question of which will win out, socialism or capitalism, is still not really settled." [6]

Maoists would later argue that the chairman had directed these comments against Vice-Chairman Liu Shao-ch'i's by then nefarious theory that struggle was no longer necessary since the socialist transformation of the means of production had been completed by 1956.[7] But that was an afterthought. The immediate reason for Mao's concern was the convulsion in eastern Europe. If the Communist regimes of Poland and Hungary could so easily threaten to totter, what then of China's?

Mao's sensitivity to this danger was heightened by his particular historical consciousness of dynastic rise and fall. For instance, his reference during the last years of the civil war to "sugar-coated bullets" (*t'ang-tan*) was deliberately associated with the sin then known as "Liu Tsung-min thought." Liu was the notoriously rapacious general who served the peasant rebel, Li Tzu-ch'eng (1605?–1645), in 1644. After Li defeated the Ming armies outside Peking, his forces entered the capital under General Liu Tsung-min's direction, jeopardizing popular support for the new dynasty by robbing and torturing the inhabitants. Manchu troops soon expelled Li Tzu-ch'eng from the city and founded their own long-lived dynasty. The parallel between these peasant rebels and the Red Army seemed obvious to the poet Kuo Mo-jo, who published an essay on Li Tzu-ch'eng in 1944. If the Communists, like Li's men, entered the capital only to stuff themselves complacently on the riches of rule, their "dynasty" might be just as shortlived. Mao soon adopted the idea as well: "Recently we have reprinted Kuo Mo-jo's

essay on Li Tzu-ch'eng so that comrades may also take warning from
this story and not repeat the error of becoming conceited at the moment
of success." [8]

Similarly, Mao—whose boyhood heroes were emperors like Han
Wu-ti (reigned 140–87 B.C.)[9]—could not have helped but relate his
own triumph to that of a founding ruler. Like such a dynast, he must
also have been conscious of the difficulty of perpetuating that victory.
And even if Mao failed to make the connection himself, others in the
party did so for him, comparing Mao at one point to Ch'in Shih huang-ti
(reigned 221–210 B.C.), whose regime collapsed because of his heavy
demands on the people.[10] This awareness of the dynastic cycle, common
to all Chinese, was aroused in Mao by his formal education (which exposed him to Ssu-ma Kuang's *Tzu-chih t'ung-chien* [Comprehensive
mirror to aid in government]) as well as by the chivalric novels he had
memorized as a boy.[11] *The Romance of the Three Kingdoms* begins:
"Empires wax and wane; states cleave asunder and coalesce. When the
rule of Chou weakened, seven contending principalities sprang up, warring one with another until they settled down as Ch'in, and when its
destiny had been fulfilled arose Ch'u and Han to contend for the mastery. And Han was the victor." [12] Not that Mao Tse-tung feared an
identical decline for his "dynasty." But the Chinese succession of ruling
houses and the historiography they engendered did suggest that all
regimes began vigorously, inspired by the zeal of their founders, only to
give way to laxness as the political legacy was squandered away by its
heirs.*

This historical disposition must have seemed all the more universal
when Russia appeared to betray the revolution by allowing factories to
run according to Yevsey Liberman's notorious market system, by show-

---

* The connection between dynastic retrogression and revisionism was also
stressed by Lin Piao later. Addressing the Politburo in 1966, Lin examined the
issue of a capitalist restoration "from the standpoint of our national history."
For, "there are many examples in which we see that political power was lost
through coups d'état before a dynasty was established for ten, twenty, thirty, or
fifty years." Lin then cited the examples of the Ch'in, Sui, Yuan, and Ch'ing
dynasties, as well as mentioning Yuan Shih-k'ai's seizure of power from Sun
Yat-sen after the Republic was founded. "These reactionary coups d'état should
have terrified us and hastened our vigilance. Our seizure of political power has
already lasted sixteen years. Will this regime of the proletarian class be overthrown and usurped? If we are not careful enough, we shall lose our political
power." Lin Piao, "Informal Address at Politburo Meeting" (May 18, 1966),
cited in Marton Ebon, *Lin Piao: The Life and Writings of China's New Ruler*
(New York: Stein and Day, 1970), p. 255.

ing Hollywood films ("America's spiritual opium"), or by letting "bourgeois scholar tyrants" monopolize the universities and make examination marks the sole criterion for admission to advanced study.[13] "In the Soviet Union the bourgeois headquarters took shape, headed by Khrushchev. It usurped the leadership of the party and the state, and the whole country rapidly changed its color. We have to take warning when the cart in front overturns." [14]

To ensure that his party avoided revisionism, Mao told members of the working conference of the Central Committee, in January of 1962, that the party would have to follow the mass line more devotedly. It must ". . . develop democracy by encouraging and listening to criticism. . . . In short, letting other people speak will not lead to the sky falling down on us nor to one's own downfall. What will happen if we do not allow others to speak? In that case one day we ourselves will inevitably fall." [15] At about the same time, Mao also began to emphasize the possibility of a capitalist restoration in China.

Socialist society covers a fairly long historical period. In the historical period of socialism there are still classes and class contradictions and class struggle, there is the struggle between the socialist road and the capitalist road, and there is the danger of capitalist restoration. We must recognize the protracted and complex nature of this struggle and we must tighten our vigilance. . . . Otherwise a socialist country like ours will turn into its opposite and degenerate, and a capitalist restoration will take place.[16]

By May of 1963, Mao had come to feel that if the continuing class struggle were forgotten, a counterrevolutionary restoration might even transform the Chinese Communist Party into a fascist organization.[17] In fact, the party itself was perhaps already a prime source of those restorationist tendencies.

Over the next eighteen months, Mao Tse-tung developed a designation—the "capitalist road"—for this tendency within the party, as well as an epithet for party "rightists" like Liu Shao-ch'i—"those persons within the party who are in authority and are taking the capitalist road." [18] And by the autumn of 1965, the chairman was asking his own fellow Central Committee members: "What are you going to do if revisionism appears in the Central Committee? This is highly likely; this is the greatest danger." [19] Finally, on May 16, 1966, Mao actually stated in a circular, "There are persons like Khrushchev . . . who are still nestling beside us." [20]

In the past Mao had many times decided that party members needed to be reeducated.* But these rectification campaigns were basically intended to be reforms within the organization, not ideological revolutions launched from outside the party. Now, overtaken by the determination that counterrevolution was imminent, Mao confronted his party as though it were a hostile political regime. Declaring that "in order to overthrow a regime, [we] must first of all take control of the superstructure, the ideology, by preparing public opinion," [21] Mao resorted to society itself, hoping to mobilize public opinion in his favor instead of conducting a Stalinist political purge. This inclination to engage public opinion was shaped by three influences. His classical Chinese studies had stressed the necessity of morally inspiring the people in order to "renovate" them (hsin-min), his Marxist–Leninist training had sensitized him to the concept of consciousness, and his civil war years had taught him the importance of mass mobilization.

The last of these was doubtless the most decisive. But the first influence—his classical studies—suggests the traditional sources of Mao's belief in moral redemption as well as institutional precedents for the kind of public indoctrination he employed in the People's Republic. At the same time, the contrast between, say, the Ch'ing system of "village covenants" and Mao's "neighborhood pacts," reveals important differences beneath the surface similarity.

The concept of "renovating the people" (hsin-min) also meant "the new people" created by that moral inspiration. This, at least, was the significance attached to the Hsin-min hsueh-hui (The New People Study Society) founded by Mao when he was a student at Ch'ang-sha in 1917. The nomenclature was directly inspired by an earlier reform magazine, Hsin-min ts'ung-pao (The New People Magazine), edited by one of Mao's early heroes, Liang Ch'i-ch'ao (1873–1929). But the origins of the term were far more ancient. The opening lines of the Ta hsueh (Great Learning)—one of the "Four Books" all Chinese students then memorized—read: "What the Great Learning teaches, is to illustrate illustrious virtue; to renovate** the people; and to rest in the highest excellence." [22] To most Confucian literati, this passage

* Mao's technique of resolving intraparty conflict by educational methods can be traced back to the Ku-t'ien conference of 1929. It was perfected on a sweeping scale during the cheng-feng (rectification) movement of 1942 in Yenan. See Mark Selden, The Yenan Way in Revolutionary China (Cambridge: Harvard University Press, 1971), pp. 188–200.

** Originally ch'in-min (to be intimate with the people), it was changed to hsin-min (to renovate the people) by the Sung Neo-Confucianists.

stressed the gentleman's duty to inspire the passive masses by behaving as a moral exemplar. But there were also traditional institutions devised to renovate by means of a more active form of indoctrination. One of these was the *hsiang-yueh* (village covenant) system devised by the great Ming (1368–1644) philosopher, Wang Yang-ming (1472–1529). Instituted in 1518 in southern Kiangsi where Wang had suppressed a revolt, the village covenant was designed to rehabilitate rebels by drawing them back into civil society. The covenant itself reflected the assumption that evil was an antisocial act produced by degenerate customs. Although officials were ultimately responsible for maintaining *li* (propriety) among the people, the officials would not succeed in their task unless it was shared with members of local communities. Because few men were strong enough to reform themselves, Wang Yang-ming was actually trying to organize a series of moral-reinforcement societies. The inhabitants of a village covenant area were supposed to elect chiefs (*yueh-chang*) to record their daily deeds. Individual contributions paid for monthly banquet meetings. At each gathering, the assembled company pledged aloud to the ritual punctuations of drums:

From this day forth we covenant members will together reverently obey warnings and instructions. Joining our hearts and uniting our wills, we will return together to goodness. If any should be of two or three minds, openly good and secretly evil, then may the gods exterminate them.[23]

Each member's behavior during the past month was then meticulously discussed. Good deeds were ceremoniously praised; bad ones were criticized, and the miscreant was urged to kneel and recant. The essential aim of the assembly, constantly reiterated, was not to punish but to reform. When evildoing was discovered, every effort was made to help the man rather than turn him over to the judicial authorities.

If there is an evil [habit] which is difficult to change, do not report it and put the guilty one in an intolerable [situation] because that may arouse him to give full rein to his evil. The *yueh-chang* and his assistant should first urge him secretly to confess himself. The membership together [should] induce, persuade and encourage him so as to arouse his good thoughts. . . . And only after he has been unable to reform again should he be seized and handed over to the government.[24]

The *hsiang-yueh* system lapsed during the later part of the Ming. But, partly to restore civil society after the disorders of the mid-seventeenth century and partly to ensure the persistence of his dynasty, the first

Ch'ing (1644–1911) ruler, the Shun-chih emperor (1644–1661), revived the *hsiang-yueh* system when he promulgated "Six Edicts" (*Liu
yü*)* to "enlighten the people." [25] To explain these edicts, a *hsiang-
yueh* official was chosen by each community from among its *sheng-
yuan* (holders of the lowest examination degree) and virtuous elders.
Twice a month, the *hsiang-yueh* leader and his assistant were to assemble the inhabitants and read the Six Edicts, which urged the people
to be filial, to honor their elders, to live in harmony with their neighbors, to instruct and discipline their progeny, to let each man work
peacefully for his own livelihood, and to not commit crimes.

As time passed, the *hsiang-yueh* system grew more elaborate. In
1729, three more assistants were appointed to help the leader expound
the imperial maxims, and a special site in each locale was designated
a *chiang-yueh-so* (pulpit for the covenant). Moreover, the original Six
Edicts were amplified. Back in 1670, the K'ang-hsi emperor had ex-
panded the number to sixteen *Sacred Edicts* (*Sheng yü*), adding emotion and rationale to the formula. Instead of being told to "perform
filial duties to your parents," the people of China were ordered to
"perform with sincerity filial and fraternal duties in order to give due
importance to social relations." The desired social end of virtuous behavior was explained in each instance. Harmony with one's neighbors
was designed to prevent litigation, propriety was manifested to carry
out good manners, schools were to be extended and false doctrines rejected to honor learning, and so forth. Above all, increased emphasis
was placed on contentedly occupying one's proper and productive place
in society. "Hold economy in estimation in order to conserve your
money and goods." "Work diligently at your proper calling in order
to give settlement to the aims of the people." The empire's population
was thus divided into those who were its stable citizenry and those
who were its unreliables (*wu-lai-che*). It was the former upon whom
the emperor depended to "explain the laws in order to warn the ignorant and obstinate" and to serve as intermediaries between civil society and its outcasts.

The Yung-cheng emperor's (1723–1735) amplified instruction of
1724 was even more concerned with social order. His ten-thousand-
word adjuration assumed that each man was given his proper assignment by heaven and that it was his duty to adhere to that calling. "For

* The original six edicts, or admonitions, were issued by the Ming founder in
1397. See: *Huang Ming T'ai-tsu shih-lu* [Veritable Records of the Ming Emperor
T'ai-tsu] (Taipei: Photolithographic reprint, 1966), p. 3677.

if each man keep and pursue his own occupation, there will be no un-accomplished missions." The tone was ever more paternal and—ap-propriate to a period of prosperity and urban wealth—as bourgeois sounding as Guizot's *Aidez-vous et Dieu vous aidera* or Samuel Smiles' *Self Help.*

If you realize that what the court worries over and concerns itself with day and night is nothing but the affairs of the people. . . .

Even though not much is left after paying public [taxes] and private [rent], yet by gradual accumulation day after day and month after month, you can achieve an ample living for yourselves and your families, with property for your sons and grandsons to inherit.[25a]

The appeal was therefore directed toward society's primary units: its family associations were to observe order, its individuals were to get ahead on their own. The hierarchical family and the ambitious individ-ual were so encouraged, because they stood dependently obedient below the state as miniature replicas of the familistic emperor and the bureau-cratic careerist. Corporate autonomy and voluntary association were forbidden, because free-floating and egalitarian societies were illegiti-mate within the pale and therefore assumed to be illegal by intent. "Lascivious and villainous persons . . . form brotherhoods; bind themselves to one another by oath; meet in the night and disperse at the dawn; violate the laws, corrupt the age, and impose on the people, and behold! one morning the whole thing comes to light, they are seized and dealt with according to law." [25b] The (secret) societies' members had to be proscribed and punished, not because their individ-ual wills opposed the collective but because they conspired mutual defense against the political patrimony and social patriarchies.

The Ch'ing *hsiang-yueh* system lapsed during the late eighteenth century. Even though it was occasionally revived by nineteenth-century officials like Tseng Kuo-fan (1811–1872, the Hunanese statesman revered by Mao Tse-tung in his youth) to indoctrinate the peasantry with moral values, the institution had been overtaken by the Ch'ing emperors' obsession with control via hierarchy. A purely bureaucratic formation, the *hsiang-yueh* therefore lost its vitality as its passive audi-tors were treated to imperial bromides.

In fact, the late Ch'ing *hsiang-yueh* was far less like the original six-teenth-century covenant than was the socialist or patriotic pact of the early years of Mao's People's Republic. Such patriotic pacts were neighborhood organizations based on "agreements among neighbors to

observe certain standards of conduct on the grounds that interests of
state or socialist construction are involved." [26] The task of such pacts—
as well as of the ubiquitous small study groups—was to achieve not
only passive obedience but also active engagement in political issues.[27]
Members realized the import of these issues as a result of cadre leadership. Eventually, though, other means were developed for arousing
political consciousness in the masses, ways which bypassed such intermediaries.

The *Quotations from Chairman Mao Tse-tung* was first published
in May of 1964. Called the *Yü-lu,* it might be better translated as the
Proverbs, since the term *yü-lu* first came into usage during the T'ang
dynasty when Ch'an Buddhist monks wrote down their masters' preachings in the vernacular to help them preach to the masses.[28] The *Quotations from Chairman Mao Tse-tung* was originally intended for members
of the People's Liberation Army, although it was regularly handed out
as a gesture of reward to young citizens who had attained distinction
as students of the thought of Mao Tse-tung. On August 18, 1966, the
Quotations was widely distributed in public for the first time in T'ien-
an-men Square, and it quickly came to be known as *The Little Red
Book.* Over one billion copies have since been printed; and by 1967
study classes of Mao Tse-tung's thought (*Mao Tse-tung ssu-hsiang
hsueh-hsi pan*) had sprung up throughout the entire country, meeting
regularly to recite the litany of the *Yü-lu.*[29]

The *Quotations* has some of the same Samuel Smiles stress on the
importance of conscientious attitudes as had the *hsiang-yueh's Sacred
Edicts*:

What really counts in the world is conscientiousness, and the Communist
Party is most particular about being conscientious.[30]

Be resolute, fear no sacrifice, and surmount every difficulty to win victory.[31]

Diligence and frugality should be practised in running factories and shops
and all state owned, cooperative and other enterprises. The principle of
diligence and frugality should be observed in everything.[32]

Oppose extravagant eating and drinking and pay attention to thrift and
economy.[33]

Thrift should be the guiding principle.[34]

An emphasis on attitudes has always marked Mao's thought, which so
strongly values courage ("The peoples of the world must have courage,

dare to fight, and fear no hardships. . . . In this way, the world will belong to the people and all the demons will be eliminated." [35]) and effort ("Think hard!" [36]). In fact, Mao often defined a revolutionary more by his state of mind than by his class origin: not who a revolutionary is, but how a revolutionary ought to be. One must, for instance, act ". . . with complete sincerity; it is fundamentally impossible to accomplish anything in this world without a sincere attitude." [37] The *how* therefore described norms instead of goals. Although Mao Tsetung was certainly capable of speaking to specific and concrete issues, he often took the aim of action for granted, and directed himself instead to the manner of acting.

The *Quotations* may thus bear a certain attitudinal resemblance to the *Sacred Edicts,* but there the likeness ends. The *Sacred Edicts* were read *to* the people. The *Quotations* was specially designed to be read *by* them. Its attachment is to the individual rather than to a member of a microcosmic hierarchy of the empire. Instead of being engraved on stone and attached to the locale, the *Quotations* is portable, mutable, and capable of being possessed by a single man. While the *Edicts* commanded the individual to submit to a "natural" social hierarchy defined by Confucian tradition, the *Quotations* destroyed hierarchy boldly and urged every man to be his own master among a revolutionary mass whose regulating force is change, not tradition. Thus, both in physical form and in ideological content, the *Quotations* is inherently less stable than were the *Edicts.*

Perhaps this can be best demonstrated in the ambivalence toward authority implied by four main motifs of the *Quotations.* First was the drumming theme of the primacy of the masses.

To link oneself with the masses, one must act in accordance with the needs and wishes of the masses. All work done for the masses must start from their needs and not from the desire of any individual, however well intentioned. . . . There are two principles here: one is the actual needs of the masses rather than what we fancy they need, and the other is the wishes of the masses, who must make up their own minds instead of our making up their minds for them.[38]

Along with the paradox of attributing personal independence to mass man, of realizing individual fulfillment through collective immersion, there was the momentary fusion of party and populace. Hence the second motif: the *Sacred Edicts* were addressed only to the people, but the *Quotations* applied to both cadres and citizens. In fact, the reference to the masses (above) was originally delivered to party members alone, so that the *Quotations* had at times the flavor of a *shou-ts'e,* a manual for official use. "Place problems on the table. This should be done not only by the 'squad leader' but by the committee members too. Do not talk behind people's backs. Whenever problems arise, call a meeting, place the problems on the table for discussion, take some decisions and the problems will be solved." [39] But what had originally been an inner-party document was now addressed to the public at large. The ubiquitousness of the *Quotations* attested to the principle behind it: universal political participation. Official and subject, cadre and citizen, were to be melded into one. The party might be "the core of the leadership of the whole Chinese people," [40] but the separating line between leader and led *below the level of prime legitimizing authority* was blurred. Indeed, one of the strongest thrusts of Mao's philosophy after the Kiangsi Soviet period was to demythify rule itself. Manuals explain the puzzles of the unknown and make the complex ultimately appear simple. "You can't solve a problem? Well, get down and investigate the present facts and its past history! When you have investigated the problem thoroughly, you will know how to solve it." [41]

A third major theme was the appeal to youth as the hope of revolutionary society.

The young people are the most active and vital force in society. They are the most eager to learn and the least conservative in their thinking.[42]

The world is yours, as well as ours, but in the last analysis, it is yours. You young people, full of vigor and vitality, are in the bloom of life, like the sun at eight or nine in the morning. Our hope is placed on you. . . . The world belongs to you. China's future belongs to you.[43]

But the appeal was ambivalent. Although Mao did single out youth for its higher capacity to revolt against convention, he also expressed deep concern lest this new post-victory generation forget why the revolution had occurred in the first place. The Cultural Revolution deliberately reenacted the heroic hardships of the civil war period, for Mao feared that the Red Guards (hailed as the *hsin-jen* or new people) would lag as his revolutionary successors *(ko-ming chieh-pan jen).*[44] Thus the *Quotations* in its fourth aspect demanded faith ("We must have faith in the masses and we must have faith in the party. These are two cardinal principles. If we doubt these principles, we shall accomplish nothing." [45]) so that the Great Proletarian Cultural Revolution was ultimately to touch "the souls of the people." [46] Faith was best aroused by the prospect of Manichean struggle. Within Mao's speeches lurked an enemy constantly ready to capitalize on the revolution's mistakes.

Revisionism, or Right opportunism, is a bourgeois trend of thought that is even more dangerous than dogmatism. The revisionists, the Right opportunists, pay lip service to Marxism; they too attack "dogmatism." But what they are really attacking is the quintessence of Marxism. They oppose or distort materialism and dialectics, oppose or try to weaken the people's democratic dictatorship and the leading role of the Communist Party, and oppose or try to weaken socialist transformation and socialist construction. After the basic victory of the socialist revolution in our country, there are still a number of people who vainly hope to restore the capitalist system and fight the working class on every front, including the ideological one. And their right-hand men in this struggle are the revisionists.[47]

An army of faithful must arise to oppose these enemies, watch over its own ranks, even determine the rectitude of its officers. For, faith—in the protestant sense used here—makes of every man a judge. The *Quotations* itself might appear to restrain eccentric authority, but like a bible it also empowers individual judgment. The *Sacred Edicts* had suffered from no such contradiction between authority and freedom, had none of the *Quotations'* tension "between the determination to make everyone think the same correct thoughts, and the desire that they should do so spontaneously";[48] the *Quotations*—despite its current authority—urges every man to question dogmatic authority.

"To rebel (*tsao-fan*) is justified," went the Red Guard cry.[49] *Tsao-fan,* once synonymous with treason, was early used by party members to condemn the Red Guards' iconoclasm. But on August 24, 1966, its seditious connotation was utterly erased. That day *People's Daily* printed a previously unknown speech by Mao which declared: "The immense complexity of Marxism can be summed up in one sentence: It is justifiable to rebel [*tsao-fan*]." [50] That slogan—so Marshal Lin Piao later explained—was designed to arouse "the masses in their hundreds of millions to air their views freely, write big-character posters, and hold great debates" [51] to expose the capitalist-roaders in the party. *Tsao-fan* was still broadly restricted, however, because only the correct use of Mao's thought permitted cultural revolutionaries legitimately to attack institutional embodiments of delegated authority. A perfect example of this was given by *Hung ch'i* (Red Flag) in 1967:

Proletarian Revolutionaries, Unite!

> "The golden monkey wrathfully swung his massive cudgel
> And the jade-like firmament was cleared of dust." [52]

Guided by the proletarian revolutionary line represented by Chairman Mao Tse-tung, the glorious Shanghai working class has formed a million-strong, mighty army of revolutionary rebels. In alliance with other revolutionary organizations, they have been meeting head-on the new counterattacks by the bourgeois reactionary line, seizing power from the handful of party persons in authority who are taking the capitalist road, and establishing the new order of the Great Proletarian Cultural Revolution. With an irresistible, sweeping force, they are following up this victory and brushing aside the rubbish that stands in the way of the wheel of history.[53]

An almost superhuman hero (the poetry describes Monkey's fight with the gods in the novel, *Hsi-yu chi*) gathers a popular army to assault those in authority within the Communist Party. There might well be two wellsprings of authority, the party and Mao himself; but there was only one fount of legitimacy. That (Mao's thought—the monkey-god's cudgel) was sanctioned by its direct connection with and mobilization of the masses, million-strong, whose "colossal scale" [54] was imagistically contrasted to the *mere handful* (a term of opprobrium in Communist Chinese) of people in the party. True, the party as such was not condemned; but how divorce the institution from its leaders? [55] This novel vulnerability of Leninism before a Marxist righteousness of sheer numbers significantly detached ideology from organization.

What *ultimate* legitimacy justified that arrogation? In the editorial quoted above, the supreme arbiter was the wheel of history, expressed by the necessity for consummating revolution. Mao the Founder was thus identified with those he hoped would perpetuate his—no, their—revolution, which was not a single act, not a finite moment of consolidation. The bourgeoisie, once overthrown, was "still trying to use the old ideas, culture, customs, and habits of the exploiting classes to corrupt the masses, capture their minds, and endeavor to stage a comeback." [56] Even though the Cultural Revolution had succeeded, power "may be snatched away [from us] again." [57] The people "must not think that after one, two, three, or four great cultural revolutions there will be peace and quiet." [58]

We have won a great victory, but the defeated class will continue to struggle. Its members are still about and it still exists. Therefore we cannot speak of the final victory, not for decades. We must not lose our vigilance.

From the Leninist point of view, the final victory in one socialist country not only requires the efforts of the proletariat and the broad popular masses at home, but also depends on the victory of the world revolution and the abolition of the system of exploitation of man by man on this earth so that all mankind will be emancipated. Consequently, it is wrong to talk about the final victory of the revolution in our country lightheartedly; it runs counter to Leninism and does not conform to facts.[59]

Mao's anxiety was shared by others. A member of the Shanghai Revolutionary Committee told a foreign visitor:

Every revolution should be consolidated some time after its initial success. The class enemy will not be reconciled to his fate. After being dispossessed the bourgeoisie struggles for restoration. . . . Many times in history a revolution has been succeeded by a restoration. In the Soviet Union, counter-revolution was defeated, private property had been transferred to the state, but they failed to make a Cultural Revolution. Bourgeois ideology was not remolded, and proletarian power was corrupted by it. A kind of restoration of capitalism was made by Khrushchev in 1956. . . . The sad lesson of revisionism in the Soviet Union gives us warning that removing property is not enough; the revolution must be carried into the superstructure of the economic system.[60]

By rejecting institutional intermediaries and appealing directly to the masses, the revolutionary founder had made his stake the people's.

2

The Red Sun

In February of 1965, Chairman Mao told the American journalist, Edgar Snow, that "perhaps there was some basis for Soviet criticism that China had fostered a 'cult of personality.' It was said that Stalin had been the center of a cult of personality, and that Khrushchev had none at all. . . . Was it possible that Khrushchev fell because he had no cult of personality?" [1] Two years later, a fifty-three-year-old Chinese peasant woman described her ruler with these words:

Chairman Mao is the great leader of the Chinese people, the great teacher of the revolutionary people of the world, the very red sun that shines most brightly in our hearts. We poor and lower-middle peasants ardently love and support our great leader Chairman Mao, who has the greatest faith in us poor and lower-middle peasants and shows the greatest care and concern for us. He is to us as blood is to flesh, water to fish, and the vine to the melon. Our hearts beat as one. He is our guide, benefactor, and savior.

As a ship at sea depends on the helmsman, as all living things depend on the sun, so we poor and lower-middle peasants can never for a moment be separated from our great leader Chairman Mao.

We will obey Chairman Mao, be his good commune members, and his good pupils.

We must study and apply Chairman Mao's works better and more creatively, raise higher the great red banner of Chairman Mao's thought and turn our whole village, our whole nation, into a great big red school for Mao Tse-tung's thought.[2]

The strongest emotion expressed by this panegyric is reciprocal love between ruler and ruled. That sentiment—whether ideal or real—

could also be used to characterize any one-to-one relationship between a single leader and his people. In its classical Chinese version, the notion was both patrimonial and populist, so that at a shallow level of analysis there is no distinction between the "red sun" and the son of heaven, nor for that matter between an ideal emperor and a modern fascist ruler, because personalism seeks to level political elites in order to erase barriers between leader and mass. Populism can therefore unintentionally abet dictatorial rule by virtue of its sheer egalitarianism. Modern forms of this marriage of populism and despotism—whether in the guise of National Socialism or Peronism—depend on the emergence of mass movements. China's imperial system, however, was rhetorically populist without being either totalitarian or egalitarian; and even though its populism was institutionally qualified by Confucian officials, that rhetoric was more continuously present than in any other bureaucratic empire. Actually deprived of direct access to political power, the common people were still reified as undifferentiated legitimators of imperial authority. European monarchs tested the justice of their reigns against the reactions of political estates. Chinese emperors only acknowledged unincorporated public opinion. Therefore, the modern despotic ideal of one-ruler/one-people occurred earlier in China than in the West, providing a much stronger disposition toward totalitarian populism than might otherwise have occurred. Nor was this solely from the state's point of view. However suspect idealized official accounts of peasant gratitude to their father-emperor may be, there was a strong popular tradition of loving loyalty toward good emperors which reflected the conviction that stability and prosperity depended to a large degree upon the personal virtue of the ruler.

The peasants' love for Mao Tse-tung is also accompanied by a sense of dependence upon the chairman—but in a much more total and intimate way. The red sun upon which life depends is not high above in the heavens. It glows *within* the hearts of men: an enormous cosmic orb which encompasses everything, both religious and secular. In fact, the latter distinction hardly exists within the cult of Mao.* As he had de-

---

* In the Marxist lexicon, cult describes devotion to a person rather than to a dogma. In the sociology of religion, it refers to an ecstatic or mystical group which has broken with religious tradition and concerns itself mainly with the problems of individuals. To say "the cult of Mao" is to risk melding usages, so that the term sounds deprecatory, implying superstitious idolatry. Yet, like a purely religious cult, the veneration of Mao does help secure a theodicy in the form of a person. But Mao, however charismatic, has been no exemplary prophet; his cult, though liturgical, distinctly lacks ritual specificity. This typology is, of course, Max Weber's: *The Sociology of Religion* (Boston: Beacon Press, 1964),

stroyed feudal superstitions, religion was completely secularized; as his
presence sustained all life, the secular was entirely sanctified. A Ch'ing
peasant might religiously depend upon the emperor to maintain the
cosmic balance, but—although the latter was sometimes likened to a
sun in the sky—he was never an independent force. Instead the emperor, as the most sanctified representative of civil religion, united nature and man by offering sacrifice to heaven. An emperor might adopt
the guise of Buddha,[3] but Amithabha's portrait—not his own—occupied the altar in a peasant household. Today, Mao's picture has replaced both altar and portrait.

At the same time Mao's thought is called "a locomotive, a compass,
a lighthouse, a bright lantern lighting up the road," and even a magic
weapon with which to accomplish "miracles in the mundane world." [4]
Once Mao himself had been the great helmsman; by the time of the
Cultural Revolution his thought alone guaranteed safe passage for the
Chinese people. This transition from person to thought served two
purposes. By providing each citizen with his own talisman, Mao's
thought promoted initiative without independence. By divorcing the
living leader from his testament, it also helped ensure the transmission
of his legacy. In a certain very limited sense, this canonization of Mao
into his own thought recalls the sanctification of dead emperors by
their heirs—the cultification of an immortal *persona* when the actual
person ceases to exist.

This separation of person and *persona* is common to most rulers—
even noncharismatic ones. Emperors, too, were canonized by heirs
hoping to legitimize their reigning houses apart from transitory dependence upon heaven's will. But only the dead were canonized; the
persona could not be mortally present because its sanctity was a function of its promotion to a spiritual rank that much closer to heaven.

For Mao it was the identification with history, not heaven, that
mattered.

Chairman Mao has experienced many more events than Marx, Engels, or
Lenin. Marx, Engels, and Lenin, to be sure, were all great personages. Marx
lived for sixty-five years and Engels for seventy-five. They both had excellent foresight. They inherited the progressive thinking of mankind and foresaw the development of human society. Unlike Chairman Mao, who personally directed at the forefront many political and particularly military

especially pp. 10 and 77. Also see Geoffrey K. Nelson, "The Concept of Cult,"
The Sociological Review, New Series, 16.3:351–362.

campaigns, Marx and Engels, on the other hand, never personally led any proletarian revolution. Lenin lived for only fifty-four years, and died six years after the victory of the October Revolution. He never experienced a protracted, complex, acute, and multifarious struggle, as did Chairman Mao. The population of China is over ten times larger than that of Germany and four times that of Russia. Chairman Mao enjoys very high prestige in the entire country and throughout the world as a most outstanding and great person, because of his richer experience in revolution than anyone else. . . . Chairman Mao is a natural talent. In what way are we different from Chairman Mao? Among those engaged in struggle together, some are older than he is, but we are not, even though we, too, have some experience. We also read books, but we do not understand, or do not always understand. Chairman Mao always understands.[5]

As this paean by Lin Piao shows, Mao Tse-tung's personal identification with the Chinese revolution gained universal acceptance. It was suggested earlier that this fusion forced him to perpetuate revolution, so that he has been, in a sense, the prisoner of his historical self-image. But from another point of view that identity of history and biography freed him from ordinary restraints, because he alone could sanction his own actions. Hannah Arendt has written that men live in a "web of human relationships, with its innumerable, conflicting wills and intentions," so that action never achieves its purpose. Within that web, though, action does produce a story of each man. "Although everybody started his life by inserting himself into the human world through action and speech, nobody is the author or producer of his own life story. In other words, the stories, the results of action and speech, reveal an agent, but this agent is not an author or producer." [6] By authoring his own story, Mao really could seem to become a free agent.

This did not mean that Mao alone has been his own source of legitimacy. However charismatic his leadership, it has been repeatedly justified by its connection with the masses. If emperors demonstrated their closeness to heaven by ritual aloofness, Mao shows his nearness to his prime source of legitimacy by repeatedly trying to reach through government directly to the people: *shen-ju chün-chung* (enter deeply into the masses).[7] Of course, this was explicitly presented as a model of democratic centralism for the entire Communist Party. Mao told the Central Committee in 1962:

Concerning the question of democratic centralism, . . . some comrades are afraid of the masses, their criticism, and what they say. Are there any grounds on which a Marxist–Leninist can justify the fear? . . . Without democracy it is impossible to have the right sort of centralism. This is because centralism cannot be established on the basis of a confusion of views, in the absence of a unified [common] understanding.[8]

Mao's "wish is to join all the comrades of our party to learn from the masses, to continue to be a schoolboy." [9] This made him a paragon for other Communists, even though ordinary cadres (dependent upon position rather than presence) might find it somewhat harrowing to submit to mass criticism. Opening wide the doors of party headquarters, exposing once-awesome authority to increasingly unawed outsiders, ran counter to the self-protective instincts of party officials. Sensing the cadres' fear, Mao repeatedly denounced their caution, and exultantly urged them to overcome timidity. "Is the backside of a tiger really untouchable? We *will* touch it!" [10] He knew how severe public criticism could be, but those who had to experience it should not "become ashen with despair." For, fear in the face of the masses was self-defeating. "We must go out, not with the word 'fear' (*p'a*) but with the word 'dare' (*kan*) [in our minds]. . . . If we go out with the word 'fear,' [the opponents] will make more and more demands." [11]

Mao could afford to give this advice because he was not only the pupil of the masses; he was their teacher as well. At first glance, this confusion of roles (who, after all, was teaching whom?) seems perfectly clear if expressed as a dialectical relationship. However, that clarity is quickly lost the moment one examines the content of the lesson being taught. Mao, we have said, grew increasingly concerned after 1962 with norms rather than with ends, with attitudes rather than with classes. In fact, even a proletarian class background was not enough to "guarantee correct attitudes," especially after the cultural revolutionaries defined the struggle within the party as between "proletarian and bourgeois world outlooks." [12] Class consciousness, party service, and the mastery of dialectical materialism were all replaced by the possession of a proper world view defined in terms of studying Mao Tse-tung thought "with profound proletarian feelings." [13] By the end of 1970, even veterans of the Long March were confessing "that it was impossible for me to study Mao Tse-tung thought consciously just because I had a class feeling." [14] If not class derived, then from where did "profound proletarian feelings" come? According to those same party cadres, "only through uninterrupted study can one develop proletarian feeling for Chairman Mao." [15] Did that kind of circular reasoning then simply mean that study produced proletarian feelings, while those same proletarian feelings enabled study? As one official explained: "To study and apply Chairman Mao's philosophical thinking well, it is necessary to have profound proletarian feelings. . . . I understand that a person's consciousness as regards study is determined by the profundity of his feelings for Chairman Mao." [16] In short, a correct world view resulted from studying Mao Tse-tung's thought with proletarian feelings, which were in turn aroused in proportion to the revolutionary's intensity of feeling for Mao the individual. Here, finally, person and *persona* were structurally—not dialectically—formed into a complete gestalt.

Or, to put it another way, there were at least three embodiments of Mao: the historical revolutionary whose past exploits inspired present action, the current chairman—red sun to all—whose person was (except for occasional acts like the famous Yangtze swim in 1966) a living presence rather than a living exemplar, and the *persona* expressed by his thought. All three of these placed the man, Mao, at a remove from mundane activities. Consequently, other human beings had to be discovered—or contrived—to act as models for the attitudes which Mao wished to inculcate in the Chinese people.

Mao's revolutionary generation had found its first identity in the guise of traditional heroes of Chinese history and fiction—especially the knight-errants (*wu-hsia*) of chivalric novels.[17] These same warriors —Wu Sung (*Water Margin*), Huang Chung (*Romance of the Three Kingdoms*), Mu Kuei-ying (the legendary woman general of the Sung), and so forth—were held up as exemplary heroes for the masses of the early People's Republic. But there were to be two drawbacks to such paragons. First of all, these heroes usually found their noblest moment in the extremity of defeat, choosing honor before submission—hardly the best examples for a country pledged to human victory over adversity. The second disadvantage was their connection with the feudal past. During the first years of the republic, traditional culture seemed long dead, buried by the May Fourth generation. By the early 1960s, however, the ghosts of the past appeared once again.[18] Not only was the quixotic individualism of romantic knights contrary to collective ideals; Communist intellectuals were actually hailing traditional heroes for their courage to oppose despotic authority. Besides, such figures (however ghostly) had outlived their usefulness. During the Great Leap period, peasants had been aroused from their fatality in the face of nature by comparing themselves to martial bravoes willing to dare everything. Once that lesson was learned, why encourage a new dependence upon individualistic historical models? As early as 1958, Premier Chou En-lai complimented the older men of one agricultural collective by saying, *"Lao-nien sai-kuo lao Huang Chung"* (the aged have surpassed so many old Huang Chungs).[19]

The transition from traditional to modern heroes was carried out by means of three great models (*pang-yang*): Norman Bethune (the Canadian surgeon with the Eighth Route Army who was felled by blood poisoning in 1939), Chang Tsu-te (a soldier killed during the civil war), and Yü Kung ("Mr. Foolish," who dared to challenge nature by trying to remove the mountain blocking his view). The last was most admired of all. "The Chinese are exhorted not only to emulate Yü Kung but to become a Yü Kung, a *huo,* or living Yü Kung, or a *hsin* Yü Kung [new Yü Kung]. Even the word *shan* [mountains] has come to denote metaphorically a hindrance, a difficulty or something counter-revolutionary." [20] But of these traditionally independent models, one was an ahistorical myth-figure and another not even Chinese. Moreover, they were models, selfless enough, but lacking the conviction of individual heroes. What was needed was someone combining the best traits of both: the subjective fervor of traditional heroes and the collective commitment of modern models.

In March of 1963, such a figure was devised—or discovered—in the guise of Lei Feng, by the Political Department of the People's Liberation Army. The nation was soon to witness a series of such heroes (*ying-hsiung*) appearing in rapid succession, each designed to illustrate one virtue or another. A soldier might be chosen to exemplify the army's benevolence, a worker to stress the importance of salvaging scrap iron, a student to encourage voluntary rustification. Each possessed one universal characteristic: invariably he committed every act by the light of Mao Tse-tung's thought.

A fairly typical example was Chin Hsun-hua, a Shanghai Red Guard, who joyfully responded in May of 1969 to Chairman Mao's call to urban youth for reeducation by the peasantry. Settling in a rural brigade in Hei-lung-chiang in May of 1969, this particular hero (like almost all of the others) kept a diary which recounted his adaptation both to Mao's thought and to the rigors of rural life. Noting his difficulty binding millet stalks, for instance, he compared his bleeding hands with the peasants' calloused palms. "This shows," he observed, "that my thinking and my hands have long been out of touch with the workers and peasants and manual laborers, and that I have been poisoned by revisionist ideas." [21]

On August 15, 1969, Chin Hsun-hua was drowned in the flooding Hsun River when he tried to save some pieces of state property for his brigade. As the swift current pulled him under, he shouted to others standing on the bank: "When you die for the people, it is a worthy death." [22] The editors of his diary added that after this misfortune, "Group after group of educated youths and children come to the martyr's tomb amidst the evergreen pines and pledge that they will follow his brilliant example, learn from him, march along the path trodden by him, perform heroic deeds, and devote their life to the defense and building of the frontier areas." [23] The property for which Chin had sacrificed his life consisted of two wooden light poles floating downstream.

It is difficult for outsiders to take such accounts seriously. No one would scoff if Chin had lost his life trying to save another's, but could so mundane, so pointless an act be truly heroic? Two attributes of the deed may relieve it of absurdity: its relevance to everyday (and therefore petty) tasks, and its expression of total commitment to Mao's thought. The intention of the forgers of such heroes was not only—against all senses of human proportion—to transform the petty into the majestic, but also to confer dignity upon any action expressive of true "proletarian feelings." The outer discrepancy between the nobility of Chin's intention and the vulgarity of the end (self-sacrifice for two electric light poles) mattered less than the inner battle to overcome the basic instinct for self-preservation and to commit the soul to the general will by "offering one's loyal heart to Chairman Mao." [24]

3
The Dictator

Leninism denied any contradiction at all between the seizure of power by a dictatorship of the proletariat and the eventual withering away of the state. Indeed, the socialist dictatorship, by transforming citizens into equally salaried employees of the state, would teach all of the members of society how to administer and regulate themselves without mutual exploitation. Then would arrive "democracy complete": "The *necessity* of observing the simple fundamental rules of human intercourse will become a *habit* and then the door will be wide open for the transition from the first phase of communist society to its higher phase, and with it to the complete withering away of the state." [1] Therefore, the transitory form of the instrumental state—even if a dictatorship—did not matter. The end was not democracy, nor civil rights; the objective was social transformation and economic liberation.

Mao Tse-tung partly agreed with Lenin. "Democracy," he said, "sometimes looks like an end in itself, but in fact it is merely a means to an end." [2] But, like Rosa Luxemburg, he diverged from Lenin by doubting the willingness of the bureaucratic managers of the dictatorship to allow their own state to wither away. Luxemburg had foreseen the danger of a dictatorship "in the bourgeois sense":

Without general elections, without unrestricted freedom of press and assembly, without a free struggle of opinion, life dies out in every public institution, becomes a mere semblance of life, in which only the bureaucracy remains as the active element. Public life gradually falls asleep, a few dozen party leaders of inexhaustible energy and boundless experience direct and rule. Among them, in reality only a dozen outstanding heads do

the leading, and an elite of the working class is invited from time to time
to meetings where they are to applaud the speeches of the leaders and to
approve proposed resolutions unanimously—at bottom, then, a clique affair
—a dictatorship, to be sure, not the dictatorship of the proletariat, however,
but only the dictatorship of a handful of politicians, that is a dicatorship
in the bourgeois sense, in the sense of the rule of the Jacobins.[3]

Mao was to go much further than that by declaring bureaucrats a class
as such. "The bureaucrats and the workers and the middle-poor peasants are acutely antagonistic classes. Such people [as the bureaucrats]
are already or are becoming capitalist vampires to the workers." [4]

That kind of statement could be dismissed as Maoist hyperbole:
political epithets in the conventional language of Marxist class analysis.
But Mao was not just being a vulgarian when he identified bureaucrats
as a class apart from the proletariat. As some European Marxists—
Milovan Djilas, for example—have argued, party bureaucrats did indeed
function like a "new class" in socialist societies. Moreover, in the context of Mao's own developed political philosophy, struggle per se defined class stances. If bureaucrats proved to be antagonistic to the proletariat, then they effectively existed as a class enemy.

Lenin had insisted that mankind would progress to the higher stages
of communism when there ceased to be an antagonism between mental
and physical labor as a result of the growth of productive forces—that
is, when superstructural attitudes were transformed by changes in the
mode of production. Although this ideal goal would never be abandoned by Marxist–Leninists, the actual effect of industrial growth in
countries like the Soviet Union was a strengthening of those very political forms which were supposed to wither away. But Mao Tse-tung was
to refuse to accept such an outcome. The ultimate instrument of socialist transformation was to be struggle, not the state.

At first, to be sure, Mao pursued an orthodox Leninist approach
toward the dictatorship of the proletariat. During the early 1950s, when
China took the Soviet Union as its model for industrialization, Mao
emphasized the importance of extensive organization, especially as it
consolidated the Chinese people against their enemies. "It is a good
thing that 'the overwhelming majority . . . belong to one organization
or another.' There has not been such a good thing for thousands of
years. The possibility for the people to transform themselves from the
state of a mass of loose sand easily exploited by the reactionaries . . .
came only after a long and bitter struggle." [5] Organization thus imposed
unity upon the people. But, even as he stressed political solidarity, Mao

also identified it with struggle. Consequently, his vision of socialist society was bipolar. And because Mao also believed that progress consisted of the serial succession of contradictory stages, in practice a period of organized unity was to be followed by one of struggle or disunity, then to give way to unity again. As the years went by, however, these epicycles were placed within the larger sweep of struggle alone. Indeed, struggle not only ideally determined organization in the People's Republic—it virtually replaced it *as a political form.* "The form of revolutionary organization is determined by the requirements of revolutionary struggle. If an organizational form does not meet the requirements of a revolutionary struggle, it must be abandoned.".[6]

From a Marxian philosophic standpoint, therefore, Mao was acting as though his country had already attained the highest level of communism, despite the lack of structural change in the mode of production. The purist would also question the sacrifice of freedom to the historically premature illusion of a socialized humanity. In modern China, socialist man did not determine his social self by his own labor; he was fashioned by internalizing noneconomic ideas imposed upon him by a personalistic state.

Whatever the justice of these charges, they would at least have to be framed in terms of a political tradition quite different than Mao's own. The foremost question of European political thought between the French Revolution and the revolutions of 1848 had been the connection between human nature and social organization. Two theories of society were developed according to each school's view of the immutability of human nature.[7] The Benthamites took it to be unchanging, and therefore advocated within the framework of English liberalism an interest theory of society in which power was distributive rather than integrative. The Hegelians rejected the empirical realities of human nature in favor of normative ideals consonant with an historical *Geist.* Hegel himself was able philosophically to overcome the contradiction between actuality and ideal by reifying civil society (*bürgerliche Gesellschaft*) into an aggregate of human relations connecting each individual to the normative community. But because Hegel's doctrine of state authority made the individual exist for the sake of the polity, these two theories posed a cruel dilemma for Karl Marx: the tyranny of social reality versus the tyranny of the idealized state.

To avoid being caught on either horn, young Marx asserted the belief that values inhere to history *itself,* which in turn is made by man *himself.* Hegel's Gordian knot was cut with a practical blade: the notion of human labor. Society resulted from, and was philosophically dependent upon, human labor. Man could therefore remake society by his own effort into a genuine community, a truly "socialized humanity." The remaining philosophical issue, that of the social determination of human nature, could be resolved by using Hegel's own theory of mutual causation, which was sharpened into Marx's distinct version of the dialectic. Man makes society in his own image; but because man is a social creature, society sets new conditions which thereby change human nature, making yet higher forms of society possible.

Marx presented this thesis most starkly in *The German Ideology,* where he desired to reveal the philosophical errors of Hegel's school: "The Young Hegelians are in agreement with the Old Hegelians in their belief in the rule of religion, of concepts, of an abstract general principle in the existing world." [8] If one begins as a materialist instead, taking as a first premise of human history the existence of living individuals, distinguished from animals by the production of their own means of subsistence, then it is logical to state that production expresses each individual's own life. What man *is* coincides with what he *produces.* Marx believed that he had thus made it possible for individuals to exist as they really are, "as they are effective, produce materially," [9] and not as they appear in their own or in others' imaginations. Hence, "life is not determined by consciousness, but consciousness by life";[10] and "consciousness is therefore from the very beginning a social product, and remains so as long as men exist at all." [11]

Despite his polemic with the Hegelians, Marx did share Hegel's instinct to transcend the given state. That instinct was most visible in the early Hegel, who wrote at the time of the French Revolution: "I shall demonstrate that, just as there is no idea of a machine, there is no idea of the state; for the state is something mechanical. Only that which is an object of freedom may be called an idea. We must, therefore, transcend the state. For every state is bound to treat free men as cogs in a machine. And this is just what it ought not to do; hence the state must perish." [12] But Marx went even further by distinguishing the idea of freedom from the concept of civic or natural rights. "None of the supposed rights of men go beyond the egoistic man, man as he is, as a member of civil society. That is, an individual separated from the community, withdrawn into himself, wholly preoccupied with his private interest and acting in accordance with his private caprice." [13] In that sense rights might well deserve to be alienated; freedom, certainly not. Until freedom is ultimately attained by socialized humanity, men must emancipate themselves via the state, but that requires a permanent revolution which would contradict the state itself.

Certainly, in periods when the political state as such comes violently to birth in civil society, and when men strive to liberate themselves through political emancipation, the state can, and must, proceed to abolish and destroy religion, but only in the same way as it proceeds to destroy private property, by declaring a maximum, by confiscation, or by progressive taxation, or in the same way as it proceeds to abolish life, by the guillotine. At those times when the state is most aware of itself, political life seeks to stifle its own prerequisites—civil society and its elements—to establish itself as the genuine and harmonious species-life of man. But it can only achieve this end by setting itself in violent contradiction with its own conditions of existence, by declaring a permanent revolution.[14]

Marx had therefore adopted Hegel's concept of a civil society only to distinguish it from—and pit it against—the state, with the hope of exceeding both by socializing humanity, so that "freedom consists in converting the state from an organ standing above society into one completely subordinated to it." [15] By way of contrast, Mao Tse-tung might be said to have taken each and included them in a larger political society. This would suggest that Mao utterly lacked a concern with the Marxian problem of alienation, which was itself aroused by the apparent conflict between man's political and his social interests. If traditional Chinese political conceptualizations denied such a contradiction, then this might account for its absence in radical Chinese thought. For, without that dialectical assumption the state cannot be apotheosized; alienation does seem irrelevant.

By stating the argument in this roundabout way, I run the risk of suggesting that there existed no distinction between public and private spheres in classical Chinese political theory. Such was certainly not the case. However, the putative conflict was resolved by consciously seeking to absorb the private in the public, politics in ethics. Particularisms may have been the mainstays of the ideal society of the *Sacred Edicts*; but precisely because of this social ubiquitousness, particularism was denied a place in the bureaucratic polity. Even emperors were sometimes supposed to sacrifice personal interests: *t'ien-hsia wei kung* (render public all-under-heaven), a phrase from the *Record of Rites,* was usually glossed to mean "when the Son of Heaven bequeaths his position to the worthy instead of bequeathing it to his son." In that ideal sense—Yao naming Shun his successor—the private familial interests of even an emperor were considered selfish insofar as they ran counter to the public duties of guaranteeing selfless rule for the sake of the people. By the seventeenth century, in fact, there had developed a standard interpretation of Chinese history (probably best known through Huang Tsung-hsi's *Plan for the Prince*), which declared that the public-mindedness of the ancient sage-kings had given way to the *ssu* (selfishness) of contemporary rulers who regarded all-under-heaven as their personal empire. This became a commonplace notion during the nineteenth century, when writers like Cheng Kuan-ying (b. 1841) pleaded for imperial reform in the name of public-mindedness.

Because Cheng's *Sheng-shih wei-yen* (Words of Warning in a Seemingly Prosperous Age)—which equated individuality with an antisocial form of selfishness[16]—greatly impressed Mao Tse-tung when he was a schoolboy, and because *t'ien-hsia wei kung* became such a well-known Maoist slogan, it would be natural to attribute Mao's primacy of public over private to a traditional Chinese source. But even if Mao was so influenced, his own conception of an entirely public political society departed radically from imperial China's, which tolerated a private sphere even for bureaucrats. Eremitism, the refusal to serve an alien dynasty, and resignation from office on moral grounds were each accorded imperial toleration and Confucian admiration. This was not because public action was divorced from private judgment. Rather, respect for individual criticism confirmed the inseparability of bureaucratic politics and gentlemanly ethics: a cause at once of strength and weakness in Chinese intellectuals.

The traditional Chinese scholar-official's conception of his role prevented him from joining others to form independent political groups. Factions were forbidden within the bureaucratic arena since they were considered divisive to the harmony of just rule. They were also psychologically repugnant because they demeaned the individual scholar-official, who had to compensate for his political dependence by taking pride in his personal autonomy. A literatus' private (and even haughty) assessment of the emperor might be impotent, but it meant more to him than either political organization or professionalism, which (however efficacious) would either have subordinated his judgment to others' or sacrificed his moral independence to routine role. Most emperors, in turn, realized that the ideal of a personal relationship between ruler and official favored the throne's interests by exalting the individual Confucianist's fundamentally powerless (except at times of dynastic change) morality in exchange for depriving the bureaucracy of collective influence. So high an evaluation of individual integrity was bound to accompany the refusal of despotic government to accord legitimate autonomy to particular groups in society. Therefore, what we might later take to be a Maoist form of Jacobinism in its opposition to particular interests really stemmed from quite different historical circumstances.

The imperial animus against associations had extended both to social groups and political factions (*p'ai*). Communist opposition was at first generally reserved for the latter.[17] But factionalism had become a virtue by the time of the Cultural Revolution, when Mao declared such fragmentation an inevitable part of intraparty struggle. "Do we have a party outside our party? I think we have a party outside it and factions inside it. When the Kuomintang said that 'there should not be a party outside this party and factions inside it,' we criticized it by saying: 'No party outside this party means autocracy; no factions inside it is in fact an optical illusion.' We are exactly the same." [18] In 1966 he was even willing to sanction spontaneous associations (presumably Red Guard units): "Like-minded youth often club together; this is nothing unusual." [19] To be sure, these were far from autonomous associations. But their prevalence showed that public *groups* confirmed Mao's theory of struggle, while private—even pluralistic—*interests* were considered too independent of the commonweal. Nor was this originally Mao's sentiment alone. When Liu Shao-ch'i earlier reported on the draft constitution of the People's Republic, he declared: "We permit no one to impair the interests and freedom of the majority, the public interests of the country and society, for the sake of the interests and freedom of any individual or individuals. . . . Personal interests are indivisible from the public interests of the country and society. . . . They are one and the same." [20] Individuals or individualism—a state of mind—denied the public interest. As a *Jen-min jih-pao* (People's Daily) editorial remarked during the commune movement: "Individualism and particularism are like a stubborn skin disease: today you drive it out, tomorrow it rushes back. . . . Individualism and particularism will not be truly exterminated until every commune member possesses communist ideology." [21]

During the early years of the People's Republic, however, intellectual autonomy and private judgment were tolerated, as long as they were ostensibly apolitical. In the slogans of the time, thought and politics were separated. At a meeting of the People's Political Consultative Conference in 1953, for instance, the philosopher Liang Shu-ming criticized the Communist Party. Mao Tse-tung angrily attacked Liang until Ch'en Ming-shu (former commander of the Nineteenth Route Army) intervened. When Ch'en asked the chairman if he was attacking Liang for his politics or for his thoughts, Mao relented. The party's account of the conference added that:

Now the Chinese Communist Party makes a great distinction between a man's thought and his politics. A man may be extremely backward in his thought and not be guilty of any crime, for thought may be corrected by political education. A man's politics on the other hand lead to action, and the Chinese Communist Party will not tolerate even the slightest deviation where politics are concerned. Politics are treated with political means.[22]

This claim of tolerance was nevertheless exaggerated. Procedures for intellectual self-reform (*tzu-wo kai-tsao*) had already been developed during the Yenan rectification campaigns of the 1940s; by 1951 Mao Tse-tung was heard arguing in public for the thought reform (*ssu-hsiang kai-tsao*) of intellectuals. "Now this suggestion [for self-education] has already developed gradually into an actuality. Thought reform is first of all the thought reform of every sort of intellectual. It is the important condition for our country's thoroughly carrying out democratic reform in every aspect and gradually implementing industrialization." [23] The insistence on thought reform diminished in succeeding years, as party leaders represented by Chou En-lai insisted on the importance of intellectuals (geologists, engineers, national defense scientists, cultural workers) to socialist construction and industrialization. In 1956 Chou announced the importance of recognizing that: "Certain unreasonable features in our present employment and treatment of intellectuals and, in particular, certain sectarian attitudes among some of our comrades towards intellectuals outside the party have to some extent handicapped us in bringing the existing power of the intelligentsia into full play." [24] Official tolerance was expressed first in the theory that "the natural sciences including medicine, have no class character";[25] and secondly in Liu Shao-chi's belief that socialism was already so triumphant in China that it was wrong to want every member to be of one color ("red" and "expert" side by side).

At the time, it seems, Mao shared Liu's optimism over past accomplishments: the primary revolution—that of materialism over idealism in the ideological sphere, and socialism over capitalism in the economic realm—had been won in China. In fact there had been enough basic transformations in both the structure and superstructure of Chinese society to permit a cycle of struggle or disorder (*luan*) that would resolve tensions between the party and the people without endangering the greater national unity. In his speech of May 2, 1956, ("Let a hundred flowers bloom") Mao thus expressed a high degree of faith in the capacity of intellectuals to criticize particular errors of the regime without questioning its fundamental legitimacy. The party itself could stand a little public dissent; for, already Mao was coming to identify the danger of ultimate revolutionary failure with bureaucratization ("bourgeois tendencies"). Not only had elements in the party questioned his policy that spring of rapidly leaping from semisocialist to fully socialist cooperatives; by fall, the Polish and Hungarian uprisings would have shown just how wide a gap could spread between entrenched Communist parties and a citizenry. And so, declaring that "it is amid great storms that human society progresses," [26] Mao served notice to his own party that it would have to undergo criticism from others, especially intellectuals, outside the regime. However, the "blooming and contending" of 1957 quickly surpassed acceptable limits. When the regime was compared to Hitler's rule, it was obvious that legitimacy was at stake, so that Mao's trust in the good faith of revolutionary intellectuals was soon destroyed. They would not again be relied upon to counterbalance party revisionists. In fact, they would become linked in Mao's mind, if not in fact, with those very elements within the party.[27]

This connection was made after the party split over the difficulties of the Great Leap Forward. In July of 1959, the eighth plenary session of the Eighth Central Committee was convoked at Lushan. There Mao was harshly criticized by a clique under Marshal P'eng Teh-huai known as the Military Club. Mao was compared to Stalin and Tito in his arrogance, castigated for his vanity, and accused of letting "the errors reach the bottom before [he] would turn the curve, and once making the turn it would reach 180 degrees." [28] One can gain a sense of the tension of the conference from Mao's own demands to be heard.

Our party is a Marxist political party. It is incumbent not only upon those of the first side to listen to others, but also upon those of the second side. People on both sides must listen to others. Did I not say that I want to speak? The first thing is that I want to speak; the second thing is that I want to listen to other people's talk. I was not in a hurry to speak, and have endured it by stiffening my scalp. Why can't I do it now? For twenty days I have shown my forbearance, and now the conference will soon be adjourned.[29]

Never before had the revolution looked so fragile to Mao, although at first he denied that the new order would collapse. "The rightists said:

why did Ch'in Shih huang-ti collapse? Because he built the Great Wall. Now that we have constructed the T'ien-an-men, we would also collapse; that's what the rightists alleged." [30] Yet he at the same time betrayed his fear of retrogression by refusing to allow the party to publicize the mistakes which production brigades had performed during the Great Leap. "What will be the result [of publication]? Our nation will collapse, and if by that time the imperialists did not come, our own people would also rise up to overthrow us." [31] It was then that he made his famous assertion that if the republic did collapse, he would start the revolution all over again.

Suppose we do ten things, and nine of them are bad and are published in the newspapers. Then we are bound to perish, and should perish. In that event, I would go to the countryside to lead the peasants to overthrow the government. If the Liberation Army won't follow me, I will then find the Red Army. I think the Liberation Army will follow me.[32]

As it turned out, Mao did not have to go back to the countryside after all. When the Central Committee voted to support its chairman against P'eng Teh-huai, Mao felt confident once again that there was enough solidarity within the party to resolve such difficulties by private convocations.

The method of convocation is one which everybody has endorsed. This is to proceed from the wish for solidarity—the solidarity of the Central Committee Plenum which involves the fate of socialism in China. From our standpoint, we must have solidarity. There is now a kind of disruptive tendency. At the Eighth Congress last year, I said that the perils were none other but, first, world war and, second, splits in the party. There were then no salient signs, but they have appeared now. The method of solidarity is to proceed from the wish for solidarity, and then through criticism and self-criticism to achieve the goal of solidarity on a new basis.[33]

The key to this dialectical relationship between solidarity and conflict was to be explained by means of a special metaphor. At the Lushan conference, Mao had recalled a poem by the Han *fu* writer Mei Sheng (before 200–140 B.C.) who described the moral illness of the debauched Prince of Ch'u. Doctrinal errors—said Mao—could also be treated like a kind of illness.

What Mei Sheng said is somewhat like our method of dealing with comrades who have committed errors. We would shout to them, warning that their ailment has become most serious and that they might die unless they were cured. Thereafter, the patient might, for a few days, weeks, or months, be unable to sleep, thus becoming confused and restive. In this way, there came hope. . . . We call this method "stringent criticism". . . . We should invite such fellows as Engels, Kautsky, Plekhanov, Stalin, Li Ta-shao, Lu Hsun, and Ch'ü Ch'iu-pai "to a discourse on the quintessence of the universe and to distinguish the merits of all things," to speak about the necessity of the great leap, the causes of communes, and the extreme importance of putting politics in command. Thus, Marx would "survey it" and Lenin "would calculate it meticulously in order to be sure of its utility." [34]

Because the awareness of sickness was confounded with submission to it, illness was regarded by Mao as salutary in itself: a necessary prerequisite to health. One comrade involved with P'eng Teh-huai's Military Club even received a letter from Mao Tse-tung which said: "You must undergo a serious illness. . . . There are two words for you: rectify painfully." [35]

The illness simile* had probably first occurred to Mao more than forty years earlier, when he read and reread the eleventh issue of Liang Ch'i-ch'ao's famous journal, *Hsin-min ts'ung-pao* (The New People Magazine).[36] Liang had argued then that social evils had to be destroyed before positive construction was possible. Comparing decadence to sickness, he insisted that one must be willing to "vomit and purge" the ailment before a cure would be expected.[37] Mao went on to develop his own version of the metaphor during the Yenan rectification campaign of the early 1940s. Just as his theory of contradiction proposed that opposites were resolved by being forced into antagonism, so would rectification succeed if the fever were brought to its height. "The first step in reasoning is to give the patient a powerful stimulus: yell at him, 'you're sick!' so the patient will have a fright and break out in an overall sweat; then he can actually be started on the road to recovery." [38] However painful this might seem, it did serve to mitigate the ultimate harshness of struggle, since the diseases—not the patients—were purged.

---

* The organic analogy was not very novel in Chinese political thought. Chu Hsi, the Sung philosopher and statesman, once compared the realm to an ill man whose four limbs were damaged. The man—said Chu—was not prevented from following his normal daily routine even though he was critically sick, as would be evident to anyone versed in medicine. What was needed were the marvelous medicines of Lu Pien (third century B.C.) or Hua T'o (Han) "to cleanse his bowels and wash his stomach." "If he receives this medical attention, he will be saved. If, however, he is not treated, the illness will daily increase in seriousness without the man realizing it." Cited and translated in Conrad M. Schirokauer, "The Political Thought and Behavior of Chu Hsi" (Ph.D. diss., Stanford University, 1960), p. 174.

But our object in exposing errors and criticizing shortcomings is like that of a doctor in curing a disease. The whole purpose is to save people, not to cure them to death. If a man has appendicitis, the doctor performs an operation and the man is saved. If a person who commits an error, no matter how great, does not bring his disease to an incurable state by concealing it and persisting in his error, and if in addition he is genuinely and honestly willing to be cured, willing to make corrections, we will welcome him so that his disease may be cured and he may become a good comrade. It is certainly not possible to solve the problem by one flurry of blows for the sake of a moment's satisfaction. We cannot adopt a brash attitude toward diseases in thought and politics, but an attitude of "saving men by curing their ills." This is the correct and effective method.[39]

This attitude persisted throughout the next twenty years ("Take a friendly and helpful attitude toward people who have made mistakes. . . . Do not create the kind of atmosphere in which no mistake is permitted, in which a mistake is a great crime." [40]) and was reiterated by Mao during the Cultural Revolution: "Our policy is 'to punish those who have committed mistakes so that others will not follow them and to cure the disease in order to save the patient.' " [41] Naturally the chances for recovery depended ultimately upon the patient's own attitude. Granted, it was easy to make "mistakes"; "the thing is to correct them conscientiously." [42]

Were all doctrinal diseases curable? At times it certainly seemed so. Chang K'ai-fan, Anhwei party secretary, was linked with the Military Club group of "opportunists who have infiltrated into the party"; but even when those opportunists were in turn identified with the "Kao Kang conspiratorial antiparty clique," Chairman Mao declared that:

If they are willing to wash their brains, it would still be possible to win them over. . . . We should rescue them; we should thoroughly expose them among the broad mass of cadres so that their market will be more and more circumscribed. It is necessary to implement the policy of healing illness and saving life by the method of presenting facts and talking reason.[43]

However, at this point Mao's concern over doctrinal illness helped lead him to identify deviation as a reactionary residue that both reflected continuing class struggle and foretold the necessity for a later Cultural Revolution in the superstructure of society.

The struggle that has arisen at Lushan is a class struggle. It is the continuation of the life-or-death struggle between the two great antagonists of the bourgeoisie and the proletariat in the process of the socialist revolution dur-

ing the past decade. In China and in our party, it appears that such a struggle will continue for at least another twenty years, and possibly even for
half a century. In short, classes must be completely eliminated before the
struggle will cease. With the cessation of old social struggle, new social
struggle will arise. In short, in accordance with materialist dialectics, contradiction and struggle are perpetual; otherwise, there would be no
world. . . . In the present time, though economic systems have changed,
the reactionary ideology left over from the old times remains in the minds
of a large number of people. . . . This is the class struggle in society, and
the intraparty struggle has merely reflected the class struggle in society.[44]

In this confused formulation, "serious" errors of thought were not only
diseased vestiges of reactionary ideologies; they also reflected existing
class struggles. Class consciousness was thereby determined less by the
stage of development of production by social individuals than by the
political motivation of members of a socialist state.

Marx and Engels had certainly valued purposive motivation. Man,
in fact, was defined by consciousness insofar as it had replaced instinct
in the realm of production.[45]

What distinguishes the most incompetent architect from the best of bees
is that the architect raises his structure in imagination before he constructs
it in reality. The labor process ends in the creation of something which,
when the process began, already existed in an ideal form. Not merely does
he bring about a change of form in natural objects, but he also realizes, in
the nature that exists apart from himself, his own purpose, the purpose
which gives the law to his activities, the purpose to which he has to subordinate his own will.[46]

But the mode of consciousness was a function of economic transformation. As the *Manifesto* asked, "What else does the history of ideas prove
than that intellectual production changes its character in proportion as
material production is changed?" [47] Or, as it was more specifically described in the *German Ideology:*

The ideas of the ruling class are in every epoch the ruling ideas; that is,
the class which is the ruling material force of society is at the same time
its ruling intellectual force. The class which has the material means of
production at its disposal, has at the same time control over the means of
mental production, so that thereby, generally speaking, the ideas of those
who lack the means of mental production are subject to it.[48]

Marxian analysis consequently disposed Maoists to define opponents
within their ranks as class enemies, so that the semantic accusatives of

the Cultural Revolution (reactionary, revisionist, capitalist road) designated onetime agents of the revolutionary order, agents whose interpretation of socialism differed from the chairman's. But the sting was partly removed by Mao's continuing insistence upon leniency and moderation (cure the illness to save the patient). By combining the illness metaphor with the most extreme and even inappropriate Marxist diatribe, he thus produced terror through rhetoric alone: a Cultural Revolution without very many mortal victims. But, precisely because heterodoxy was the determinant of bourgeois class behavior, thought and politics were finally fused.[49]

The Cultural Revolution therefore began with an attack on intellectuals, accusing Teng T'o, Liao Mo-sha and Wu Han—the authors of the popular essays, *San-chia ts'un cha-chi* (Notes from Three-Family Village)—of political conspiracy. Wu Han (a noted historian who had worked in the Communist underground while teaching at Pei-ta, and who became deputy mayor of Peking in 1952) was especially castigated for his association with Mao's opponent at Lushan, P'eng Teh-huai. A month before the Lushan Conference, Wu Han had published an essay (*Hai Jui ma huang-ti,* Hai Jui Scolds the Emperor) about a famous Ming minister who had dared to criticize the Chia-ching emperor (1522–1566). After the secret condemnation of P'eng, which resulted in his dismissal from office, yet another essay on Hai Jui was published by Wu Han. Finally, in 1961 (while P'eng was distributing five "investigation reports" designed to rally support to his own side), Wu Han finished a play on the same theme (*Hai Jui pa kuan,* Hai Jui Dismissed from Office). The conjunction of dates and theme (after all, hadn't P'eng Teh-huai been scolding *his* emperor?) certainly did suggest a conspiracy. At least, Mao Tse-tung repeatedly declared so to the Central Committee: "The crux of the dismissal of Hai Jui lies in the dismissal itself. Emperor Chia-ching dismissed Hai Jui; in 1959 we sacked P'eng Teh-huai. P'eng Teh-huai *is* a Hai Jui."[50] This seemed to be publicly confirmed after P'eng was openly denounced in the fall of 1967. Then, a Red Guard publication asserted that P'eng Teh-huai had made a last attempt in 1962 to gain vindication by submitting an eighty-thousand character "memorial" with the shout: "I cannot remain silent any longer. I want to be like Hai Jui!"[51] Furthermore, the published record of his interrogation (P'eng had been arrested in Ch'eng-tu by Red Guards on December 28, 1966) quoted P'eng as saying: "He [Mao] dismissed me from office; I agreed, but had my reservations. I felt very much relieved without any official position. As I was no good and others were better than I was, I must be replaced. Since the Lushan meeting, I, as 'Hai Jui' was finished." [52]

There may well have been a conspiracy, but its content, not its existence, should interest us most. For, Wu Han and others were attacked because they seemed to be justifying the right of particular *individuals* freely to exercise critical judgment within a socialist society. Earlier it was shown that an imperial scholar-official was certain of his moral right to criticize the throne—whatever the cost to himself. It was exactly this form of personal autonomy which men like Wu Han or Teng T'o praised. Teng, a famous journalist, had edited a column called *Yen-shan yeh-hua* (Evening Chats at Yen-shan), which ran in newspapers throughout the country during 1961–1962. The column repeatedly mentioned the uncompromising integrity (*ku-ch'i*) and spirit of resistance (*fan-k'ang ching-shen*) of Confucian officials like Li San-ts'ai, Cheng Pan-ch'iao, or Mi Wan-chung, who had bravely censured emperors for corruption or for dictatorialism. Teng particularly admired the Tung-lin academicians, who had been purged by the emperor's eunuchs in the 1620s. This group of scholars, which included relatives of Ku Yen-wu (1613–1682) and Huang Tsung-hsi (1610–1695), had long been a paragon of Confucian heroism; and the "righteousness" of the group continued to receive praise under the Nationalist Republic.

The offensiveness to the People's Republic of Teng T'o's admiration for the Tung-lin scholars was detailed in 1966 by the literary critic, Yao Wen-yuan, who had achieved earlier fame for dogmatically chopping up Yü P'ing-po's interpretation of the *Dream of the Red Chamber*. Yao, who was Mao Tse-tung's son-in-law, also joined the Cultural Revolution Small Group of Party Central. His review of "Evening Chats" which appeared in Shanghai's *Chieh-fang jih-pao* (Liberation Daily) accused Teng T'o of using Ku Hsien-ch'eng's (1550–1612, founder of the Tung-lin Academy) famous lines, "Family, state and world affairs / I show concern for them all," to express his own hidden wish to "live up to his 'political ideas.' " [53] Teng T'o was thus pilloried for venerating "corrupt" officials of a "feudal" regime, for espousing the individual's right of social criticism, and even for suggesting that a new Tung-lin faction be formed.

Teng T'o pinned his hope of restoring capitalism especially on the persons of the "honest, incorrupt officials" who had been relieved of their offices, the insubordinate "arrogant scholars," and other antiparty and antisocialist elements. He exerted his utmost to laud their "deportment" of "considering themselves as the masters and refusing to serve as slaves." He repeatedly eulogized the Tung-lin faction—the "opposition faction within the landlord class of the Ming dynasty"—and showed great appreciation for their "political ambitions." He called on the antiparty and antisocialist elements to form a contemporary "Tung-lin faction." He urged them "not to indulge themselves in scholarly discussion" but "to show concern for politics." In order to achieve "their political aims," they must not fear "death and bloodshed" and must "steadfastly fight against the crafty statesmen in power." [54]

Some criticisms of Wu Han's praise of Hai Jui were just as vitriolic as this; but because Hai Jui was only an individual, and not the leader of a political faction, Wu Han incited a slightly less strident debate over the proper attitude which one should take toward "good" officials from China's "feudal" past. One critic, Chu Li-chang, published the following analysis:

Comrade Wu Han has called [Hai Jui] a pure official who "genuinely scolded the emperor; indeed he scolded him exceptionally bitterly." This "Memorial to Govern and Pacify" is precisely the memorial which "Hai Jui himself tendered" and which was supposed to be written at the people's request. The minute we glance into the memorial authored by this "pure official" we see clearly expressed: "The first priority in the empire is to speak truly in order to rectify the ruler's Way, clarify the minister's charge, and entreat the myriad generations to govern and pacify." There it also says: "[The subjects of] this empire are Your Majesty's kin. There has never been a man who has not looked after his kin. Within and without [the imperial presence] a minister is diligent about his official duties and his responsibility to speak out just to honor Your Majesty's family and make [Your reign] as stable as a rock". . . . It is not hard to see that Hai Jui stands within the landlord class, and, inspired by the thought of loyalty to his ruler, only submits his memorial urging the emperor to live up to the duty of a supreme ruler in order to attain the long-term consolidation of the feudal rule. . . . Of course, as far as a genuine appraisal of a "pure official" or "good official" is concerned, the "supreme" emperor is always unhappy [to hear criticism]; and so Hai Jui's submission of a memorial to the Chia-ching emperor truly meant taking his life in his own hands. But how can one support this kind of action on the part of Hai Jui as some kind of abstract "sense of courageous righteousness and high responsibility"? Rather, this is a feudalistic and theoretical concept of a minister daring to die for the sake of loyalty to lord and master, and of the minister having no choice but to die when the ruler wills it. When the memorial speaks of "daring to die and exhausting all attentiveness" it is a genuine reaction [within the terms] of Hai Jui's thought. In that case how is it possible for this kind of stupid and overwhelming loyalty to the emperor to be regarded as being for the sake of the people instead of a trait of individualistic indulgence? [55]

Mao had much earlier faulted sympathetic portrayals of Confucian officials as "praise" of "vile conduct"; such films or plays glorified men who "did not lift a finger to disturb the tiniest fragment of the feudal economic base or its superstructure." [56] But it was not only a question of misrepresenting the true nature of "feudal" collaborators; other remarks by Chairman Mao made it clear that he too regarded mere personal responsibility as a form of dangerous self-indulgence. He had announced in 1955, for example, that: "It must be known that collective leadership and personal responsibility are not antagonistic to but are integrated with each other. Personal responsibility and personal dictatorship which violates the principle of collective dictatorship are two entirely different things." [57] Admirers of the critical autonomy— "personal responsibility"—of some Confucian officials therefore erred to suppose that simple, individual humaneness could overcome class oppression.* Or, to use Yao Wen-yuan's more succinct dismissal of Hai Jui: "In this play, only Hai Jui is the hero. . . . Hai Jui *goes it alone* in making a great economic and political revolution." [58] Audacity might be a virtue, but only if it relied upon the general will of the masses.

* This interpretation is confirmed by James R. Pusey's careful study, *Wu Han: Attacking the Present through the Past* (Cambridge: Harvard East Asian Research Center, 1969). On p. 69, Pusey remarks that, "In the eyes of Mao Tsetung, Wu Han could only have been an exasperating reapparition of the demonic force of 'bourgeois thought' that he had so long endeavored to extinguish. Wu Han was a symbol of the failure of thought reform. He was evidence against Mao's cherished hope that men could change and that old intellectuals could become new intellectuals, and he was a sign that the battle of socialist education had not been won."

4

The Great Legislator

In his *Social Contract,* Jean-Jacques Rousseau (1712–1778) had insisted that:

If the people came to a resolution when adequately informed and without any communication among the citizens the general will would always result from the great number of slight differences, and the resolution would always be good. But when factions, partial associations, are formed to the detriment of the whole society, the will of each of these associations becomes general with reference to its members, and particularly with reference to the state; it may then be said that there are no longer as many voters as there are men, but only as many voters as there are associations. . . . It is important, then, in order to have a clear declaration of the general will, that there should be no partial association in the state.[1]

In his view particular groups (*associations partielles*) or factions (*brigues*) created miniature collective wills which detracted from the general will of the entire people. Citizens, to retain their worth as deliberating members of the larger society, would have to stand as individuals, abandoning primary associations and eschewing voluntary groupings. For Mao, on the other hand, to stand alone was to stand apart. Liberalism stems from petit bourgeois selfishness,[2] while conceit (*tzu-ta*) is derived from an individualism which overlooks the strength of the masses and "lags subjectively behind objective reality." [3] Because individualism stresses the capability of the singular self, it underestimates the collective potentiality of the masses and inhibits national accomplishments. Consequently, the individual must "wage revolution against oneself" (*ko tzu-chi ko-ming*) and the very word "I" must be smashed and vanquished (*ta-tao wo-tzu, ya-sui wo-tzu*). As a *People's Daily* editorial argued in early 1966, "If one could utterly ignore *wo* [I], one would dare to climb a mountain of swords and climb into a sea of fire." [4] In the same spirit Mao also declared, "The basic ideological program of the Great Proletarian Cultural Revolution is 'to combat selfishness and criticize revisionism.' " [5] We might say, therefore, that the Maoist version of a general will diverged from Rousseau's insofar as it tolerated associations while condemning independent citizens.

Different, too, would be Mao's version of Rousseau's Great Legislator. In the latter's political universe, the Legislator was designed to replace law.

If Sparta and Rome have perished, what state can hope to endure forever? If we wish to form a durable constitution, let us, then, not dream of making it eternal. In order to succeed we must not attempt the impossible, nor flatter ourselves that we are giving to the work of men a stability which human things do not admit of. The body politic, as well as the human body, begins to die from its birth, and bears in itself the causes of its own destruction. But both may have a constitution more or less robust, and fitted to preserve them a longer or shorter time. The constitution of man is the work of nature; that of the state is the work of art. It does not rest with men to prolong their lives; it does rest with them to prolong that of the state as far as possible, by giving it the best constitution practicable. . . . The principle of political life is in the sovereign authority. The legislative power is the heart of the state; the executive power is its brain, giving movement to all the parts. The brain may be paralyzed and yet the individual may live. A man remains an imbecile and lives; but so soon as the heart ceases its functions, the animal dies. It is not by laws that the state subsists, but by the legislative power.[6]

Within Rousseau's world of decline and fall, laws had a higher rate of mortality, a quicker speed of transit, than legislation. Human pride, which was man's mockery of eternal creation, myopically enshrined laws. Inflexible and rigid, such laws, in the end, prevented the state from adjusting to historical change. Only the sovereign Legislator was capable of divining men's intent through history. His divination could not be mistaken because he himself was the sum of his subjects' individualities.

Now the sovereign, being formed only of the individuals that compose it, neither has nor can have any interest contrary to theirs; consequently, the sovereign power needs no guarantee toward its subjects, because it is impossible that the body should wish to injure all its members. . . . But this is not the case as regards the relation of subjects to the sovereign. . . . Indeed, every individual may, as a man, have a particular will contrary to, or divergent from, the general will which he has as a citizen.[7]

The sovereign Legislator thus existed above that rationalistic, universal, and sovereign natural law which was conceptualized in sixteenth-century Europe out of a tradition running back to the Stoics. In one sense, the tradition culminated in Rousseau's version of the social contract. In another, it was replaced altogether by the theory of the general will. But this ambivalence is understandable, since Rousseau could not have conceived of a Legislator above law had law not been sovereign in the first place.

The Western theory of absolute sovereignty was engendered by the extraordinary tension between temporal and spiritual authority within the Holy Roman Empire. The ideal of a theocracy with two elected heads, one secular and one sacred, subordinate to Christ, was seldom realized. By the fourteenth century, in fact, an intense political conflict between pope and emperor had developed. To deny the principle of a body politic with two heads, Boniface VIII issued a bull (*Unam Sanctam*) in 1302 which argued for the unquestioned supremacy of a single authority whose acts could not be subject to legal criticism. When imperial apologists countered this declaration of *plenitudo potestatis* with their own theory of an emperor's divine right to rule, the foundation had been laid for the sixteenth-century doctrine of the divine right of kings.[8] Although the fully developed doctrine recognized the notion that there exists in the state an authority which can make laws and is therefore ultimately above law, sovereignty at first took its place within the scholastics' scheme of *lex naturalis*. Because that system of natural law owed so much to Aristotle, "natural" (the immanent human potentiality for development) and "conventional" (the development itself, shaped by art) were not sharply divided. But an equally important concept, influenced by Roman theories of law, was the absolute distinction between Zeno's universal law of nature and simple *jus civile*.[9] This became a contradiction between nature and convention when the scholastics' unified scheme of natural law was dissolved by the skepticism of the sixteenth and seventeenth centuries. Then *lex* became an ideal to which *jus* should, but did not necessarily, correspond.

There were various ways of attempting to resolve this conflict. One, as we have seen in Rousseau's *Social Contract*, ambivalently juxtaposed two previously contradictory concepts of the state: the idea (often absolutist) of a constitution guaranteeing universally natural human rights, and the notion (usually democratic) that the majority of men can by particular acts determine their political destiny. But another way, prior to this one, was to free the state completely from restraint by universal law. Assuming that men were dominated by passions which had to be curbed by laws (here, no more than judicial decisions), Niccolo Machiavelli (1469–1527) had argued that the state made civil society possible and must therefore exist above it as an untrammeled legal and military authority. As one scholar has described Machiavelli's attitude toward law:

For him law is not prior to the state, nor is justice. There are no universal laws or objective standards upon which the laws of the state could be founded, and to which her government is subordinate. On the contrary law is devised (and differently) within each state to assist in its preservation and growth, and is secondary to and dependent upon, military strength.[10]

Because conventional laws were now directed against naturally base instincts, the state of Machiavelli or Thomas Hobbes (1588–1679) was designed to replace "natural man" with a civilized citizenry. Even Rousseau, despite his nostalgia for an earlier state of nature, held this belief.

He who dares undertake to give institutions to a nation ought to feel himself capable, as it were, of changing human nature; of transforming every individual, who in himself is a complete and independent whole, into part of a greater whole, from which he receives in some manner his life and his being; of altering man's constitution in order to strengthen it; of substituting a social and moral existence for the independent and physical existence which we have all received from nature. In a word, it is necessary to deprive man of his native powers in order to endow him with some which are alien to him, and of which he cannot make use without the aid of other people. The more thoroughly those natural powers are deadened and destroyed, the greater and more durable are the acquired powers, the more solid and perfect also are the institutions.[11]

Rousseau thus felt that the citizen should be denaturalized, his physical existence transformed by appropriating from him those elements of nature which permitted him individual independence. In their place entirely new social and moral characteristics should be infused by— literally from the French—"he who dares to undertake the task of instituting a people" (*celui qui ose entreprendre d'instituer un peuple*). Rousseau's citizen had to be man-made and civic virtues artificial, because only then was the individual truly dependent upon the higher artificiality called the state. The institution of a people could therefore be likened to creation, god-like as it partook of the Enlightenment's characteristic faith in man's ability to overcome nature.

Mao Tse-tung believed as well in man's struggle against nature, but he did not thereby deny man's natural being. To him, nature as such was inimical where it hindered man's advance: the river to be dammed, the mountain to be moved. This was a struggle with and not against nature, which was not in principle called into question. Indeed, for Mao freedom was the unfettering of man's nature-given capacities. In his concluding speech at the Seventh National Congress of the Chinese Communist Party, for example, he told an ancient fable about Yü Kung, "The Foolish Old Man Who Removed the Mountains." Because two great mountains obstructed the view from an old man's doorway, he ordered his sons to begin digging away at their slopes. A neighbor (the Wise Old Man) ridiculed him for expecting that such a small number of people could dig up an entire mountain.

The Foolish Old Man replied, "When I die, my sons will carry on; when they die, there will be my grandsons, and then their sons and grandsons, and so on to infinity. High as they are, the mountains cannot grow any higher and with every bit we dig, they will be that much lower. Why can't we clear them away?" Having refuted the Wise Old Man's wrong view, he went on digging every day, unshaken in his conviction. God was moved by this, and he sent down two angels, who carried the mountains away on their backs. Today, two big mountains lie like a dead weight on the Chinese people. One is imperialism, the other is feudalism. The Chinese Communist Party has long made up its mind to dig them up. We must persevere and work unceasingly, and we, too, will touch God's heart. Our God is none other than the masses of the people.[12]

However, the God of the parable was only a *deus ex machina*. The real creative force was the generic (and natural) procreation of man, who remained the center of the tale—rewarded, unlike Job, for his serene confidence. But Mao insisted at the same time that man can only realize his nature by "reshaping the objective world." [13] Thus, "The working class remolds the whole of society in class struggle and in the struggle against nature, *and at the same time remolds itself*." [14] It was as though Mao could combine the best of two traditions: a culturally inherited sense of unity with cosmic forces, and a Western-derived notion of Darwinian struggle and Marxist self-determination. Were the people then both of nature and against it? Not entirely, for the phrase "conquest of nature" was literally *tui t'ien hsüan chan* (to declare war against heaven),[15] so that the farmers who led the storm attacks (*t'u-chi*) of plowing and manure collecting during the Great Leap were wresting their livelihoods away from heaven. Although that does suggest a sharp distinction between *t'ien* (heaven, which was traditionally associated with external authority and uncontrollable destiny) and nature as such, man's relation to the latter was still imprecise.

Mao's fusion of man and nature was especially visible in his poetic images.

The Occupation of Nanking by the People's Liberation Army

The wind and rain arise at Mount Chung yellow-green,
A million sturdy soldiers cross the Yangtze stream.
Tiger crouching, dragon coiling—present conquers past
As the cosmos overturns—generous and keen.
With all remaining courage pursue the foe on to the end!
We cannot emulate Hsiang Yü just to buy esteem.
Had heaven feelings it would age as well,
But here among men the right path is from sea-blue to mulberry-green.*

Men first appear in this poem like a natural force, a storm sweeping over Mount Chung, yet their victory is expressed by the crossing of the river, an act of overcoming nature. Though the final image seems to transform the sea into mulberry trees by the natural force of time, Mao inserts a purposive connotation with the phrase "right path" (*cheng-tao*), which makes the domestication of outer nature an obligation of man's inner nature. It is this human nature (*hsing*), distinct from natural forces (*t'ien-jan li*), which realizes itself by transforming the outer world. Consequently, civilized men—"socialized humanity"—are not unnatural; they epitomize the basic instincts of mankind, itself a natural phenomenon. And although civil society and the state of nature are clearly differentiated, the two exist along a compatible continuum.

---

* "Tiger crouching, dragon coiling" are former names for Nanking; "Pursue the foe on to the end" (*chui ch'iung k'ou*) is the opposite of the old adage, *ch'iung k'ou wu chui* (do not press the foe too far). What is translated as Hsiang Yü is in the original *pa-wang* (the hegemon). Hsiang, who revolted against the Ch'in in the third century B.C., so called himself. In his desire to appear magnanimous, he refrained from killing Liu Pang, the founder of the Han, who went on to defeat him. "Sea-blue" and "mulberry-green" in the last line evoke the Chinese legend of a woman who lived so long that she witnessed the seas dry up and turn into fields covered with mulberry trees.

Therefore even socialist man does not have to deny his own basic nature in order to forge a new social being. Mao did not believe that all natural human desires coincided with society's aims. For, we have already seen the important place that struggle (against both external nature and internal selfishness) occupied in his vision of communism. Rather, his consideration of this relationship did not follow a line of inquiry which began by assuming that social and natural man were two different creatures. This was not because classical Chinese political conceptualizations were uniformly optimistic about human nature. On the contrary, one influential school of thought sounded at times more pessimistic even than Hobbes.

Legalism has been traced back to the seventh century B.C. However, it did not really take form until the time of Hsün Tzu (ca. 298–238 B.C.), when it was formulated as policy by Han Fei (d. 233 B.C.) and Li Ssu (d. 208 B.C.) for the authoritarian Ch'in rulers who unified China in 221 B.C. Ch'in's empire grew out of the chaotic period of Warring States (403–221 B.C.), when new methods of warfare (iron weapons and massed cavalry) forced chivalric principalities to conceive of institutions which would permit them to conscript the populace into standing armies. The sheer extent of warfare persuaded many observers that monarchic government should halter the independence of the nobility. Consequently, one of the strongest impulses of legalist administration was to level its subjects by reducing feudal intermediaries standing between the ruler and the ruled. Another was to deny the "virtue" theory of Confucian governance. The people, like children, could not care for themselves. They needed prophylaxic discipline, not some formless version of paternal love. Han Fei wrote:

The way in which a mother loves her child is unsurpassable. But if the child has wicked habits, he is disciplined by a teacher; if he is sick, he is treated by a doctor. Without the teacher's discipline, he might some day receive capital punishment by the law; without the doctor's treatment he might die. In both cases no amount of mothers love would avail either to alleviate the penalty of the law or to rescue him from the grim clutches of death. If a mother cannot preserve a family by her love, how can an emperor keep a state by love? [16]

And another legalist philosopher, somewhat like Hobbes, pessimistically asserted that: "[The] human disposition is to hate; because of the wickedness of the human heart, laws had to be brought into existence." [17]

This theorist, Kuan-tzu,* believed that humanity had, by nature, always been disorderly, selfish, and benighted. The ruler (not divine, but simply endowed with higher intelligence) created civil society to bring men out of this mire.

In ancient times the people made no distinction of superiors and subordinates, of emperors and officers. Nor even did they respect the relationship of husband and wife either among the ordinary people or in the imperial family. They lived promiscuously like beasts, they attacked one another by force. Consequently the intelligent took advantage of the ignorant, the strong oppressed the weak, the young or the fatherless. In later times the intelligent people prohibited cruelty and oppression, and by means of united efforts they stopped violence.[18]

Han Fei was less able to escape entirely the prevailing belief in an earlier Golden Age of man, and therefore employed a determinist argument which made "virtue" dependent upon social conditions.

In the days of old, men did not need to till the soil; the natural supply of fruits and seeds was sufficient for their needs. The women did not have to weave; the supply of animal skins was sufficient to clothe them. There was an abundance of supply without the need of labor; there was scarcity of people and superfluity of wealth. Fighting was not necessary. But now a man is not content with only five children; ten is the vogue. It is common for a grandfather to have twenty-five grandchildren. This increased population is confronted with a diminution of wealth; prolonged labor is rewarded with an inadequate return. Under such circumstances fighting is the natural consequence. . . . This is . . . because supply and demand are different. Therefore the communistic life of people of the olden times is accounted for not by virtue but by superabundance. Today people fight for possessions. It is not the lack of virtue but the paucity of wealth which causes it.[19]

But whatever the accounting for human depravity, all of the legalists agreed that the people had to be given strict regulations for behavior: "Law is that which is observed by the government in orders and regulations, and observed by the people as standards of reward and punishment. Reward lies in obeying the law; punishment is meted out to those who disobey." [20]

The rule of law entailed both constancy and codification by those fit

* Traditionally identified as Kuan Chung (died 645 B.C.), the chief minister of Duke Huan of Ch'i. The *Kuan-tzu,* or book by that name, was not compiled until at least the fifth century B.C.

to govern. Uniformity corresponded to the centralizing ambitions of Ch'in ministers frustrated by the differing dialects, customs, and traditions of the Warring States. Because the right of any man to rule was so ambiguously challenged, invariable rules promulgated by those in power would clarify the source of sovereignty. Kuan-tzu declared: "Orders came from above. But if their application is discussed below, then the authority descends and resides in the people." [21] Above all, law divorced virtue (*te*) and sovereignty, intimately connected in the Chou (1122–249 B.C.) theory that heaven (*t'ien*) would recall its mandate (*ming*) from a tyrannical ruler and bestow it upon another, more virtuous house. The Confucian school had refined the Chou theory to identify legitimacy even more closely with the moral self-cultivation of individual monarchs, rather than with the genealogy of their succession. In the *Ta hsueh* (Great Learning), for instance, the sage-ruler was one who simply "makes his virtue illustrious" (*ming te*).[22] Or, in the words of the *Doctrine of the Mean:* "Knowing how to cultivate his own character, he knows how to govern other men." [23]

Confucianism thus added a high degree of princely voluntarism to the original mandate of heaven concept, but it also made the tenure of a ruling house depend rather insecurely upon the generation-to-generation capability of its scions. Legalism therefore helped guarantee constancy of rule, which both served the interests of individual dynasts and reassured political theorists that institutions, rather than persons, preserved good government. No one denied that sage-rulers governed best, but must "the saint system die with the death of the saintly ruler"?

Power is not something which can force itself into the hands of the virtuous and withdraw itself from the hands of the worthless. Used by the virtuous, power produces order; used by the worthless, power produces the reverse. . . . When Yao and Shun have power order prevails; when Chieh and Chou [two evil emperors] have it, disorder prevails. Here I do not mean to minimize the greatness of Yao or Shun, but to emphasize that their condition is not within their own control. . . . Men like Yao and Shun or like Chieh and Chou are born once in a thousand generations. . . . The average man is not as virtuous as Yao and Shun nor as vicious as Chieh and Chou. If they all observe the law, order will reign; if they all violate the law and wait for Yao or Shun to bring order out of disorder, then there would be only one generation of order out of a thousand. On the other hand, if the people observe the law and wait for the advent of Chieh or Chou to create disorder, then there would be only one generation of disorder out of a thousand generations.[24]

The legalists thus controlled the circumstance of virtue by abolishing it.

The dismissal of virtue also reflected the momentary decline of the mandate of heaven theory. The third-century descendants of those Chou rulers who had conquered China a millennium earlier were mere figureheads. The Chou's own extrication of heaven from the Shang ancestral spirits had already done much to universalize the king-head; the legalists rationalized one step further by freeing rule from charisma. Such routinization, perhaps the bureaucrat's best weapon, justly aided legalist functionaries by making the emperor's person just a *persona*. To that end the legalists could fortunately evoke another political figment: the Taoist *wu-wei* (nonaction) sage who ruled wisely by ruling not at all, so that society ran itself. The legalists secularized this religious nonattachment into the instrument of law. "If the supreme ruler exercises law and suppresses personal feelings, then the affairs of the state will move by the standard of law." [25] Personal involvement obviously hampered the rule of law because it entailed despotic whim. "Favoritism is what the emperor exercises, and law is what the state follows." [26] Hence the rule of law may have placed great symbolic stress on the sanctity of the emperor, but it put actual legislation in the hands of his officers. Therefore, later monarchs naturally inclined toward the original mandate theory in order to recover personal importance, even though that meant paying some deference to the so-called Mencian right of rebellion.

Mencius had once been asked by Wan Chang to explain how the sage-ruler Yao ignored his own heirs to give the empire to Shun. Mencius' immediate answer was to say that no emperor could simply give the kingdom to someone else; that was heaven's right alone. However, impersonal heaven did not provide instructions with its grant. "Heaven does not speak. It simply showed its will by [Shun's] personal conduct, and his conduct of affairs." [27] As Wan Chang pressed for more specifics, Mencius explained that Yao had first let Shun administer the empire as a kind of trial. "He caused him to preside over the conduct of affairs, and affairs were well administered, so that the people reposed under him;— Thus the people accepted him [*min shou chih yeh*]. Heaven gave [the empire] to him. The people gave it to him." [28] To cap his declaration, Mencius quoted from the *Shang-shu* (Book of Documents) that "Heaven sees according as my people see. Heaven hears according as my people hear." [29] He might as well have cited another line from the same section of that classic: "What the people desire, heaven will be found to give effect to" (*min chih so yü, t'ien pi ts'ung chih*).[30]

How close this could skirt to the threat of popular rebellion was amusingly illustrated by another dialogue between Mencius and Prince Hsuan of Ch'i: "[Mencius] proceeded, 'Suppose that the chief criminal judge could not regulate the officers [under him], how would you deal with him?' The king said, 'Dismiss him.' [Mencius again] said, 'If within the four borders [of your kingdom] there is not good government, what is to be done?' The king looked to the right and left, and spoke of other matters." [31] Because peasants often did revolt, and because such talk was treason to the ears of more powerful rulers, Mencius' boldness was qualified in two ways. First—and most faithful to the original—monarchs ruled for the sake of the people. The comfort of the ruled was the prime end of government, because heaven gauged it to judge a ruler's possession of virtue. Second, a new theory of dynastic change, which was elaborated during the Han period (206 B.C. to 220 A.D.), identified popular revolts as omens of heaven's displeasure. Like a comet or an earthquake, rebellion became a signal, rather than a cause, of the imminent withdrawal of the mandate. The major author of that explanation was Tung Chung-shu (c. 179 to c. 104 B.C.), who incorporated a cyclical *yin-yang* theory from the canonical *Book of Changes* into the esoteric divination principles of the "Five Elements": "Heaven possesses the Five Elements: first, wood; second, fire; third, earth; fourth, metal; fifth, water. Wood commences the cycle of the Five Elements; and while water ends it, earth is in the middle. Such is their natural progression. Wood produces fire, fire produces earth, earth produces metal, metal produces water, and water produces wood." [32] Heaven and humanity therefore moved in tandem cosmic sequence, as evidenced by omens. "Just before an emperor or ruler arises, auspicious omens first appear. Just before he is to perish, inauspicious omens appear. Consequently, things of the same gender summon each other." [33] It was true that a ruler could partially influence the process by the extent of his moral rectitude: "If the ruler is upright, the primal material force will be in harmony. Wind, rain [will come on] time. Auspicious stars will appear. The yellow dragon will descend. If the ruler is not upright, strange changes will occur in Heaven and bandits will appear." [34] But to Han emperors the fundamental appeal of Tung Chung-shu's syncretism was its replacement of ineffable virtue with thaumaturgic ritual. "Only after one has received the Mandate of Heaven can he become the ruler. The ruler determines the first day of the calendar for his dynasty, changes the colors of court costume, establishes regulations for rituals and music, and unifies the entire empire." [35] In this manner, King T'ang replaced the red of Hsia with the white of his own Chou dynasty; King Wu, the white of Yin with the black of Chou; and so forth. This may have routinized the task of "correct" rule, but it also rendered a monarchy's tenure dependent upon cosmically determined agents. "All this [changing of colors] manifests the change of dynasty [so that] the ruler is not succeeding [another] human being; and it reveals that he has received the Mandate from Heaven." [36] As heaven rolled into a new conjunction of the five elements, so would one dynasty inevitably fall to the next.

Some of this mechanical determinism was alleviated by theories of restoration formulated during the T'ang period (618–906). But it was above all the Sung period (960–1279) which saw fundamental changes in the conceptual primacy of an untouchable heaven. The Ch'eng brothers—Ch'eng I (1033–1107), and Ch'eng Hao (1032–1085)— key figures in what is styled Neo-Confucianism, first argued that human self-control distilled the essential goodness of human nature. Man could determine by effort his own degree of virtue. "Men must try ever harder to purify [the muddy water or evil in their nature]. The water will clear quickly if there is unceasing and vigorous effort. The water will clear slowly if effort is slow and lethargic. When it has cleared, the water has [recovered its] original [nature]. . . . This is the principle of the Mandate of Heaven." [37] Above the sequential flow envisaged by Tung Chung-shu was an immediate principle of nature which could be tapped at any moment to liberate rulers from the dictation of nominal concordance. "It, the principle of nature, is not in existence because of Yao, the sage-emperor. It does not stop existing because of Chieh, the wicked [ruler]." [38] It was Chu Hsi (1130–1200) who spelled out this new limited freedom from determinism in a dialogue with his schoolmen:

Question: At present the school of occultism, such as that of Shao Yung, asserts that all is predetermined and cannot be changed. What do you say?

Answer: They can only show the general course in which the principle of the prosperity and decline and the augmentation and diminution of *yin* and *yang* is revealed. Such theories were not held by sages or worthies. At present people expounding Shao Yung's [system based on] number assert that he had said that everything and every event succeeds or fails at a predetermined point of time. Such exposition is superficial. . . .

Further Question: If so, then Heaven produces sages and worthies only accidentally and not with any intention.

Answer: When does Heaven say that it purposely wanted to produce a sage or a worthy? The mere fact is that whenever the courses of material force reach certain points and meet, a sage or a worthy is born. After he is born, it does seem that Heaven had such an intention. . . . It is true that each man has his destiny, but he should not fail to obey the correct destiny. For example, the man who understands destiny will not stand beneath the precipitous wall. If he should say that everything depends on the Mandate of Heaven and goes to stand under a precipitous wall, and if by any chance the wall should crumble and crush him, he cannot blame it on destiny. Whenever a man has done his very best, there he has his destiny alone.[39]

Here was a philosophy of action—if not entirely of free will—to enable rulers to adjust the rate of historical mechanics. Because of its connection with the mandate of heaven theory, the dynastic cycle could not be abandoned altogether, but its span could be broadened according to the degree of the emperor's pursuit of virtue. And, because the management of an increasingly complex bureaucracy required just decisions as well as moral conduct, rulers had to seek the counsel of history. To this end Ssu-ma Kuang (1019–1086) compiled his massive *Tzu-chih t'ung-chien* (Comprehensive Mirror for Aid in Government; 294 *chüan* of annals completed in 1084).

A prince amid his ten thousand daily concerns must wish to know comprehensively the merits and demerits of former ages. . . . Disregarding my inadequacy I have constantly wished to write a chronological history roughly in accordance with the form of the *Tso* tradition, starting with the Warring States and going down to the Five Dynasties, drawing on other books besides the official histories and taking in all that a prince ought to know—everything pertaining to the rise and fall of dynasties and the good and ill fortune of the common people, all good and bad examples that can furnish models and warnings.[40]

While the prince consciously mastered the past well enough to avoid its mistakes, the Confucian historian's own position was concurrently strengthened. After all, it was he who catalogued and patterned that past.

In a way, this aggrandizement of the individual *ju* (Confucianist) ultimately hobbled the collective elite of scholar-officials. This same period also witnessed the rise of a gentry social estate whence literati usually emerged. As the local influence and power of that group increased, it did show some signs of evolving into a kind of political estate.

It was probably most hindered from this development by the sheer rate of vertical mobility upward and downward in the meritocracy. But the Neo-Confucian theory of dynastic legitimacy was an obstacle as well. As individual literati felt themselves capable of divining heaven's will, they understandably mediated the bestowal of legitimacy. Consequently, even exponents of greater local autonomy—like the seventeenth-century political philosopher Ku Yen-wu (1613–1682)—had very little incentive to develop an independent gentry theory of sovereignty.

Ku Yen-wu is still one of the most widely read theorists of the Confucian state. Loyal to the Ming dynasty, he refused to serve the succeeding Ch'ing, living out his years as an independent and extraordinarily prolific scholar. His works greatly influenced the statecraft (ching-shih) school of the eighteenth and nineteenth centuries, and enjoyed wide currency at the turn of the twentieth century among young nationalists like Mao Tse-tung, who cited Ku in his own writings.[41] One portion of Ku Yen-wu's best known work, the Jih-chih lu (A Record of Daily Learning), investigated the etymological origins of ch'ing-i (pure discussion), which was usually taken to mean the right of loyal scholars to censure the emperor for deviating from the correct "Way" (Tao) of governance.* His research instead showed that ch'ing-i was developed by the Han emperors as a way for villagers to recommend local notables for official appointment. Rather than expressing a right of dissent, pure discussion, Ku argued, was originally a bureaucratic instrument allying central and local government against the feudal aristocracy which once stood between them. However, it did have a purely social function. Because ch'ing-i in practice involved public praise and criticism of local office-seekers, it had the additional effect of shaming evildoers. By so influencing customs, pure discussion made harsh legalist punishments unnecessary, and consequently permitted society to regulate itself without imperial intervention: an ideal Confucian equilibrium.

If ch'ing-i was once enlightened enough to guide imperial appointments, then a degree of rectitude or virtue (which in its Chinese form, te, is almost equivalent to Rousseau's souveraineté) must have rested inherently with the masses. Ku admitted that people did have their own virtue, but it was "small," and needed the greater virtue of the ruler to be articulated. For, heaven alone inspired the proper ordering of society into the nine Confucian divisions of human relations; there were no natural or mechanic relations (Ku himself was quite Durkheimian

* See the Appendix.

in his sensitivity to that distinction) derived from society as such. They were organically conferred on the people by the king, heaven's instrument. In fact, heaven's plan overrode the monarch's responsibility to his own subjects, so that the compact of rule was made with heaven, not with the ruled.

Perhaps there once was in China a compact between an elected chief and his tribesmen, but by the Shang (conventionally, 1726–1122 B.C.), the emperor was responsible only to his ancestral spirits and *shang-ti* (the lord on high). No matter how meticulous Ku's researches, he could not—like European scholars—have historically justified some form of early social contract. Western theorists, on the other hand, did redefine political sovereignty in this way. By examining the history of the early Franks, Francois Hotman's *Francogallia* (1573) demonstrated that early French kings were elected magistrates who shared their authority with the community.[42] Hotman's theories were systematically transformed into a constitutionalist doctrine of the state by the Huguenot Theodore Beza. His *Right of Magistrates* used scriptural examples of the election of Jewish kings, as well as early European oaths of coronation, to show that monarchs were originally installed by the people. Because the latter granted authority, it would only stand to reason that the people had imposed civil law upon the king to protect their own interests. Beza would not go so far as to sanction personal disobedience on these grounds, but he did argue for the right of corporate resistance by the estates which composed society.[43]

Ku Yen-wu, on the other hand, could only check despotism by appealing to the sageliness of the ruler. His scriptures (*The Book of Documents*) extolled the paradigmatic Emperor Shun for heeding the counsel of his subjects. "He deliberated with the [chief of the] four mountains, how to throw open all the doors [of communication between the court and the empire], and sought to see with the eyes and hear with the ears of all [*ming ssu mu, ta ssu ts'ung*]." * An emperor's ability to fulfill the mandate consequently depended on his willingness to listen to the advice of those happy few in the empire who could judge the morality of his reign. Virtue—as defined by Confucianists—was to be paramount over law. Ku's political stance was therefore both an ideological reac-

* *Shang shu*, 2.1.5.:15. James Legge, *The Chinese Classics* (Hong Kong: Hong Kong University Press, 1970), vol. III, part I, p. 41. Ku evoked this passage in his own essay on *ch'ing-i* by using the phrase *ssu ts'ung*. Most traditional commentaries agreed that the entire phrase meant that Shun made himself accessible to the counsel of the empire's gentlemen (or what we would today call the gentry) by "widening the pathway [of words] for the worthy" (*kuang hsien lu*).

tion to the Ch'in school of law and an expression of the social consequences of legalism's centralizing policies. During its brief but forceful
tenure, legalism had destroyed feudal pluralisms and thus withered any
growth of fundamental law. Because fundamental law in the European
feudal sense was the defense of natural particularisms, it could not be
man-made, and consequently prevented any single source of human
authority from acting as the source of law. Therefore, when Jean Bodin
(1530–1596) and other sixteenth-century continental theorists saw
how centralist authority was diffused by fundamental law, they were
inspired to conceive of a theory of sovereignty which explicitly separated
social and political realms.[44] Because of the evolution of Chinese society, Ku Yen-wu found no source of authority—no fundamental law—
in social groups, and hence no inspiration to describe sovereignty in
autonomous terms.[45] Instead, state and society remained in his eyes
loosely tied together by a single figure whose authority was trammeled
by Ku's defensive insertion of his own *Stand* at the nodal point of political and social connection. And because the literati lacked their own
socially separate corporate identity, they could neither share in trans-
scendental rule nor possess a fundamental right to govern on their own.
Nothing was left for them but mediation between the society below and
the bureaucratic polity above. And because this sociopolitical elite occupied both spheres at once, it was not inclined to articulate a defense
of individual or corporate rights against the state. Man was thus placed
within a total order, so that even in the eyes of Mao Tse-tung's generation the individual was fettered by an entire net of politically sanctioned
social relations, rather than by society or polity alone. Consequently,
when the theory of the social contract was discovered at the turn of the
century, Chinese interpreters of Rousseau simply identified individual
freedom with national sovereignty in the hope of discovering a new
political society to free them from the old one.

Mao, for example, was first exposed to Rousseau by reading Liang
Ch'i-ch'ao's exposition of the social contract in the popular journal
Hsin-min ts'ung-pao.[46] For Liang, the most exciting implication of
Rousseau's theory of the contract was natural right, because such an
agreement could only be made between free and equal individuals. In
that event, political responsibility (once bestowed by heaven on individual rulers) had to be shared by all. For, "How can we speak of a
contract if one possesses responsibility while the other lacks it?" [47]
Every member of society had to be a part of this organic whole—not
because that assured a proper apportionment of social duties, but be-

cause "the state alone possesses a complete body while an individual is no more than a limb or organ." [48] In Liang's eyes the social contract therefore diminished each citizen's individuality. Rousseau could argue that there was a gain in exchange as the individual benefited from the cumulative strength of the entire citizenry, but Liang Ch'i-ch'ao continued to fear that if each person "contributed himself to the state, then he would be swallowed, dissolved." [49] Still, even though this seemed to him the most dangerous quality of Rousseau's political system, Liang ended by insisting that Rousseau only wished to have the individual "contribute a portion, and not the sum total of his sovereignty" in return for the "massed strength" of a nation which would "protect and preserve his own freedom and sovereignty." [50]

Liang's conclusion was ambivalent, arguing both for a strong nation and for the rights of the individual. There was a theoretical exit from this dilemma by way of Hegelianism, but that solution was not yet available to the Chinese. Forced to an antithesis, Liang and many of his liberal contemporaries—however suspicious of the Jacobin state's absolute claims upon its citizens—did concede the necessity of personal sacrifice in terms which supposed a greater collective realization of human sovereignty than the individual alone could attain. This was expressed in the Chinese sense of sovereignty, *ch'üan,* which means rights as well as strength: perfectly appropriate to a period in her history when China seemed "a sheet of loose sand" before the concerted onslaught of imperialism. Indeed, Liang Ch'i-ch'ao had prefaced his discourse on Rousseau with a quote from Kant declaring the *Social Contract* to be a theory for the establishment of a nation. Even classical liberalism was then seen as the political philosophy best designed to strengthen the nation by freeing the individual's spirit of independence in order to transform slaves into citizens. Whether because of a Confucian bedrock of ethical conviction, or because of a predilection to judge institutions by their effects upon social behavior, modern Chinese political theory perpetually suggested that norms alone determined, if not replaced, institutions as such.

5

The Myth-Prince

If institutions are replaced by norms, then society is determined by consciousness. That is why the ideological resonances of Mao's revolution vibrate so strongly in the works of Neo-Hegelian Marxists.[1] Georg Lukacs (1885–1971), for instance, criticized his own influential work, *History and Class Consciousness* (1923), for having "messianic, utopian aspirations" which were "violently opposed to bureaucracy."[2] As he later put it, he was "absolutely convinced" then that "the purely contemplative nature of bourgeois thought had to be radically overcome. As a result the conception of revolutionary praxis in this book takes on extravagant overtones that are more in keeping with the current messianic utopianism of the Communist left than with authentic Marxist doctrine."[3] In 1923 Marxism had seemed to Lukacs a scientific philosophy which liberated men from the inhuman domination of capitalist economic laws in order to create a communist society controlled by human reason alone.[4] This idealist desire to restore autonomy to human reason was classically Hegelian, so that one of Lukacs' strongest impulses was to turn back to the young Marx in order to stress his connection with Hegel. Arguing that all of Marx's important categories stemmed directly from Hegel's logic, Lukacs believed then "that all good Marxists should form, in Lenin's words 'a kind of society of the materialist friends of the Hegelian dialectic.' "[5] Indeed, Hegelianism had been sublated (*aufgehoben*) in Marxism, so that *History and Class Consciousness* was devoted to transforming the Hegelian concept of concrete totality into a fundamental Marxist category: the identical subject-object which existed in history as the proletariat conscious of its own self-awareness.[6]

By stressing totality, Lukacs hoped to show that Marx and Engels had revolutionized social theory because they no longer studied objects in isolation. Rather, a society was a total complex of interacting elements which constantly adjusted one to the other with each single shift. Once men grew conscious of their class position—once they understood "reality as a social process"—they could willfully rearrange those elements and so escape the tyranny of economic laws.

For only this conception [of reality as a social process] dissolves the fetishistic forms necessarily produced by the capitalist mode of production and enables us to see them as mere illusions which are not less illusory for being seen to be necessary. These unmediated concepts, these "laws" sprout just as inevitably from the soil of capitalism and veil the real relation between objects.[7]

Defining Marxism as a method of perception meant assigning great importance to subjective human intervention. As one analyst of Lukacs' thought has commented: "The system in short depends upon the men. A social system is not something given in history but is a social object that is selectively interpreted and is actively conceptualized by men in the here and now; it is seen as the product of the interaction of 'subject' and 'object.' "[8]

The temporality of social systems was certainly not Lukacs' perception alone. Whether in the West or in China, modernity and the awareness of fundamental mutability went hand in hand. What did particularly characterize this school of Marxism, however, was the conviction that, business cycles or not, one made a revolution by arousing the consciousness of workers enmeshed in capitalist social relations and enslaved by the tyranny of custom. For Lukacs, the agent of the awakening was the Leninist party. For the Italian Marxist, Antonio Gramsci (1891–1937), it was more figuratively the modern myth-prince.

Gramsci's myth-prince was ostensibly a metaphor for the political party which embodied the collective will.

The modern prince, the myth-prince, cannot be a real person, a concrete individual; it can only be an organism; a complex element of society in which the cementing of a collective will, recognized and partially asserted in action, has already begun. This organism is already provided by historical development and it is the political party: the first cell containing the germs of collective will which are striving to become universal and total.[9]

But that organism, like Machiavelli's prince, was a personification of Jacobin political creation, representing the process of formation of the collective will "not through dispositions and pedantic classifications of the principles and criteria of a mode of action but through the qualities, characteristic traits, duties, necessities of a concrete person." [10] It was the historical example of a Sorelian myth: not coldly rational ideology but the specific clustering of the collective will of disparate individuals. George Sorel's (1847–1942) concept of myth was too much predicated on the immediate, even mindless, action of syndicalist unions. Such a total emphasis on spontaneity and immediacy alarmed Gramsci because of its tendency toward fascism. Besides, it was easy enough to engender destructive myths, but once society's existing moral and legal relations had been destroyed, the myth's *raison d'être* would expire, fragmenting and dispersing the collective consciousness into individual wills before genuine revolution had been reached. Under extreme conditions, a concrete "prince"—an actual person—could overcome the negative character of Sorelian myth and embody a constructive ideology.

In the modern world only an immediate and imminent historicopolitical action, characterized by the necessity for rapid and lightning movement, can be mythically embodied in a concrete individual: this rapidity can only be rendered necessary by a great imminent danger, a great danger which in fact brings about simultaneously the enflaming of passions and fanaticism, abolishing critical sense and the corroding irony which can destroy the "divine" character of a *condottiero*.[11]

But because successful revolution required a greater duration than the "immediate and imminent" acts of the *condottiero,* the true myth-prince had to be an organic party. Why not then abandon the metaphor and simply call for a party as such? Because:

The Modern Prince must contain a part dedicated to Jacobinism (in the integral significance which this notion has had historically and ought to have conceptually), as an example of how a collective will was formed and operated concretely, which in at least some of its aspects was an original creation, *ex novo.* It is necessary to define collective will and political will in general in the modern sense; will as working consciousness of historical necessity, as protagonist of a real and effective historical drama.[12]

In this manner Gramsci's modern prince actually surpasses metaphor. As a figure of history (instead of speech), it was designed to stand above humanity, drawing together both articulated political and inchoate collective wills, both state and society. It not only focuses the two, being the projection of them, but also acts creatively to make them components of, or actors in, history. Like Machiavelli's own prince (tagged by Gramsci as Jacobin in manner), it would bring even the peasants into political life. As John Cammett pointed out:

Machiavelli analyzed [the classes and institutions of society] in a thoroughly "Jacobin" manner: beginning with the actual social structure, he established a goal that was attainable through resolute political direction of forces in the structure. Gramsci, in fact, concluded that only this Jacobin attitude is realistic, because it alone can deal with historical reality.[13]

Gramsci's identification of the realistic assessment of social forces with archetypal Jacobinism recalls Mao's long struggle to force doctrinaire Marxists to recognize the revolutionary importance of the peasantry. But it is the question of *resolute direction* which is most intriguing—especially because Gramsci and Mao's variants of Jacobinism may both have salvationist roots: the Catholic Church for the former,[14] the Confucian gentleman's duty to renovate the people for Mao Tsetung. Of course, the comparison might make better sense in terms of negative reactions instead of positive influences. One would expect a member of the May Fourth generation to show as much concern for moral or spiritual authority as a socialist plotting revolution in Catholic Italy. As Gramsci viewed common sense in terms of its religious elements,[15] so did Mao describe the tyranny of popular superstition in rural China as "theocratic authority."[16] And, like Gramsci, the young Mao indignantly responded to the social figments of that authority with anarchism, assaulting the despotism of the traditional family.[17]

It was perhaps because Mao began with indignation and only later acquired a revolutionary ideology that he viewed Marxism primarily as an instrumentality rather than as a revelation. "When we say Marxism is correct it is certainly not because Marx was a 'prophet' but because his theory has been proved correct in our practice and in our struggle. We need Marxism in our struggle. In our acceptance of his theory no such formalistic or mystical notion as that of 'prophecy' ever enters our minds."[18] But there were two other reasons which were far more important than impulse. First, Mao felt that Marxism, of Western provenance, had to be adapted to the particular necessities of China's historical setting so as to be refined into "a theory which is our own and of a specific nature."[19] Second, party intellectuals must not be allowed to become academic dogmatists who failed to realize that "application is the sole object of this mastery."[20] Or, as Mao put it much more earthily in another speech during the party rectification movement of 1942:

Our comrades must understand that we do not study Marxism–Leninism because it is pleasing to the eye, or because it has some mystical value, like the doctrines of the Taoist priests who ascend Mao *shan* to learn how to subdue devils and evil spirits. Marxism–Leninism has no beauty, nor has it any mystical value. It is only extremely useful. . . . Those who regard Marxism–Leninism as religious dogma show this type of blind ignorance. We must tell them openly, "Your dogma is of no use," or to use an impolite phrase, "Your dogma is less useful than excrement." We see that dog excrement can fertilize the fields and man's can feed the dog. And dogmas? They can't fertilize the fields nor can they feed a dog. Of what use are they? [21]

Statements like these, deliberately intended to shock party cadres into demystifying Marxism, made Mao seem to be a revolutionary pragmatist for whom ideology was merely a choice of weapons. Yet he simultaneously emphasized the uniqueness of Marxism–Leninism as "true theory . . . drawn from objective reality and then verified by objective reality." [22] No other political philosophy possessed this quality in Mao's view, so that his revolutionary certainty was sustained by the conviction that Marxism truly described the world he saw around him. But what of the inconsistencies between a proletarian ideal and a peasant reality, between a Marxist pattern of development and the specific Chinese situation? Certainly, Mao recognized those discrepancies as he argued again and again that dogma must be tempered by practice and that China had to adapt Marxism to its own needs. But did he not at the same time have to believe that this "true theory" was capable of being extracted from (not imposed upon) Chinese history, that China was only a particular instance of universal patterns inhering to mankind's history?

The tension between subjective perception and objective reality, between abstraction and specificity, was not simply Chinese; it characterized the foundation of Marxism itself. Engels had repeatedly insisted that dialectical materialism did not impose abstractions upon history. Rather it derived general laws by observing the connections between events.

Modern materialism sees history as the process of the evolution of humanity, and its own problem as the discovery of laws of motion of this process. [23]

In characterizing the process [of capitalist production begetting its own destruction] as the negation of the negation, Marx does not dream of attempting to prove by this that the process was historically necessary. On the contrary: after he has proved from history that in fact the process has partially already occurred, and partially must occur in the future, he then also characterizes it as a process which develops in accordance with a definite dialectical law. That is all.[24]

At the same time—even in the language used here—Engels revealed his certainty about the correctness of Marx's perception of those dialectical laws, and in turn projected them onto history with enough assurance to create an illusion of necessity, making subjective action possible. For, the original aim of dialectical materialism was to allow man to control his destiny by dominating, even destroying, the forces of nature and society extraneously imposed upon him by his religions, "phantastic reflection[s] in men's minds of those external forces which control their daily life." [25]

The forces operating in society work exactly like the forces operating in nature: blindly, violently, destructively, so long as we do not understand them and fail to take them into account. But when once we have recognized them and understood how they work, their direction and their effects, the gradual subjection of them to our will and the use of them for the attainment of our aims depends entirely upon ourselves.[26]

It is important to note, then, that the heart of Marxism is the belief that knowledge is power. Once man *knows* correctly, once religion is unmasked, then he can begin to perform those acts which will finally bring social forces under the control of society.[27] Praxis: prophecies fulfill themselves.

Yet no matter how unorthodox the Marxist revolutionary, praxis always had to be informed by correct theory, lest action become mindless. This task was hardest in the non-European world where revolutions were often identified with a single guerrilla leader of nonproletarian origin. Although Che Guevara, for instance, agreed with Lenin's premise that "without a revolutionary theory there is no revolutionary movement," he had to insist that "revolutionary theory, as the expression of a social truth, surpasses any declaration of it." [28] Or, put another way, revolutionaries like Fidel Castro, careless of theory, can succeed if they correctly interpret the historical reality which theory supposedly describes. "We, practical revolutionaries, initiating our own struggle, simply fulfill laws foreseen by Marx, the scientist. . . . That is to say . . . the laws of Marxism are present in the events of the Cuban Revolution independently of what its leaders profess or even know of those laws from a theoretical point of view." [29]

Of course, this could border on adventurism or revolution for revolution's sake. Guevara's quixotic farewell letter to his parents seemed a *condottiero's* testament:

Once again I feel beneath my heels the ribs of Rosinante. Once more, I hit the road with my shield upon my arm. . . . My Marxism has taken root and become purified. I believe in armed struggle as the only solution for those peoples who fight to free themselves, and I am consistent with my beliefs. Many will call me an adventurer, and that I am—only one of a different sort, one of those who risks his skin to prove his truths. . . . Give a thought once in a while to this little soldier of fortune of the twentieth century.[30]

At the other extreme, however, theoretical integrity at the expense of action not only made intellectuals out of revolutionaries; it denied Gramsci's definition of the genuine doctrine of Marx, according to which "man and reality, the instrument of labor and the will, are not separated but come together in the historical act." [31]

Action in history, praxis realizing theory, was a vital part of Marx's philosophical system. The historical actor, his will resolving determinism, became a crucial element in the thought of many of Marx's followers. To Lukacs, for instance, only Lenin had been able to break with mechanical fatalism, ". . . both with the concept of proletarian class consciousness as a mechanical product of its class situation, and with the idea that the revolution itself is only the mechanical working out of fatalistically explosive economic forces." [32] In fact, to believe that Marx's predictions were a scientific guarantee of revolution, rather than a methodology for action, abolished human decision.[33] Indeed the major concern of *History and Class Consciousness* was to deny the immutability of scientific laws, the eternal truths of Marxism, in order to recover the possibility of true freedom. Like Hannah Arendt, Georg Lukacs was profoundly aware of man's confinement in the web of social relations, but he believed that praxis (truly a mystique when expressed this way) could liberate the individual from these restrictions.

Man finds himself confronted by purely natural relations or social forms mystified into natural relations. They appear to be fixed, complete and immutable entities which can be manipulated and even comprehended, but never overthrown. But also this situation creates the possibility of praxis in the individual consciousness. Praxis becomes the form of action appropriate to the isolated individual, it becomes his ethic.[34]

Lenin therefore demonstrated the possibility of escaping from necessity without denying history—or, rather, without denying historical materialism. Since the latter was really nothing more than "the theory of the proletarian revolution," Lenin's own theoretical stature could be measured by his ability "to detect beneath the appearances of bourgeois society those tendencies toward proletarian revolution." [35] After all, the dialectic was "not a finished theory to be applied mechanically to all the phenomena of life"; it awaited application to be given a "more complete and *theoretically more developed form*." [36]

The development which Marxism thus underwent through Lenin consists merely—merely!—and in its increasing grasp of the intimate, visible, and momentous connection between individual actions and general destiny— the revolutionary destiny of the whole working class. . . . Lenin alone took this step toward making Marxism . . . concrete. That is why he in a world historical sense is the only theoretician equal to Marx yet produced by the struggle for the liberation of the proletariat.[37]

Thus the individual who could perceive humanity's collective destiny, and then concretely associate himself with that sociohistoric totality, both realized Marxism and pushed it to a higher theoretical level. Lukacs' Lenin was therefore doubly Hegelian. He on the one hand married necessity and will by perceiving the "destiny" (the subjective realization of idea) of history, and on the other he individually mediated the concrete universal through actual practice. "For Marxists the concrete analysis of the concrete situation is not the opposite of 'pure' theory; on the contrary, it is the culmination of all genuine theory, its consummation, the point where it therefore breaks into practice." [38] But this did not make Lenin an abstract philosophical agent. On the contrary, Lukacs most admired Lenin's personal courage to act. Other Marxists had been so concerned with doctrinal purity that they paid "lip service to revolution without understanding what revolution is." [39] Lenin realized, however, that "whoever expects a 'pure' social revolution will *never* live to see one." [40] In fact, he seemed to Lukacs the very epitome of the Stoic-Epicurean sage. Standing as a model of "permanent readiness," Lenin came to represent "an ineradicable value" for an age during which manipulation was absorbing praxis, and bureaucracy was replacing revolution.[41]

The generation of the mid-1920s had seen the failure of socialist revolution in Germany and Hungary and its routinization in the Soviet Union. Lukacs was all the more alert to this discrepancy between Marxist ideals and actuality because of his early studies in Neo-Kantianism, which stressed the difference between what was (*sein*) and what ought to be (*sollen*), between reality (*Wirklichkeit*) and value (*Wert*). He therefore tried to resolve the Marxist contradiction between necessity and freedom by arguing that the proof of the potential for human choice in the face of social determinants could be found in the individual's recognition that he *ought* to change his way of life. The same kind of consciousness of the gap between promises and reality characterized the social criticism of the Frankfurt Institute, which sought to create a dialectical social science that transcended the limits of immediate experience without falling too deeply into Hegelian idealism. By combining the *Lebensphilosophie* of a Nietzsche or Dilthey with Marxist rationalism, Max Horkheimer had hoped to harmonize individual and social interests.[41a] One major offshoot of his *kritische Theorie* was the integration of psychoanalysis and history, both in the idealism of Erich Fromm and in the connections made by Herbert Marcuse between industrialism and alienation. This particular strain of Marxism influenced members of the American New Left in the 1960s. It is difficult to make sweeping generalizations about so eclectic a movement, but one dominant impulse behind it has certainly been a deep concern with the dehumanization of the individual in technologically advanced societies, and a consequent tendency to look to Maoist China for evidence of the reconcilability of individual and mass. Those in search of a humane Marxist order were sometimes embarrassed by Mao's personality cult, but misgivings were often overcome by the wish to believe that man can construct a socialist society beyond alienation. For, like the young Lukacs, members of the New Left tended to assign man the capacity to mold a socialist utopia despite the great disillusionment of Stalinism. The impulse was profoundly humanistic: a commitment to keep Marxism from turning into a sociology which accepted the irresistability of technocratic allocation, socialist stratification, and revolutionary bureaucratization. If the realm of freedom were ever to be reached, such "laws" would have to be broken, and that in turn called for Rousseau's legislator, Gramsci's myth-prince, Lukacs' Lenin, or Mao himself. Laws, in short, would be opposed by ideals: a coherent vision which was necessarily individual.

Here, where Mao Tse-tung and Hegelian Marxism seemed to run together, it is important to remember that they did ultimately remain apart. Lukacs, for example, had stressed the importance of socializing, "denaturalizing," the means of production in order to liberate man.[42] Mao, as we have seen, drew the natural and the social poles of Marxism together, <u>mass man being a force of nature as such</u>. Furthermore,

Mao—influenced by T. H. Green rather than Bruno Bauer or Arnold Ruge—saw individual fulfillment *in* society, rather than merely by associating with it. For both of these reasons, he tended toward a mass, rather than elitist, line. Lukacs, on the other hand, believed that only the intellectual could "awaken the genuinely independent personality, whose possibility has been created by previous economic development." [43]

Another way of distinguishing Mao from the Western myth-prince would be to consider the problem of praxis. The Marxist hero constantly risks falling to either side of practice: empirical pragmatism versus messianic militancy.[44] A French Marxist has described the empiricist danger:

Let us be extremely schematic: under these circumstances [that is, a disassociation of social and personal consciousness] one can say and do anything one wishes. This "works" or that "doesn't work at all." Anything which "works" (even if it tends towards disaster) is good. There are no longer principles, line [of development], nor successive struggle. And since bourgeois ideas are those which "work" the best in a bourgeois society, the empiricist will consider "his" ideas successful when they are in reality no more than bourgeois ideas which have become successful.[45]

Messianism, on the other hand, overcomes knowledge with will. One critic of Hegelian Marxism has identified this as an anti-intellectualism which sees theory "as a subversion of revolutionary militancy," calling "ritualistically for the 'unity of theory and praxis.' " [46]

The same contradiction between objective knowing and subjective doing existed in philosophical guise as the Marxian problem of "false consciousness," which has been brilliantly summarized by George Lichtheim.

There is only truth about history, and only one criterion for judging the discrepancy between what men are and what they might become: this criterion is supplied by philosophy, specifically by its understanding of man as a rational being. Thus philosophy, as the norm of reality, entails an implicit critique of this reality. Yet Marx also held that the philosophy of every age is the "ideological reflex" of determinate social conditions. How then could it function as the source of normative judgments pointing beyond the existing state of affairs? . . . [After becoming a materialist] he took over from his French predecessors the critical demolition of traditional metaphysics, yet he also went on ascribing a rational content to history. The rationality was a hidden one and had to be discerned in the logic of the "material" process itself. . . . The historical character of the Marxian dialectic, and with it the problem of ideology in the modern sense, is a consequence of the discovery that there is not—as Feuerbach had thought—a single universal human standpoint from which to judge the alienations imposed by history; there are only particular human standpoints, corresponding to forms of society. . . . There is not in Marx a clear distinction between sociological statements relative to particular situations, and philosophical generalizations pertaining to history as a whole. How is the dilemma to be met? . . . *A rational order is one in which thinking determines being.* Men will be free when they are able to produce their own circumstances. . . . [Thus, Marx] took it for granted that, though consciousness is conditioned by existence, it can also rise above existence and be a means of transcending the alienation which sets the historical process in motion. The *truth* about man is one and the same for all stages of history, even though every stage produces its own illusions.[47]

But the dialectical resolution remained a contradiction, which seemed to some an existential dilemma. The French existential Marxist Lucien Goldmann therefore placed Marxism alongside Christianity as a faith which "explained the paradoxical and double nature of man and the world." [48]

Subsequently Hegel, and especially Marx and Lukacs, have been able to substitute for the wager on the paradoxical and mediatory God of Christianity the wager on a historical future and on the human community. In doing so, however, they have not given up the main demands of tragic thought, that is to say a doctrine which explains the paradoxical nature of human reality, and a hope in the eventual creation of values which endows this contradiction with meaning and which transforms ambiguity into a necessary element of a significant whole. In my opinion this is one of the best indications which we have of the existence, not only of a continuity in what I would call "classical thought" from Greek times to our own day but also of a more particular continuity in modern classical thought, within whose framework the tragic vision of Pascal and Kant constitutes an essential stage in the movement which goes beyond sceptical or dogmatic rationalism toward the birth and elaboration of dialectical philosophy.[49]

To avoid injecting transcendental values into history, a Marxist had to start from an existential act of faith which assumed that the values Marx used to define history were present in history to begin with. "Values are founded in an objective reality which can be relatively if not absolutely known (God for Saint Augustine, history for Marx). . . . If we are to arrive at a scientific knowledge of man, we must begin by the wager, or assumption, that history has a meaning. We must therefore set out from an act of faith." [50] Within the European intellectual tradition—argued Goldmann—Marx renewed the Augustinian and Jansenist affirmation of a *Deus absconditus*. His rationalist assertion that there are objective laws in history stems not from *cogito ergo sum* as much as from *credo ut intelligam*. And once having understood, Marx could then abandon transcendentalism without sacrificing teleology, and believe in objective truth while still admitting illusion.

Contemporary Marxists like Louis Althusser have used the concept of praxis to elaborate this existential notion that man defines himself by his own "project." Arguing that "true" theory was itself a form of praxis, a "theoretical practice" because it reshaped and altered primary representations of reality, Althusser insisted that the dialectic must not simply be applied to external phenomena; it must "change truth received from without." [51] And further, "The application of the 'laws' of the dialectic to such and such result of physics, for example, is not a theoretical practice, if that application does not change by an iota the structure of development of the theoretical *practice* in physics." [52] Because pure theory was idealist, real theory had to be both concrete and—like Marx's dialectic in *Kapital*—capable of changing the very object it studied.[53] Knowledge thereby became itself an act of production. Thus, it was the act (the doing) as well as the production (the making) which constituted the totality of theoretical practice. The impulse for the act depended upon the resistance of external objects, which demanded a reformulation of both subject and object: the praxis of a revolutionary figure who was consciously aroused

. . . when his object (the existing world of the society which he transforms) opposes to him sufficient resistance to oblige him to overcome this hindrance, to interrogate and reflect upon his own method in order to produce adequate solutions, the means of producing it, and especially in order to produce in "theory" which is its own foundation (the theory of the social formation which exists) the *new* understanding which corresponds to the content of the new stage of its development.[54]

Obviously, it was this revolutionary person who remained the key to praxis, so that Althusser was to praise Mao Tse-tung for not confusing "the [falsely] theoretical practice of a classical historian who analyzes the past, with the practice of a revolutionary leader who reflects upon the present in the present, upon the necessity of accomplishments." [55] An awareness of that "necessity" was what made men like Mao great revolutionaries. For, Mao was daring enough to deny the reality of merely cognizable knowledge and to seek "true" knowledge by "taking the risk" of putting his theses to the test of real theoretical practice.[56] But was Mao himself actually conscious of such a risk? However important his accomplishments seemed to some European Marxists, could he perhaps have acted without making that existential wager?

It may be inaccurate or even deprecatory to style European Marxism a Christian heresy, but it did comprise a new theology, especially for those of Catholic background. To Che Guevara, for instance, revolution was a moral antidote to alienation, to the singular isolation of the individual in capitalist society. His *Notes on Man and Socialism in Cuba*[57] thus poeticized the great public communions between Fidel Castro and the masses who vibrated together "like a counterpoint between two musical melodies." Someone who had not actually experienced a revolution could hardly appreciate "this close dialectical unity between the individual and the mass, in which the mass, as an aggregate of individuals, is interconnected with its leaders." [58] Guevara's romantic apotheosis of such a collective communion was not just a Jacobin form of civil religion. In his view, the "counterpoint" between leaders and led would actually enable the Cubans to build communism in the absence of capitalist economic formations. Like Mao, therefore, Guevara rejected the Leninist insistence on transforming men into employees of the state so that the acquisition of the habit of wielding the instruments of control would abolish democracy and achieve freedom. Instead of reaching socialism by means of "the dull instruments which link us to capitalism," the Cubans would fashion new "moral instruments" for mobilizing the masses.[59] Of course, it was easy enough during "moments of great peril" to "muster a powerful response to moral stimuli" (*vide* Gramsci), but over the long run a socialist state had to develop this novel form of consciousness in a more permanent and routine fashion. That would only be possible when a new "priority of values" had been inculcated by converting society "into a gigantic school." [60]

The school analogy immediately recalls Mao's social vision, which was also suggested by Guevara's call for a "unified march forward." [61] But the two Marxists' prescriptions actually differed. Guevara's "unified march" had always to be led by a vanguard which was ideologically more advanced than its followers, the masses. Moreover, the vanguard would create that new social consciousness by establishing "a series of mechanisms, of revolutionary institutions," by—in short—an "institutionalization of the revolution" [62] which would overcome human alienation. The "unified march" did not just collectivize individuals; it organized "this great throng." And ". . . its clarity of program corresponds to its consciousness of the necessity of organization. It is no longer a dispersed force, divisible into thousands of fragments, thrown into space like splinters from a hand grenade." [63] Consequently, Guevara's "institutionalization of the revolution" was—unlike Mao's "permanent revolution"—a quest to liberate man "from his alienation," to identify perfectly "the government and the community in its entirety" without transplanting bourgeois democratic commonplaces like legislative chambers "into the society in formation." [64] Like many revolutions in the third world, Cuba's was not strictly bound by Marx's scenario. In fact, claimed Guevara, this period of transition to communism had no historical precedents whatsoever, because for him the root of alienation was not sociological but theological. "What we must create is the man of the twenty-first century. . . . New generations will come who will be free of original sin. . . . Our task is to prevent the present generation, torn asunder by its conflicts, from becoming perverted and from perverting new generations." [65] Guevara's desire to free man from the "original sin" of his past assumed a utopian future: an antihistorical age when men would no longer struggle against each other, but instead would unite in the harmony of collectivity. Mao Tse-tung shared no such assumption. In place of the utopian "new man" of the twenty-first century were the "poor and blank" masses of the present, who moved through history by taking struggle for granted. Indeed, conflict was not a sign of deviation from the ideal, a fall from grace, but the very image of nature's patterns of change. If man could learn to accept those patterns then he might be able to channel change —a concept which was at the very heart of the Chinese philosophical tradition which informed Mao's thought.

6

The Image Seeker

With the exception of a few philosophers of the absurd, traditional Chinese thinkers attributed a regular pattern to events. Their difficulty lay in discerning the concealed regularity of those events. For, reciprocally determined relationships, unlike laws of development, existed in constant mutual flux. Cycles of discerned recurrence therefore seemed the most logical explanation of change. And, fortunately, there existed the classics to proffer essential clues for unraveling the pattern. As the great Sung philosopher, Chu Hsi (1130–1200), wrote:

The *Book of Changes* is based on what is concealed in order to move purposefully toward what is manifest. The *Spring and Autumn Annals* [conversely] infers what is concealed from what is visible. Together, the *Book of Changes* and the *Spring and Autumn Annals* are the Tao of Heaven and Man. The *Changes* takes what is beyond form and projects it into [or explains it outward in terms of] the phenomenological [actual] world. The *Spring and Autumn Annals* takes the phenomenological world and projects it upward into the metaphysical.[1]

Consequently, the individual's power to affect history proceeded from his ability to discern its course. This admission of restraints on absolute freedom—this consciousness of history and the times in which one lived—enabled the superior man to know when and how to act.

Freedom within necessity constituted the fundamental message of the *Book of Changes*. It was perhaps best expressed in the *Wen-yen* section, which is supposed to be Confucius' own personal commentary on *ch'ien,* the first hexagram of the *Changes.* The hexagram itself conthe Chou *Changes*), also explained ease in terms of human knowledge and immediate attainment.

Since the virtue of *ch'ien* can be said to be "ease," then if it carries out what it seeks, it "knows with ease". . . . The *"ch'ien* knowing with ease" and the *"k'un* being capable with simplicity" can be said to be the essence and function of *ch'ien* and *k'un*. "Knowing with ease" and "being capable with simplicity" means that since *ch'ien* and *k'un* possess this nature, men can also [know and act] with ease.[9]

Consequently, one only had to seek to understand that *ch'ien's* wish was its fulfillment, and one's own perception of this luminous truth would come just as easily as that cosmic act had occurred in the first place.

At first glance, this reasoning appears identical to the Jansenist act of faith behind *credo ut intelligam*. The logic is more tortuous, however, as it might be expressed in *t'i-yung* (substance-function) terms.

Given substance: "*ch'ien* knows with ease."

Assumed function: "To know with ease is to know the self."

Demonstration: "Man knows the self."
"Man knows the self with ease."
"Man knows the self can know with ease."
"Man knows with ease that selfness (*ch'ien*) can know with ease."
"Man knows *ch'ien*."

This structure of thought hangs on more than the use of self intent to demonstrate cosmic intent. After the original passage, the *Hsi tz'u* goes on to say, "If you know easily then you possess the self. If you follow easily then you possess merit." Chu Hsi then explains that to know easily is simply to be self-aware. To be self-aware is to know the heart, to be at one with the emotions and hence truly to "have the self [under control]." To follow easily is to control one's strength, domesticate the will, and control random desires (*yü*); and therefore to possess merit or skill. Possession of the self and of merit likens one's personality to heaven as it encompasses all beings. "If it is easy to know, then your feelings of being at one [with others and the universe] are many. Therefore you are near [to the Tao of heaven]." Such a likeness helps in turn define the superior man's mission on earth, which is to fashion a social order corresponding to the pattern of relationships evident in the cosmos. As the original *Hsi tz'u* put it: "Ease and simplicity are the principle and acquiring of all under heaven. The principle and acquiring of all under heaven is developing [one's proper] position in its midst."

K'ung Ying-ta's interpretation of these lines was that:

> The principle of all under heaven is that everything accords with ease and simplicity by acquiring its specific position (*fen wei*). . . . This is to enlighten the sage so that he can implement [patterns of] heaven and earth. If the transformation [is carried out] with ease and simplicity, then he is capable of spanning (*t'ung*) the principles of all under heaven. Therefore to be able to fulfill and establish the hexagrams and the images in the midst of heaven and earth is to be an equal with heaven and earth.[10]

Consequently, the superior man's task is to fulfill the hierarchy of ranks which he perceives in the heavenly order, and to which he actually gives expression by the creative act of discernment. To perceive patterns is to realize them, so that the sage shares creation with the cosmic forces themselves. In Chu Hsi's words: "To 'fulfill position' means to fulfill men's positions [in the world]. 'In the midst' means 'in the midst of heaven and earth.' If this is reached then [the sage will have acquired] the extraordinary merit of the *Tao* of [heaven's] essence. As the sage is able to serve [this order] so can he participate in heaven and earth." [11]

Chu Hsi's conception of self-fulfillment only partly resembled the Renaissance ideal of self-determination. Pico della Mirandola's (1463–1494) God had told man, his creation, that:

> I have given thee, oh Adam, neither a fixed seat, nor a face of thy own, nor a gift peculiar to thee, in order that thou mayest have and possess by thine own wish and decision whatever seat, or face, or gift, thou consciously choosest. The determinate nature of other things is bound by the laws which I have imposed upon them. Thou art confined by no bonds except the free judgment in whose hands I placed thee so that thou mayest determine thy nature for thyself. . . . Thou art the molder and maker of thyself.[12]

But man could still only make himself within the hierarchy of beings created by God. Even Nicholas of Cusa's (1401–1464) notion of pure potentiality (*Non ergo activae creationis humanitatis alius extat finis quam humanitas*)[13] was defined by the species of creatures which man could become: a human god, a human angel, a human beast, a human lion, a human bear, and so forth. In contrast, Neo-Confucian thought allowed man to share creation by encompassing the entire universe of being. Chu Hsi's divinity was nonanthropomorphic: a self-knowing of polar forces rather than a holy craftsman shaping species from without. To be sure, the Neo-Confucian sage did recognize natural hierarchical relationships which he hoped to realize in society. As the opening to the *Hsi tz'u* reads: "Heaven is high, the earth is low; thus the Creative and the Receptive are determined. In correspondence with this distinction between low and high, inferior and superior places are established." [14] But these were relationships—not a chain—of being, so that man fulfilled himself by acquiescing in these patterns with ease and simplicity. Confucian humanism did not, therefore, contain a Promethean dimension. Man had no creator to rival, no call to tamper with nature.

The Neo-Confucian recognition of a natural order was not the same as the Western concept of natural law. Chu Hsi's pupil, Ch'en Hsun, might seem to have been describing natural law when he wrote of "formless" *li* (pattern or organization): "*Li* is a natural and unescapable law of affairs and things. . . . The meaning of 'natural and unescapable' is that [human] affairs and [natural] things are made just exactly to fit into place. The meaning of 'law' is that the fitting into place occurs without the slightest excess or deficiency." [15] But, as Joseph Needham has pointed out regarding this passage, *li* was simply "the principle of organization" inherent to a universe in which the only law (*tse* or *fa*) was that "parts of the whole have to conform to [it] by virtue of their very existence as parts of wholes." [16] Neo-Confucianism, therefore, held in place of a celestial lawgiver the internality of principles of organization, so that their natural law (like Whitehead's) was distinctly organismic. In fact, the only tradition of Chinese thought containing a possibly external law of nature was the *Yin-yang* and Five Agents school of the Han period.[17] As we shall see, it was to this school that the nineteenth-century utopian philosopher K'ang Yu-wei would return in search of absolute laws with which to construct an autonomous ideology of social criticism. However, he was only alerted to that possibility after becoming aware that categorical laws of nature existed in Western thought. For, it was otherwise impossible to imagine an absolute discrepancy between an ideal set of principles (capable of objectification outside of growth and change) and the real world itself. Granted, there was almost always a gap between ideal institutions and actual historical conditions. But the ideals were either historicist or expressed as imperatives for individual moral cultivation within the existing order. The integrity of Neo-Confucianism was thus inviolate until the Chinese discovered the possibility of substantial principles existing outside the mutually reinforcing functions of the Tao. The Jesuits did introduce independent mathematical principles to the Chinese in the sixteenth and seventeenth centuries, but as far as we know,[18] no major Chinese philosopher had related these laws to social theory. Confidence in the Way of Chinese civilization made them seem irrelevant to the majestic ambiguities of the *Changes*. Not until the late nineteenth century was that confidence shattered. Then, desperately seeking new principles of civilization, men like K'ang Yu-wei would try to determine the connection between the objective laws of Western science and human progress.

However, those Chinese who discovered the theorems of Euclid or the laws of Social Darwinism near the turn of the century did not entirely abandon the Neo-Confucian concept of patterned change. Intellectuals of that generation screened Western learning through their own tradition, by selectively discriminating certain portions of the works to which they were exposed (that in itself a matter of translators' preferences) or by so casting them in Chinese linguistic and symbolic terms as to infuse the perception of these new ideas with a Sino-Western significance.[19] Furthermore, many of these transitional thinkers innovated from within their own extraordinarily rich tradition, incited by the times to reopen doors to writers long neglected or forgotten. Naturally, this was not a pure rediscovery; it was not as though tradition suddenly revealed these ideas in pristine form. At first, the past was combed in search of sanctions for reform. Later, men sometimes sought equivalence with the West, attempting to find native roots for foreign ideas. But even when the search was so motivated, the new concepts discovered in the past did possess a force of their own. They not only created a magnetic field which subtly altered the trajectory of the particles of Western thought which entered it; they also created new elements of their own.

One native thinker rescued from oblivion was the seventeenth-century Hunanese philosopher, Wang Fu-chih (1619–1692). During most of the Ch'ing, Wang's writings—some of them strongly anti-Manchu —had been quite obscured. In fact, the first complete collection of his works did not appear until 1842, edited and compiled by a local Hunanese historian and classicist named Tsou Han-hsun. The printing blocks of the edition were destroyed and Tsou himself killed when

Taiping armies occupied the province. But after the civil war, the great Hunanese statesman Tseng Kuo-fan sponsored a reprinting of the work. Interest in Wang Fu-chih continued to grow during the next half-century. By 1915 there had been founded, in Ch'ang-sha, a Wang Fu-chih Study Society (*Ch'uan-shan hsueh-she*) which published its own magazine.[20] In fact, Wang's influence was so strongly felt in Ch'ang-sha's normal school that Mao Tse-tung was inspired to attend the weekly lecture meetings of the study society.[21] Thus, without being certain that Mao Tse-tung lingered long over the more abstruse passages of Wang's philosophical writings, we can at least assume he acquired some sense of Wang Fu-chih's theory of change.

Wang Fu-chih himself wrote in reaction to the metaphysical dualism of the Sung Neo-Confucianists. It would be an exaggeration to claim that Chu Hsi had sharply separated the realm of principles (*li*) from the material world of energy or force (*ch'i*). For, there was no such noumenal-phenomenal distinction in Sung ontology. But he had elevated principles to a higher sphere, implying in many passages that intellectual illumination could be acquired by moving through and beyond the material world to perceive the principles behind (and therefore potentially outside) it. Material energy or *ch'i* was thus relegated to a lower, dependent position—guided from aimlessness into purpose by those higher principles. This shattered the integrity of being, creating a kind of essence/existence dichotomy which was distasteful to thinkers influenced by holistic philosophical Taoism or Ch'an (Zen) Buddhism. Wang Fu-chih, therefore, was attempting to recover philosophical integrity when he attributed all natural bounty to the moving power of material force (*ch'i*).

It fills the universe. And as it completely provides for the flourish and transformation of all things, it is all the more spatially unrestricted. As it is not spatially restricted, it operates in time and proceeds with time. From morning to evening, from spring to summer, and from the present tracing back to the past, there is no time at which it does not operate, and there is no time at which it does not produce.[22]

According to this, one of *ch'i's* attributes was the autonomous force of growth. This contrasted sharply with the Sung school's (and especially Chang Tsai's) belief that the motive force behind material energy was heaven itself. The *li* or principle of the Tao of heaven (*t'ien chih tao*) manifested itself in growth or creation (*sheng*), which consequently represented the gift of heaven to living creatures, and hence its essential kindness or humaneness (*jen*). Man's sense of gratitude for this perpetual bounty—realized in the perception of his own essentially good nature—permitted him to share that sentiment of common humaneness (*jen*) with heaven. *Jen* was thus the bridge between the simply material and the sphere of *li*.

Wang Fu-chih ceased attempting to transcend the material by shifting his emphasis from the substance to the function, from *jen*—the principle behind growth, to *tung* (movement)—the operation of growth. The material sphere therefore seemed to have an inner motor of its own: the evolution of *yin* and *yang*, the interaction of the five agents, and so forth. And as the motor drove, as things grew, even the apparently immutable mandate of heaven had to move in accompaniment. "By nature is meant the principle of growth. As one daily grows one daily achieves completion. Thus by the mandate of heaven is not meant that heaven gives the decree (*ming*) only at the moment of one's birth." [23] Heaven-granted human nature would become tarnished as man grew away from infancy, unless heaven constantly intervened to realize (complete or *ch'eng*) it. Consequently, there were two related but separate processes of life. Heaven altered physical form in order to produce *excellence*. Material force of itself engendered *growth*. This reunited *li* and *ch'i* by making them mutually dependent. In order to equalize the two, however, Wang Fu-chih had to grant autonomy to growth as a principle of evolution in the material world alone. Because this implied that change as such was both necessary and good, the student of Wang's thought was disposed to assume that phenomenal movement was purposive *without reference to external idea*. Thus Wang's thought was the embryo of an independent materialist conception of history: distrustful of pure principle, interested in immanent social relationships, and in some ways sounding themes vaguely reminiscent of Marx himself.

Marx	*Wang Fu-chih*
The human essence (*das menschliche Wesen*) is no abstraction inherent in each separate individual. In its reality it is the *ensemble* of the social relations.[24]	Without a concrete thing there cannot be its Way. . . . Correct virtue [is a matter of] the relationship between ruler and minister, father and son. If one described these and sought for that which existed before concrete things, even if he spanned past and present, went through all the myriad transforma-

tions, and investigated heaven,
earth, man, and things to the utmost, he would not be able to give
it a name. How much less could he
find its reality! [25]

There were even moments when Wang sounded like Engels: "At bottom principle is not a finished product that can be grasped. It is in-
visible. The details and order of material force is principle that is visible.
Therefore the first time there is any principle is when it is seen in material force. After principles have thus been found, they of course appear to become tendencies. We see principles only in the necessary aspects of tendencies." [26]

As Wang Fu-chih identified the discernment of pattern with material
self-movement ("the necessary aspects of tendencies"), he would actually have seemed to some Marxist philosophers a more absolute historical materialist than Lenin himself. Karl Korsch, for instance, accused Lenin of reinfusing Marxism with an unnecessary eschatology.
In his philosophical naïveté, the Russian revolutionary had dragged
the debate between materialism and idealism back to a pre-Hegelian
stage, for:

The dissolution of the metaphysical systems of Leibniz and Wolff began
with Kant's transcendental philosophy and ended with Hegel's dialectic.
Thereafter the "absolute" was definitely excluded from the *being* of both
'spirit' and *'matter'* and was transferred into the dialectical *movement* of
the *'idea'*. Materialist conversion by Marx and Engels of Hegel's Idealist
dialectic merely consisted of freeing this dialectic from its final mystifying
shell. The *real movement of history* was discovered beneath the dialectical
"self-movement of the idea" and this revolutionary movement of history
was proclaimed to be the only "absolute" remaining.[27]

Lenin had thus abandoned the true dialectic to "present knowledge as
a fundamentally harmonious *evolutionary progress* and an infinite
progression toward absolute truth." [28] Because Wang Fu-chih clearly
had not made the meaning of phenomena depend upon an ultimate
completion, he had no such eschatology. His rationalization of history
was not even a theodicy. For, as Leszek Kolakowski has pointed out,
while theodicy may not seek justification in ultimate completion, it
remains an heir of theology as it "tries to justify partial evil by linking
it to the order of a wisely conceived whole." [29] Because Wang Fu-chih
began with Chang Tsai's attribution of humaneness to heaven's life-

giving, he did not need to find any justification for movement other than in movement as such. That is, life itself was a proof of good, so that man did not have to endure the evil of secular life while awaiting the City of God. In fact, without the dichotomy between secular and sacred, life and death, sin and salvation, Wang did not need absolute justifications at all: the pattern (which one could both know and affect) alone sufficed. Consequently, whether influenced specifically by Wang Fu-chih or more generally by traditional notions of change, a Chinese revolutionary like Mao Tse-tung did not have to confront some kind of existential choice: action for action's sake, the great helmsman pushing boldly off into the void, the magician of praxis. Instead, movement made sense for itself—not always as defined by abstract ends, perhaps, but at least as expressed by concretely universal images. In fact, Mao both represented and inspired the force of change by substituting images for ideas.

The line between Mao's private imagery and the larger repertoire of popular symbols he employs is not always clear, particularly because some of his language has been so widely disseminated among the masses. Color imagery was one example of this amalgam. In his New Year's poem of 1930, Mao wrote of Wu-i Mountain: "Below the mountain, below the mountain/ The wind unfolds our red flag like a scroll." [30] That same red color of revolution was to have become, thirty-five years later, the very symbol of doctrinal purity. One of the most important tasks during the Cultural Revolution was to retain one's "basic color" (*pen-se*), so that those once tolerated as being "both red and expert" (*yu hung yu chuan*) now had to let "redness guide expertness" (*yi hung tai chuan*).[31] The Red Guards may have been modeled on the *Krasnaya gvardia* of the Russian Revolution and the red flag recognized worldwide as the sign of revolt. But the color did have Chinese connotations of its own: auspicious joy (*hsi*), triumph, the banner of command. When party leaders declared at the time of the Great Leap that "politics must take command" (*cheng-chih hua-shuai*), for instance, they immediately evoked the traditional opera *Mu Kuei-ying Takes Command,* and the image of "a middle aged woman, still handsome and elegant in embroidered armor, carrying a seal wrapped in red satin." [32] Against red was posed black (*hei*), the color of villainy. Intellectual opponents of the Cultural Revolution were called *hei-pang* (a black gang of criminals) or their writings *hei-hua* (black talk, the language of the underworld in the popular novel *Monkey*).[33] Of course, colors were not the only indicators of good and bad. "Erroneous ideas," said Mao in 1957, were "bull ghosts and snake gods (*niu-kuei she-shen*)," a phrase drawn from the eighteenth-century novel, *Dream of the Red Chamber*.[34] Revisionists were described as "voracious wolves, poisonous snakes, parasitic worms, and injurious vermin," while Mao's thought was extolled as a "demon-exposing mirror." [35]

In contrast, then, to the way Western Marxists attributed distinct heresies to the deviant, Chinese Communist political diatribe was cast in a much earthier and ideologically vaguer form. Enemies were not specifically sinful; they were generally inhuman. And even though political positions were sometimes identified with personal labels, or social attitudes quite definitely characterized ("commandism," "bureaucratism"), Mao as often as not dipped into the folkloric imagery of good and bad to stir the people's consciousness.

Mao's skill in using folk associations, usually drawn from the vernacular core of the language, did not prevent him from creating metaphors. One such cluster centered on the image of the mountain: a towering structure sometimes endowed with life-force, rearing like "ten thousand horses drunk with battle," "piercing the green heavens" which would topple without its support.[36] At other moments, it represented the elemental face of the earth, the great "void" which must be traversed "to leave the world." Vast and mighty K'un-lun Mountain, standing between Mao and the terminus of the Long March in 1935, endures beyond mortal time, challenging man's temporality. If Mao could only lean on heaven to draw his "precious sword," then he would slice K'un-lun in three and share its energy with the world to realize the era of great peace (*t'ai-p'ing*).[37]

The Taoist sage accepted nature, blending with the mountain. Mao exulted in its challenge, admiring those beings who overcame adversity.

> Only heroes can quell tigers and leopards
> And wild bears never daunt the brave.
> Plum blossoms welcome the whirling snow.
> Small wonder flies freeze and perish.[38]

Merely to survive the challenge of nature—like the plum blossom fighting through winter toward spring—was a victory in itself.

Ode to the Plum Blossom

(Upon Reading Lu Yu's Plum Blossom *Tz'u,*
Countering His Meaning while Using It)

Spring's escorted out by wind and rain.
It's welcomed back by flying snow.

Though looming cliffs are thick with ice
There's still a branch there blooming so.

So fair, she'll not contend for spring,
But tells its coming with thanks.
Then, when mountain flowers glow all round
She'll smile among their crowded ranks.[39]

The famous poem which Mao countered—"The Plum Blossom *Tz'u*"
—was written by the twelfth-century Sung loyalist, Lu Yu.*

Outside the courier post, beside the severed bridge
Unowned, she blooms deserted and alone.
In the growing yellow dusk she grieves for solitude
And makes the wind and rain her own.

Striving selflessly for spring
She has to stand the others' spite.
But though her petals scatter, ground to mire,
Her fragrance lives on through the night.[40]

Lu's plum blossom stood in heroic solitude, displaying the individual's
courage to resist the temper of the time. "Unowned" (*wu-chu,* literally
"without a lord"), it stood beside the severed bridge to office and the
North. Its loneliness was necessary because "others" (*ch'ün,* the common "coterie" of officials) had accepted the prevailing policy of ap-
peasement and were enviously spiteful of anyone who remained aloof
from politics on moral grounds. Because such an *Abstand* could be
mistaken for an empty gesture, Lu Yu feared that his integrity would
be besmirched. But even if his reputation were destroyed, his petals

* Lu Yu (1125–1210), styled Wu Kuan, was born the year before North
China was abandoned to the Jurced dynasty of Chin. Lu passed the Southern
Sung exams with poetic distinction and became a noted official who consistently
opposed the "peace" policies of Ch'in Kuei, hoping to restore Sung rule in the
North. Later, after exemplary service in the provinces, Lu was put in charge of
military planning in the capital. Just before his death, with the North still in
Chin hands, he wrote his son:

Death comes.   When the conquering armies
I know at last   Northward go
The myriad acts   At the family altar
Of life are vain,   Do not fail
But yet I mourn   To tell
For China's   Thy sire.
Disunited provinces.

Translated by Clara M. Candlin in *The Rapier of Lu, Patriot Poet of China*
(London: John Murray, 1946), pp. 20–21.

scattered, the poet was convinced his "fragrance" would survive in the end—not so much because the spring of Sung restoration in the North was inevitable, but rather because his stance was so similar to that of the heroes of Confucian antiquity.*

Although written around the same central theme of the plum blossom, Mao's ode replaced the softness of dusk with the harsh brightness of flying snow and mountain ice. "Better than the glow of spring," he tells us in another poem, are "Ten thousand frosty leagues of desolate skies and waters." [41] In such a landscape the plum blossom stands above wind and rain, frozen to complement the cliffs of ice. Whereas Lu scans a horizon of abandoned human things—the courier post and the ruined bridge—Mao's poem looks up vertically at the climbing outlines of natural objects where the blossom's beauty is but "fair" (*ch'iao*, "likeness"), an epitome instead of an exception. Fighting among— rather than against—many, its sole uniqueness in the ranks is its confident ability to await the springtime, so that where Lu Yu gazes at the past for self-justification and political restoration, Mao looks to the revolutionary future for fulfillment.

Human and natural struggle also coincided in many of Mao Tsetung's other poems, especially those inspired by the civil war. Celebrating the Red Army's capture of Chang Huai-tsan during the first encirclement campaign of 1931, Mao described how the "Heavenly troops' rage soars up to the firmament," so that the "thousand peaks of dragon ridge† dim." Military victory was cosmic victory, his soldiers' rage "heavenly" enough to scorn the firmament itself and even overshadow the spirits of the Chinese landscape: "Below Pu-chou Mountain‡ the red flags roil." [42] The same war with heaven was waged by Monkey in Mao's poem about the awesome hero of *Hsi-yu chi*, where the ape symbolized man's natural capacity for brutal and destructive action unless restrained by Buddhist compassion. Monkey warred with

---

* The last words of Lu's poem, translated as "through the night," literally read *ju-ku*, "like of old."

† According to legend, a dragon had lived in these mountains for so many years that his skin and bones had formed the peaks themselves.

‡ Mao here invoked the ancient myth of Kung-kung (which in modern Chinese means collective workers) who once struggled for the hegemony of the Underheaven with another giant, Chuan-hsu. During the battle Kung-kung knocked off the summit of Pu-chou Mountain, severing the pillar that supported the sky, which subsequently slanted. Written versions of the myth left Kung-kung's fate in doubt, so Mao asked: "Did he die or not? It doesn't say. It looks as though he didn't die, so Kung-kung actually won." Mao Tse-tung, *Mao chu-hsi shih-tz'u* [The Poetry of Chairman Mao], (Peking: Jen-min wen-hsueh ch'u-pan she, 1963), p. 11.

the gods as though he were himself a force of nature, arising suddenly from the great earth like "wind and thunder." [43] Revolution was such a storm as well. When Mao's men attacked Nan-ch'ang, he wrote: "The lamenting melody of the Internationale/ Descends upon me from heaven like a swirling gale." [44] And as the revolution was made by men, they too were wind and thunder, rain and lightning.

The folkloric figure of Monkey shows that Mao's image of the people as a force of nature was not novel. Even Confucianists so viewed the peasantry in revolt, perhaps because it was consoling to believe that popular turbulence could be as ritually controlled by imperial rule as the course of the seasons. Consequently, when the mandate of heaven theory was fully elaborated during the Han dynasty (which also witnessed the appearance of large-scale peasant rebellions) revolts were categorized as divine omens portending heaven's displeasure, so that the governors of China could admit the masses' influence in history without having to concede them a causal role. And even in later times, when the theory of omens had lost much of its magic for Confucian theorists, popular revolts were still regarded almost as a natural force to be used by others. Wang Fu-chih, for example, had this to say about the employment of "massed rebels":

Using massed rebels is either an affair of great profit or of great risk. There is power to be found by gaining their alliance. There is mastery to be found by gaining their support. Kuang-wu [founder of the Latter Han, who reigned from 25–57] received [the support of] T'ung Ma [a bandit chief defeated near Ch'ang-an] and became emperor. Ts'ao Ts'ao [founder of the Wei dynasty, who reigned from 220–226] allied with the Yellow Turbans and seized power. Conversely, though, T'ang Shao [-tsung, who reigned from 889 to 904] used Chu Wen [who was also called Chu Ch'üan-chung and founded the Liang dynasty, reigning from 907 to 915], and [his dynasty] perished.[45]

Mao Tse-tung may have thought in similar instrumental terms when he investigated the peasant movement in Hunan from January 4 to February 5, 1927, but he was not gingerly weighing the "profit" and "risk" of using the peasant movement; he was insisting that this torrent (*t'ao-t'ao*) of rural revolution had to be boldly met.*

* Nor am I suggesting that Mao's populism was exclusively acquired from a firsthand reading of Wang Fu-chih. Maurice Meisner's excellent study, *Li Ta-chao and the Origins of Chinese Marxism* (Cambridge, Mass.: Harvard University Press, 1967), traces much of Mao's populism to the theories of his mentor, Li. However, another work by Meisner—"Leninism and Maoism: Some Populist Perspectives on Marxism–Leninism in China," *China Quarterly*, 45:2–36—seeks

For the rise of the present peasant movement is a colossal event. In a very short time, in China's central, southern, and northern provinces, several hundred million peasants will rise *like a tornado or tempest,* a *force* so extraordinarily swift and violent that no power, however great, will be able to suppress it. . . . To march at their head and lead them? Or to follow at their rear, gesticulating at them and criticizing them? Or to face them as opponents? . . . In force and momentum, the attack is *like a tempest or hurricane;* those who submit to it survive and those who resist it perish.[46]

Mao not only welcomed the momentum of those elemental mass forces; he grew exuberant in their midst. That same summer, when the revolutionary surge seemed even stronger, he wrote: "In wine I drink a pledge to the surging torrent./ The tide of my heart rises as high as the waves." [47] And by 1966, when the Cultural Revolution was underway, the image of a rising tide, a surging wave, had become a major motif of his thought. "No need to be afraid of tidal waves; human society has been evolved out of 'tidal waves,'" he told his comrades.[48] "Let it come, I think it is a good thing to have this tidal wave." [49] Indeed, as his poetic imagery forty years earlier had suggested, Mao viewed life itself as a breasting of the tide.*

---

to understand how Mao could so consistently believe in the revolutionary spontaneity of the peasant, the advantage of backwardness, the importance of will, and the preponderance of the countryside over the city, without having read Herzen or Chernyshevsky. Meisner recognizes the possibility of indigenous sources for Mao's populism. But he stresses "the independent appearance of certain similar revolutionary modes of thought" in Russia and China resulting from uniform external causes such as the breakdown of traditional rural life in the face of capitalism, the absence of a bourgeoisie in both countries, and so forth. "Populism can be seen as a protest against modern capitalism and its human and social costs, particularly as those costs are borne by the peasantry. It is not a peasant ideology, but a protest ideology of intellectuals speaking for the rural masses." I am interested here, however, in showing that Mao may have been sensitized to the force of peasant movements by traditional Chinese influences.

* This was the symbolic significance of Mao's famous Yangtze swim in 1966. A year later, fifty thousand "proletarian revolutionaries of Wuhan" and soldiers of the People's Liberation Army commemorated his feat at the same spot. Together they made a "breakthrough in the storms and waves of class struggle" by swimming "triumphantly across the Yangtze River, following the course pioneered by their great leader, Chairman Mao." (*Peking Review,* 33:13, August 11, 1967.) The same imagery was used to describe the death of the young hero, Chin Hsun-hua (see Chapter Two): "Young Chin battled the tempestuous waves bravely in the torrents. One big wave dashed him into a whirlpool but he raised his head again and made for the nearby pole. Another wave whipped him back into the whirlpool but again he emerged and rushed ahead for the pole. A third big wave descended upon him; with tenacity he pushed his head to the surface again and dashed towards the pole. . . . The tests young Chin experienced in battling the three wave onslaughts involving a life and death struggle are a

One hundred barges struggle against the flow
Hawks strike the wide sky
Fish roam the shallows
The myriad creatures contest their freedom in the frosty air.[50]

Just as human and external nature sustained each other in the parable of Yü Kung, so did contestant and contended merge and assume significance in the same torrential image of struggle. In fact, it was through this conflict that man realized himself to the fullest. For, man—even as a collective unity—was only latently powerful. Revolutionary activity emancipated his "productive forces," actually "promot[ing] the development of productive force." [51] Therefore, revolution as such was converted from a result into a force,[52] from a destination into the very "locomotive of history." [53]

Still, the locomotive did require an engineer; the motor of revolution, however mighty once begun, had to be started and fueled. That was why Mao came to feel such a desperate sense of urgency: aroused, the masses were capable of anything; subsided, they might settle into apathy.

why
Revolution —

So many deeds cry out to be done
And always urgently;
The world rolls on,
Time presses.
Ten thousand years are too long,
Seize the day, seize the hour.[54]

And because it was actually Mao who did the seizing, he was able to inscribe his own images upon the Chinese people, "poor and blank" as an unmarked sheet of paper where "the freshest and most beautiful characters can be written, the freshest and most beautiful pictures can be painted." [55]

A lifetime earlier Mao Tse-tung had begun from indignation to seek the images of historical change. The ones he found and tested in the turmoil of civil war aroused the imaginations of many besides himself.

---

powerful denunciation of the revisionists' 'philosophy of survival.' Young Chin's strength began to fail with each struggle and he was carried deeper and deeper into the water and farther and farther away from shore. And yet he was making nearer and nearer for the ideological peak of 'fearing neither hardship nor death.' Charge forward, charge forward! Seizing the pole means victory! The pole was only one meter away but just then another torrential wave roared over young Chin." *A Model for Revolutionary Youth* (Peking: Foreign Languages Press, 1970), pp. 25–26.

As he came to paint his own portrait across the canvas of China, those images overtook ideology. To be sure, even so feverish a movement as the Great Proletarian Cultural Revolution, which varied by the week from restraint to excess, could be measured in precise ideological degrees: a self-conscious policy of two steps forward and one step backward, or a program based on Mao's theory of contradiction ("Struggle-Criticism-Transformation"). Yet so often the slogans seemed rationalizations after the fact of impulse. So often it appeared as though the slowing of the locomotive had brought Mao Tse-tung to such a pitch of concern that he turned instinctively for inspiration to the very images he had helped create.

But this does not make Mao a prisoner of his own metaphors; it does not imply a bifurcated mind, veering abruptly from intellect to imagination and back again. Images prevailed at times, but behind them there did exist a consistency of intent, an integrity of perception, that is better explained by the history of ideas.

PART TWO

Transition to Ideology

If one thinks that the only purpose of political philosophy is to provide serviceable guides to action for politicians and political groups, then indeed utopia was a useless enterprise. If critical understanding and judgment, however, are also real ends, then the construction of such models is not only justifiable, it is a perfect instrument.

Judith N. Shklar, *Men and Citizens: A Study of Rousseau's Social Theory*

7
Affinities and Influences

Despite his later prominence, Mao Tse-tung's early intellectual development is only sketchily understood. Some historians have emphasized his
family life, examining the psychological effects of Mao's relationship
with his father, a dour and stern figure who early provoked rebellious-
ness in his son. Others (including Mao himself on occasion) stress the
impact of public events: the 1910 rice riots in Ch'ang-sha (capital of
his native province) or the revolution of 1911 (which he briefly joined
as a soldier in the Revolutionary Army). Even so, his youth was not
exceptional; Mao simply swam in the ideological currents of his time.

The Chinese sources of these currents can be divided into five categories. First came the five Confucian classics, routinely memorized by
Mao at Shao-shan primary school between the ages of eight and thirteen.
Sometime later, he also studied Taoist philosophical works, and he has
occasionally employed some rather startling archaisms from those
sources.*

* "It is true that most of the time he makes genuine efforts to utilize 'the
people's vocabulary.' Yet the impression is clear that at times he becomes carried
away, forgets his announced principles, falls back on his classical education.
Mao's predilection for composing refined traditional poetry is of course well
known but in his prose as well it seems that Mao is prone to the use of obscure
words and recondite allusions." H. C. Chuang, *The Little Red Book and Current
Chinese Language* (Berkeley: Center for Chinese Studies, August, 1968), p. 34.
Mr. Chuang also points out by way of example that Mao consistently used the
archaic form of *pao* (to protect or nurture), written with radical 140 at its top,
which comes from the *Kuan-tzu* and *Chuang-tzu*. Thus, a phrase like "The Com-

Next were vernacular novels and historical romances (*wu-hsia*), to which Mao escaped from his regular studies. His favorites by the age of eight were *Hsi-yu chi* (Monkey), *Shui-hu chuan* (All Men Are Brothers), and *San-kuo chih yen-i* (Romance of the Three Kingdoms), to which he later added the biography of the heroic Sung loyalist, Yueh Fei (*Chin chung chuan*), and the eighteenth-century novel, *Hung-lo meng* (Dream of the Red Chamber). Mao himself testified: "We learned many of the stories almost by heart and discussed and rediscussed them many times. We knew more of them than the old men of the village who also loved them and used to exchange stories with us. I believe that perhaps I was much influenced by such books read at an impressionable age." [1] Military values, theories of dynastic change, the stereotyping of characters into villainous and heroic roles, even a certain populism, were all found in these tales. To be sure, Mao would later fault the novels for their feudal class content. "All the characters were warriors, officials, or scholars; there was never a peasant hero. I wondered about this for two years and then I analyzed the content of the stories. I found that they all glorified men of arms, rulers of the people who did not have to work the land because they owned or controlled it and evidently made the peasants work it for them." [2] But that was a post-Marxist awareness, and even after the judgment was made Mao continued to use the language and imagery of these vernacular classics: "Either the east wind prevails over the west wind or the west wind prevails over the east wind" was drawn directly from the pages of *Hung-lo meng*.[3]

The third and fourth categories consisted of orthodox historical chronicles like Ssu-ma Kuang's *Tzu-chih t'ung-chien* (Comprehensive Mirror for the Aid of Government, completed in 1084), and of the seventeenth-century writers (such as Wang Fu-chih, Ku Yen-wu, Ku Tsu-yü, Yen Yuan, Hou Fang-yü) revived during the late Ch'ing.

Finally, there was contemporary political criticism. Some consisted of nothing more grandiose than political pamphlets which described the conquest of Taiwan by Japan or of Annam by France, and urged their readers to assume personal responsibility for China's fate (*p'i-fu yu tse*). Many years later Mao was still able to recall the pamphlets' exact

---

munist ideological and social system alone nurtures (*pao*) its fine youth and vitality, sweeping the world with the momentum of an avalanche and the force of a thunderbolt," was written with a recondite Taoist character. Jerome Ch'en has also demonstrated that Mao's usage of words veers strongly toward the classical, for example, *yü-chou-kuan* instead of *shih-chieh-kuan* for "world view." Jerome Ch'en, *Mao Papers: Anthology and Bibliography* (London: Oxford University Press, 1970), pp. xiii–xxxi.

phrasing as well as their effect on him. "When I read these phrases I felt that the future of the fatherland deserved extraordinary pity. I began to recognize that it was each person's calling to exert himself to save the country." [4] He was further inspired by a much more ambitious work, Cheng Kuan-ying's *Sheng-shih wei-yen* (Words of Warning in a Seemingly Prosperous Age), which called for industrial development, western studies, and constitutional reform. The book's stress on education actually persuaded the fourteen-year-old to resume his studies after a year of farming for his father.[5]

There was a curious discontinuity between the events which inspired these works and their impact upon Mao Tse-tung. Annam had been conquered twenty-three years earlier, and Cheng Kuan-ying's study originally was published around 1893. Mao was only fourteen in 1907, just coming of political age, but the time lag still suggests the insularity of his childhood. And even though Shao-shan was barely forty miles west of the provincial capital of Ch'ang-sha (which had been such an important base for the reformers of 1898), Mao experienced the same fresh excitement in 1909 when his cousin presented him with a book describing K'ang Yu-wei's (1858–1927) reform activities, along with the eleventh issue of Liang Ch'i-ch'ao's *Hsin-min ts'ung-pao*. "I read and reread these until I knew them by heart. I worshipped K'ang Yu-wei and Liang Ch'i-ch'ao and was very grateful to my cousin. . . . Indeed I considered the emperor as well as most officials to be honest, good and clever men. They only needed the help of K'ang Yu-wei's reforms." [6] Two years later, when Mao had gone to Ch'ang-sha to attend Hsiang-hsiang Middle School, he still idolized K'ang. Reading for the first time of the republican program of Sun Yat-sen's (1866–1925) Revolutionary Alliance (which bitterly opposed K'ang Yu-wei, the constitutional monarchist), he was naïvely inspired to post a proposal of his own on the school bulletin board, calling for a new government with Sun as president, Liang Ch'i-ch'ao as foreign minister, and K'ang as premier.[7] Mao soon realized what an incompatible trio this was and quickly abandoned his faith in constitutional monarchy. But K'ang Yu-wei did not lose relevance for him altogether. Almost a half century later, Mao Tse-tung declared that: "The family appeared in the latter period of primitive communism. It will vanish in the future, thus completing the cycle. In his *Universal Harmony* [*Ta-t'ung shu*] K'ang Yu-wei realized this point." [8] This time, though, Mao was viewing K'ang in quite a different guise. The pragmatic reformer he had so admired in 1911 now appeared a utopian socialist, a visionary like Saint–Simon or

Fourier, whose prediction of a communist society would be realized sometime in the future.

The turnabout was not Mao's doing. K'ang really had been a utopian thinker, even though his contemporaries were hardly aware of it during his lifetime. In fact, the contradiction between K'ang Yu-wei's public reform programs and his more private writings on social progress still puzzles historians. How could one man be politically moderate and theoretically extreme, practical and fanciful, at one and the same time? The answer was to be found in K'ang's own intellectual affinities with the novel nineteenth-century tradition of *Kung-yang* Confucianism—a tradition which was transmitted obliquely through T'an Ssu-t'ung to Mao and his fellow students in Ch'ang-sha, and which enabled the transition from orthodox Confucian values to autonomous ideologies of radical social criticism.

8

The Kung-yang Revival in the Nineteenth Century

Orthodox Confucianists of post-Han times did not believe in an ideal state of nature without the benefit of enlightened kingship. Nevertheless, there was a classical source for arcadian bliss in addition to the well-known Taoist utopias (Chuang-tzu's "state of established virtue" and Lieh-tzu's "country of the extreme north"). The *Li-yun* (Evolution of Rites) section of the *Li-chi* (Record of Rites) had Confucius describe an era "when the great Tao was in practice, and the world was a commonweal (*t'ien-hsia wei kung*)." Men had no thought of profit because particularistic affections were not yet known; each loved the other as though his kin. The sick and elderly were cared for by all, and doors hung open for lack of thieves. The Great Harmony (*Ta-t'ung*) prevailed. But then the Tao was suddenly obscured. People split into families, loving only their own. As men sought profit, princes protected their holdings behind walled cities which now covered the land and were passed selfishly on to their heirs. It was then that rules of propriety (*li*) and the obligation of righteousness (*i*) had to be created as devices of rule, "skeins to rectify the ruler-minister [relationship]." The *Ta-t'ung* waned and mankind entered the era of Small Tranquility (*Hsiao-k'ang*).[1]

Even in the *Li-yun,* the *Ta-t'ung* was lost forever: Confucius plaintively "sighed" to think that he had been born too late to witness the age when all was common (*kung*) and selfishness (*ssu*) had not yet torn mankind apart. The text's nostalgia for the irretrievable helped confirm later Confucianists' belief that one has to accept the human condition as it is, and do the best one can to guide men to good behavior. Still, the nostalgia was occasionally translated into ideals for the present, if only because the mundane society of the *Sacred Edicts* was so obviously held together by appealing to selfish particularities. Flight to the realm of *kung* might be expressed on one level by Wang Yang-ming's desire to embrace the entire world as his own, and on another by the periodic dreams of religious rebels to restore the Great Harmony. *Ta-t'ung* seeped into the civilization's system of perception in such a diffused manner as to be truly described as a fundamental (although nonintegrated) value of the culture. Its situational use and its ubiquitousness are visible even in modern times. The largest electric appliance manufactory on Taiwan today is called the Great Harmony Company, while students across the Straits of Formosa can open their copies of Mao's "On the People's Democratic Dictatorship" to read: "State power and political parties will die out very naturally and mankind will enter the realm of Great Harmony." [2] However, Mao's use of the *Ta-t'ung* was quite novel from the viewpoint, say, of a sixteenth-century reader of the *Record of Rites*. What was, by the mid-twentieth century, common intellectual currency—the Great Harmony as an ideal *future* stage of development—is solely owing to K'ang Yu-wei's identification of the *Ta-t'ung* with another Confucian tradition: the *Kung-yang* school of the Han period.*

The Confucius of the *Li-yun* dwelt on the past. The Confucius of the *Kung-yang* school predicted the future. According to tradition, the one classic that Confucius indisputably wrote was the *Spring and Autumn Annals* (*Ch'un-ch'iu*). His authorship of this chronicle of the state of Lu is explained in *Mencius*:

Again the world fell into decay, and principles faded away. Perverse speakings and oppressive deeds waxed rife again. There were instances of ministers who murdered their sovereigns, and of sons who murdered their fathers. Confucius was afraid, and made the *Spring and Autumn*. What the

* The *Kung-yang* school of the Han was not a single entity. Jack Dull has shown that there were at least two wings. The first was the early "school" of Tung Chung-shu, whose own work was largely revised by later Han Confucianists. The second was that of the "apocrypha" (*ch'an-wei*) tradition which stressed Confucius' ability to predict the future. Ho Hsiu may represent yet a third school, which responded to the attacks of the Old Text disciples by returning to sources which antedated Tung Chung-shu. (I am grateful to Professor Dull for making these observations to me. The development of the Han *Kung-yang* school is detailed in his paper: "History and the Old Text–New Text Controversy in the Han," Seattle: University of Washington, 1966).

Spring and Autumn contains are matters proper to the emperor. On this account Confucius said, "Yes! It is the *Spring and Autumn* which will make men know me, and it is the *Spring and Autumn* which will make men condemn me." [3]

But what are men to know of Confucius' legacy when they actually turn to the sparse entries of the *Spring and Autumn*? If this was to be the text by which he would be judged in the eyes of later generations, why would Confucius content himself with the routine of a court chronicle, which—in a sample taken at random—describes an entire year in the reign of Duke Huan as follows? "In the fourth year, in spring, in the first month, the duke hunted in Lang. In summer, the king [by] heaven's [grace], sent the [sub-] administrator, Ch'ü Po-chiu, to Lu with friendly inquiries." [4] The very leanness of the text must have been purposive. Every word must have been weighed with the greatest care by the master, skilled as he was at "rectifying names" and bestowing praise and blame in the subtlest fashion. Even—argued the commentators—his omission of certain details must convey meaning. Here, for instance, it was suggested that Confucius did not list any autumn or winter entries in order to express his displeasure with Duke Huan for conspiring to murder his (the Duke's) brother, the former ruler.

How was one to know this? Either out of respect for the ruling house of his native state or for fear of being accused of *lèse-majesté,* Confucius simply stated that the former duke had died. According to the Han scholar Liu Hsin (46 B.C. to A.D. 23) what Confucius had then done was orally to inform one of his disciples, Tso Ch'iu-ming, of the truth. Tso then wrote a special additional commentary (the *Tso-chuan*) to be read alongside the *Spring and Autumn*. Two other commentaries also existed: the *Kung-yang chuan* and the *Ku-liang chuan.* However, the great majority of Confucianists after the second century A.D. believed the *Tso* version to be the most correct, largely because it was supposed to have been authorized by Confucius himself.

One reason for the *Tso-chuan's* preferability over the other two was its historicity. The information it added was often anecdotal, enlivening the *Ch'un-ch'iu* with background details and historiettes. The original *Spring and Autumn* may, for instance, briefly record the execution of an officer of Lu. The *Tso's* addition for such an entry would likely expose the drama behind the event (perhaps the officer had derided the *faux pas* of a court favorite), discuss the fairness of the trial, and opine that the duke had been at fault in his judgment. Of course, the *Tso-chuan* did more than satisfy idle curiosity. As the Old Text school later employed it, the *Tso* commentary provided an historical record in which were imbedded metahistorical truths. The ultimate of these were social relations, such as between father and son or ruler and minister. Naturally, therefore, when nineteenth-century scholars like K'ang Yu-wei wished to attack the finality of such relationships, they were driven to other texts.

The *Tso-chuan* had already in Han times failed to satisfy those who sought ultimate cosmic truths in the *Spring and Autumn*. Thus scholars turned to the *Kung-yang* commentary, which did much more to ferret out the "hidden" meanings of Confucius in the text. For instance, the last *Spring and Autumn* entry for the first year of Duke Yin (721 B.C.) reads: "Duke's son I-shih died." [5] As there was no day given, the *Tso* commentary explained that "Chung-fu [the other name of I-shih] died. The Duke did not take part in the *hsiao-lien* [ceremony of placing the corpse in the coffin]. Therefore no date is written." [6] For the same passage the *Kung-yang* asked, "Why is there no date?"—and answered itself:

It was far away.
(*Note:* It was not seen by Confucius.)
What was seen [is expressed in] different words. What was heard [is expressed in] different words. What was hearsay [is expressed in] different words.
(*Note:* What was seen refers to events of [Dukes] Chao, Ting, and Ai [from 540 to 467 B.C.] which were at the time of [Confucius] himself and his father. What was heard refers to events of Princes Wen, Hsuan, Ch'eng and Hsiang [from 625 to 541 B.C.] which were at the time of [Confucius'] father. What was hearsay refers to the Eminent Ancestors Yin, Huan, Chuang, Min, and Hsi [from 722 to 626 B.C.] which were at the time of [Confucius'] ancestors.) [7]

The *Kung-yang's* judgment was that Confucius adjusted his style to accord with the era he described. Of the three eras (*san-shih* or *san-teng*) which divided the twelve ducal reigns of the house of Lu, the most recent included events which Confucius had personally witnessed. Because its rulers were intimate to him, he consciously "made subtle" (*wei*) his descriptions, omitting disrespectful phrases. The second age covered those years whose contemporaries Confucius had interviewed. Less directly involved, he was nonetheless compassionate enough to express deep grief as he recounted the calamities of that era. For the last and most distant age, Confucius afforded nothing but impartiality, setting aside compassion to judge that era as it was. [8]

The *Kung-yang* commentary's "three ages" did not stand by themselves as esoteric revelation. That principle was added by the later *Kung-yang* school of classical interpretation, led by Tung Chung-shu (c. 179 to c. 104 B.C.) of the Han dynasty. Tung's metaphysical cycle of three phases (*san-t'ung,* represented by the colors black, white, and red) was partly inspired by the *Kung-yang's* three ages. Claiming that each phase evolved from simplicity to refinement before giving way to the next, Tung Chung-shu attributed the same principles to Confucius' organization of the reigns of the Dukes of Lu. But the principles were not simply analytic categories, used to order the chronicle. Instead, they were paradigms of cosmic-historic stages of universal development, so that the Dukes of Lu were merely examples of a vision which Confucius had received of the pattern of all history, good for any time and any place. Consequently, Tung made of the *Spring and Autumn Annals* a revelation, an expression of heaven's bestowal upon Confucius of a mandate to order the world.

Tung Chung-shu's theory of Confucius' mandate came from the very last entry of the *Ch'un-ch'iu:* "In the fourteenth year [of Duke Ai], in the spring, [some] hunters in the west captured a *lin.*" [9] The *lin* (a unicorned antelope with the tail of an ox) was believed to appear once every five centuries to augur the arrival of a sage on earth. Did this final omen of the *Spring and Autumn* mean that Confucius-the-sage had been inspired to write the *Ch'un-ch'iu* upon seeing the animal? Or was it heaven's signal that the completed work established Confucius as a sage? The *Family Sayings* of the Confucian school underscored Confucius' own modesty when he was supposed to have experienced the event.

Confucius went to see it, and said, "It is a *lin.* Why has it come? Why has it come?" He took the back of his sleeve and wiped his face, while his tears wet the lapel of his coat. When Shu-sun [an officer of the state of Lu] heard what it was, he sent and had it brought [to the city]. Tzu-kung asked the master why he wept, and Confucius said, "The *lin* comes only when there is an intelligent king. Now it has appeared when it is not the time for it to do so, and it has been injured. This is why I was so much affected." [10]

But to Tung Chung-shu the appearance of the *lin* was certain evidence of divine inspiration.

There are things which, while incapable of being brought about by effort, arrive of themselves. Hunting in the west they captured a *lin;* this was an omen of [Confucius'] receiving the mandate. Afterwards he entrusted to the

Ch'un-ch'iu to rectify what was not correct therein and revealed the meaning of changing institutions. He [sought to] unify [the world] under the Son of Heaven and added his own grief to the grief of the empire. He devoted attention to eliminating the calamities of the empire, while wishing to penetrate [the principles] of the earlier five emperors, and extend [the principles] of the later three kings. Penetrating the Tao of a hundred kings and following heaven's [process] from beginning to end, he encompassed the results of acquiring and losing [power] and examined the operation of the expression of the mandate.[11]

By the same token, Confucius partook of divinity, so that Tung's judgment of the sage accompanied a wider tendency of thinkers of the Han to portray Confucius as a kind of Gnostic demiurge. The many apocryphal texts which were made canonical by Emperor Kuang-wu (who reigned from A.D. 25 to 57) described Confucius' divine genesis, his superhuman strength, his godly wisdom. For example, the "Expository Chart on Confucius" of the *Subtleties of the Spring and Autumn (Ch'-un-ch'iu-wei, Yen-k'ung-t'u)* explained that his mother, Cheng-tsai, fell asleep one day on a tomb mound, where she dreamed of being ravished by the Black Emperor.* The child she later bore in a hollow mulberry tree had writing on his chest—"The act of instituting [a new dynasty] has been decided and the rule of the world has been transferred" [12]— and grew to be ten feet high, awesomely resembling a crouching dragon whenever he sat down.

As Tung Chung-shu helped transform Confucius into an uncrowned king (*su-wang*), so he also made a prophet of the sage. And what had been a text became (like the *Book of Changes*) a testament to plot the future and guide the present.

Men of the past had a saying to the effect that though we do not know the future we can see it in the past. Now the *Ch'un-ch'iu*, as it is studied, speaks of the past and elucidates the future. However, its phrases incorporate the subtlety of heaven and are therefore difficult to understand. If one is not capable of investigating its subtlety, it is as though it has no [meaning]. If one can investigate it, there is nothing which is not within it.[13]

To this was added a final elaboration of the *Kung-yang* school. Two and a half centuries after Tung Chung-shu's death, Ho Hsiu (129–182) tried to free the *Kung-yang* from the influence of the apocryphal texts by going back to Tung Chung-shu's point of departure. He further refined

---

* *Hei-ti*, the god of winter, associated with the planet Mercury.

the evolutionary theory of three ages (*san-shih*) by equating them with a tripartite division of history into an early era of disorder (*shuai-luan*), one of approaching peace (*sheng-p'ing*) before Confucius was born, and a final stage during his lifetime of universal peace (*t'ai-p'ing*).

In the age of which he heard [through oral testimony], he made visible that there was an order arising of Approaching Peace. Therefore he considered the Chinese hegemony as the center and treated the outlying barbarian tribes as something outside [his scheme]. . . . Coming to the age which he [personally] witnessed, he made evident that there was an order arising of Universal Peace. Thus, the barbarian tribes became part of the feudal hierarchy, and the whole world, far and near, large and small, was like one.[14]

Eventually these two conceptions of the *Kung-yang* school blended together. Tung's prophecies loaned Ho's three ages an air of future history: a recent age of disorder, a current one of ascending peace, and a final and even imminent one of universal peace—the very *t'ai-p'ing* of which nineteenth-century rebels saw themselves the agents.

The *Kung-yang* school posed something of a threat to the monarchy because of its religious potential.

The Old Text [that is, *Tso-chuan*] scholars were arguing that there was only one good in the state—the ruler's immediate good. The New Text [that is, *Kung-yang*] scholar-official had a certain amount of freedom of action in any given situation, but the Old Text philosophy taught that in all circumstances the official had only one route to follow: loyalty and subordination to the ruler. . . . In place of the emperor to whom the official owed complete loyalty, the New Text scholar-officials felt that they were ultimately answerable to God on high or to heaven.[15]

Therefore, despite the corroboration it lent to the throne-supporting theory of omens which Tung had inspired, the *Kung-yang* school was eventually displaced. This was not simply carried out by imperial fiat; in fact, many emperors favored the *Kung-yang*. The victory of the *Tso* tradition was brought about by a portion of the literati themselves who benefited from—perhaps even engineered—a major textual controversy.

In 213 B.C., the Ch'in despot, Shih huang-ti, had ordered the burning of the classics. During the succeeding Han dynasty, various schools of Confucianism had reproduced from memory the words of the canon in the New Text (*chin-wen*) seal writing of the period. The *Kung-yang* was such a New Text version. At the end of the Former Han (206 B.C.

to A.D. 9), though, scholars claimed to have discovered extant copies of the pre-Ch'in classics written in the Old Text (*ku-wen*) style and hidden away to preserve them from Ch'in inquisitors. The Old Text version of the *Book of Documents,* for instance, was supposedly discovered in a wall by K'ung An-kuo, Confucius' descendant. When these texts, which included the *Tso-chuan,* first appeared, the foremost scholar urging their acceptance was Liu Hsin. They did become briefly canonical during the early years of Kuang-wu's reign; but that emperor soon favored the New Text school, which at this time managed to regain its position by introducing the apocrypha described above. However, by the later years of the Han, most scholars simply followed the masterfully synthetic annotations of the eminent Confucianist, Cheng Hsuan (127–200), so that the distinction between the Old and New Text schools virtually ceased to exist. When the dynasty fell, so did the New Text tradition altogether.

The *Kung-yang* tradition was largely ignored for the next fourteen centuries. True, Chu Hsi had expressed doubts during the Sung of the authenticity of the Old Text portion of the *Book of Documents;* but it was not seriously questioned until the seventeenth century. Then a loosely defined school of empirical research (*k'ao-cheng hsueh*) and Han learning (*Han-hsueh*) arose at the inspiration of Ku Yen-wu. Some scholars, like the famous Fei family (Fei Ching-yü, Fei Mi, and Fei Hsi-huang), argued that Han literati had been much closer to antiquity and were far more interested in practical matters of government and philological reconstruction of the canon than the Sung Neo-Confucianists. The latter injected all kinds of illusory metaphysical meaning into the classics, which were made "bags to contain the wind and fog which seemed at times to be real and at other times to be unreal." [16] Other Ch'ing empiricists, like Ch'en Ti, who wrote a critical study of the Mao recension of the *Odes,* began to experiment with inductive methods of philological research, often using internal phonetic evidence to disprove the consistency of certain texts. Ku Yen-wu helped perfect this phonetic technique in his study of the Five Books, which in turn influenced his friend Yen Jo-chü (1636–1704).

Yen applied this new philological method to the ancient text portion of the *Book of Documents.* In 1745 his *Shang-shu ku-wen shu-cheng* (Inquiry into the Authenticity of the *Shang-shu* in the Ancient text) was published, astonishing mid-Ch'ing literati with its bold and incontrovertible demonstration that the sixteen chapters of the *Book of Docu-*

ments written in the Old Text style, along with the commentary by K'ung An-kuo, were actually forgeries which probably had appeared during the Eastern Chin (317–419). Only the New Text portions were authentic! [17] Although the following account by Liang Ch'i-ch'ao probably exaggerates the impact of this discovery, contemporaries truly were stunned.

Ever since the Emperor Wu (140–87 B.C.) of the Han apotheosized the Six Arts and suppressed the Hundred Schools, our countrymen had been allowed only citation and exegesis but no criticism of the Six Classics. . . . If a man harbored even the slightest intention of doubting or criticizing a single word or sentence in a classical text, he felt instantly as if he had fallen into a position of "vilifying the saints and disregarding the law"; he would be uneasy and conscience-stricken, not only in dread of legal prosecution and irresponsible criticism. As a rule, matters of a religious nature cannot be treated as a problem for scholarly research; once it has become a problem its sacrosanct position is already shaken. Now, not only had [the *Book of Documents* in "ancient text"] become a problem, but the results of the study had revealed that what had been previously honored as sacred was in part trash, and the [resulting] mental arousal, turmoil, and *volte-faces* are easy to imagine. From that time on, all classical texts could become problems for study.[18]

If part of the *Shang-shu* was forged, then why not also the Old Text *Tso-chuan*? The first to extend the same skepticism to the *Tso-chuan* was Chuang Ts'un-yü (1719–1788), member of a scholarly Kiangsu family which claimed descent from Chuang-tzu. Although Chuang's conclusion that the subtler meanings of the *Ch'un-ch'iu* were to be found in the *Kung-yang* was not published until 1827, he earlier influenced his grandson, Liu Feng-lu (1776–1829), to pursue similar researches. Liu read Tung Chung-shu's *Luxuriant Gems,* mastered Ho Hsiu's interpretation, and decided that the *Tso-chuan* merely emphasized detail at the expense of the true meaning of the *Spring and Autumn.* Through the early years of the nineteenth century, he published a series of works illustrating this theory. The most consequential of these, the *Tso-shih ch'un-ch'iu k'ao-cheng* (Critical Verification of the *Spring and Autumn* of Messr. Tso) advanced what was to become the central thesis of the *chin-wen* (New Text) school of the Ch'ing: the *Tso* commentary was originally an entirely separate chronicle of its own written in the style of the *Kuo-yü* (Discourses of the States). It had been altered, rearranged—perhaps even partly fabricated—by Liu Hsin to appear to be an expressly written commentary on the original *Ch'un-ch'iu*. Liu Hsin had thereby driven the true *Kung-yang* commentary out of circulation and willfully obscured Confucius' true meaning.[19]

The philological rehabilitation of *Kung-yang* mysticism accompanied a much broader revolt against convention during that period. Many late eighteenth-century thinkers seem to have been repelled by the congealing of Neo-Confucian *li-hsueh* into a rigid and hierarchical system of inflexible rules that denied spontaneous emotion. One of the greatest philosophers of the time, Tai Chen (1724–1777), argued that desire and reason were not respective attributes of "vulgar" matter (*ch'i*) and "divine" principle (*li*). Man's rational sense of duty, his capacity for feeling that he ought to refine his intelligence was as much a part of his nature as the sexual drive. His "ought"—as Hu Shih (1891–1962) later paraphrased Tai—"does not oppose 'spontaneity' [that is, nature, *tzu-jan*]; it is simply the 'utmost extension of the spontaneity' which is indicated by human intelligence." [20] And a few years after Tai Chen, the famous essayist Yun Ching (1757–1817), urged his contemporaries to realize that rigid and formalistic adherence to the institutions of the past would not solve the problems of the time. "The sages governed the empire not by grasping the stylus but by acting for the [current] situation." [21] Perhaps reacting to the luxury of the Ch'ien-lung emperor's court and the misery of the White Lotus rebellion, Yun urged economic moderation on the country and more regard for the feelings of the people. Above all, the empire's administrators must adjust to circumstances. "Although there is a central Tao, the former kings' Tao gradually changed with the times. Their laws were not in accord [with formal prescriptions], yet upon examination they were without blemish, and in use they were without evil practices." [22] Yun's writings called for institutional flexibility, and so appealed to would-be reformers who for the same reason turned to the *Kung-yang's* doctrine of the *chün-tzu's* (superior man, gentleman) responsibility to adjust to the times.

This prevailing theme of the *chin-wen* tradition was found in the *Kung-yang's* discussion of the *Spring and Autumn* entry for the eleventh year of Duke Huan: "Men of Sung seized the cadet Chi of Cheng." Why, asked the *Kung-yang,* was Chi's given name not mentioned? Confucius must have intended to honor Chi by not using his familiar. Indeed, Chi's behavior had been exemplary. Then chief minister to the newly acceded ruler of Cheng, he was captured by neighboring nobles who tried to force him to dethrone his lord in favor of a younger brother related to them by marriage. Chi realized that if he resisted, the neighboring Sung would simply invade Cheng. To save his state Chi carried out their orders, even though he knew he would be vilified for betraying the person of his ruler. His sacrifice was a noble one—*under the circumstances.*

What is [acting according to] circumstances (*ch'üan*)? [Acting according to] circumstances is going against [normal] standards of conduct (*ching*) such that consequently there will be good [results]. A program of [acting according to] circumstances cannot be adopted unless death or extinction are entailed. Carrying out [this acting according to] circumstances has a Tao [of its own]. To effect [this acting according to] circumstances, degrade and injure one's own self. To effect [this acting according to] circumstances, do not harm others. Killing others in order to keep himself alive, extinguishing others in order to preserve himself, is not done by the superior man (*chün-tzu*).[23]

In his freedom to make this decision, the superior man stands above all others. The very phrase *chün-tzu* (son of the lord) almost likens him to an uncrowned ruler by virtue of self. Yet as symbolic descendant of the lord, his presumptuousness must entail self-sacrifice; the superior man must draw censure upon himself to justify his independence.

Thus, the New Text *chün-tzu's* martyrdom was an apotheosis of the self—an expression of individuality which was anathema to restrained conservatives of the nineteenth century like Wo-jen (d. 1871). His and Tseng Kuo-fan's teacher, T'ang Chien (1776?–1861), seemed almost to fear self-expression. T'ang Chien believed, as did most othodox students of Sung learning, that one realized the good by conquering the self (*k'o-chi*), denying it, even punishing it. And so the resurgence of *chin-wen* individualism was as much a reaction to this self-restraint as the consequence of philological discoveries. The young expressionists of the New Text school wished to reunite the self through the heroism of the superior man, who would stand at the center of a universe where subject and object, individual and society, were integrated by his humane love (*jen*).[24] Thanks also to his superior discrimination of change (another powerful source of New Text theory was the *Book of Changes*), the *chün-tzu* would restore to man his control over events. Free of conventional prejudices, he would judge better than others when action must be modified to suit circumstances, and—like the minister of Cheng—he would value the preservation of the state above all other considerations. As the *Kung-yang* commentary's note to "circumstances" read: "*Ch'üan* [that is, circumstances] is to estimate, and therefore to distinguish between the important and the unimportant. Illustrating that, Chi Chung knows the state (*kuo*) is important and the ruler is unimportant." [25] Even though the ideal *chün-tzu* was no Japanese *shishi**—his heed to circumstances keeping him within the *Changes'* tradition of self-accommodation—his commitment to *kuo*, his appreciation of exigency (not necessity), and his limited right to ignore conventional standards or *ching* (literally, "warp," which also means "the classics") entranced many nineteenth-century literati concerned with the future of the empire.

By the 1820s and 1830s, many Ch'ing scholar-officials had begun to share a deep sense of worry about the dynasty's declining fortunes and the growing Western presence on the southeastern coast. Among other symbols of degeneration, the *T'ien-li chiao* (Doctrine of Heavenly Principles) rebels' attack of 1813 on the imperial palace, the opium problem, and the waterworks crisis made even philosophical conservatives —men like Wo-jen who would later oppose reform—feel enough anxiety to argue for "maintaining tradition in order to save the age" (*shou-tao chiu-shih*).[26] Bolder thinkers turned to the *Kung-yang* for self-definition.

Of these, Kung Tzu-chen (1792–1841) was probably at first the most influential. Grandson of an iconoclastic philologist, Tuan Yü-ts'ai (1735–1815), Kung was a precocious genius whose poor handwriting disqualified him for high office. In place of the bureaucratic career he had expected, he became a pamphleteer, writing essays on the political and administrative practices of his time. His *Ting-an wen-chi* (The Collected Writings of [Kung] Ting-an), first published in 1868 and later read by K'ang Yu-wei,† attacked the formalism of state examinations, condemned the binding of women's feet, and urged that the court abandon demeaning rituals. Behind all these specifics were many of the more general themes of New Text scholarship: adaptation to the times, the importance of the superior man, and so forth. In naming equality the

---

* Literally, knight of resolve, usually translated as patriot or public-spirited man. The *shishi*, who played such an important role in the Meiji restoration, acted by necessity. Their individuality was much more self-justifying than the *chün-tzu's*. In this regard, they more closely resemble the *hsia* or knight-errant of earlier periods of Chinese history.

† "Most of the so-called Scholars of New Learning of the Kuang-hsu period (1875–1908) went through a period in which they worshipped him. A reading of his *Ting-an wen-chi* electrifies a man at first, but after a time one gets tired of his shallowness. Nevertheless, the development of the Modern Text school actually began with him." Liang Ch'i-ch'ao, *Intellectual Trends in the Ch'ing Period* (Cambridge: Harvard University Press, 1959), p. 89.

highest virtue, Kung invoked the Mencian tradition of limited popular sovereignty: "The eyes and ears of the people are fundamental to heaven." [27] And, as he sought to liberate the self, he recalled the six-teenth-century iconoclasts' glorification of individual (*ssu* or selfish) desires: "*Kung* (public) and *ssu* (private) mutually sustain each other." [28] Kung was also one of the first Chinese scholars to warn in 1820 of the new dangers of the foreign presence in Canton, and to urge that relations then be severed. His concern with foreign relations undoubtedly influenced Lin Tse-hsu, imperial commissioner at the beginning of the Opium War; and Wei Yuan, the famous New Text scholar and expert on barbarian affairs. Just as the three of them joined the same literary society in Peking, so are traits of *Kung-yang* thinking to be found even in the diplomatic policies of Commissioner Lin.[29]

Partly owing to Lin Tse-hsu and Wei Yuan, Canton became identified as a major center of *Kung-yang* learning. However, the New Text influence there actually antedated them because so many early *Kung-yang* thinkers were sponsored by the famous man of letters, Juan Yuan (1764–1849), who was governor-general of Liang-kuang from 1817 to 1826. During that tenure, Juan founded the prestigious *Hsueh-hai* Academy which, for instance, published some of Kung Tzu-chen's studies in its massive collection of classical commentaries, the *Huang Ch'ing ching-chieh* (1829). Of course, Juan Yuan was more than editorially intimate with these intellectuals. His sons were tutored by the *Kung-yang* scholar, Ling Shu (1775–1892), author of a famous annotation of Tung Chung-shu's *Luxuriant Gems of the Spring and Autumn* while many other New Text interpreters studied under Juan's closest friend, Ch'eng En-tse (1785–1837).[30]

Juan Yuan shared with the *Kung-yang* scholars a strong belief in the vital force of *jen* even though his source of inspiration was the Old Text philosopher, Cheng Hsuan, whose definition of *jen* as the simple but effective notion of people living together was much more appealing to Juan than the Neo-Confucian use of it as a metaphysical principle of life. Because Sung abstractions seemed to deaden this vital emotion, Juan Yuan preferred to revive the earlier concept of *jen* "as human beings living together," [31] generating among themselves a deep and powerful force of mutual attraction which might then be projected outward onto the society at large.

In a way Juan's own vision of the Academy as a self-sustaining and socially engaged community of fellows was an illustration of this belief, and it infused the philosophical circles of Canton with life and enthusiasm. Consequently, most Cantonese scholars, whether they were New Text *dévotés* or not, laid a great deal of stress on personal involvement in current affairs. Ch'en Li (1810–1882), for example, tried to steer between Sung and Han learning while studying geography (he was to advise Wei Yuan on his geography of the West) and mathematics. Similarly, Chu Tz'u-ch'i (1807–1882), Ch'en's close friend, emphasized the call of the seventeenth-century thinkers for social commitment. And, like most of the Cantonese intellectuals of the time, Chu held that same philosophy of vitalism, of the power of *jen* in the hands of a superior man. It was this conviction above all others which he would convey later to his most famous student, K'ang Yu-wei.

9
Syncretic Utopianism

K'ang Yu-wei was the most intriguing—if seemingly inconsistent—Chinese intellectual of the late nineteenth century. Fecund and imaginative, he left a corpus of writings which roam from visionary utopian socialism to utterly pragmatic programs of gradual reform. Like Saint-Simon, another great seer, K'ang turned different faces to different people. Unlike the French socialist, his boldest work was hardly known to contemporaries. The *Ta-t'ung shu* (The Book of Great Harmony) was probably conceived in the 1880s, written during his 1902 exile in Darjeeling after he conspired to overthrow the Dowager Empress, published in snippets in 1913, and not entirely available until after 1930 when K'ang Yu-wei was already several years dead. When its import was finally realized, the K'ang of 1898, valiantly attempting reform from above and change from below without scrapping the monarchy, seemed utterly belied.

The contradiction between K'ang in theory and in action has troubled many historians. If K'ang were the hard-headed reformer he appeared to be in 1898, working through the emperor for relatively moderate institutional change, then the *Ta-t'ung shu* must have been compiled in later disappointment after the Dowager Empress's coup deposed the emperor and either drove into exile or executed the reformers. Perhaps the *Ta-t'ung shu* should even be explained away as a utopian dream, divorced from K'ang's real political life—an exercise in fantasy. Of course, the most learned students of K'ang's thought, like K. C. Hsiao, have understood that K'ang was a gradualist. He aimed toward the utopia of Universal Harmony, but had sense enough to pace his steps along the way in rhythm with mankind's historical progress at that particular moment.[1] Yet even Hsiao necessarily conceived of K'ang's thought as being staggered.

On one level, he directed his attention to the practical affairs of China, in the last decades of the nineteenth century when he endeavored to salvage the sinking empire through reform and, later, in the first decades of the twentieth when he engaged himself in scathing criticisms of the tottering republic. On another level, he disengaged himself from concerns with immediate situations and sallied forth into theorizations and speculations which had little direct contact with reality. Often he moved simultaneously on both these levels; sometimes he shifted back and forth from one level to another. In this way he assumed a double role: as a practical reformer and as a utopian thinker.[2]

This impression of duality, of a mind swinging between fantasy and reality, fractures the integrity of K'ang Yu-wei's thought. However, utopian thinker and practical reformer really went hand in hand, for K'ang's genius was to syncretize past and future, Chinese and Western, into a coherent vision which employed Western science—analytic laws and concepts of evolution—to project an almost forgotten ideal of China's past into his country's future.

Joseph R. Levenson once analyzed this syncretic effort as the injection of new (Western) values into an accepted (Chinese) tradition. K'ang—Levenson argued—stood for a generation of troubled men who searched for Western ideals of progress in Chinese civilization in order to reconcile history and value, *their* China and *true* universal principles of history now set by the West. Because those principles, even if they had existed in China's past, were not really part of K'ang's culture as it existed in the present, the source of his civilization had to be adroitly redefined. K'ang managed this by believing that generally accepted versions of the classics were actually distortions of Han compilers, deviating from the versions Confucius had written. His own reconstructions would transform Confucius into a reformer, while making Confucian records of the past into divine predictions of the future.[3]

In contrast, the interpretation given here will try to show that K'ang was able to syncretize Western and Chinese thought because of a much higher degree of cultural confidence than Levenson believed to exist. Not that Levenson's interpretation was entirely wrong; it subtly illuminated K'ang's emotional search for China's equivalence with the West. But it suggested that K'ang's Confucianism was more an instrumentality than a source of his convictions. Levenson's exposition of K'ang Yu-wei therefore began with the latter's redefinition of Confucianism, mentioning—as though it were the first stage of K'ang's development—his *Hsin-hsueh wei-ching k'ao* (On the Spurious Classics of Hsin Learning, completed in 1891)* which "challenged the authenticity of certain texts of the Confucian canon (especially the *Tso-chuan*), texts which he wished to see superseded by others more 'exploitable' [for setting a course for Chinese history in the stream of Western optimism, and calling it a Chinese stream]." [4] Levenson therefore emphasized the means of reconciliation without explaining why K'ang's syncretism assumed that particular guise; and, by opening his analysis with the *Hsin-hsueh wei-ching k'ao*, Levenson seemed to set the origin of K'ang's intellectual odyssey in 1891—six years after the actual moment of illumination which had so fundamentally altered K'ang's entire perception of world history.

K'ang Yu-wei was born in 1858. His family, well established in Nan-hai near Canton, had long produced local yamen clerks and secretaries. The Taiping rebellion provided the family, as it did so many other fringe-gentry lineages, with an opportunity to raise its station. The elderly K'ang's led militia defense bureaus, directed local schools, and mastered the fiscal intricacies of famine relief well enough to become ranked officials with high gentry status. K'ang Yu-wei's grandfather actually held a *chü-jen* degree and was appointed director of studies in a mountainous district of Lien-chou, where he took the young boy after Yu-wei's father died in 1868. It was perhaps because of the hard-willed family's social success that the old gentleman was subsequently able to instill such a remarkable sense of confidence in the boy. Perhaps, too, this was due to an absence of normal father-son tensions, since young K'ang seems to have been pampered with praise by his grandfather and made to feel a truly exceptional youth.

Full of boyish self-esteem, I would emulate the men of the past: when I did something, I would believe myself to be the equal of Chang Ch'ih; when I wrote an essay, I would think of myself as the equal of Su Shih (1036–1101); when I conceived an idea, I would consider myself the equal of the Sixth Patriarch (Hui-neng, 638–713) or of Ch'iu Ch'ang-ch'un (1148–

---

* Levenson was probably following Liang Ch'i-ch'ao, who indicated in *Intellectual Trends in the Ch'ing Period* (Cambridge: Harvard University Press, 1959), on p. 92, that "the first book K'ang wrote was the *Hsin-hsueh wei-ching k'ao.*"

1227), and I would assume an air of superiority over the other students in the department.[5]

This enthusiasm was stifled when K'ang entered adolescence and settled into the conventional rut of preparing for examinations. Back in Canton by 1871, he spent those stultifying hours of exercise so necessary for mastery of examination-essay style and calligraphy; but the effort failed to earn him the *chü-jen* degree in 1876. Eighteen years of age, he then persuaded his family to let him study under the far more exciting regimen of the noted Cantonese scholar, Chu Tz'u-ch'i. Chu, deeply influenced by Ku Yen-wu and Wang Fu-chih, offered K'ang the same counsel that he gave his other students: the learning of the ages was empty, devoid of meaning, unless one devoted oneself to the service of humanity. Coming as it did after his daydreams of superiority had been frustrated by the monotonous grind of examinations, this adjuration to dare to act like the worthies of the past made K'ang feel "like a traveler finding a place of lodging or a blind man seeing light." Overnight his confidence was restored, and he came to believe

. . . that it was possible for me to be a sage, that it was possible for me to read all the books before I was thirty, that I alone could establish myself in life, and that I could remake the world. From this time on, I gave up the writing of examination-style essays and thoughts of becoming rich and exalted. I stood, towering and lofty, above the common people, associating myself with the great and good men of the past.[6]

By relegating bureaucratic careerism to a secondary place in the gentleman's scheme of things, Chu Tz'u-ch'i's teachings helped K'ang recover his self-esteem and suggested that practical scholarship was just as legitimate a road to worldly excellence. Of course, for all its supposed practicality, scholarship remained scholarship. For the next two years action was translated by K'ang into a frantic reading program, as he pored over the writings of the seventeenth-century philosophers, the histories, and the classics. Then, in 1878, he suffered serious misgivings about the value of all this academic effort.

I gradually grew weary of books and began to conceive new ideas. Of what use, I asked myself, were the works of such scholars of textual research as Tai Chen (1724–1777), whose books filled his whole house? I therefore gave up this type of learning and privately sought ways to the achievement of peace of mind and fulfillment of my mission in life. I abruptly abandoned my studies and the reading of books, locked my door, and refused to see friends. I sat alone to cultivate my mind. My schoolmates thought that my behavior was strange because our teacher stressed practice and scorned Ch'an Buddhism, and none of us studied it. Sitting quietly by myself, I would suddenly come to the realization that the universe and its myriad of things were all a part of me. A light dawned within me, and believing that I was a sage, I would be happy and laugh; then, thinking of the suffering of the people in the world, I would be sad and cry.[7]

K'ang embraced quietism just as fervently as he had erudition, reproducing in a brief span the life pattern of many earlier Chinese thinkers. And like many other idealists of the Ming and Ch'ing, he exulted in that strong, but threateningly vacuous, identity with the cosmos. There was also in him a familiar Mahayana Buddhist strain as he recognized the duty of the once-enlightened to save others less fortunate.

That motif emerged prominently after K'ang left Master Chu's school and, in 1879, retreated to Hsi-ch'iao Mountain near his home. Further eremitic cultivation there strengthened his calling. "I reflected upon the perils and hardships in the life of the people and upon how I might save them with the powers of wisdom and ability granted to me by heaven. Out of commiseration for all living beings, and in anguish over the state of the world, I took it as my purpose to set in order all under heaven." [8] But the conviction was not firm enough to resist constant family pressure to sit for the examinations. Although his perseverance would eventually gain him official rank, crucial to his later reform program, it seemed for the moment mundanely irrelevant to his superhuman visions. There was thus a continuously disparate and strained coexistence between lofty fantasies, and the tedious chore of convincing his uncles that he was serious enough about an orthodox career to deserve an allowance; while all around K'ang more and more Chinese began to wonder where imperialist pressures on China would finally take their country, their world, as they knew it.

K'ang was sensitive to these concerns as well. As early as 1879, he had visited the British crown colony of Hong Kong to satisfy his curiosity about the West. From that trip he retained vivid memories of clean streets, large buildings, orderly policemen. "I was impressed by the organization and administration of the foreigners, and I realized that we must not look upon them as barbarians, as our older and more conservative people have done." [9] Three years later when he sat for the metropolitan examinations, he passed through the international settlement in Shanghai, where he bought Kiangnan Arsenal translations of foreign books and arranged for a subscription to the missionary journal, *Wan-kuo kung-pao* (Cosmopolitan Gazette). During the following year he read all he could find in these Western sources on acoustics, optics, chemistry, electricity, and mechanics; and in 1884 he alternated his studies of Neo-Confucianism (Chu Hsi's sayings, Huang Tsung-hsi's anthology of Ming thought) with mathematics and geometry.

The impression of these years which one gleans from K'ang Yu-wei's autobiography is of an odyssey only partly detailed: titles listed, trips recounted; forays from book to book, from Chinese philosophy to Western science. The search is for unity, for synthesis. K'ang seems to gaze across dizzying vistas of experience, always looking for the one summit of knowledge that will bring the landscape together: the visionary conviction in his own mission of 1879, the ambivalent admiration for Western discoveries, the belief that the writings of his own past must somewhere contain an answer.

And this was now no eremitic search for his own sake alone. For all his reading, K'ang was not immune from the heightened anxieties of his countrymen. During the spring and summer of 1884, he dwelt in the southern sector of Canton city. By autumn that provincial capital had been turned into a regional military headquarters for the first declared war between China and a European power in almost a quarter of a century. As hostilities spread in northern Vietnam between France and China, war fever gripped the Cantonese. Their vigorous governor-general, Chang Chih-tung (1837–1909), believed that the empire could not afford to stand by and watch a vassal state be overrun by Jules Ferry's administrators. The French would soon blockade the Chinese coast, sink the bulk of the Ch'ing's modern navy at Foochow, and even invade Taiwan. In anticipation, martial law was declared in Canton; and K'ang Yu-wei, like many others, returned to the relative safety of his native countryside.

K'ang spent most of the fall and early winter of 1884 alone in the House of Calm and Contentment (*Tan-ju lou*), a villa in the shadow of Hsi-ch'iao Mountain near the small town of Yin-t'ang. The house, which faced a large private library built by his granduncle,* dominated a garden graced with gazeboes, juniper trees, and a pond arched with bridges. There K'ang momentarily gave up reading and tried to draw his thoughts together. In the twelfth lunar month† his understanding suddenly and decisively deepened.

Because in a microscope a tick can be magnified to the size of a wheel and an ant to an elephant, I came to realize the principle of relativity of sizes.

---

* K'ang Kuo-ch'i, former governor of Kwangsi.
† January 16 to February 14, 1885.

Because electricity or light can travel hundreds of thousands of *li* in a second, I came to realize the principle of the relativity of speed. I came to understand that beyond the biggest objects there are objects bigger still and that within the smallest objects there are smaller objects still, that an object can be divided and subdivided infinitely and that no two things among the myriad of things are the same, and that in the intermixture and interaction of primeval influences one can foresee the dawn of the millennium.[10]

This was K'ang's second illumination, and even more germinal than his vision of 1879. During the next three years, he would write two books exploring his discovery. The first, *Esoteric and Exoteric Essays of Master K'ang* (*K'ang-tzu nei-wai p'ien*), analyzed the consequences of relativity. The second, *Substantial Truths and Universal Principles* (*Shih-li kung-fa*),* tried to formulate scientific social laws of development. Neither work was published, but each has been carefully studied by Richard Howard and K. C. Hsiao.[11] Both scholars believe, as I do, that the two books contain the fundamental principles of the later *Ta-t'ung shu,* in which K'ang Yu-wei detailed his fully developed utopian system. This would tally with K'ang's own declaration that he had firmly established his entire intellectual position by the time he was thirty.[12]

K'ang's vision in 1885 was apparently bifold. All was relative. Yet at the same time there existed a single absolute force, the prime ether (*yuan ch'i*), which incorporated a process of evolution beginning from the dawn of the millennium. The two were connected as his perception of relativity embodied the multiplicity of life. He now *saw* with the lens of the microscope what had been only in his mind's eye on Hsi-ch'iao Mountain: the variety of beings, the sweep of generations, the diversification of societies. Such variegation demanded meaning—a purpose he now shared with cosmic creation.

Yet they were all created with a purpose. So I felt that it was not for me merely to wish [to save them] or to resign myself. The purpose of my creation was to save the masses of living things, even if instead of residing in heaven, I would go to purgatory to save them; and even if instead of being an emperor or a king, I became a common scholar in order to save them.[13]

Relativity not only sustained him; it also liberated K'ang, enabling him to realize that principles assumed by orthodox Confucianists to be eternal patterns of the relationship among heaven, earth, and man were nothing more than the products of circumstantial social forces. *Hsiao*

* Probably a revised version of a draft entitled *Axioms of Mankind* (*Jen-lei kung-li*).

(filial piety) was rather like the skeins of the *Li-yun:* a social institution suited to a particular time, instead of an expression of eternal divine intent.

To exalt the sovereign and to look down upon the subject, to attach importance to men and to slight women, to show consideration to honorable people and to repress dishonorable ones—these constitute China's custom and right conduct. [In the past] the positions of the subject and wife had been depressed to the lowest possible level. Coming down to the present, ministers of state, kneeling in abject submissiveness [before the sovereign] are so awed by his majestic presence that they dare not speak out. Wives, downtrodden and repressed, remain untutored and unenlightened. . . . I am afraid all these are merely the results of convention; they do not accord with the highest principles of justice and reason. . . . I say, at the end of one hundred years all these will change.[14]

Such a revelation may in turn have helped ease some of K'ang's personal anxieties, just as the anxieties themselves may have shaped the revelation. He had for more than a decade been pressed between family demands to become a safely respectable bureaucrat and the riskier urges of mission. Now to believe that the sages' own pronouncements had been conditioned by society was to conclude that *hsiao* was mere convention. "Even when the sages undertook to make [new] laws, they could not but formulate them with due regard to the existing circumstances and old customs." [15] This freed K'ang "completely of discrimination, personal involvements, selfish desires, and covetousness," so that he could take "love and benevolence exclusively as [his] operative principles." [16]

But this discovery was far, far more than personally relevant; it was capable of ideally destroying the entire Confucian family system. If social institutions corresponded to particular stages of human development, then no social institution was intrinsically good. The family may have been a useful way of organizing humans during a period of anarchic disorder, but as a parochial unit it bred parochial sentiments which could destroy the sense of broader comradeship necessary for a period of complete social harmony. In this sense, K'ang Yu-wei's perception announced the birth of ideology for modern China. In the Confucian past, fathers were unfit when they failed to behave as proper fathers; emperors erred when their demeanor did not suit their proper role; officials were faulted when they did not live up to accepted norms. But the propriety of norms, and of the familial, monarchic, and bureaucratic values and institutions behind them were not basically questioned.

In K'ang's eyes, however, structures of authority were only circumstantial.* A father was needed when a son's selfishness had to be curbed. He was unnecessary, even pernicious, if mankind evolved beyond selfishness. Then emperors and officials would not be replaced because they failed to live up to their obligations. They would be dismissed, even overthrown, precisely because they were emperors and officials.

K'ang was not thereby converted to social anarchism. Although relativity called into question the permanence of social figments, it did not automatically sentence them to immediate destruction. K'ang Yu-wei was, after all, influenced during these years by *Kung-yang* learning. The relativity vision may have even in the first place been the sudden jelling of the theory of circumstances (*ch'üan*) with his elementary knowledge of modern scientific discoveries. Certainly, K'ang repeatedly insisted in the *Esoteric and Exoteric Essays* that one must accept the social circumstances of the time regardless of ideals of future harmony.

Former kings had instituted the relationship between sovereign and subject, father and son, husband and wife, elder and younger brothers, and between friends. As I was born into these relationships I should comply with the established tradition: I should recognize as sovereign who is sovereign, as subject who is subject, as father who is father, as son who is son, and so forth. And as I was born in a particular period of time, I should accept whatever style of dress and dwelling, whatever calendar system, whatever form of writing and speaking, whatever sort of moral principles that are accepted by society at that time.[17]

Although the acknowledgment of circumstantial constraints forced K'ang to distinguish between ideal and actuality and so explains his role in the Reform Movement of 1898, it also suggests that he may have been nothing more than a traditional *Kung-yang* theorist. And so he might have been, if his theory had not exceeded circumstances alone. Or, to put it more positively, the *Kung-yang* school, as conceived by Tung Chung-shu and Ho Hsiu, had avoided the abyss of relativism by constructing an elaborate metaphysic of harmonies: colors, elements, or

* I do not mean by this that K'ang Yu-wei was the first Chinese philosopher to identify Confucian institutions as functions of social development. This was not only present in the writings of Hsun-tzu (fl. 298–238 B.C.); it was also a pronounced strain in the thought of Chang Hsueh-ch'eng (1738–1801). See, for example, *Yuan tao* (On the Way), in Chang Hsueh-ch'eng, *Chang-shih i-shu* [The Extant Writings of Mr. Chang] (Chia-yeh t'ang Library, 1922), p. 37. However, Chang and others—even when denying the autonomy of absolute moral principles (*li*)—did attribute immanent good to the *Tao* manifested in human institutions.

numbers, whose accord was an end in itself, demanding an ideal coincidence between circumstances and institutions. What metaphysic could K'ang Yu-wei define to provide him with similarly ultimate principles above and beyond the vagaries of each circumstantial era?

The one additional element allowing K'ang to move beyond the traditional formula was his awareness of Western science, *as it proved the existence of objective laws.* Until he used that awareness to avoid mere relativism, he at least unconsciously knew himself to be lost. And so, having completed his *Esoteric and Exoteric Essays* around the principle of circumstantial relativity, he began in the spring of 1887 to try to work out the "universal principles of mankind on the basis of geometric principles." [18] The effort almost finished him. After April 7, he was continually assailed by a terrible, possibly psychosomatic headache, so violent "that [he] thought [he] would die." [19] Keeping to his room and swathing his head with bandages, he desperately spent the next several months checking his notes in search of an answer before the death he assumed to be imminent. Gradually the headache eased, perhaps because he had managed to conceive of a connection between universal principles and the Great Harmony (*Ta-t'ung*) of the *Li-yun*. This partial recovery made it possible for him to go once again to the retreat on Hsi-ch'iao Mountain. There he cured himself completely and finally worked out to his own satisfaction the relationship between geometric axioms and human relations.

That solution was detailed in the *Shih-li kung-fa.* The purpose of the work, as its title (*Substantial Truths and Universal Principles*) suggests, was to define the one set of human values applicable to all nations of the world. Thus, one motive behind K'ang's quest for synthetic human unity surely was to overcome cultural relativism, proceeding from the disturbing revelation that Western institutions as they appeared to K'ang in Shanghai or Hong Kong were superior to Chinese ones. This point—another demonstration of the search for equivalence—hardly needs to be labored. What should be stressed, particularly as it bears on the argument here, is that logical universality was at stake for him as well. K'ang's desire for universality was certainly impelled by the West. But the possibility for that same universality only existed thanks *to* the West, from which K'ang learned of the category of analytic truths: an isosceles triangle penned by quill had the same two equal sides as one drawn with a brush. Method replaced means. Consequently, the *Shih-li kung-fa* was based on the expectation that he could derive ethical rules by using Euclid's method which proved noncircumstantial theorems from axioms. This would guarantee their universal truth for all men, not just Chinese or English.

If these universal laws proceed from the axioms of geometry, their principles are relatively true; if they proceed from the laws that have been established by man, their principles are relatively false. Again, the laws that proceed from the axioms of geometry are termed "necessary truths" or "eternal truths"; laws established by man are termed "equivocal truths." [20]

If there existed mathematical laws, then there also could exist universal laws for other realms of being. Fixed laws derived from geometrical axioms were part of an entire system of universal laws—laws which were the starting point for K'ang's utopian *Ta-t'ung shu:* every man has the right to be his own master, all man-made laws must accord with the ideal of equality, every social institution must be determined by universal public discussion, and so forth.

Although inspired by Euclidian analytics, K'ang Yu-wei's actual proofs muddled synthetic and analytic statements. Some universal human principles were said to be merely related to geometrical axioms. Others were actually called "human axioms of geometry." But K'ang remained aware of the distinction between norms and rules. His characteristic solution to the logical gap was to stress universality as such: to be eternal, necessary, and universal, human laws had to be both deduced by all men and applied to all men.

There are many institutions in the world to which the axioms of geometry do not apply; and not having laws that proceed from the axioms of geometry, we must rely on laws that are established by man. Laws established by man are fundamentally lacking in certainty, and so we can only deduce those that are most beneficial to human morality and regard them as "universal laws." But these must be deduced in common by all mankind. We may say, then, that they are universally deduced.[21]

Since truth was now supposed to inhere to relationships, it was no longer imposed upon them as divine principle or sage-given revelation. The sages themselves were not givers of the law, but rather men gifted enough to discern the universal principles of mankind behind the veils of circumstantial customs.

The sage holds no authority which pertains to all men. Ancient and modern doctrines shall be judged in the light of truth; they shall not be measured by [the words of] sages or worthies. All dicta shall be evaluated on the basis of their intrinsic validity, without considering the persons who uttered them.[22]

Like the European rationalists, K'ang had begun to move toward critical theory by establishing the possibility of necessary truths, trying to attach ethics to a logical base without recourse to revelation. However, the universality of his principles was in the end nothing other than their character of extension and authorship.

In other words, although he rested his new belief on the existence of necessary and noncontingent truths, K'ang did not deduce necessary and noncontingent ethical imperatives. Science's objective laws were *his* revelation of "Truth"; but science was not necessarily part of the end result.* His touchstone, after all, was *kung:* what was common to (and therefore good for) society as well as what was universally validated by it, decided by *all* men in joint discussion. Society, not transcendental Idea, determined the good. For that to occur, though, society itself would have to change. Indeed, it would have to become a transcultural humanity, devoid of specific (and therefore contingent) cultural content. Thus, K'ang would ultimately fall back on teleology—not derived from necessity but necessary to his system of ideas. And that teleology itself depended on a further revelation of K'ang Yu-wei's which, inconsistent with the iconoclasm of the *Shih-li kung-fa,* enhanced the authority of one above all other sages: Confucius himself.

In describing his vision of relativity, K'ang Yu-wei had explained that his starting point was to be the Prime (*yuan,* or origin). This cosmological concept of the Prime, or primal energy (*yuan-ch'i*), came to him from the *Book of Changes* by way of Tung Chung-shu. The *Changes* reads: "How great is the Prime of creativity [that is, *ch'ien*]! The myriad things owe their beginning [to it] and it permeates heaven." [23] Like the later philosopher, Wang Fu-chih, Tung Chung-shu associated the Prime with material force. *Ch'i,* not *li,* was the essence of divine creation.

The material force of heaven is above. The material force of earth is below. And the material force of man is in between. . . . There is nothing as

---

* K'ang Yu-wei did not try to prove the Great Harmony of the *Ta-t'ung shu* with geometrical axioms. His later view of science was as a theory of materialism, a study of technology, which enabled states to grow powerful. As *wu-chih hsueh* (literally, the study of matter), science was just a technique for ordering societies into growth. See K. C. Hsiao, "In and Out of Utopia: K'ang Yu-wei's Social Thought," pt. 3, "Detour to Industrial Society," *The Chung Chi Journal,* 8:1:5.

refined as *ch'i*, nothing as fecund as earth, nothing as divine as heaven. Among the beings created by the essence [*ching*] of heaven and earth, none is more noble than man. Man received the mandate (*ming*) from heaven. Therefore he surpasses other creatures.[24]

Tung's material force was the instrument of operation of the Prime, which K'ang Yu-wei transformed into a principle of evolution. Commenting upon Tung Chung-shu's theory, he wrote, "Evolution is based on Origination [that is, Prime], which unites and commands heaven and earth." [25] Hence, the "scientific" key to creation was for K'ang to be found in embryo in the Han philosopher's work.

The universe seems empty but is real. Material force enters into man as a fish enters into water. Material force is to water the same as water is to earth. It is real no matter where it goes. . . . Master Tung's theory goes to the bottom of the sources of heaven and man. Can chemists of today go beyond it? [26]

The Sung Neo-Confucianists had believed that the creative force of the universe was a manifestation of its benevolence or *jen*. K'ang made the same connection, but added Tung Chung-shu's equation of Prime with *ch'i* to transform the Sung's *jen* from a principle of intuitive mind into an objective and material force tying together the entire universe. Schematically expressed, the evolution of the idea went through four stages: (1) *Changes:* Cosmic creation = Prime (*yuan*); (2) Tung Chung-shu: Prime = material force (*ch'i*); (3) Sung: Prime = principle of benevolence (*jen*); (4) K'ang Yu-wei: Prime = material force = benevolence.

In short, K'ang made of material force a vital form of energy in itself, which combined spirit and matter and united the individual with the cosmos. Just as the universe was permeated with the primal energy (*yuan-ch'i*), so was man himself filled with soul-matter (*hun-chih*).

Vast is the primal energy (*yuan-ch'i*), the creator of heaven and earth. Heaven is a single spiritual substance (*hun-chih*), and man, too, is a single spiritual substance. Though different in size, they both share the vast energy derived from the Great Origin (*t'ai yuan*). . . . Confucius had said: "Earth contains the spiritual energy (*shen ch'i*) which [produces] the wind and thunderclap. By the wind and thunderclap the [seeds of] forms are carried along, and the multitude of creatures show the appearance of life." *
This spiritual thing is electricity, possessed of consciousness. As electric light, it can be transmitted everywhere; as spiritual energy, it can activate

* *Record of Rites*, Sec. 30, *K'ung-tzu hsien chü.*

everything. . . . There are no creatures who are devoid of this electricity, this spirit. It is a conscious energy (*chih ch'i*). . . . To whoever possesses consciousness it gives the power of attraction, like that of the lodestone, but how much more so in the case of man! The inability to endure (*pu jen*) [seeing the suffering of others] is a manifestation of this power of attraction. That is why both love (*jen*) and wisdom are stored [within the mind] where wisdom holds precedence; it is why both love and wisdom are exercised [in internal conduct], where love is more noble.[27]

This fascinating passage illustrates once again the heuristic way K'ang used his sometimes hazy knowledge of Western science to corroborate, and then fundamentally alter, principles of Chinese philosophy so that they became dynamic factors of change. By suddenly associating *jen* with electricity, K'ang infused the intuitive principle with material reality. It was this—his discovery that there was such a "thing" as electricity—that inspired his synthesis of Tung Chung-shu and the Neo-Confucians to give life-force to what theretofore, even for Wang Fu-chih, had only been discernible patterns of being. K'ang's new *jen,* that spiritual electricity, at once did away with the separation that had always existed between spirit and nature in post-Sung thought, and attributed purposive identity to the forces of matter.

To K'ang, that was only one part of his structure of thought. To his disciple, T'an Ssu-t'ung (1865–1898), it was the core of a new philosophical system. T'an, one of the executed martyrs of the Reform Movement and a hero to the students of Mao's normal school, was the author of a brilliant if eccentric work (*Jen-hsueh,* A Study of Benevolence, 1896) which is an even better example of the attempt to unite traditional idealism and scientific materialism into an analytic of life. The *Jen-hsueh* begins:

The foremost principle of *jen* is penetration (*t'ung*). Ether (*ch'i*), electricity, and the force of the mind are all instruments of operation for penetration. Ether and electricity are coarse and shallow instruments. We will borrow their name to materialize the force of the mind. The principle of penetration is to make the Tao hold all in its embrace. . . . *Jen* is the source of heaven and earth and the myriad things. Therefore, it is mind alone. Therefore, it is knowing alone. . . . The essence of *jen* is nonbirth and nondeath. If nonbirth and nondeath are equal then birth and death are equal. Nonbirth and nondeath, plus birth and death are also equal. Birth is close to renewal. Death is close to extinction. Renewal and extinction are equal. Therefore, the present and the future are equal. There is a past and there is a future. There is no present. The past and future are both the present. . . .

We will express it algebraically. Let birth equal *chia;* let death equal *i.* Let death be represented by *pu.* Then it can be ordered as follows:

$$chia = \text{birth}$$
$$i = \text{death}$$
$$\text{multiply} = pu$$
$$pu \times chia = pu \times i$$
$$i \neq pu \times i \ ^{28}$$

And so on. Although T'an was also deeply influenced by Hua-yen Buddhism, the impact of Western science on his thought is obvious here. By turning *jen* into a universal denominator and sole *élan vital,* T'an figuratively completed the demolition of other Confucian principles, systematically obliterating the harmony of differentiated virtues. After all, the specific doctrines of obligation to superiors and kindred—the *san-kang* and *wu-lun**—were as much condemned by an overriding virtue of universal humaneness, or an equal unity of opposites, as by Mohism or the Great Harmony of the *Li-yun.*

Although T'an Ssu-t'ung applied *jen* to the analysis of current institutions, that virtue had a certain suprahistoric quality for him. In trying to prove the existence of such a transcendent ethical force, T'an therefore actually departed from K'ang Yu-wei, who wished to work *jen* out through history toward a utopian end not yet arrived:

I made benevolence (*jen*) the center of my philosophy, which was to follow the will of heaven in bringing about unity to the earth, the unity of nations, the unity of races, and the unity of religions. I also speculated on the changes in the speech, writing, food and drink, clothing, and housing of mankind after the world is united, on equality for men and women, and universal laws for everyone, so that a paradise on earth for all men might be attained.[29]

Here again, K'ang's definition of *jen* as an evolutionary principle, the source of his teleology, stemmed from a recombination of traditional themes enhanced by Western scientific discoveries.

He began with *Kung-yang* learning, studying the commentary itself in 1881, but soon afterwards rejected it for what he took to be Ho Hsiu's errors of interpretation.[30] The theory of the three stages alone clearly meant little to him at that point in his intellectual development. But at the very moment of K'ang's 1885 vision of relativity and primal movement, he *immediately* conceived of the past in terms of Tung

---

* The "three net-ropes" (duties of a ruler, a father, and a husband) and the "five relationships" (between ruler and minister, father and son, husband and wife, elder and younger brother, friend and friend).

Chung-shu's three sequences, "and when I looked to the future, I based my view on the concept of the three stages." [31] *Kung-yang* historiography suddenly made sense to K'ang Yu-wei because he had connected it with his readings on the doctrine of evolution in the *Cosmopolitan Gazette*. He had learned, for instance, of scientific proof that man had evolved from more primitive creatures; and although K'ang did not specifically refer to this at the time of his illumination, he did a few years later tell his disciple, Ch'en Ch'iu-liu, that:

The cultural states of Yao, Shun, and the Three [Ancient] Dynasties were actually hypothesized by Confucius, and he believed and found supporting evidence. I suggested to him that the horse could descend from man, or man from the horse, and that men had evolved from primates; he believed and found supporting evidence. . . . I told him of the three stages of evolution to reach the world of Universal Peace, and of the Three Sequences; and he believed and found supporting evidence.[32]

As species evolved in the past, so must they continue to change in the future. If human history was not a patterned repetition of events or cycles, but rather a linear movement forward, then the three stages might—indeed, must—describe events to come. In sum, the evidence of evolution convinced K'ang Yu-wei that the *Kung-yang's* schema should be projected into the future. Confucius himself must somehow have discovered the principles of human progress long before they were known to the West. Suiting his doctrine to the circumstances of the age in which he lived, Confucius falsely appeared a conservative for all time. Were he alive today, he would be the first to preach progressive reform.*

K'ang thus used Darwin's principles of evolution to redefine Chinese thought. Yet once that had been accomplished, the Western theory ceased to interest him. In that fashion his formulation resembled catalysis. The agent, evolution, precipitated a contact reaction by which it was not ultimately absorbed. One might explain this by arguing that K'ang had to find unimpeachable sanction for contemporary reform: Darwin packed much less weight than Confucius. That point is weakened, however, when one realizes that probably nothing was more injurious to his actual reform program than the two works which supposedly created that sanction in the first place: the *Hsin-hsueh wei-*

---

* In 1886, K'ang first began writing his study of Confucius as a reformer (*K'ung-tzu kai-chih k'ao*). In 1889, during one of his periodic depressions over political affairs, he worked on it again. It was not completed until 1892, when he finished it with the help of his students.

ching k'ao (for which the plates were ordered destroyed by the authorities in 1894)* and *K'ung-tzu kai-chih k'ao* (A Study of Confucius as a Reformer). As we will see later, they created a reputation for K'ang which frightened away many would-be supporters. The other explanation, far more logical, is Levenson's: K'ang could not rest easy with a Western explanation for Chinese history. Or, to use the chemical analogy once more, his final compound had to bind integrally by means of nothing but traditional elements.

This argument is supported by K'ang's own hesitation at that moment. The combination of the *san-shih* (three stages) with evolution did not really seem to be a satisfactory proof for him. Something was lacking, something which he would ultimately find in the *Li-yun's* Great Harmony.

Although K'ang Yu-wei's *Li-yun chu* (Annotation of the *Evolution of Rites*) was not published until 1912, the preface was dated Kuang-hsü 10 (1884). The intellectual historian Ch'ien Mu believes that it was actually written about 1902.[33] For, had K'ang written it in 1884, then the *Li-yun*—not the *Kung-yang* commentary—would have been the original inspiration for his theory of evolution. And that is clearly refuted by his chronological autobiography.

It is easy to see why K'ang might have antedated the work. The impression one gets from reading the *Li-yun chu* is that he was almost consciously trying to show an entirely Chinese origin for his concept of progress, making no mention of the influence of Western learning. The entire thrust of the book is to demonstrate how K'ang painfully worked his way back through a layer of Chinese commentaries to reveal a vision of man long deliberately concealed by enemies of the true Confucius.

The *Li-yun chu* opened proudly by extolling Confucius' influence on the rest of Asia: Korea, Annam, Japan. But the spread of his teachings was circumscribed, his true message hidden, by the ancient-text scholar, Liu Hsin. What remained after Liu had finished butchering the original texts was further cut down by Chu Hsi, "so that the great Tao of the uncrowned king was eclipsed and darkened," forcing Chinese to live

---

* On August 4, 1894, the Kuang-hsu Emperor told the Grand Council that he had received memorials saying that the *Hsin-hsueh wei-ching k'ao* "calumniates [our Confucian] predecessors and deludes later disciples." If investigation proved it "really does depart from the canon and deviates from the true path," then the book should be destroyed. See Chien Po-tsan, et al., eds., *Wu-hsu pien-fa* [The Reform Movement of 1898] (Shanghai: Shen-chou kuo-kuang she, 1953), 2:1.

out a millennium in the benighted state of *Hsiao-k'ang* (Small Tranquility), unable to receive the "blessings of the Great Harmony." [34] K'ang explained that he had vaguely sensed the loss as a young student. By the age of twenty-seven, he felt that he had exhausted the classics with their Han, Wei, Six Dynasties, T'ang, Sung, Ming and Ch'ing commentaries. Still he kept going back, looking for a different Confucius than they presented, not the sage or *sheng* of which he was told, but a truly divine or *shen* being. Following one path after another through the texts, he finally came to the writings of the New Text school, and through them to the *Kung-yang* and *Ku-liang* commentaries. Although they enabled him finally to grasp the "meaning of the *Changes'* transformations of *yin* and *yang*, and the *Spring and Autumn's* Three Stages," he still could not relate that meaning to Confucius' ulterior intent. Then he reached the *Li-yun*.

I read up to the *Li-yun;* and, overwhelmed, sighed, 'The transformations of Confucius' Three Stages and the truth of his great Tao are here! The Tao of the Great Harmony and Small Tranquility are explained with clarity, distinguished with subtlety. The causes of progress from ancient to modern and the profound commiseration of the divine sage are here. Implementing when times are favorable, not being perverse when acting in tandem: the transforming penetration and the utmost advantage of the sages of the time are here. This text [contains] the subtle words and true preachings of Confucius. It is a treasured canon without superior among the myriad countries, and a divine formula for resuscitating all mankind under heaven.[35]

Now he could understand why the "true" Confucius had been so carefully hidden from him. Not only were his enemies at work; the sage himself had also been deliberately esoteric. To preach of a Great Harmony where goods were shared by all and princes barely ruled was to court death at the hands of living monarchs. K'ang's pen thus turned "true" Confucianism into a conspiratorial creed. "Inner" meanings of the sage had to be orally transmitted to Han scholars because of political danger. The only written references were necessarily concealed in the obscurities of the *Kung-yang* and *Ku-liang,* and so forth.[36]

In fact, the "inner" meanings K'ang claimed to rediscover were a completely novel invention of his own which melded the *Li-yun's* version of the perfect society with the *Kung-yang's* theory of the three stages as already altered by the catalyst of evolution. Together they appeared a single grand scheme.

| Kung-yang | Li-yun |

$\left.\begin{array}{l}\text{PAST: } \textit{Shuai-luan} \text{ (Disorder)} \\ \text{PRESENT: } \textit{Sheng-p'ing} \text{ (Approaching Peace)}\end{array}\right\} = Hsiao\text{-}k'ang$ (Small Tranquility)

FUTURE: *T'ai-p'ing* (Great Peace) $= Ta\text{-}t'ung$ (Great Harmony)

Each of the three stages also equaled eras of political and social development:

Age	Social	Political
Disorder	Tribe	Absolutism
Approaching Peace	Nation	Constitutional Monarchy
Great Peace	World	Democracy

To K'ang, therefore, the hidden meaning of the *Li-yun* was the reversal of sequence. *Ta-t'ung* was not a pined-for past; it was a projected future. Seen in that way, the two texts held the same basic meaning: Confucius had foretold what was to come; and that made him, in K'ang's eyes, as much a divine being as he had been in the Han apocrypha. As his introduction to *A Study of Confucius as a Reformer* explained:

Heaven, having pity for the many afflictions suffered by the men who live on this great earth, [caused] the Black Emperor to send down his semen so as to create a being who would rescue the people from their troubles—a being of divine intelligence, who would be a sage-king, a teacher for his age, a bulwark for all men, and a religious leader for the whole world. Born as he was in the Age of Disorder, he proceeded, on the basis of this disorder, to establish the pattern of the Three Ages, progressing with increasing refinement until they arrive at Universal Peace.[37]

The Sung philosophers had believed that men could control change by training themselves to acquire the same faculty of perception which the sages possessed. There were no abstract, metahistorical rules which alone determined fate. K'ang Yu-wei substituted principles for perception, not only because he shared in the Ch'ing revival of Han philosophy, but also because the realization of his ethical system depended upon a loose teleological construction. Now he could look ahead to a world of Great Harmony defined by the premise of the *Li-yun* that "all under heaven is for the commonweal" (*t'ien-hsia wei kung*). The future age would not be marred by *ssu* or selfishness. To abolish the selfishness of autocratic rule, authority would shift to the people. To destroy the selfishness of man, parochial institutions would disappear: property, the family, even race. The fundamental notion of his *Ta-t'ung shu* was the erasure of the boundaries that kept human beings apart. Private dwellings would cease to be built. Temporary mating would replace permanent marriage. By miscegenation all races would start to blend into one, until the dark races he assumed to be inferior changed into light-skinned humans like the yellow and white men. Nations would dissolve into a loose world government that barely needed to reign over a common society of citizens living in self-governing communal farms or factories, each economically self-sufficient.

There were two major contradictions in this scheme. First, the homogeneity of the *Ta-t'ung* conflicted with K'ang's prediction that as society developed economically, it would grow more and more specialized. To ensure communality, therefore, he invented organic institutions to regulate society. A new labor unit, military in cast, would assemble collective work brigades. Officials, whose titles and tasks were carefully detailed in the *Ta-t'ung shu,* would muster farmers according to quotas and hourly work schedules, and issue commands to till the fields and harvest the crops. Although K'ang did spell out precise details of his self-governing communities, he did not make allowance for the contrariety between advanced economic specialization and collective labor, nor for that matter between individual fulfillment and communal engagement. François Fourier (1772–1837), in contrast, imagined *phalanstères* which at least tried to reconcile individuality and solidarity by meeting every imaginable desire.

The second contradiction was a much greater failing. How would this ideal society be realized; how would the evolution occur? For obvious reasons, K'ang was strongly repelled by the Darwinian concept of evolution which apparently made competition among creatures a natural state of affairs.

People who had a little knowledge and held mistaken views, such as Darwin, invented the theory of evolution, making out that it was natural [for men to compete]; he taught men that competition was a great principle. As a result, competition, which proves to be an extremely evil thing for the whole world, past and present, is being carried on openly and accepted even by honorable men without shame. Thus the earth becomes a jungle in which all is "iron and blood." [38]

In a way, K'ang's repudiation of strife also lay at the heart of the first contradiction. Fourier's genius was to acknowledge egoistic passions.

K'ang believed in the fulfillment of desires but somehow hoped for the disappearance of egoity. And, when writing of man's future progress toward utopia, he universally denied the agency of competition or struggle between men. At the same time, however, his assurance of humanity's arrival at Harmony, of its growing together into one great, undifferentiated unity, was acquired from historical examples of unification actually produced by strife. To prove that mankind had already moved part way toward ultimate incorporation, for instance, he reminded his readers of the creation of the Chinese empire when strong warring states swallowed weaker ones during the third century B.C.[39] Would the same process of conquest accompany the creation of world government? Certainly not in K'ang's view; and if the question had been posed to him in this way, he probably would have answered that it was the existence of selfish nationalisms in the first place which made disarmament and a world government so desirable for man. But was this a necessary evolution? Why not some other outcome?

K'ang's personal faith—such an amazing mixture of apocryphal and realistic elements—cohered by attributing divine authority to Confucius, and by relating natural human evolution to universal principles of justice and truth. But were these universal principles eternally valid even in his own eyes? Apparently not. For, at one point while discussing his utopia, K'ang remarked that:

According to the universal principle (*kung li*), nothing is inherently good or evil. Right and wrong are all according to what the various sages have established. . . . Indeed, as good, evil, right, and wrong are all man-made, universal principles themselves are determined by the [circumstances] of a given time.[40]

Even *jen* was only a relative virtue. "History goes through an evolution, and *jen* has its path of development. As the path may be large or small, so *jen* may be large or small. Until the proper time comes, it cannot be forced." [41] And if *jen* were conditioned by history, then what conditioned history itself?

Of course, K'ang firmly believed that equality was a necessary principle because heaven had created men—a belief he shared with some nineteenth-century westerners whose works he probably knew. John Fryer's *Tso-chih chu-yen* (Homely Words to Aid Government), which K'ang no doubt read, explained that:

Having endowed men with life, heaven must also give them capacity and power to protect their life. . . . Thus irrespective of nationality, race, or color, each man being his own master cannot [yield his right of independence] to another even in the slightest degree. . . . Civilized states should bring equality to all races of men; then there would no longer be the phenomenon of oppression and aggression.[42]

Civilized states *should* bring equality: a desideratum rather than an imperative. K'ang, too, told his readers that the usurpation of human rights was a violation of heavenly principles; but even though all men *should* be equal ("a universal principle"), "the inequality of creatures is a fact." [43]

There is quite a span between desire and fact, possibility and necessity, should and must; and here it is the difference between utopian socialism and Marxism. Mao Tse-tung once reproached K'ang for lack of means—"K'ang Yu-wei wrote the *Ta-t'ung shu* or the *Book of Great Harmony,* but he did not and could not find the way to achieve Great Harmony" [44]—and just as well implied the lack of imperative, of sharper teleological bite. What laws of progress, what dialectic, what historical agent would bring about the Great Harmony? The existence of necessary scientific truths delivered the certainty to jolt K'ang's interpretations of the past into recipes for the present and plans for the future; the theory of evolution helped him review certain elements of the Confucian tradition which suggested a sense of development. But because of *kung,* he could not accept the mechanism of struggle, of competition between species. And so he reaffirmed the peaceful nature of cosmic unity as a natural process headed by sages in concert (rather than in competition) with the cosmos. In a sense, therefore, the sage of the *Kung-yang* tradition was a device to avoid struggle, and K'ang Yu-wei's teleology was an aspiration instead of an obligation of history. Change, when it came, would have to be effected by individual agents.

10

Construction and Destruction

K'ang Yu-wei's first individual attempt at reform, though intellectually cautious, was politically audacious. In 1887, after completing his *Shih-li kung-fa,* he sent bold petitionary letters to such higher officials as Weng T'ung-ho. Seeking sponsorship for moderate political change, K'ang did not deliberately conceal his utopian views. In fact, his obdurate retention of those early visions jeopardized his political acceptability. When he sat for the metropolitan examinations in 1888, Hsu T'ung (both grand secretary and examiner) supposedly insisted, "He is a madman. We should not pass him." [1] K'ang passed nonetheless.

What would damn K'ang most severely later on was his "impious" study of Confucius as a reformer. At one point, for instance, K'ang was well on his way toward securing the backing of Chang Chih-tung, the most influential viceroy of the empire, for his reform program. During those crucial negotiations, Chang's private secretary told K'ang that his patron would only support a reform society in Nanking if K'ang refrained from preaching his wildly heterodox theories about Confucius' theory of the future. But K'ang's aggressive commitment to his vision was not to be shaken. He answered the secretary: "The institutional reforms of Confucius are a great truth. How can I change it merely for the support of a governor-general of Kiangnan and Kiangsi? If because of the need for financial support I were to abandon my teachings, how would I deserve Chang Chih-tung's esteem?" [2] Later on the same conflict between expediency and ideals occurred in the capital. Political strategy demanded that K'ang repudiate his by-then notorious theories of Confucius in order to retain the support of the southern clique led by Weng T'ung-ho (1830–1904), the emperor's former tutor. But K'ang would not abandon his heresy, and appeared to Weng a "wild fox" full of megalomaniacal ideas.[3]

K'ang himself even lost hope occasionally of realizing his dreams of change in so resistant an atmosphere, and at these times thought of emigrating to Brazil to "build a new China." [4] What postponed departure and kept pulling him back into contemporary politics was his concept of circumstance, of according with the times (*ho-shih*). By that notion there was no discrepancy between a future utopia and limited current reform. K'ang could hardly relinquish his theory of Confucius as a reformer because it buttressed the idea of *ho-shih*, but he could work to improve a monarchy in the belief that democratic institutions must await their time: "Linens for summer; furs for winter." [5] Besides, although high officials might be too hidebound to adapt the state to modern times, K'ang could rely on other agents of change: younger, more progressive scholars, and the emperor himself.

As the Chinese were swept by agitation after the Japanese victory of 1894–1895, K'ang Yu-wei was only one among many literati convinced of the necessity for reform. He stood, for example, at the head of 603 metropolitan degree candidates like himself, assembled in Peking for the examinations and willing to endorse K'ang's ardent proposals for change.[6] These scholars, especially the ones from K'ang's native Kwangtung and the group from Hunan, worked together through study associations (*hsueh-hui*) and provincial clubs. Not since the florescence of literary and philosophical societies during the seventeenth century had so many scholars gathered together on a regional basis. Because such organizations had been expressly forbidden in early Ch'ing times due to their independent political character, K'ang's reform movement was a conscious if illegal revival of the club (*she*) and party (*tang*) movement of the late Ming.[7] The seventeenth century was also a source of theoretical inspiration as the reformers recalled the pleas of Huang Tsung-hsi or Ku Yen-wu to place more power in the hands of the gentry. Ku Yen-wu, for instance, wished to imbue prefectural (*chün-hsien*) centralism with the spirit of feudal (*feng-chien*) localism by permitting districts to select their own gentry as law clerks and yamen officials. This would better represent local interests and would balance the overwhelming power of the central bureaucracy. It also corresponded with Ku Yen-wu's conception of the gentry as mediators of imperial sovereignty—all themes revived in the mid-nineteenth century by such statecraft (*ching-shih*) theorists as Feng Kuei-fen (1809–1874), whose arguments for local self-government gained wide currency among young scholar-officials of the 1890s.[8]

K'ang Yu-wei was therefore both building extrabureaucratic political support and sounding a familiar reformist note when he urged the throne to accept and even to sponsor the "righteous zeal" of the country's *shih* (gentlemen). If the emperor would bypass stodgy senior officials and appoint new counselors from among the most talented while accepting petitions and memorials from all the younger scholars of the empire, then fresh blood would revive the body politic.[9] Of course, K'ang's reform proposals did not just echo conventional appeals to "widen the pathway of words." Quite unlike Ku Yen-wu, he was calling for a parliament—not because the sage-rulers Yao and Shun sought counsel from the empire's worthies but because one must choose from among the regulations of all the countries of the world exemplary laws "to establish constitutional distinctions between public and private." [10] While traditional sanctions went by the board for the (new) sake of national survival, officials were—in K'ang's view—unfit to hold public office until they had been sent abroad to study. And when they finally did assume their positions, the policies they administered were to be decided upon by the emperor only after he had deepened his understanding of ways to change the laws (*pien fa*) by consulting a parliament. That parliament would not yet be a popular assembly, for the people were still too backward to govern themselves. Constitutional consultation was momentarily restricted to only the most talented and educated, but the peasantry would eventually be schooled in local self-government by specially appointed gentry in charge of *min-cheng chü* (bureaus of people's government).[11]

The theories behind this pattern of political mobilization were more explicitly discussed by K'ang in a study which was not published until after the reform period. His study, entitled *Discussion of the Function of Officials* (*Kuan-chih i*) first appeared in 1903. In it K'ang agreed with Ku and Feng Kuei-fen that a degree of self-government was desirable, because district control was then in the hands of men better apprised of local needs. And although to K'ang the prime example of this administrative arrangement was the English system, he also concurred with the statecraft theorists' judgment that the best combination of centralized power and local initiative in post-Han China had been the Sung government. The barbarian Mongols (the Yuan dynasty,

1280–1368) had destroyed this structure by creating an intermediate *sheng* (province) that interspersed a bureaucratic barrier between district magistrates and the emperor. However, there was a significant difference between K'ang's argument in *Kuan-chih i* and the statecraft school. K'ang esteemed the Sung less because it encouraged self-government than because it had destroyed the stranglehold of local notables on regional politics by deputing *chou* (district) magistrates directly from the Ministry of Personnel. Furthermore, he thought that the Sung ideal would be restored by creating a parliament.[12] After the people selected representatives from among the "worthy talents" of the country, the parliament (*i-yuan*) would assemble these "noted gentlemen" from the four quarters of the country to advise the emperor.[13] As throne and district were once more connected in this schema, K'ang's version of local government stressed its benefit to the central regime more than to the local gentry, reversing the emphasis of seventeenth-century theorists who had been consciously reacting against the increasing power of the monarchy. For, even though some reformers in 1898 wished to create sovereign expressions of local gentry power, K'ang Yu-wei (at least in these published writings) was not anxious to develop local self-rule. He valued constitutional government because it was more *kung,* more public, than the selfishness of pure autocracy.[14] And by increasing participatory understanding of government, parliamentary monarchy would help elevate the entire nation's well-being. As constitutional rule "unites the hearts of the people of the entire country and elevates the worthy talents of the entire country," so does the country itself benefit. "As the people's qualifications progress, so does a standard of the nation's qualifications progress." [15] The best example of this was the Meiji government of Japan, which employed mass literacy and public political involvement to strengthen the cohesion between emperor and subject.

By celebrating the Meiji monarchy during the reform movement and working for an imperial restoration in the early 1900s, K'ang seemed to belie his disciples' assertion that he consistently favored popular sovereignty (*min-ch'üan*). Liang Ch'i-ch'ao tried to explain the discrepancy by arguing that K'ang had always favored popular rights but that he felt reform more likely if one worked with, rather than against, the throne. "My teacher's proposal was that we ought to use the monarchy to carry out the intent of popular sovereignty" (*min-ch'üan*).[16] But did Liang's rationalization really tally with K'ang's own arguments in the *Kuan-chih i?* Mencius-inspired theorists before the nineteenth century had pleaded for *min-pen:* ruling for the sake of the people. Late nineteenth-century writers, beginning with the compradore-intellectual, Cheng Kuan-ying (1842–1923), claimed that authority issued from and should be granted by the people (*min-ch'üan*).* K'ang's *kuo* (country) was neither *min-pen* nor *min-ch'üan*. Despite the egalitarianism of the Great Harmony, statements like the *Kuan-chih i* advocated most of all national sovereignty (*kuo-ch'üan*). A *kuo* was, to him, "A body (*t'i*) composed of many people drawn together. Though there is no contract (*yueh*) [between these people], it [the *kuo*] cannot exist without a government to maintain it." [17] For, a state has its attributes—treasury, army, bureaucracy—and upon these depends its existence. Officials must "protect the people" but this is primarily in order to "strengthen the body of the *kuo*." [18]

Although Hsiao believes that K'ang's concern for *kuo*—his patriotism—was a temporary and instrumental goal, designed to realize world society by bringing China into step with the other powers of the family of nations,[19] the "blood and iron" flavor of K'ang's political statements made the nation an end in itself, and parliament the true instrument in question. In a memorial to the emperor in the early summer of 1898, he wrote:

The secret of the strength of Japan and Western countries lies solely in their adoption of constitutional government and convening of parliament (*kuo-hui*). Parliament is a body through which the sovereign and the people deliberate together the laws and policies of the country. Since the appearance of the doctrine of three powers [there has come into being a political system in which] laws are made in parliament and enforced by the judiciary, and administrative matters are conducted by the government, while the ruler stands above them all. A constitution is enacted, which binds the ruler and all others alike. The ruler's person is inviolable; he can do no wrong, as administrative responsibilities are shouldered by the government. In this way the sovereign and the people are welded together into one body politic. How can the nation not be strong? [20]

* Even the identification of Cheng as a *min-ch'üan* advocate is ambiguous. Part of his reasoning, like K'ang's, was that a parliament (*i-yuan*) would help unite ruler and ruled for the sake of national unity: "The absence of a parliament will engender much alienation between the ruler and the people." And his famous analogy of the people upsetting imperial rule could be read as an attribution of sovereignty to heaven in the traditional fashion: "Heaven gives birth to the people while establishing a ruler. The ruler is like a boat and the people are like the water. The water can either turn over or support the boat." See Cheng Kuan-ying, *Sheng-shih wei-yen* [Words of Warning in a Seemingly Prosperous Age], cited in Chien Po-tsan, et al., eds., *Wu-hsu pien-fa* [The Reform Movement of 1898] (Shanghai, 1953), 1:55, 56.

Certainly, K'ang Yu-wei's appeal for national strength may have been strategically intended for the client of his reform and the climate of the times. Yet here once again the reference to Japan underscored K'ang's selection of the sovereign monarch as the key agent of historical change.

On January 29, 1898, K'ang singled out preliminary steps toward the reform of the empire. First, the emperor should pledge an oath of governance before his assembled officials. Then an Institute of Response to Questions of Policy (*Tui-ts'e so*) should seek the opinions of the ablest men in the empire. Finally there should be established a Bureau of Institutions (*Chih-tu chü*) to draft a constitution. For each act K'ang specified a Japanese example: the Meiji Charter Oath of April 6, 1868; the Meiji emperor's *Kōgisho* (created to poll public opinion, *kōgi,* at the time of the restoration); and the *Seido torishirabe kyoku* (Bureau for the Investigation of Constitutional Systems), established in 1884 at Itō Hirobumi's request to plan for a constitution.[21] Naturally, Japan's success at self-strengthening was foremost in the minds of K'ang and the reformers after their own country's defeat in the war. However, K'ang Yu-wei was not seeking to imitate Japan just because it was the victor. He and his emperor believed that Japan was the best example of a new definition of monarchy based upon the single notion of creating an intimate tie between the emperor and his subjects. Instead of portraying that connection as mediated through a hierarchy of officials, however worthy they might be, K'ang envisaged a direct one-to-one relationship between each citizen of the empire and its ruler. The emperor's *person* would radiate downwards to every individual in the realm. For the emperor's birthday in 1898, K'ang "recommended a display of the emperor's picture; the issuance of an edict expressing his care and concern for the people in order to rally them; and the publication of an edict proclaiming the new policies, which was to be printed on yellow paper and posted in the most remote corners of the empire to broadcast the benevolent intentions of the emperor." [22]

At the time K'ang's justification to the emperor for a parliament did confirm the importance of sharing the responsibility for decisions (thereby judiciously implying an equal sharing of the blame which now fell to the regime for losing to Japan and conceding fresh privileges to the West), but it also incorporated that ideal of intimacy between monarchic person (not just *persona*) and the people—an intimacy which would preserve both by preserving the state. For the latter—

once an instrument of governance and now its end—was necessary to the preservation of the entire trinity.

Yet the state was, after all, a monarchy. Could we not continue to claim that K'ang simply accorded with his times by electing to work through the emperor? Again, the reasoning was more complicated than it first appears, because for K'ang the emperor as agent of change brought together the reform program and his own utopian thought. Or, to put it even more directly, K'ang Yu-wei's new age could not dawn without a monarchic agent.*

To be sure, his attitude toward the emperor was not free from ambivalence. After all, autocracy corresponded to the Age of Disorder; monarchic absolutism had led China, "the first nation to evolve culture on earth, . . . to shun progress, to stagnate, and to be jeered at as an uncivilized nation." [23] At the same time, though, there is much evidence of K'ang's personal admiration for the young Kuang-hsu emperor (who reigned from 1875 to 1907), as well as his conviction that the emperor's support was really all he needed to engineer change. In fact, most historians believe that K'ang's major political failing was his overconfidence in the effectiveness of ukazes. What else can one make of K'ang's famous interview with the emperor the morning of June 16, 1898? "With your majesty's intelligence," he told his sovereign, "the self-strengthening of China should be as simple as turning the palm of your hand." [24] Surely this was intended to cajole him into action; but it is hard to disbelieve K'ang's own credence in his repeated assurances that, "As soon as [Your Majesty] hands down an imperial rescript, the empire will move [as if shaken by] thunder." [25] When the emperor finally did decide to abolish the traditional eight-legged civil service examination, K'ang asked himself, "Who [else] could have been so courageous as to do away with this evil institution which has been with us for a thousand years?" [26] And when the emperor told a grand councillor that he was willing to cede some of his authority to a parliament if it would help save his people, K'ang judged the phrase worthy of a

---

* It is not surprising that utopian thinkers often fell back on the device of a great man. Saint-Simon's "critical" and "organic" ages were dissonant, not dialectical. Consequently, he was almost forced to believe that if he could just get Napoleon to understand his encyclopedic plans for society, then the new harmony would be carried out. With some of the same illusions, Fourier returned daily to his room at an appointed hour to await the millionaire who might be persuaded to finance his *phalanstères* and so realize man's liberation. Without an internal historical mechanic, what other agent did they have?

ruler "who sincerely intended to make the empire a commonweal" (*kung t'ien-hsia*).[27] Later, although K'ang's own followers (including even his brother, K'ang Kuang-jen, who would be executed soon after the conservative *coup*) warned him that he was relying too heavily on the emperor's authority for reform, K'ang still refused to let his confidence in that chosen agent waver.[28]

It was not only a matter of his belief in the man beneath the crown; the imperial institution as such was an instrument of history. K'ang's *Kung-yang* commentary predicted a democratic future, but by the same token he believed in transitional leadership from above. Perhaps he even secretly viewed himself as a *su-wang* in his own right: an uncrowned king like Confucius, working through secular authority to decisively influence history. He insisted time and again that he really only stood behind the emperor as an advisor. "All I did was to send in my books; and the emperor, deriving ideas from my reference notes, would then issue the edicts." [29] These modest-seeming disavowals were certainly intended to contradict his enemies' accusations that K'ang had bewitched the emperor like some kind of court eunuch and actually ran the government behind the scenes. But might they not also express K'ang's view of himself as a New Text *chün-tzu:* the superior man realizing the potential of all men, the visionary planner dealing in revelation, the prophet inspiring kings to act? There may be more than fancy in the charges of some officials that K'ang Yu-wei was transforming Confucius into a god and Confucianism into a cult so that he could be the new religion's pope. For, when K'ang proposed that a Confucian cult society be formed, or when he suggested that the year be dated from Confucius' birth instead of the inception of the current reign,[30] he was elevating Confucius above the temporal emperor. As the monarch would then serve that higher authority, so would he in some respects be an instrument of K'ang himself. At the same time, K'ang's role as *chün-tzu* made it impossible for him to stand in place of the emperor. His was no usurpation of secular authority; it simply transferred legitimization away from heaven and its mandate to Confucius himself.

K'ang Yu-wei's conception of the sage may also have been influenced by Tung Chung-shu, who wrote in the *Luxuriant Gems of the Spring and Autumn:*

Nature is like a cocoon or like an egg. The egg must wait to be hatched before it becomes a chicken. The cocoon must wait to be unwound before it becomes silk. Nature must wait to be instructed (*chiao*) before it becomes good. This is called the [nature of] heaven. Heaven has given birth to human nature so that it has the material (*chih*) for good which is not yet capable of being good [without instruction]. For this [reason, heaven] established kings in order to make it good. This is heaven's intent. People receive from heaven a nature which is not yet capable of being good and they turn to the king to receive instruction to complete their nature. The task of the king is to undertake heaven's intent in order to complete the people's nature. Now to say on the basis of his true material [substance] that man's nature is already good is to lose [sight of] heaven's intent and discard the task of the king. If the nature of the myriad people's nature were already good, then what task would remain for the king when he receives [heaven's] mandate? [31]

As Tung's ruler unfolded the potential of each being's nature, K'ang's sage realized the equality that was supposed to exist between them.

Though all are born of heaven, men differ among themselves in being intelligent or simple-minded, strong or weak. Not being of the same quality they naturally compete with one another. The strong win, whereas the weak lose. In this process of natural selection there can be no equality. But while inequality is heaven-made, equality is the work of the sage man. Therefore all [his] institution and moral principles aim at eventual equality. [32]

In each case, the key to entelechy was that higher, divinely endowed figure of the crowned or uncrowned king whose duty to man was even higher than self-regard. Only after human equality was ultimately in force, K'ang believed, should the sage seek the final goal of personal fulfillment. In that sense, the culmination of social development was to be found in the singular individual's religious cultivation. Mentioned at the end of the *Ta-t'ung shu,* and explored more deeply in his "Lectures on the Heavens" of 1926, was K'ang's desire that the divines of the Great Harmony pass through immortality and Buddhahood to the highest attainment of all: celestial peregrination. Perhaps influenced by the science fiction of Inoue Enryō and certain there was life on other planets, K'ang dreamed of soaring through a universe studded with inhabited planets clustered in higher and higher spheres of celestial harmony.* He even believed this transcendental wandering to be the essence of Confucius' doctrine.

---

* Although apparently not influenced by European theosophy or theories of metaphysics, K'ang seemed to have the same taste for astronomical speculation as Fourier. It is almost as if the orderly passion of both utopian thinkers was not sated by their detailed conceptions of earthly utopias. Of course, K'ang did not relate his heavens to principles of attraction as did Fourier. Nor were his descriptions of life on other planets as detailed.

The doctrines transmitted through the Six Classics . . . deal with the non-essential matters concerning governance and legislation; they do not represent Confucius' transcendental thought (*shen-ming chih i*). There is [besides these a doctrine concerning] the limitless, numberless heavens which are absolutely intangible—a heaven-constituted world (*t'ien tsao chih shih*) unthinkable and ineffable. There the Sage roamed, wishing to share the celestial transformation [which he had achieved] with all the living beings. This is the ultimate doctrine of Confucius.[33]

These transcendental speculations were the highest representation of K'ang's belief in the cosmic role of the sage. His reform efforts were the highest expression of his confidence in the transforming role of the emperor as advised politically by the sage. Thus, there should be no inconsistency between his authorship of the egalitarian *Ta-t'ung shu* and his sponsorship of the imperial *Pao-huang hui* (Protect the Emperor Society, founded in Vancouver in 1889). Just as both implicitly converged on the single figure of the sage, so were his ideological and political interests coincidental during the hectic one hundred days of reform in mid-1898.

Although K'ang frequently called for parliamentary monarchy, in practice he consistently strengthened the throne. More important than a parliament to his proposals was the plan to create a Bureau of Institutions manned by junior reformers serving just under the emperor, exactly like the new Japanese-style general staff which K'ang also favored. Similarly, he recommended that his supporters—T'an Ssu-t'ung, Lin Hsu, and so forth—be appointed secretaries to the Grand Council so that they could see the emperor's orders directly carried out by higher sinecured officials.

Therefore, while the key office was to be the emperor-advising Bureau of Institutions instead of a parliament, men like T'an were regarded more as imperial delegates than representatives of the gentry reform movement in provinces like Hunan. In other words, K'ang's two original agents of change, the reform clubs and the emperor, were by the end of the reform period reduced to only one. Then, as T'an and Lin urged him to concentrate on working for a parliament, K'ang insisted that reform would best be carried out from the top via his favorite, the Bureau of Institutions.[34] Although this choice was colored by his appreciation of the degree of conservative opposition to a parliament, it further reflected his instinct to rely on the emperor alone.

Unfortunately, the emperor was a weak reed, especially since K'ang

Yu-wei's definition of his, the Kuang-hsu emperor's, role as steward of the *kuo* (country) conflicted with the ruler's duty to the imperial family. Royal family conflict had helped open the door to K'ang Yu-wei in the first place. His proposals so obviously strengthened the throne that Weng T'ung-ho, the emperor's tutor and leader of the southern clique, believed a reform movement would both strengthen the government against imperialism and help free the emperor from the influence of the Dowager Empress, Tz'u-hsi (1835–1908). Instead, the reformers' attacks on sinecure-holding Manchus brought the Dowager Empress out of retirement; and she, after inspiring the September 21 military coup, condemned the Kuang-hsu emperor to imprisonment in the lacquered pavilions of Ying-t'ai Island with the scornful charge that he had been contemptibly beguiled by that plotter K'ang to forget his familial and racial duties to the Aisin Gioro clan.

Tz'u-hsi's judgment—phrased in terms she herself would probably not have used—was that the Kuang-hsu emperor had neglected his *kuo,* the dynastic state of the Ch'ing, to serve a new *kuo-chia,* the nation of China. But could she really blame his motives? After all, the emperor had been convinced that the dynastic *kuo* could not be preserved unless the entire nation was kept free from foreign domination. When he was once accused of unfilially tampering with ancestral laws, he asked in response, "If the ancestors' land is not preserved, what about their laws then?" [35] And to defend that land the emperor hoped to draw close to his people in a concerted program of national reform.

As of now, let my intention to change the laws be promulgated throughout the empire so that the people are completely acquainted with my mind and together realize that they can depend upon their ruler. I am overcome with the earnest hope that above and below all will be of joint mind to effect the new government, to strengthen China.[36]

The Dowager Empress could not accept his identification of *her* state with the entire *kuo-chia,* but she could share his belief that this new unity between the emperor and his subjects, this strengthening of the bond between the throne and the people, might lend the dynasty a mass support it badly needed at the time. Tz'u-hsi herself would later try to draw close to the people. But her motives possessively defended the dynasty apart from the country, because she wanted Manchu rulers and Chinese subjects to come together while still maintaining dynastic autocracy. This desire was as characteristic of her approval of the seemingly obscurantist Boxers in 1900 as of her support for the progressive Constitutionalists in 1906. However much these two social groups differed, they were both representations in her mind of popular movements, and of opportunities for the ruling house to adopt a populism of its own. Unfortunate to the dynasty's survival was her misconception in each case.

The Boxers, for example, would have been readily outlawed by early Ch'ing monarchs as dangerous rebel cultists. But by 1899 the Dowager Empress was so aware of increasing anti-Manchuism in the South, and so desperate to identify the throne with the masses, that the Boxers appeared to her the very symbol of acceptably righteous popular zeal. And in 1906, when she sponsored constitutional reform, Tz'u-hsi was similarly hoping to bypass provincial officials (now approaching the fiscal and military independence of the later warlords) to link directly up with the people—mainly local gentry—beneath. In that regard, hers was the culmination of the Kuang-hsu emperor's plan, except that her program was based on the more traditional *min-pen* conception of sovereignty. For, in spite of the constitutional principles involved, she really thought only to share *hsin* (feeling), not *ch'üan* (authority, power), with the people. This was a crucial miscalculation, because the constitutional movement itself stemmed from a major impulse of the original reform movement now in full momentum.

The founders of the *hsueh-hui* and reform clubs of 1898 had wanted to modernize the country by transforming provinces like Hunan into centers of reform. Many of the young reformers became revolutionaries after the 1898 failure had convinced them that the Manchus must be overthrown by force. But their instinct to develop new provincial political movements was realized between 1902 and 1911 by more moderately inclined local gentry. Floating railway bonds, founding chambers of commerce, setting up modern schools, and above all meeting in provincial assemblies to prepare for a national constitutional convention, this provincial elite implicitly challenged traditional theories of sovereignty—a consequence which the dynasty seemed to ignore when it permitted the establishment of local assemblies. First to the Dowager Empress, later to the Manchu princes surrounding the child-emperor P'u-i (Hsuan-t'ung, who reigned from 1908 to 1912), the assemblies were supposed to be advisory bureaus to help the government keep in touch with local sentiment and to garner popular support for the regime. The monarchy's misunderstanding was politically fatal when the Constitutionalists' national convention was postponed as far into the future as the Manchus dared—"dared," because by 1910 the paradox of K'ang Yu-wei's political thought (egalitarianism by superior fiat) had become a major political contradiction: imperial autocracy versus local self-government.

K'ang Yu-wei's conception of constitutional monarchy did not even help that new provincial elite to construct a viable theory of parliamentary sovereignty, because K'ang denied the legitimacy of a political system defined by competing interests. True to the image of *kung* throughout, he opposed pluralist struggle. As we have seen, his continuing search for understanding was colored constantly by that initial revelation of the world as multiplicity united in commonality. His 1885 vision of relativism was thus the sudden and liberating awareness of *other,* and of his identification with it. To believe, as he did, that all things are at once different and the same, would have hardly been difficult for a Sung Confucian who thought that the sage encompassed all things. Even Cheng Hsuan's earlier idea of *jen* as "people living together" would have expressed K'ang's sentiment, partially because *jen* is a homonym for the word man, as well as carrying that radical in its character. K'ang in one sense only enlarged its sweep, redefining *jen* (and man) to include those from beyond the pale. Other men were kin to him just because all human relationships exist in terms of the same kind (*lei*): *jen-lei* (mankind) is mutually self-loving because *lei* is humanness, not Chineseness nor Englishness nor Japaneseness. K'ang's *jen* was therefore less a principle of universal love contained within the self than love for mankind; the self *was* mankind, and *jen* the force of attraction between all these members of the same species.[37]

This conception of a universal human condition not just his own helped alleviate his deep concern for the fate of China. If all mankind was changing, then so too would China, without losing her place in the march of social progress. As a cosmopolitan, K'ang would cease regretting the loss of particular values and rejoice in the pattern of human evolution. All men are brothers—"Being that I was born on earth, then mankind in the ten thousand countries of the earth are all my brothers of different bodily types."[38] And so his fate was theirs: "Do they [the men of Greece, India, France] progress?—then I progress with them; do they retrogress?—then I retrogress with them."[39] Society would eventually lose the distinctions dividing family from family, man from wife, owner from owned, self from other; the boundaries between nations would dissolve as that one world of the Great Harmony was born. Then *jen* would extend to enlighten all humanity, so that each person's love held the entire world its family and China but a single member.[40]

K'ang Yu-wei's theory of *jen* and *kung,* especially as it appeared in the work by T'an Ssu-t'ung which he influenced, provided the first ideological weapon with which to attack the particularistic relationships of orthodox Confucianism. And, even though flawed, his reform theories also inspired hundreds of thousands of young Chinese like Mao Tse-tung to ponder the possibilities of political change. But K'ang's intellectual currency was very brief because humaneness, cosmopolitanism, and harmony seemed hopelessly idealistic to a generation imbued with Social Darwinism and convinced that the Chinese nation was about to be exterminated. They responded instead to journalists like Liang Ch'i-ch'ao, who preached a much harsher message.

Less than four years after the demise of the 1898 reform movement, Liang published an editorial in his journal, *Hsin-min ts'ung-pao* (The New People Magazine), which argued vigorously for the necessity of *p'o-huai,* or destruction.[41] Sick of double-talk, he declared that any scholar of resolve (*chih-shih*) must absolutely refuse to condone the corruptions of the time—corruptions which would soon destroy the entire system. Moreover, those who refused to recognize that "destruction in the end cannot be avoided" simply extenuated the difficulties of the present, for history proved that human progress was impossible without destruction. England could not have reached her current great power status without the civil war of the seventeenth century, which cleared away feudal debris; the United States of America owed its strength to the experience of the War of Independence and the Civil War. The very arts of civilization (*wen*) were the fruits of violence and warfare (*wu*), which obliterated traditional impediments to progress (*chin-pu*). Luther, Bacon, Montesquieu, and Copernicus had each been forced to sweep away the old before creating the new, construction always being preceded by destruction. This was the price of progress: in the economic sphere, the destruction of cottage handicrafts by the industrial revolution or the replacement of small business enterprises by great corporations; and in political history, the destruction of aristocracy and monarchy by democracy. Some always suffered, but it was worth diminishing the profit of a few to advance the well-being of the majority. Besides, suffering simply could not be avoided: an ailment must be completely "vomited and purged" before health was possible.

Halfway measures, like moderate political reforms, merely postponed the cure. The Ch'ing government could establish all the new schools and chambers of commerce it wished, but there would be no genuine improvement until the old order (*cheng-t'i,* the essence of government) and its buttress, "the rotten and sycophantish theories of these several thousand years," were entirely destroyed.

Not that Liang Ch'i-ch'ao believed in extinction regardless of human cost. There were, after all, two forms of destruction: a bloodless sort like Japan's Meiji Restoration, and the bloody terror of a French Revolution. China was certainly capable of the latter; by cataloguing every peasant rebellion that had occurred since the end of the Ch'ien-lung reign (1736–1796), Liang could show "that during this past century there has not been a single place in all our eighteen provinces which was not drenched in blood." Nevertheless, he hoped and prayed that China could have a bloodless destruction even though it might already be too late to avoid something like a French Revolution. Montesquieu had pointed out that despotism sowed the seeds of its own demise. The Ch'ing government had done nothing to prevent the slaughter of its subjects, either by rebels or by state executioners; it had done nothing to forestall the death of others by starvation. Thousands had died without anyone blinking an eye, while in the West the death of a single citizen did not go unnoticed. Furthermore, the great powers crouched like tigers beyond the country's borders, poised to leap hungrily upon their prey. If Liang's readers simply realized that China could easily follow India's path into colonial subjugation, "then they will be able to believe my words, 'destroy and there will be destruction, do not destroy and there will still be destruction,' are not exaggerated." Only decisive action by the righteous (*seigi,* wrote Liang, quoting the Japanese *shishi,* Yoshida Shoin) would avert that fate, so that destruction for the moment was in the long run an act of healing, of compassion, of humaneness. Mazzini had been right: to destroy in order to construct was the highest ethical goal. Faintheartedness was a moral abnegation. "Those who say, 'Do not destroy, do not destroy,' I call people devoid of human feelings."

One of Liang's readers was young Mao Tse-tung. Indeed, it was precisely this issue of *Hsin-min ts'ung-pao* that Mao "read and reread" until he knew it "by heart." [42] Whether or not Liang's editorial inspired Mao's belief—later elaborated by his famous work "On Contradiction" —in the necessity of provoking a potentially destructive historical crisis to its revolutionary climax, it certainly did affix in Mao's mind the connection between destruction and construction.* During the Great Proletarian Cultural Revolution, Chairman Mao would repeatedly insist that "Without destruction there can be no construction," adding dialectically that "Without blockage there can be no flow; without stoppage there can be no movement." † It is toward the development of such a dialectic that we must now turn.

* The very concept of *hsin-min* (new people, or renovate the people), which was the hallmark of Liang's thought during this period, also profoundly influenced Mao. In 1917, he and some friends formed the nucleus of a study society called the *Hsin-min hsueh-hui* (New People's Study Society). The society had seventy to eighty members, many of whom later became well-known members of the Communist Party. The majority were killed during the counterrevolution of 1927. This information is provided in "Mao's Autobiography," recounted in: Edgar Snow, *Red Star over China* (New York: Grove Press, 1961), p. 146.

† Mao Tse-tung, "Construction and Destruction" (June 8, 1966), translated in Jerome Ch'en, *Mao Papers: Anthology and Bibliography* (London: Oxford University Press, 1970), p. 113. Another example of this connection was given in Mao's talk to party leaders on July 21, 1966: "Oppose, especially oppose the bourgeois 'authoritative' thought; that is destruction (*p'o*). Without this destruction, there cannot be the construction (*li*) of socialism." (*Ibid.*, p. 25). The terminological parallel was not absolutely identical: Liang Ch'i-ch'ao used *p'o-huai* (destroy) and *chien-she* (construct, build); Mao employed *p'o* (destroy, break) and *li* (construct, establish). The latter became part of many Cultural Revolutionary slogans: *p'o-ssu li-kung* (destroy selfishness and construct selflessness), *p'o-chiu li-hsin* (destroy the old and construct the new), *hsien-p'o hou-li* (first destroy, later construct), *p'o chung yu li* (in the midst of destruction there is construction). These examples are all given in H. C. Chuang, *The Great Proletarian Cultural Revolution* (Berkeley: Center for Chinese Studies, 1967), p. 40. Liang's own theory of "destructivism" (*p'o-huai chu-i*) may have been derived from Itō Hirobumi's writings: see Hao Chang, *Liang Ch'-i-ch'ao and Intellectual Transsition in China, 1890–1907* (Cambridge: Harvard University Press, 1971), p. 145.

PART THREE

Freedom

Since I have robbed the will of all impulses which could come to it from the obedience to any law, nothing remains to serve as a principle of the will except the universal law of action as such, that is: I should never act in such a way that I could not also will that my maxim should be a universal law.

Immanuel Kant, *Werke*
(Berlin, 1922)

11

New Youth

Mao Tse-tung was demobilized from the Revolutionary Army in February of 1912. Adrift in Ch'ang-sha, he scanned the daily newspapers in search of a career. After dallying with the notion of becoming, respectively, a policeman, a soap-maker, and a lawyer, he enrolled in a business school. But because most of the texts were in English—a language of which he knew little more than the alphabet—he soon withdrew and took the entrance examination for the First Provincial Middle School. There he spent the next six months studying Chinese history and literature until he came to the conclusion "that it would be better for me to read and study alone" in the provincial library.[1]

Still politically unshaped,[2] Mao was avidly interested in learning more about Western geography and history. The provincial library's shelves gave him that opportunity.

During this period of self-education I read many books, studied world geography and world history. There for the first time I saw and studied with great interest a map of the world. I read Adam Smith's *The Wealth of Nations* and Darwin's *Origin of Species* and a book on ethics by John Stuart Mill. I read the works of Rousseau, Spencer's logic, and a book on law written by Montesquieu. I mixed poetry and romances and the tales of ancient Greece with serious study of history and geography of Russia, America, England, France, and other countries.[3]

Mao's daily readings (which also included Thomas H. Huxley's *Evolution and Ethics*[4]) during this autodidactic interlude marked his first extended exposure to Western thought. Yet the ideas he encountered were not entirely unfamiliar. He had, for example, already learned from Liang Ch'i-ch'ao to equate national strength with economic individualism. *The Wealth of Nations* simply reinforced that notion. This was especially so because the Chinese version of Smith's work had been translated by Liang's close friend, Yen Fu (1853–1921), who repeatedly stressed:

. . . that the system of economic liberalism developed in the book of Smith and demonstrated in the living example of Victorian England is a system admirably designed to achieve the wealth and power of the state. Here again we come back to the theme we have met before—that the wealth and power of the state can only be achieved by a release of energies and capacities (in this case specifically economic) of the individual.[5]

Individual capacity was also emphasized in another of Yen Fu's translations, Huxley's *Evolution and Ethics,* which introduced Social Darwinism to the Chinese in spite of Huxley's intention to oppose Spencer's theory of cosmic progress with a doctrine of ethical social progress.

Social progress means a checking of the cosmic progress at every step and the substitution for it of another which may be called the ethical process. Just as human art runs athwart the cosmic process in horticulture so does human morality run athwart the cosmic process. If the conclusion that the two are antagonistic is logically absurd, I am sorry for logic. . . . The history of civilization details the steps by which men have succeeded in building up an artificial world within the cosmos.[6]

But Yen Fu, who had identified Neo-Confucian principles (*li*) with Spencer's Unknowable, felt that Huxley was wrong to oppose civilized man to a universe which was ethical in nature. It was not that Yen Fu identified the cosmic process with *jen* (humaneness). Rather, he was inspired by Spencer to believe that the effect of those driving and self-assertive forces of the evolutionists' universe was ultimately good because of human progress. Some earlier thinkers like Li Chih (1527–1602) had suggested that egoism (*ssu*) was the ultimate source of altruism (*kung*), but they had not thought to show that the universe itself operated according to such a principle. Now, scientific evidence seemed to prove that self-assertion was a primary cosmic impulse, so that Yen Fu was able to combine the Chinese value of unity between individual and natural forces (as in the *Changes* tradition) with a new ethos of personal striving.

The historical role of individual will was also stressed in Yen Fu's translation of Montesquieu's (1689–1755) *Spirit of the Laws*. Montesquieu had been accused by later thinkers like Durkheim or Spencer of confusing art and science, invention and discovery. Lacking Spencer's faith in mechanical progress, Montesquieu had to believe in the efficacy of the individual legislator's willing intent to shape society. But Yen Fu's paraphrasing of *Spirit of the Laws* infused Montesquieu's reliance upon human will with Spencer's faith in the future.[7] Mao's first systematic introduction to Western political theory therefore confused invention and discovery by combining legislative craft with spontaneous historical laws of evolution.

In the spring of 1913, after six months of private reading, Mao was accepted as a scholarship student at the Fourth Normal School, which had been founded the previous year. That fall his school was absorbed by the more prestigious First Normal School. Thanks to the merger, Mao was soon able to study philosophy under the highly influential professor, Yang Ch'ang-chi (1870–1920).

> The teacher who made the strongest impression on me was Yang Chen-ch'i (sic), a returned student from England with whose life I was later to become intimately related.* He taught ethics, he was an idealist and a man of high moral character. He believed in his ethics very strongly and tried to imbue his students with the desire to become just, moral, virtuous men, useful in society.[8]

Yang was nicknamed "Confucianist" by his students because of his stern regard for morality. Educated in Chinese classical philosophy, he had learned English at the age of thirty in order to travel abroad in 1902 and study Western thought—first in Japan, then in Edinburgh (where he took a philosophy degree), and finally in Germany (where his studies involved him in Neo-Kantian thought). After returning to Ch'ang-sha in 1912, he was appointed professor of ethics, psychology, and education at the First Normal School. There he quickly gathered a following of devoted students, including Mao, Ts'ai Ho-sen (Mao's best school friend and later a founder of the Chinese Communist Party), and Ch'en Chang-fu (who would be executed shortly after joining the party). These students almost literally sat at Yang's feet—visiting him frequently at home and following to the last detail his moral injunctions and Rugby-like insistence upon physical education, which included deep breathing exercises and year-round cold baths. Mao and his comrades

---

* Mao married Yang's daughter, K'ai-hui, in October of 1921. She bore him two children. Arrested in 1930 by the governor of Hunan, she refused to renounce Mao and was executed.

thus made a habit of swimming as late into the fall as they dared, and spending their winter holidays meditating in the mountains.[9]

Yang's classroom lectures were usually woven around a comparison of Chinese philosophers, such as Wang Fu-chih and T'an Ssu-tung (he especially admired the *Jen-hsueh*), and Western thinkers like Kant, Spencer or Rousseau.* Although he consistently attacked the Confucian rules of propriety in the manner of T'an Ssu-t'ung, Yang did teach the *Analects* in his own specially annotated version, the *Lun-yü lei-ch'ao* (Categorized Excerpts from the *Analects*). The opening section of his new arrangement was entitled *Li-chih* (Establishing the Will), an emphasis that persisted throughout the text thanks to Yang's gloss. "Those who are strong of will can control the deviant lusts of their own desires, and oppose the social oppression of authority. . . . [For those who] possess a will which cannot be taken away, there is nothing which cannot be realized." [10] A strong will not only manifested a strong conscience (*liang-hsin*); it was also a measure of human immortality. Martyrs lost their mortal lives, but the spirit of their will was preserved to influence later generations. Moreover, the ideals defended by that will should not be sacrificed to any form of authority. When Confucius wrote that "the will even of a common man cannot be taken from him," [11] he was not denying one's responsibility to society. Rather, like some modern ethical philosophers, he meant that:

. . . man belongs to a society and so must devote himself to the profit of his society. If there is a time when his own interest and society's interests conflict, then he must sacrifice his own interest to society's. However, even though it is permissible to sacrifice one's own interest, it is not permissible to sacrifice one's own ideals. To be unwilling to give up one's own ideals is what was meant by not being able to take away even the will of an ordinary man.[12]

* These men are frequently referred to in Mao's school notebooks. The notebooks had been stored at his home in Hsiang-hsiang. After Mao became a revolutionary, his relatives—fearing trouble from the authorities—decided to burn them. One person did manage to salvage two of the school notebooks from the fire, so that Li Jui, Mao's semi-official biographer, was later able to quote long citations from them. One book consisted of over ten thousand words of essays and was ninety-four pages long. The other notebook contained class notes, which referred to pre-Han philosophers, history, T'ang and Sung classical prose writers, Sung and Ming Neo-Confucianism, and seventeenth-century philosophy. There were several brief historical essays on Napoleon, Caesar, and Fukuzawa Yukichi, as well as notes on natural science. Li Jui, *Mao Tse-tung t'ung-chih ti ch'u-ch'i ko ming huo-tung* [The Early Revolutionary Activities of Comrade Mao Tse-tung] (Peking, Chung-kuo ch'ing-nien ch'u-pan-she, 1957), p. 22.

Retaining one's ideals was also a matter of endurance (*chien-ch'ih*). Talent or genius (*t'ien-ts'ai*) was certainly important, but the best exemplars of will were those capable of enduring long enough to see a task completed. Because accomplishment (*ch'eng-chiu*) was a gauge of one's "strength of endurance," one had to "focus all one's spirit" on an undertaking, taking care not to get involved in too many things at once. This meant that a person had first of all to plan a realistic sequence of acts, and secondly not try to "carry out [his] own will alone" like the reform-movement martyr, T'an Ssu-t'ung.[13]

Despite this criticism, Yang Ch'ang-chi's faith in the immortality of individual will may well have been influenced by T'an Ssu-t'ung's declaration in *Jen-hsueh* that:

Wang Ch'uan-shan [Fu-chih] has the theory that when a sage dies his pneuma (*ch'i*) is divided among the mass of worthies (*hsien-jen*). When it resides in the country it is called "soul"; it is called "immortality." In Buddhism it is called "reincarnation"; it is called "dying in this [existence] and being born in another." Can we doubt that Confucius' doctrine lacked this [quality of immortality]? The [*Hsi-*]*tz'u* of the *Changes* assuredly declares that, "Returning to the beginnings of things, we can probe to the very end, thereby knowing the reasons for birth and death. Spirit and energy constitute all things. Escaping soul brings about the transformations [of things]. Because of this we can know the conditions of the spirits." How can this be said not to be true?[14]

T'an's union of eternity and immortality, which transformed men's fame into an epiphenomenal pneuma, was far more religiose than the notion that historic exemplars gained immortality in later men's eyes.*

The contrast between immortality and eternity also suggests Hannah Arendt's definition of fabrication, as distinct from action:

* This was also a crucial element in Liang Ch'i-ch'ao's theory of group consciousness, developed after 1903 and also influenced by the Buddhist doctrine of *karma* (an individual after his death left behind a *karma* which eternally influenced other beings). Liang connected this idea with what he took to be the Darwinian discovery that human improvements were transmitted by heredity from one generation to the next. "The physical existence of the human individual did not, he stated, have any intrinsic worth, for it was ephemeral and would pass into oblivion very soon. What really counted was the collective whole of the group, because it was this collective whole which embraced in itself all the spiritual values of individual members and would have an everlasting existence. The physical existence of the human individual Liang called 'small self' (*hsiao-wo*); the collective whole of the group to which one belonged Liang called the 'great self' (*ta-wo*)." See Hao Chang, *Liang Ch'i-ch'ao and Intellectual Transition in China, 1890–1907* (Cambridge: Harvard University Press, 1971), p. 277.

Fabrication, the work of *homo faber,* consists in reification. . . . *Homo faber,* the creator of the human artifice, has always been a destroyer of nature. . . . The actual work of fabrication is performed under the guidance of a model in accordance with which the object is constructed. This model can be an image beheld by the eye of the mind or a blueprint in which the image has already found a tentative materialization through work.[15]

Although one judges the fabricator by his finished product, the actor is estimated by his quality as an exemplar. In China this judgment often emphasized the sincerity behind action, so that the actor's state of mind mattered most. Indeed, consciousness sometimes became so important that some Neo-Confucians exalted *ching* (tranquility) at the expense of accomplishments. Yang's discussions of the will were therefore quite novel. They did not replace action with fabrication, but action was certainly recast in terms of achievement. A great man neither made nor acted but rather *did.* Consequently, the act of accomplishment, instead of the accomplishment alone, became the touchstone of self-fulfillment.

Yang also expressed his belief in the importance of will and self-realization in a two-part essay published in the popular journal *New Youth (Hsin ch'ing-nien).*[16] Although the second installment mainly emphasized the importance of timeliness, the first part of the article dealt with the current political crisis (a defunct republic and growing warlordism), not by suggesting specific constitutional reforms but by explaining how to "manage the people's livelihood," because a nation could not become strong without an invigorated citizenry. To renew the people, Yang would at least refer to the Confucian canon—not in search of clues to the proper inner motivation, but because he thought that the *Ta hsueh* (Great Learning) exposed some of the external characteristics of a good society. "Let the producers be many and the consumers few. Let there be activity in the production and economy in the expenditure. Then the wealth will always be sufficient." [17] However, Yang countered the basic intent of the *Ta hsueh* by using this physiocratic creed to attack the Chinese extended family system. If each individual were encouraged to produce and consume for himself, then the young would end their economic and psychological dependence on the family. Self-deprivation thus helped liberate the individual by nurturing the inner will to break his reliance on the family's charity. Conversely, the dissolution of the lineage would ultimately create the economic necessity for self-reliance. For, quite unlike the *Ta hsueh,* which began with the inner self and then moved out toward society, Yang Ch'ang-chi regarded social institutions as the determinants of individual

norms.* If, for example, one person controlled the entire family's livelihood, he might have nothing but the best welfare intentions in mind.
But the actual effect was harmful, because the other members of the
lineage failed to develop a spirit of self-reliance. Even the future repay-
ment of parental sacrifice by caring for the aged was noxious because
that too denied the importance of self-preservation. The Japanese, Yang
pointed out, had learned this lesson; grandparents moved out of the
stem family so that individuals learned not to depend on others for
sustenance. Admittedly, that ran against the grain of the accepted social
—even natural—feelings a child had for its parents, but those feelings
had to be curtailed "for the sake of the progeny's lifelong happiness."
Nor did this apply solely to paternal-filial dependence. The care of
siblings had the same consequence: several people exhaust the strength
of one, the weaker pulling down those better adapted to survive.
Women, too, should learn to become self-sufficient by attending voca-
tional schools, marrying at a later age, and leaving the confines of their
households to earn their own incomes.†

Yang Ch'ang-chi's individualistic beliefs, which were strongly tinged
with Social Darwinism, forced him to pit egoism against altruism. He
had begun by noting that whatever the morality or even naturalness of
feelings like filiality, their result was inhumane. As his argument progressed, however, he was forced to extend his attack, demolishing the
very virtue (*jen* or humaneness) which K'ang Yu-wei and T'an Ssu-
t'ung had used in the first place to attack such Confucian particularisms
as *hsiao* (filial piety). Extended thus far, Yang's egoistic ethic appeared to deny altruism altogether. Would all institutions that depended
on self-sacrifice then have to be opposed? Where did one draw the

* The extended family was also attacked in another article which Yang published in *Chia-yin tsa-chih* (Tiger Magazine) in 1915. Praising the family system
of the West because it encouraged autonomy in the husband–wife relationship,
he attacked arranged marriages for perpetuating genetic weaknesses, for permitting the very young to marry before they were capable of supporting a family,
and for fostering concubinage. "Returning to the idea of the independent household, he pointed out that rural life and ancestor worship made it difficult for
Chinese to marry late and live in separate establishments. That pattern was easier
for people in the West, where city life predominated." Howard L. Boorman,
Biographical Dictionary of Republican China, vol. 4 (New York: Columbia
University Press, 1971), pp. 2–3.

† Yang, like so many others, regarded the role of women in China as one of
the basic problems which had to be solved for the sake of the entire society.
The connections between Mao Tse-tung's political views and feminism have
been analyzed in Roxane Witke, "Mao Tse-tung, Women, and Suicide in the
May Fourth Era," *China Quarterly,* 31:128–147.

line between the attack on primary units like the family and the larger collective called the nation?

Yang Ch'ang-chi's answer was to envisage society on two levels: one of particular associations, which determined norms, and another of more universal or collective relevance (country, state, society-at-large), which was determined *by* norms. In this manner, individual self-assertion could be justified both negatively (it destroyed oppressive institutions) and positively (it affirmed popular sovereignty and strengthened the nation). Democracy, argued Yang, depended on the people's realization of each individual's potential. Failing that, China would continue to be a republic in name only. If, however, it hoped to gain the national strength of a country like England, China would have to encourage "democratic participatory sovereignty" by nurturing a "spirit of independence" among its people.[18] Because such a national spirit was (and here Yang took for granted the causal connection between individual states of mind and collective attitudes) an aggregate of individual states of mind, smaller units like the family had to be sacrificed for the sake of the country. That was also why youth was so important—the young were the most capable of acquiring that sense of self-independence in order to "expand the nation's strength." [19]

The concept of national strength legitimized Yang's attack on social welfare, but a contradiction still remained. The spirit of a nation surely might reflect that of its citizens, but could not individualism conflict with collectivism? Yang tried to resolve this contradiction in three ways. First, he accepted the importance of collective responsibilities, such as universal military service, while maintaining that these would not interfere with individual development. That is, there was a time in life when it was important to serve the country, and other periods when (the service having been rendered) the individual could look entirely to himself. There were even Chinese precedents for this in the old T'ang militia system which allowed people to intersperse farming with military service. Second, service was volunteered. The best armies that China had, such as those of Yang's native Hunan, were composed not of conscripts but of volunteers—men who had realized that they could not afford to lose the "possibility of preserving themselves." And, finally, the collectivity remained in the end for Yang (as it had for Liang Ch'i-ch'ao) the best guarantee of individual well-being. Profit-making, for instance, was to be encouraged, but not at the ultimate expense of the collectivity. For, "one can temporarily accrue profit for one's own self" to the detriment of the nation, "but in the end one cannot long retain this profit." [20] In short, by Yang's time the traditional dimensions of social responsibility had utterly altered. Loyalty was not confined to the particularisms of the *Sacred Edicts*; it was owed to society-at-large.

Whichever of Yang's writings and teachings Mao Tse-tung remembered, he undoubtedly believed that will was the essence of personality —an immortal core that was fully realized when directed toward social improvement. There was thus a distinction between mere self-interest and commitment to one's ideals. The former was transitory; the latter demanded endurance and persistence. Internal commitment was insufficient. Strength of will was really only proved by external effectiveness. Consequently, it was important to get to the heart of an affair by concentrating on essentials and by ordering the concrete sequence of action as realistically and practically as possible.

Mao was also convinced by Yang of the importance of "honestly doing things, sincerely seeking learning," not by sitting in a study, cultivating self-sincerity, but by relating learning to the actual needs of the real world beyond the classroom's walls. "If one seeks learning behind a closed door then his learning will be useless. One should follow the myriad events and creatures of the Under-heaven and in the nation by studying them [firsthand]." [21] Foreshadowing themes which were later developed in his essay "On Practice," Mao's school notes consistently sought the contemporary relevance of self-cultivation. "First, esteem the ego. Seek in yourself and do not reprove others. Second, penetrate the present. If you are reading history then you must emphasize recent times so that it and the self are related." [22] Presentism also implied the need to look after the people's material needs. "When we say that the *chün-tzu* is set on the Tao rather than on food, this is to oppose scrambling after profit. It is not to say that all of the scholars and people deprecate [the necessity of] planning to make one's living." [23] How could one even write of will without regard for physical welfare? "We speak of the will as not existing without a warm body and full belly. . . . But if we speak of activity then the essence of the kingly way (*wang-tao*) is really nothing more than [providing] food and clothing to prevent starvation and exposure. How can we say that a warm body and full belly cannot be provided?" [24] Concern for the "kingly way" thus kept Mao from simply accepting either a capitalist ethic of the Manchester sort or the exclusive right of the fittest to economic survival.

Still, individualism continued to be the primary message of the day, reflected above all in the famous journal *New Youth*. Mao, who was introduced to the magazine by Yang Ch'ang-chi, spoke later of its prominence to Edgar Snow.

I began to read this magazine while I was a student in the normal college and admired the articles of Hu Shih and Ch'en Tu-hsiu very much. They became for awhile my models, replacing Liang Ch'i-ch'ao and K'ang Yu-wei whom I had already discarded. At this time my mind was a curious mixture of ideas of liberalism, democratic reformism, and utopian socialism. I had somewhat vague passions about "nineteenth-century democracy," utopianism, and old-fashioned liberalism, and I was definitely anti-militarist and anti-imperialist.[25]

A summary of the contents of *New Youth* (which was published monthly beginning September 15, 1915) would require a book in itself, but a glance at the table of contents of any single volume gives some sense of the rich fare which readers like Mao consumed. The fourth issue (December 15, 1915), for example, contained the following:

1. Several pieces of descriptive prose, a serialized short story in vernacular Chinese, and a portion of Oscar Wilde's *An Ideal Husband*.
2. Detailed news and commentaries on the international and internal situations.
3. An account of Marshal Hindenburg's life and role in the war on the eastern front.
4. "Femininity and Science": an article by a Japanese scholar which discussed the nature of sexuality in terms of bacterial differentiation, entomological hermaphroditism, and the human menses.
5. Ch'en Tu-hsiu's essay on "The Fundamental Distinction in the Thinking of Eastern and Western Peoples," contrasting the Western sense of individuality, respect for law, interest in the present, and so on, with its oriental opposites: familism, traditionalism, and anti-legalism.
6. A plan ("On Security") by Li I-min for revolution. Directed against the faint-hearted, his plan was based on the argument that movements like the French Revolution or South America's emancipation from Spain had actually created greater security in the end. Shortsighted attempts by the Chinese to avoid tumult would only perpetuate enslavement and insecurity.

7. Kao I-han's "Theory as to Why a Nation Is Not the Final Resting Place of Human Life," which retrieved the theories of German political scientists like Bluntschli and Holtzendorff.

8. "Remarks on the History of Art and Literature in Modern Europe": a piece by Ch'en Tu-hsiu in which he insisted on the social responsibility of the artist, singling out Tolstoy as a paragon in this regard.

9. A translation ("Blood and Iron") of an editorial from a "liberal" London newspaper which described the plight of Europe's working class and argued that the rulers of the West had chosen war over revolution. "Capitalism is war—socialism means peace among nations."

10. "On Schopenhauer's Self-Will": a philosophical essay by Liu Shu-ya which briefly analyzed *Die Welt als Wille und Vorstellung* and *Ueber den Willen in der Natur* (characteristically translated in Chinese to read, "The Will as Occupying Nature"—nature being *tzu-jan,* which also means "spontaneity").

Mao devoured every issue of *New Youth.* In fact, he even copied portions of articles by the editor, Ch'en Tu-hsiu (1879–1942) into his school notebooks. One piece by Ch'en, which may well have inspired Mao's first published work (an essay on physical education*), urged that the Chinese nurture the more physical and savage aspects of their nature just as the Japanese writer, Fukuzawa Yukichi (1835–1901), had suggested. According to Ch'en, Fukuzawa's theory was that children under the age of ten should be educated in bestialism (*jūsei shugi*), and only afterwards in humanism (*jinsei shugi*). Western evolutionists—declared Ch'en—had also pointed out that "Our human feelings are nothing more than a continuation of animal sensations. The activity of morality among men is no more than a continuation of an amoral stimulation [of our senses]." [26] Having evolved from animals, man possessed at one and the same time both a bestial and human aspect.† Given this dual origin of the species, man should not emphasize

* Mao Ze-dong, *Une étude de l'éducation physique.* Translated and annotated by Stuart R. Schram (Paris: Mouton, 1963). Mao would also obviously have been influenced by his teacher, Mr. Yang, by Friedrich Paulsen (who will be discussed later), by Yen Yuan (the seventeenth-century physical cultist) and by Yen's student, Li Kang-chu (1659–1733). See Li Jui, *Mao Tse-tung,* 32; and Stuart R. Schram, *The Political Thought of Mao Tse-tung,* rev. ed. (New York: Praeger, 1969), p. 31.

† This was no doubt influenced by uniformitarianism, the notion behind social evolutionism that the present is the key to the past and that the stages of

one side at the expense of the other, especially because savagery was a "will (*i-chih*) that is obstinate and ferocious, a wish to struggle without submitting." [27]

Ch'en Tu-hsiu reinforced Yang Ch'ang-chi's emphasis on individual assertion, but a passage like the one quoted just above from *New Youth* did not resolve the conflict between self-development and social good. Like Yen Fu's presentation of Social Darwinism, it simply assumed that the social organism was an aggregate of its plural cells, a singular unison of many different particular wills. Although this sort of biological explanation did confirm will as a fundamental instinct of the species, it did not unify man's implicitly dualistic nature: bestial drives versus humanistic ideals. Consequently, Mao Tse-tung had to make the leap from particular mind to universal principle, from a concept of the ambivalent species to one of unified being, by way of another set of premises altogether. Under Yang Ch'ang-chi's influence, Mao read a book on ethics by the Neo-Kantian philosopher, Friedrich Paulsen (1846–1908), and "was inspired to write an essay which I entitled 'The Energy of the Mind' [*Hsin chih li*]. I was then an idealist." [28] "All I believed in was Kant's dualism, particularly his idealism." [29] It was therefore German idealism which first convinced Mao Tse-tung that will was not just an irrational instinct, and egoism not just selfish. Instead the will was free, rational, and universal.

---

human development can be reconstructed by comparing extant human groups which occupy the scale from savagery to civilization. See, for example, George W. Stocking, Jr., "Edward Burnett Tyler," in *International Encyclopedia of the Social Sciences* (New York: Macmillan, 1968), p. 172.

12

Rationalism

Christian Wolff (1679–1754), the great logician, was ejected from Prussia by the Pietists in 1721, when he argued in a public lecture at Halle that Confucius' *Analects* proved the autonomous ability of human reason to acquire moral truth without divine guidance.[1] But cultural relativism was hardly the main source of rational inquiry in the West. Its origins are usually traced back to Aristotle's logic or to Cicero's *notitiae communes;* and then on up again through thinkers like Herbert of Cherbury (1581–1648), who tried to prove that God had implanted in every human being universal and innate truths above which there existed no higher authority.[2] In fact, the greatest impetus to rationalism was the scientific revolution of mathematicians like Johann Kepler (1571–1630), who argued that rational cognitions are based on axioms which can be understood as necessary and universal in the form of a priori propositions.

At the same time, Kepler's belief that these axioms or innate ideas (number, magnitude, and so forth) were not derived from experience posed difficult problems for all those who thought to construct a metaphysic independent of revelation. Kepler himself, along with René Descartes (1596–1650) and G. W. Leibniz (1646–1716), could only connect the rational and empirical spheres by positing metaphysical ideas: independent laws of reason according to which the real world operates because it (and the ideas) had been created by a divine intellect. Leibniz went even further in that direction by declaring that the truths of reason were the very essence of God's mind. Indeed, the entire universe was composed of a system of perceiving minds which partook of this essence as monads, each reflecting the universe with brighter or hazier clarity according to the degree of accuracy with which the particular monad perceived forms. Still, that range of perception was divided somewhat sharply in two by Leibniz' (and Christian Wolff's) distinction between confused and distinct (or intelligible) ideas, or even between synthetic and analytic statements. According to the rules of logic, every true sentence was true of the actual world, but only some true sentences were true of all other possible worlds. The latter truths were analytic statements ("grass is green"), incapable of being false, while a sentence like "Socrates died in 399 B.C." was only a contingent truth. This distinction at least provided a *possibility* for Leibniz to try to transform contingent elements into rational ones according to the rules of logic.[3] As Wolff phrased it: "Philosophy is the science of the possibles insofar as they can be." [4] But even though there existed such a possibility, Leibniz and Wolff could not do without metaphysical propositions; that is, the notion that a divine intellect created these rules in the first place. W. H. Auden put the quandary most elegantly:

> If theologians are correct,
> A Plan implies an Architect:
> A God-built maze would be, I'm sure,
> The Universe in miniature.

And he asked the very question Kant would place to logic:

> Are data from the world of Sense,
> In that case, valid evidence?
> What in the universe I know
> Can give directions how to go? [5]

The difficulty of regarding the truth of experience as self-sufficient captured the attention of the English school of reason which assumed actuality to be individualist: there does exist a concrete ego related to a broader universe around it. But how was it connected? John Locke (1632–1704), for example, tried a psychological line of inquiry. The interaction between individual mind and the outer system of things created conscious experience which consisted in turn of ideas. Yet Locke could not resolve the problem of *merely* subjective experience, so that it was left as a matter of doubt for both George Berkeley and David Hume to ponder. Berkeley (1685–1753) did elaborate on the ability of mind to explain its own experience (*esse* is *percipere*), but continued to base reality on the supreme or divine mind of God.[6] Hume's

(1711–1776) attempts were more audacious, insofar as he bluntly confessed in *A Treatise on Human Nature* that he could neither abandon nor reconcile the two principles that, on the one hand—all of our distinct perceptions are distinct existences, and, on the other—the mind never perceives any real connection among distinct existences. No existence can transcend itself.[7]

The dilemma was brilliantly resolved by Immanuel Kant (1724–1804). Kant approached Hume with a Wolffian point of view. Instead of asking, as Locke had, where experience arose, he demanded to know how the ego could link together the data of experience via cognition. In short, what were the conditions of knowledge itself? His first step was taken while studying the principles of natural theology. Knowledge must be, as Wolff had said, divided between synthesis (the construction of notions in mathematics) and analysis (the clearing up of given notions in metaphysics). Or, as Kant put it in the *Critique of Pure Reason* (1781):

In all judgments wherein the relation of a subject to the predicate is cogitated (I mention affirmative judgments only here; the application to negative will be very easy), this relation is possible in two different ways. Either the predicate B belongs to the subject A, as something which is contained (though covertly) in the conception A; or the predicate B lies completely out of the conception A, although it stands in connection with it. In the first instance, I term the judgment analytical, in the second, synthetical.[8]

Then he examined the kind of a priori proposition which had bedeviled Hume: "Everything which happens has its cause." Such a proposition contained an analytical element because it conceived of an existence preceded by a time factor. Yet the notion of cause did not form part of that concept. That notion must therefore be synthetic. But how was it derived?

How then am I able to assert concerning the general conception—"that which happens"—something entirely different from that conception, and to recognize the conception of cause although not contained in it, yet as belonging to it, and even necessarily? What is here the unknown X, upon which the understanding rests when it believes it has found, out of the conception A, a foreign predicate B which it nevertheless considers to be connected with it?[9]

Hume had clearly been right when he demonstrated that the connection between cause and effect, the *principium causalitatis,* could not be analytically derived from experiential observation, simply because the principle possessed greater universality and necessity than the connection itself. It therefore had to be completely a priori. But how could Hume's subsequent conclusion—that such an a priori proposition was entirely impossible—be correct, since according to it metaphysics was a delusion, and pure mathematics an illusion? Pure mathematics *does* exist; it *does* contain a priori synthetic propositions. By the same token, so must metaphysics exist. Indeed, Kant even foreshadowed Hegel (1770–1831) by describing the "natural disposition" of men toward metaphysics (*metaphysica naturalis*). "And now the question arises— How is metaphysics, as a natural disposition, possible? In other words, how, from the nature of universal human reason, do those questions arise which pure reason proposes to itself, and which it is impelled by its own feeling of need to answer as well as it can?" [10] To answer this question a special science, a critique of pure reason, would have to be conceived. Such a critique would contain those principles whereby man could know anything absolutely a priori. Because it would be concerned with our mode of knowing objects and not with the objects themselves, the science would be a transcendental one. Kant's task, as he set it for himself in the *Critique,* was to prove the necessity of that transcendental science.

Kant began at Hume's starting place with the classic problem of cognition. Representations of objects reach us via sensibility, which in turn yields intuitions. Because such intuitions are sensations, they are empirical. How then account for the unity of forms of these empirical sensations? Each piece of incoming data must be discrete, because the essence of knowledge is the sense of the data's unity in difference. And if they are discrete, then conglomerates of data cannot carry with them their own forms of appearance. There must be some a priori form of perception, separate from sensation.

That which in the phenomenon corresponds to the sensation I term its *matter;* but that which effects that the content of the phenomenon can be arranged under certain relations I call its *form.* But that in which our sensations are merely arranged, and by which they are susceptible of assuming a certain form, cannot be itself sensation. It is, then, the matter of all phenomena that is given to us a posteriori; the form must lie ready a priori for them in the mind, and consequently can be regarded separately from all sensation.[11]

What would then be these universal, necessary and a priori forms of perception, these "pure forms of sensible intuition"?

As Kant put the question in this fashion, he challenged his predecessors' assumptions of a generic division between a priori and a posteriori knowledge. Aristotelian philosophy had posited that reality consisted of universal essence or form and matter, the former being prior to the latter. Hence, deductive reasoning from the essence of an object was a priori; knowledge derived from the experience of observing materialized essence was a posteriori. This distinction between form and matter had been dropped after the fourteenth century by the Scholastics, who emphasized temporal distinctions: arguments from cause to effect were a priori, from effect to cause a posteriori. Finally, as Leibniz and Wolff decided, a priori knowledge was composed of judgments derived from concepts or ideas, while a posteriori knowledge was just derived from experience. What Kant did now was to cease regarding them as two *kinds* of knowledge, and instead consider them two *factors* of knowledge. Thus a posteriori factors were empirically supplied natural data, transformed into orderly experience, thanks to a priori forms which had to exist to make experience possible at all. The two a priori forms most necessary to this transformation of data were space and time. Without those two elemental notions of the sensory sphere, data would only be scattered congeries of sensations, one pulse after the other, not perceivable objects. Still, could one not argue that space was induced from the relationship between objects instead of being imposed upon them by reason?

To avoid grounding on this Locke-ean shoal, Kant performed a bold logical maneuver—perhaps natural to him but difficult for most—by arguing from principles to knowledge. This form of philosophy, which he called "transcendental exposition," sought to define concepts from which the *possibility* of other a priori synthetic knowledge could be understood. Such concepts had a reality of their own—a "transcendental ideality" as real as, but distinct from, empirical reality. For example, a statement such as a geometrical proposition announces an absolute and necessary truth which is not empirical because it cannot be derived from experiential judgments.

Now, how can an external intuition anterior to objects themselves, and in which our conception of objects can be determined a priori, exist in the human mind? Obviously not otherwise than in so far as it has its seat in the subject only, as the *formal* capacity of the subject's being affected by objects, and thereby of obtaining immediate representation, that is, intuition; consequently, only as the *form of the external sense* in general.[12]

Therefore, space does not represent any property of things in themselves nor does it represent them in their relation to one another. It is nothing more than the form of all appearances of outer sense: one of the subjective and necessary conditions of intuitive sensibility. As it presents to us outward objects, space is real. Yet if we abstract it from things in themselves, we can conceive it as pure intuition, which gives it the ideal quality of geometrical propositions. Hence, space has both empirical reality and transcendental ideality.

But—Kant warned—one should not be misled by the abstraction to believe the transcendental ideality of space or time equal to a pure category of thought. Because space and time are necessary to the limited intelligence of men, they are contingent (that is, true only under existing conditions), and so cannot be necessary categories in the realm of pure reason—a realm that can be proved to exist by these same limitations.

This last point was a stroke of the highest genius. It would have been all too easy for Kant to follow the direction of earlier rationalists by assigning space, a form or category of perception, the status of higher reason. Instead, Kant carried to its ultimate Leibniz' distinction between contingent and absolute truths. The former described *phenomena,* objects of the senses; the latter described *noumena,* objects of understanding. Christian Wolff had hoped for no limit to philosophy's possibility of probing understanding. In fact, that was philosophy's *raison d'être,* although it was thereby dependent upon inspired rules, like the *li* of Neo-Confucian philosophers. To avoid that and to solve Hume's dilemma, Kant made an extraordinary intellectual decision. If we are to proceed transcendentally to define the concepts which make experience possible, then we should by the same act realize that we are *only* defining the perception of phenomena. We can never, in other words, see more than our perceptions allow us; we can never really know a thing-in-itself (*Ding-an-sich*).

This skepticism permitted Kant what would otherwise have been an act of highest faith. For, to admit that man's intelligence was restricted was also to suggest the possibility of *unlimited* cognition, of an intelligence for which data and pure categories would coincide. This would be the realm of the noumena, for which no corresponding human intuition existed. Leibniz and Wolff had therefore been wrong in treating the difference between confused and distinct ideas as merely logical. The difference between them did not merely concern their logical form. It concerned their very origin.

For the faculty of sensibility not only does not present us with an indistinct and confused cognition of objects as things in themselves, but, in fact, gives us no knowledge of these at all. . . . When we say that the intuition of external objects, and also the self-intuition of the subject, represent both, objects and subject, in space and time, as they affect our senses, that is, as they appear—this is by no means equivalent to asserting that these objects are mere illusory appearances. . . . The object as phenomenon is to be distinguished from the object as a thing in itself. . . . It would be my own fault, if out of that which I should reckon as phenomenon, I made mere illusory appearance. But this will not happen, because of our principle of the ideality of all sensuous intuitions. On the contrary, if we ascribe objective reality to these forms of representation, it becomes impossible to avoid changing everything into mere appearance. For if we regard space and time as properties, which must be found in objects as things in themselves, as *sine quibus non* of the possibility of their existence, and reflect on the absurdities in which we then find ourselves involved, inasmuch as we are compelled to admit the existence of two infinite things, which are nevertheless not substances, nor anything really inhering in substances, nay, to admit that they are the necessary conditions of the existence of all things, and moreover, that they must continue to exist, although all existing things were annihilated—we cannot blame the good Berkeley for degrading bodies to mere illusory appearances.[13]

Because Kant began with cognition instead of assumptions about the constitution of objects, his "transcendental exposition"—as he put it himself—was the Copernican revolution of metaphysics. Rather than examining the axioms of Euclid, one should analyze the possibility of those a priori synthetical judgments in the first place, the better to derive apodeictic cognitions applicable to noumena. The product of this new logic, the "transcendental aesthetic," obviously had to be holistic. It could only exist as a system, because its concepts emerged from pure understanding according to the coherent idea of possible experience. But these concepts *were* knowable. For, as intellectual notions a priori (*Verstandesbegriffe*), as categories of transcendentalism, they were the basic conditions of the possibility of experience; and as such, as conditions of self-consciousness, they could be arrived at by examining the process of logical judgment alone.

Before Kant, categories were always predicates—concepts of assertation under which a subject was brought. Since Aristotle's *Organon*, philosophers had assumed that these modes of understanding corresponded to ultimate modes of being: substance, quantity, quality, time,

and so forth. As Kant declared that we can have no knowledge of a
thing-in-itself, he also denied that categories represented modes of being, and made them simple modes of synthetic apprehension. Of course,
that immediately raised the question of subjective experience. Does,
say, the category of cause and effect come from the objects or the subject? Because the categories of understanding do not represent the
conditions under which the objects are given to us in intuition, ". . . we
find ourselves involved in a difficulty which did not present itself in
the sphere of sensibility, that is to say, we cannot discover *how the
subjective conditions of thought can have objective validity.*" [14] Obviously, there were only two ways in which synthetical representation
(subject) and its objects could come together unless there existed a
supreme mind. Either the object made it possible by itself, or the representation made it possible by itself. If the first were true, then this would
be an empirical relation, totally without a priori representation. If the
second, then representation (which of course does not produce the object's existence) had to be an a priori determinitive to cognition. Such
a condition of the possibility of cognition would be the *conception* by
means of which the object corresponding to the intuition of the phenomenon was thought. Hume had correctly realized that such conceptions had to have an a priori origin, but he failed to explain how they
—disconnected in our understanding—were necessarily connected in
the object, "and it never occurred to him that the understanding itself
might, perhaps, by means of these conceptions, be the author of the
experience in which its objects were presented to it." [15]

Kant, on the other hand, would separate empirical apperception from
the pure and spontaneous apperception of such a representation as "I
think." The self-consciousness which that implied not only produced
the particular representation; it accompanied all representations. "It is
in all acts of consciousness one and the same, and unaccompanied by
it, no representation can exist *for me.* The unity of this apperception I
call the transcendental unity of self-consciousness, in order to indicate
the possibility of a priori cognition arising from it." [16] This principle of
unity was the transcendental faculty of the understanding which con-
joined various representations. By means of it the manifold givens of
an intuition were united into a conception of the object. Objective in
principle (and not just the subjective unity of consciousness), the unity
of apperception made possible the act of final understanding, which—
as a logical function of judgment—was determined by the categories.

In this fashion Kant hoped to show that a metaphysical deduction of the a priori origin of these categories could be proved by their accordance with the general logical functions of thought. That alone would not have overcome the skepticism of a Hume. But Kant went beyond the deduction described just above by formulating a *transcendental* process. This new kind of deduction demonstrated the possibility of the categories as a priori cognitions of objects of an intuition in general.

Accordingly, conceptions of objects in general must lie as a priori conditions at the foundation of all empirical cognition; and consequently, the objective validity of the categories, as a priori conceptions, will rest upon *this,* that experience (as far as regards the form of thought) is possible only by their means. For in that case they apply necessarily and a priori to objects of experience because only through them can an object of experience be thought.[17]

His transcendental deduction therefore rested on the proof that these categories conditioned the possibility of all experience, since without them an object could not be thought. The demonstration was staggeringly simple once he made the fundamental decision that a sufficient deduction of their existence would be given by starting *with* them, by showing that with their means an object *could* be thought.

This, then, was Kant's Copernican revolution: first, the idea that the regularity of nature does not belong to it as such, but rather depends upon the forms of our perception; and, second, the assertion that only by accepting this critical contingency can we understand how phenomena are linked together according to these ultimate and unknowable categories. Arnold Brecht has summarized Kant's position with enviable lucidity.

Conceding that neither pure reason nor experience can reveal the reality and the nature of causal relation, he taught that nonetheless the human mind cannot operate—or, at least, cannot acquire generalized empirical knowledge—but in terms of the idea that every change in phenomena must have a cause. If the universe did not project this principle into reason, then it was reason which projected it, as a necessary form of its own functioning, into the universe. This was Kant's Copernican revolution.[18]

The concession which Kant had made set limits to both intuition and understanding. But by beginning with reason, as revealed in the modalities of logic, and working outward, Kant hoped to demonstrate the existence of a "productive imagination" which was the common ground between categories of understanding and the intuition of sensations. After all, categories—abstract in themselves—were only useful when dealing with possible objects of experience. Something had to mediate the form that possibility took; something—which he called "transcendental schemata"—had to inform the workings of the productive imagination which brought the dualism together.

Returning to the difficult problem of temporal cause and effect, Kant assumed that there must be a priori determinations of time, such as:

Possibility: agreement of the synthesis of different representations with conditions of time in general.
Actuality: existence of an object in some determinate time.
Necessity: existence of an object at all times.

These schemata, these "analogies of experience," were based upon the sequence of perceptions in time. But were they not still subjective? No, answered Kant; experience was the manifold of perceptions according to synthetic unity. He had already shown that the manifold came neither from the perceptions themselves nor from the constructions of experience, and so the manifold must exist objectively in time. Or, to put it another way: because time cannot be seen for itself, the determination of the existence of objects in time necessarily reflects their connection by a priori concepts.

Our *apprehension* of the manifold in a phenomenon is always successive, is consequently always changing. By it alone we could, therefore, never determine whether this manifold, as an object of experience, is coexistent or successive, unless it had for a foundation something that exists *always,* that is, something *fixed* and *permanent,* of the existence of which all succession and coexistence are nothing but so many modes (*modi* of time). Only in the permanent, then, are relations of time possible (for simultaneity and succession are the only relations in time); that is to say, the permanent is the *substratum* of our empirical representation of time itself, in which alone all determination of time is possible.[19]

This analytic of categories, while devoted to understanding, granted Kant access to the a priori notions of pure reason (*Vernunftbegriffe*) which were beyond understanding. That realm of metaphysical ideas contained necessary concepts of reason for which sense-experience had no corresponding object. Produced by reason, these ideas existed but were quite beyond experience. "They are not mere fictions, but natural and necessary products of reason, and have hence a necessary relation to the whole sphere of the exercise of understanding. And finally, they are transcendent and overstep the limits of all experience, in which, consequently, no object can ever be presented that would be perfectly adequate to a transcendental idea." [20] Kant was thus trying to derive transcendental ideas without falling into the paralogism, the fallacy of the ego, of Descartes' rational psychology. "I think" could not be a transcendental concept in Kant's eyes because that offended the prime rule of his critical logic: when we conceive of a thing as subject alone and never as predicate, that signifies there is no object to which it corresponds. Consequently, it lacks objective reality.

Did that not equally condemn his pure concepts, for which there was no corresponding object? Not at all, he argued. Reason may not generate concepts, but it does free them from the conditioned realm of experience. By demanding a totality of conditions for any concept, reason transformed it into a transcendental idea. Transcendental ideas, in other words, were categories extended to a completion of conditions, which was the unconditioned realm of freedom itself.

This process, this extension toward transcendence, was done via a series of definitions of conditions, beginning with the condition closest to a thing's appearance and moving on toward more remote conditions through a "regressive synthesis." As that was done, philosophy quickly reached a level of absolute conflicts between *dogmatic* knowledge: conflicts which could not be resolved by appeal to fact or to reason. These were antinomies of reason, for which a transcendental antithetic, a "dialectical doctrine of knowledge," was necessary.

To prove this, Kant subsumed transcendental ideas under three major antinomies of reason: soul, cosmos, and god. Then he proceeded to demonstrate that the existence (thesis) or nonexistence (antithesis) of each could be proved with equal validity, so that the antinomy itself was an illusory opposition as well as further proof of the transcendent ideality of being: the capstone of his critical system.

Thus the antinomy of pure reason in its cosmological ideas disappears. For the above demonstration [that is, that the universe exists for Kant only in the empirical regress of the series of phenomena and not per se] has established the fact that it [that is, the antinomy] is merely the product of a dialectical and illusory opposition, which arises from the application of the idea of absolute totality—admissible only as a condition of things in themselves, to phenomena, which exist only in our representations, and—when constituting a series—in a successive regress. This antinomy of reason may, however, be really profitable to our speculative interests, not in the way of contributing any dogmatical addition, but as presenting to us another material support in our critical investigations. For it furnishes us with indirect proof of the transcendental ideality of phenomena, if our minds were not completely satisfied with the direct proof set forth in the Transcendental Aesthetic. The proof would proceed in the following dilemma. If the world is a whole existing in itself, it must be either finite or infinite. But it is neither finite nor infinite—as has been shown, on the one side, by the thesis, on the other, by the antithesis. Therefore the world—the content of all phenomena —is not a whole existing in itself. It follows that phenomena are nothing, apart from our representations. And this is what we mean by transcendental ideality.[21]

Here was the apogee of reason. By proving phenomena to be without unity themselves, yet showing by logical regression that their synthesis in both transcendent and empirical realms was indeed connected, Kant assigned creative force to reason. Its peculiarity—he said—was its striving force to achieve its own unified systematization. God, as "mere" idea, was the construction according to idea. The concept of a highest intelligence, in other words, was no more than a thing *in* the idea, a regulative schema for which no "real" object existed, but which was constructed according to Kant's analytic conditions of the greatest possible unity of reason. Idea itself should never be reified. Instead, all that Kant asked was that philosophers be willing to act as though there were such ideal objects to test his thesis: we cannot extend our knowledge beyond the objects of experience by treating speculative ideas as though they were constitutive principles; but we can deduce those ideas if we treat them as archetypes, or as regulative principles which unify the manifold of empirical knowledge.

In this way, the idea is properly a heuristic, and not an ostensive conception; it does not give us any information respecting the constitution of an object, it merely indicates how, under the guidance of the idea, we ought to *investigate* the constitution and the relations of objects in the world of experience. Now, if it can be shown that the three kinds of transcendental ideas (psychological, cosmological, and theological), although not relating directly to any object nor determining it, do nevertheless, on the supposition of the existence of an *ideal object,* produce systematic unity in the laws of the empirical employment of the reason, and extend our empirical cognition, without ever being inconsistent or in opposition with it—it must be a necessary *maxim* of reason to regulate its procedure according to these ideas.[22]

In psychology one would therefore link all appearances just as if the mind were a persistent and unified identity. In cosmology one would act just as if the series of appearances were endless. In theology one would view all possible experience as if it had a single and higher ground beyond itself in self-subsistent reason.

The terms with which Kant studied reason were *Naturbegriffe* (natural concepts) determined by the rules of causality. These were appropriate to theoretical philosophy, but could not be used to study what Kant called "practical philosophy." This epistemological distinction, which was elaborated in the *Critique of Judgment,* did not concern the contents of either theoretical or practical knowledge, but rather their *Vorstellungsant:* the ways in which they were conceived and used. The practical counterpart to *Naturbegriffe* was therefore *Freiheitsbegriff:* the concept of freedom, which operates according to the causality of autodetermination. Freedom is transphenomenal—out of reach of critical theory because it is not an object of intuition. Consequently, Kant's reason for the existence of practical philosophy was simply that it "ought" (*sollen*) to be. To be sure, theoretical knowledge suggested that the source of this "ought" was rational purpose, because the highest concept of unity which reason can derive from its own ideas is purpose itself. Purpose in the practical realm was expressed as moral law, which is man's *willing* to overcome the discrepancy between his perceptions and the ideals which his mind is capable of conceiving. The highest conceivable ideal of all, which is the possibility of unqualified good, is thus pure will, of which the very ontological character was untrammeled goodness of intent. To be faithful to its own ontological nature, however, pure will had to obey some law or categorical imperative of the intelligible order of reason. That imperative was the universal law of action as such: "Since I have robbed the will of all impulses which could come to it from the obedience to any law, nothing remains to serve as a principle of the will except the universal law of action as such, that is: I should never act in such a way that I could not also will that my maxim should be a universal law." [23] Such action would indeed make the will's ontological law one of objective reality, but what of *Freiheitsbegriff,* the will's supposed obedience to no law at all? What law could the will *will* freely? The only possible answer was its own pure independence, its autodetermination, its *willing* accordance with moral law, its obedience to "practical" necessity.

The complete accordance of the will with the moral law is holiness, which is a perfection no rational being of the sensory world is capable of at any point of time in his existence. Since in the meantime, nonetheless, it is required as practically necessary, it can be discovered only in an infinite progress toward that complete accordance: and it is necessary according to the principles of pure reason to assume such a practical progression as the real object of our will.[24]

The realization of the highest good is the necessary object of that will which is determined by moral law. In such a will, the supreme condition of the highest good would be its perfect identity with the moral law. And as our own will progresses toward that moral law, we draw all the closer to the realm of pure practical reason: idea as purposive will, teleology as well as freedom. For, Kant had wished to preserve the mathematical spirit of Descartes without surrendering ethics. He had asked himself the question, "How could you have a metaphysics beyond the sensible world without being forced to limit science's right to investigate natural reality alone?" He had answered himself, in the words of one philosopher, by limiting "the rights of theoretical knowledge in order to be able to ascribe to practical knowledge infinitely more rights than ever had been ascribed to it." [25]

Kant's metaphysic was his solution to disbelief. The antinomy of God was explained by, and accounted for, the dialectic. The dilemma of epistemological skepticism was resolved with, and gave expression to, the transcendental aesthetic. Kant, too, made Jansenist demands: believe and you will know. But the knowledge he delivered was not just intelligibility. Nor was it the Neo-Confucian promise that knowledge was the ability to accord with change. Rather, it was an astonishing demonstration of the power of reason.

Twentieth-century Chinese intellectuals encountering Kant's rationalism therefore began at the finished end of his system, without asking the same questions of being that he had posed at its inception. Unlike European thinkers, they were not whirling round and round the axis of religious disbelief. They were instead trying to find a new and universal definition of human will in a contest whose cosmic rules had suddenly been changed. Kantianism to them was the emblem of rational purpose. Think for a moment of the difference between K'ang Yu-wei's potential teleology of *jen,* and the absolute purpose of Kant's pure practical reason. Reason, unlike *jen,* did stand above history; so that Chinese intellectuals saw in Kantianism both an emancipation of the ego and an ethic which, instead of determining moral behavior by the consequences resulting from it, declared that good conduct was an unconditional law, a categorical imperative.

Marx himself once defined Kantianism as "the German theory of the French Revolution," [26] because it opposed the individual to traditional society, casting the human conscience against the state or church. However, he saw Kantianism as *merely* a philosophy of liberation—quite impotent to inspire revolution as such because it reconciled the clash between moral imperatives and political authority in a higher, transcendent sphere of practical reason, eschewing the real world of political and class interests.* Marx characteristically tried to connect this judgment with Kant's *milieu*. According to *The German Ideology*, the Prussian state was as transcendent as Kantianism for particular historical reasons. Germany had long been an economically dispersed country with weak individual social elements. The only means of conquering exclusive power was by creating an independent bureaucracy.

The necessary consequence of this was that during the epoch of absolute monarchy which appeared here in its most crippled, semipatriarchal form, the special organs (*Sphäre*) which in accordance with the division of labor were assigned to the administration of public interest, developed an abnormal independence which soon developed into the modern bureaucracy. The state constituted itself into an apparently independent power and maintained this position whereas in countries other than Germany its independence was only temporary and transitional.[27]

The bureaucracy's autonomy abetted the German illusion of the state as a transcendent political entity independent of social interests. Therefore, the German equivalent of French liberalism (which expressed genuine bourgeois class interests) was the critical philosophy of Kant.

Neither he nor the German bourgeoisie whose ideological apologist he was, observed that at the root of these theoretical ideas of the bourgeoisie lay material interests and a class will conditioned and determined by the material relations of production. Kant consequently separates the theoretical expression of these interests from the interests themselves. He transforms the materially motivated will of the French bourgeoisie into a *pure* self-determination of the *free will*, of the will in-and-for itself, of the human will. In this way he converts it into a purely ideological determination and moral postulate.[28]

Although Marx's analysis of the rise of the Prussian bureaucracy is surely open to question, his judgment of Kant is still suggestive for Chinese historians. For, Kantianism—though an influence on Mao—

* Perhaps Kantianism was only relatively impotent. After all, the Prussian cabinet—supposedly because of Frederick William II's displeasure—did forbid Kant to write about religious subjects at all after 1793 and virtually kept him from all but occasional lecturing until 1797.

was certainly no theory of the Chinese revolution. We can sense this obliquely in Mao Tse-tung's passing reference in 1965 to his early interest in Kant. Arguing that "philosophy is only possible with class struggle," Mao declared:

The present approach, from book to book, from concept to concept, is not right. . . . Which one of the universities—Peking or People's—is better? I only learned something at a school for brigands. I have studied Confucius, the Four Books, and the Five Classics. I studied them for six years and really believed in Confucius. Later on I spent seven years in a bourgeois school learning everything they had to teach—natural sciences, social sciences, and even some education. *All I believed in was Kant's dualism, particularly his idealism.* Feudal elements and bourgeois democrats originally pushed me into the revolution. I was only an inexperienced elementary school teacher who had briefly attended middle school when I joined the party. However, I knew we had to revolt. What were we revolting against? Why were we going to revolt? Naturally we were going to revolt against the imperialist old society. I did not know what imperialism was, not to mention why revolution was necessary. What was learned in thirteen years of study was not usable for making revolution.[29]

In spite of posing as less of an intellectual than he really was during his Ch'ang-sha days, Mao rightly accorded Kantianism a prerevolutionary place in his thought. Critical reason would have been a poor instrument of social revolution, even if there had been a vigorous and independent state in China after 1911, when state power was largely replaced by institutional and social interest groups. That situation alone was quite enough to warrant revolt, but Mao's recognition of its necessity was certainly aided by his exposure to German idealism.

13

Idealism

Kant's disciple, Johann Gottlieb Fichte (1762–1814), seized upon the force of practical reason to formulate an even more dynamic credo of rational purpose. His *Critique of Revelation*—mistaken when published in 1792 for one of Kant's own works—clarified the rationalist declaration that religion was a belief in divine moral law. Belief, said Fichte, was a practical postulate necessary to add force to law. As it characterized beings whose reverence for law was obliterated by baser drives, religion necessarily rested upon practical reason as a requirement of the ego.

In the succeeding series on *Wissenschaftslehre,* Fichte tried to unite practical and pure reason as he struggled with Kant's notion that the fundamental condition of knowledge was the synthetical unity of consciousness. Instead of believing that cognition was acted on by noumena beyond consciousness, why had Kant not related cognition *by necessity* to the specific nature of consciousness? He, Fichte, would design a science to completely expose the principles behind all reasoned cognition. Following Kant's Copernican revolution, he would assume the *Wissenschaftslehre* to be proved if one could deduce all cognition from its three primary principles, even though the categories themselves could not be proved. First was the principle of one unconditioned in form and matter; second, one unconditioned in form but not in matter; and third, one unconditioned in matter but not in form. From the first principle, Fichte deduced the first condition of knowledge, that the ego be self-aware. This deed-act, this *Thathandlung,* was the pure act by which consciousness, unconditioned in form and matter, comes to be what it is. Once consciousness is self-aware, another primary act occurs: its op-positing by nonego (conditioned in matter because negative), which sets an antithesis to the original thesis.[1]

But *how* can there be reality beyond ego itself? What explained op-positing as such? Fichte's logical foundation was Kant's *Practical Reason*. His own *Revelation* had intensified the driving force of practical reason as ego. Now he realized a vision of spiritual consciousness based upon dialectical resistance to that force. As the ego willed, it had to demonstrate its striving power to itself in order to be self-aware. This the ego did by creating its own resistance, by establishing a limit to itself: a negative plane or *Anstoss* from which it was deflected and where material nonego was determined. That plane was the necessary condition for the ego's consciousness of its freedom.[2]

The ego (thesis) and nonego (antithesis) were then of course in contradiction. To resolve that, Fichte conceived of yet a higher stage which would absorb the two by mutual determination. This third synthetic stage saw nonego determining ego just as it had been solely determined by ego before. Thus, the entire scheme of rationalist creation depended upon a dialectical assumption which the great English logician, F. H. Bradley (1846–1924), has critically but sympathetically described.

If we make that assumption [that is, that the Dialectic has a real way of its own], we pass naturally from the process of Recognition on to the Dialectic movement. Like recognition this starts from a single datum, and without the help of any other premise it brings out a fresh result. Yet the result is not got by mere analysis of the starting point, but is got by the action of a mental function which extends the datum through an ideal synthesis. So far the method of Dialectic is precisely the same as the common recognition which works by means of reintegration. But now comes a difference; the ideal synthesis, which in Dialectic meets and supplements the starting point, is not reproduction from past perception; or rather, and to speak more correctly, it is not *merely* such ideal reproduction. Even though the synthesis which it brings into play does repeat a connection we have got from presentation, there still is more than bare repetition. The function is felt not as what the mind does because it has thus been trained to perform; the naturalness seems more than the ease of habit, and the necessity above any *vis inertiae*. And the cause of the difference we find is this; the message in the one case seems external tidings which are so believed, since thus received; but in the other it seems like a revelation of ourselves, which is true because we have the witness in our own experience. The content in one case, itself irrational seems to come to our reason from a world without, while in the other it appears as that natural outcome of our inmost constitution, which satisfies us because it is our own selves. This *internal* necessity, of the function and of its product, is the characteristic of the Dialectic Method and constitutes its claim and title to existence.[3]

It was this internal necessity of the dialectic that seemed to Fichte to permit the logical development of his categories for the universal theory of science, thereby proving to his own satisfaction the primary principles themselves. And, in proving them, Fichte thought to show as well the existence of an absolute ego which is made, in the *Bestimmung des Menschen* (The Vocation of Man, 1800), the infinite moral will of the universe: God, a spirit conscious of itself and of its own absolute freedom.

The sole end of reason is pure activity, absolutely by itself alone, having no need of any instrument out of itself,—independence of everything which is not reason,—absolute freedom. The will is the living principle of reason, —is itself reason, when purely and simply apprehended; that reason is active by itself alone, means that pure will, merely as such lives and rules.[4]

Such a dialectical self-knowing was radically different than, say, Chu Hsi's explanation of *ch'ien's* (the creative principle) knowing itself, even though *yin* and *yang* in negative–positive tension produced being. The opposition between *yang* and *yin* was generative, not dialectic, as there was no logical principle like antinomy to point to synthesis beyond analysis. In addition, *ch'ien's* knowing itself merely required an analogy of understanding (you know with ease, *ch'ien* knows with ease), and that just suggested—but did not prove—the intuition. Or, phrased a different way, there cannot be a practical reason without a notion of pure reason. Lacking that combination, antinomies really would be irresolvable (the "illusion" of the dialectic—in Kant's term), and creation would repeat itself mindlessly. Without the will of practical reason, there was no movement toward higher self-awareness. Without a true dialectic, there was no necessity. For that to be there must exist the concept of autonomous Idea.

Hegel's Idea was not just the apotheosis of Kant's self-conscious reason and of Fichte's dialectic; it expressed his attempt to construct a genuine theory of intelligible (rather than merely sensible) realities. Hegel's extraordinarily difficult *Phänomenologie des Geistes* (The Phenomenology of Mind, 1807), started from the idealist notion of self-comprehend-ing spirit, proceeding on the assumption that there was no reality apart from individual consciousness. Kant (remembering Berkeley) had refused to doubt material reality outside of mind. Hegel (discovering History) decided that the consciousness of external reality was a matter of intellectual conceptions rather than sensations. These conceptions evolved dialectically by ontohistorical stages, beginning with undifferentiated consciousness. Because consciousness could not detect permanent objects outside itself, it became self-conscious by finding—creating—a subject besides itself *within* itself. Once created, this being defied the pure rationality of undisturbed Idea. Reason therefore exerted practical effort to perfect its rationale. At this stage it existed as mind or spirit, representing the consciousness of Idea belonging to community, but it was as unconscious of itself as were the organic human members of that community. To give man (and spirit) consciousness, reason (now in the form of culture) freed man from social conventions by using moral law clothed as religion to create new values. The final stage in the becoming of Idea would be reached with absolute knowledge: spirit finally knowing itself as spirit.

It is this that winds up this series of embodiments of spirit, for in it [that is, the reconciliation of consciousness and self-consciousness] spirit gets to the point where it knows itself not only as it is inherently in itself, or in terms of its absolute content, not only as it is (objectively) for itself in terms of its bare form devoid of content, or in terms of self-consciousness, but as it is in its self-consciousness, as it is in itself and for itself.[5]

Thus, Hegel melded Fichte's cosmic dialectic with human history, making stages of spirit equal levels of social development. He created this union by treating thought as not just a subjective action, but rather as "the thorough universal, which as such is objective in the world." [6] Such universal and objective thought existed in three progressive stages. First came abstract Understanding, which stereotypically distinguished each product of thought (its own subject matter) from the other, investing them with the form of universality as *limited* abstractions. The second stage was the Dialectic, which saw these limited and finite abstractions dissolve themselves by passing into opposing categories. Hegel pointed out that this should not be confused with the conventional sense of dialectic as a subjective seesaw of skepticism-producing arguments for and against a proposition. His Dialectic was subjectively the sympathetic sense of the *reality* of life as merging opposites, and objectively "the very nature and essence of the categories (formulated by the Understanding) of things, and of the finite as a whole." [7] In Hegel's view, Kant should be honored as the first to grant the Dialectic its due for conceiving the antinomies of reason as abstract forms of understanding naturally veering around to their opposites. But Kant had failed to use the Dialectic to get at the real, the living, the true *Ding-an-sich,* because his external abstractions were merely those of Understanding, which reified the finite and denied the vitality of reality, the Dialectic of change present in all things. Hegel's conception instead recognized the identity between life and thought. "Life, as life, involves the germ of death . . . and the finite, being at war within itself, causes its own dissolution." [8] And as the finite Understanding was dissolved into the infinite Dialectic, the third stage of thought was reached by uniting the first two in Speculative or Positive Reason. Speculative Reason *thinks* rational things, absorbing the oppositions between subject and object, substance and attribute, which mere Understanding cannot conceive. By apprehending the unity of all categories in their opposition, Speculative Reason is also concretely universal: an abstraction of thought that is not abstract.

Hegel related these stages of thought to the three parts of logic:

Being (*Sein*)—quantity/abstract principle/in its immediacy/notion in germ.
Essence (*Wesen*)—cause and effect/substance and attribute/in its reflection/the being for self.
Notion (*Begriff*)—syllogism/interpenetration of thought and subjectivity/in its return into itself/its being all to itself.

The correspondence was demonstrated by the nature of causality. Instead of simple a priori and a posteriori states of necessity, cause and effect were action and reaction, so that the causing substance and the effect were united by a single process of reciprocal causality, the one cause "losing itself so far as it is substance in its effect, and in this action as a cause first rendering itself complete." [9] Through such unification, necessity (the linking of substance to effect) was transformed into freedom (both now being elements of one and the same); for—remember—the logic of thought was to Hegel an objective universal. And this logical reunion of elements as *Begriff* was itself the third stage of Speculative Reason where essence reverted to the simple immediacy of being, liberating the actual which now possessed itself *as its own free being and creation in the other actuality with which it was once bound up by necessity.* "As existing in the individual form, this liberation is called I; as developed to its totality, it is free Mind; as feeling, it is Love; and as enjoyment, it is Happiness." [10]

Kant's *Critiques* had solved rationalism's dilemma by setting aside unknowable things-in-themselves in order to construct a connected and objective order of sensations on the assumption that there was logic to the process of cognition. To discover that order, Kant created a new synthetic logic, different from the formal analytic sort in that it could arrange the understanding of appearances. Hegel used that same critical philosophy to connect mind and world by refusing to accept Kant's agnoiology of the *Ding-an-sich*. In one sense, then, Hegel set out to employ the logic of "transcendental" synthesis (which put the world together, instead of analyzing it apart in the Aristotelian manner) in order to overcome the ontological distance which Kant had placed between mind and thing-in-itself. But because Hegel's logical idealism rejected the unknowability of the *Ding-an-sich,* neither could he accept the "identity philosophies" of Schelling and other romantics who conceived of Nature and Mind as co-attributes of the Absolute. Hegel instead tried to show that Mind and Nature *are* the Absolute: the entire universal can be penetrated by thought which integrates both in the proceeding self-revelation of Idea. The real is rational, and the rational is real.

Pure insight, therefore, is the simple ultimate being undifferentiated within itself, and at the same time the universal achievement and result and a universal possession of all. . . . This pure insight is, then, the spirit that calls to every consciousness: be *for* yourselves what you are all essentially *in* yourselves—rational.[11]

In short, Hegel's logical idealism sought to make Kant's synthetic logic —a theory of thought—into a theory of actual being. Fichte's use of the Dialectic suggested that logic was an abstraction of the actual process by which absolute spirit revealed itself as the cosmos. Hegel made that Dialectic mind-in-itself (categories as ultimate realities, not forms of thought), mind-for-itself (nature as the self-externalization of mind), and mind-in-and-for-itself: *Sein, Wesen, Begriff.* And, capping it all, he identified each of these thought systems with an historical stage in the development of Idea.

In the history of philosophy the different stages of the logical Idea assume the shape of successive systems, each of which is based on a particular definition of the Absolute. As the logical Idea is seen to unfold itself in a process from the abstract to the concrete, so in the history of philosophy the earliest systems are the most abstract, and thus at the same time have least in them. . . . Now, although it may be upon the whole admitted that every philosophy has been refuted, it must be in an equal degree maintained, that no philosophy has been refuted, nay, or can be refuted. And that in two ways. For firstly, every philosophy that deserves the name, always has the Idea for its subject matter or contents: and secondly, every system should represent to us one particular factor or particular stage in the evolution of the Idea. The refutation of a philosophy, therefore, only means that its limits are passed, and that the fixed principle in it has been reduced to an organic element in the completer principle that follows. Thus the history of philosophy, in its true meaning, deals not with the past, but with the eternal and veritable present: and, in its results, resembles not a museum of the aberrations of the human intellect, but a Pantheon of godlike figures. These figures of gods are the various stages of the Idea, as they come forward one after another in dialectical development.[12]

Consequently, Fichte's formal rule of logic was envisaged as an essential law of thought ("that by means of which the Concept forges ahead is the above-mentioned Negative which it carries within itself"[13]), of Idea, and hence of life itself. The Universe was process; and the movement of Idea, the self-unfolding of the Absolute. The a priori categories of Kant (who did not regard them as constituents of reality except in conjunction with experience) were made by Hegel a noncontingent system of their own. "Is" was "becoming"; philosophy was history.

Although Hegel's Idea overcame the post-Enlightenment separation between subject and object,* there was after his death a general materialist reaction to the doctrine of idealism. A series of scientific discoveries created profound doubts over the philosophy of mind. In 1832, the year after Hegel died, Justus von Liebig (1803–1873) and Friedrich Wöhler (1800–1882) showed in a famous discursis on benzaldehyde that the radicle benzoyl might be the unchanging material constituent of an entire series of other compounds; and Liebig later suggested that human functions were merely physiological by teaching that the spark of life—body heat—was no more than the product of combustion and oxidation.[14] Four years after Liebig's almond oil paper, Theodor Schwann (1810–1822) paved the way for Louis Pasteur (1822–1895) and

---

* As the Marxist philosopher, Lucien Goldmann, has put it: "To the *ego* of Montaigne and Descartes, Pascal responds, 'The I is odious,' and from Hegel to Marx, 'other' men become more and more, not beings which I see and understand, but beings *with whom I act in common*. They are no longer *on the object side* but *on the subject side* of knowledge and action. The 'We' thus becomes the fundamental reality with respect to which the 'I' is subsequent and derivative." Lucien Goldmann, *The Human Sciences and Philosophy*, trans. Hayden White and Robert Anchor (London: Jonathan Cape, 1969), p. 28.

Joseph Lister (1827–1912) by disproving the theory of spontaneous generation before a conference of scientists at Jena. His discoveries of the influence of organisms and fungi on fermentation and putrefaction were followed in 1839 by microscopic investigations that established the source of animal and vegetable tissues in identical cells.[15] And, eight years after that, Hermann von Helmholtz (1821–1894) pioneered the theory of the conservation of energy.[16] As spirit was called into question, scientific philosophers hearkened back to the sensationalists of eighteenth-century France. In fact, men like Jacob Moleschott (1822–1893) and Karl Vogt (1817–1895) were no more than echoing Pierre Jean Cabanis (1757–1808) when they insisted that the brain produces thought just as the liver produces bile: a cutting rejection of vitalism.[17]

Nevertheless, Mind and Will were far from defunct. Friedrich von Schelling's (1775–1854) almost poetic conviction that "will is primal being" (*Wollen ist Ursein*) was recovered in Arthur Schopenhauer's (1788–1860) apprehension of the "immediate knowledge" that below the level of rational motivation we are still conscious of our will. But for him, as for other voluntaristic idealists like Karl Robert von Hartmann (1842–1906) logic increasingly gave way to emotion. As Nietzsche (1844–1900) denied the very possibility of knowledge altogether and substituted for it the will to power, the *Ding-an-sich* continued to haunt philosophers impatient with its resistance to modern science's increasingly evident powers of investigation. Some thinkers, like Auguste Comte (1798–1857), could gladly accept the limitation of knowledge to directly observed phenomena, and could build a positivist science of culture on that base. Others, like the chemist George Henry Lewes (1817–1878), elected to leave metemperics (what we would call metascience) to the logicians and develop an ascertainable metaphysics. Arguing from the analogy of the formation of chemical compounds, Lewes' *Problems of Life and Mind* (1875) pleaded for a new metaphysical category of "emergence." Because chemists could not foretell the nature of an emergent from the structures of the constituents themselves, why should philosophers puzzle over the reason for (instead of the logic of) ontological structures? "The quest of rational research is *the ascertainable order of dependence* in phenomena, and not the futile *why* of this order. We know the causes when we have ascertained the laws." [18] Since ultimate causes cannot be known,[19] we should at least realize that "the existence of an unknown quantity does not necessarily disturb the accuracy of calculations founded on the known functions of that quantity." [20] This "scientific canon" of excluding from calculation all incalculable data would place "Metaphysics on the same level with Physics," [21] and enable philosophers to distinguish between "a rational and an irrational Ontology, an empirical and a metemperical Metaphysics." [22]

Lewes' plea to accept the unknowability of final causes was one abutment of scientism and anti-Hegelian rationalism. Another strain, starting with Helmholtz, went directly back to Kant by trying to prove that the transcendental noumena of synthetic logic were consistent with physiological evidence. Helmholtz began with a doctrine of the "specific energy of sense organs" formulated by his (as well as Theodor Schwann's) scientific mentor, Johannes P. Müller (1801–1858). Müller's psychological researches seemed to prove that an organ's constitution, not outer stimuli, determined sensations: "Light is only light when it falls on the seeing eye." Helmholtz's own experiments convinced him that perception was indeed nativistic, that is, that sensations were only signals to the consciousness of the existence of changes in the external world, but not direct images of those changes. Repelled by Hegelianism,* he used this scientific evidence to substantiate Kant's theory of the unity of perception in a famous memorial lecture given at Königsberg on February 27, 1855. As Helmholtz's biographer paraphrased the lecture, Helmholtz declared that:

Since we never can perceive the objects of the external world directly, but only from their action upon our nervous mechanism, the question obviously presents itself, how in the first instance we ever got into touch with the real world by means of our nervous sensations? We must postulate the presence of external objects as the cause of our nervous excitation, since there can be no effect without a cause: but this dictum can be no law of experience,— we already need it for the knowledge that there are any objects at all in the space around us. Yet it cannot come from the internal experience of our self-consciousness, since we regard the self-conscious acts of our will as free. Hence we must fall back on Kant's conclusion that all our thoughts and acts, the greatest as the least, are founded on our confidence in the unalterable uniformity of nature, and that the axiom, "no effect without a cause," is a law of our thought prior to all experience. [23]

* Helmholtz attacked "the philosophical vaporing and consequent hysteria of the 'nature-systems' of Hegel and Schelling" in a letter to his father dated December 31, 1857. He wrote then that he felt it "a favorable moment for voices of the old school of Kant and the elder Fichte to obtain a hearing once more." Leon Königsberger, *Hermann von Helmholtz*, trans. Frances A. Welby (Oxford: Clarendon Press, 1906), p. 159.

Helmholtz thus found himself arguing for the existence of mechanical laws governing the material world, and so confirming the metaphysics of Hermann Lotze (1817–1881), whose works were becoming very influential at this time.* Like Helmholtz, Lotze could not accept Hegel's belief that one category of self-consciousness begat another. Arguing that Being does not necessarily imply non-Being, Lotze declared that there had to be some moment of contingency in order to provide the kind of unity Hegel had constructed in the historical development of spirit. By examining the nature of perception we can tell that the world we know is only a representation of a universe of causes which act upon the soul to organize unities of sensations that form the objects of our experience. Those objects are themselves representations of real external objects acting upon the body. Thus, in the end a transcendental unity of apperception permits the mind its unity in the totality of experience which it creates through logic.[24]

However, Helmholtz's confidence in Lotze and Kant was shaken as soon as he began his brilliant study of the physiological basis of musical harmony. After defining the physiology of consonance and dissonance as continuous and discontinuous sensations of tone, he completed *Die Lehre von den Tonempfindungen, als physiologische Grundlage für die Theorie der Musik* (On the Sensations of Tone, as a Physiological Basis for the Theory of Music) in 1862. Besides explaining more about the physiological modes of auditory perception, Helmholtz's book showed that the history of music proved that scales and the harmonies of modes were determined at least in part according to aesthetic principles which changed as mankind developed. Furthermore, the law which governed melody was established by musical overtones. Although these overtones were not consciously perceived by the nerves, their consonance and dissonance were felt. Thus the octave occupied such a fundamental position in harmony because it contained more partial tones than, say, the fifth in its overtones.

Helmholtz thus had to abandon Johannes Müller's nativism for an empiricist theory of perception. Sensations were no more than signs for external things whose significance must be learned as we interpret by experience. Cognition (*das Kennen*) simply combined conceptual sensory impressions which could not be expressed in words. And if Müller was wrong—decided Helmholtz—then so was Kant. There was no

---

* Lotze's *Allgemeine Pathologie und Therapie als mechanische Naturwissenschaften* was published in 1842, and his *Medizinische Psychologie oder Physiologie der Seele* in 1852.

special intuitive sense, no innate a priori idea, no realm of transcendental categories. "It is only the relation of time, space, equality, and those derived from them, namely those of number, magnitude, and conformity, in brief mathematical relations, which are common to both the outer and the inner world, and in these we can actually strive for complete correspondence of the percepts with the things perceived." [25]

With Kant's categories so drastically reduced, Neo-Kantians took what scientific empiricists conceded to them—mathematical principles —and tried to use Leibnizian and Newtonian calculus to demonstrate that knowledge could be built up from infinitely small constituents. But where were ethics to be found in that sort of exercise? How might one relate value to being so as to recreate the categorical imperatives of Kant? In 1882 Wilhelm Windelband (1848–1915) answered that the physical laws (*Naturgesetze*) of "is" (*sein*) should be separated from the norms of "ought" (*sollen*). We know there are such norms, said Windelband, because man could never feel that he was acting freely unless he felt accountable for his acts. The feeling of accountability was expressed by *sollen,* which was the mandatory command of man's moral, logical, and aesthetic consciences.

Windelband's norms were a way of conceiving of principles of value without constructing seemingly idealist categories of practical reason. To the same end Windelband's pupil, Heinrich Rickert (1863–1936), distinguished between being and meaning; the former constituted the realm of natural science, and the latter was confined to the sphere of cultural science. Rickert thought to find an independent basis for meaning in the existential sense that to know something is to appreciate it (*Kennen ist Erkennen*). He thus transformed validity or truth into a value so that *sollen* was the transcendental necessity of positively affirming our perceptions: we "ought" to acknowledge the truth of an analytic statement like "the grass is green." The instant judgment is made, we feel an immediate sense of affirmation which shows what science can neither demonstrate nor refute—that there are ethical and aesthetical values.[26]

But Windelband and Rickert kept facts and values separate. Making knowledge a science of values, they influenced others among Kant's *Epigonen* to turn more and more toward a positivistic science of culture.[27] For, in spite of their efforts to repair the breach between reason and transcendence, norms were more open to exploration than laws. And once the gulf between is and ought had widened this far, *sollen* itself seemed to lose its necessity almost immediately, so that the entire defense of knowledge as a science of values was jeopardized. It was Georg Simmel (1858–1918), the great sociologist, who attacked it most tellingly in 1892 by pointing out the simple truth that ought was just a formal mode of thought, a grammatical imperative like past and future tense. Because *sollen* was no transcendental imperative, science could not determine values.

Georg Simmel's disposition of values inspired Max Weber (1864–1920)—who declared himself in the line of Windelband and Rickert—to write his famous essay on " 'Objectivity' of Knowledge in Social Science and Social Policy" (1904). Weber questioned Simmel's argument that scientific criticism should be suspended in the presence of value judgments. Critical analysis could at least expose the appropriateness of means for a given end, and thereby indirectly judge the end itself. Or by causally examining the consequences of an act, science might ask what the cost in the predictable loss of other values would be if the desired end were attained. The final value decision could not be made by science; it would depend on one's own conscience. But though "an empirical science cannot tell anyone what he *ought* to do," it can tell him "what he *can* do, and under certain circumstances what he wishes to do." [28]

While one wing of Neo-Kantianism inclined toward the historical pluralism of Weberian sociology, replacing ideology with the ideal type, other Kantian idealists tried to maintain the vitalistic union of scientific value and transcendental being. Although we cannot really speak of a school as such, the would-be founder of this group was Gustav Theodor Fechner (1801–1887). Like Lotze, his student, Fechner tried to prove the reality of both matter and mind without either acquiescing in the unknowability of the *Ding-an-sich* or denying scientific theories of perception. In 1860 his *Die Elemente der Psychophysik* introduced the new science of "psychophysics" to measure the relationship between sensations and stimuli. His inspiration was the work of E. H. Weber (1795–1878), the physiologist who discovered that intensities of sensation bore a ratio to the magnitude of the stimulus.[29] Fechner's refined formulation was stated as a law of psychophysics: the magnitude of a stimulus must be increased geometrically if the magnitude of sensation is to increase arithmetically. Fechner's Law was to profoundly influence the development of experimental psychology in later years. At the time, Fechner himself used it to engage in metaphysics. Indeed, psychophysics was a substitute for metaphysics: "an exact theory of the functionally dependent relations of body and soul, or, more generally of the material and the mental, of the physical and psychological worlds." [30] Denying that he was either an empiricist or an idealist, Fechner believed that he had created a new form of knowledge, founded on the assumption that the elementary laws of the relationship between mind and body could be scientifically studied even though no one could ever observe the two simultaneously.* Matter and mind were but outer and inner facets of the same psychophysical entities. There is only one world, Fechner declared. The universe is an assemblage of souls joined in purposive drives.

The man most closely associated by his contemporaries with Fechner's panpsychism was Friedrich Paulsen (1846–1908), professor of moral philosophy at the University of Berlin after 1896. Although Paulsen was frequently labeled a panpsychist, he himself denied discipleship.

I have often been counted among Fechner's followers and disciples. It can give me nothing but pleasure to see my name associated with this excellent and venerable man; but I am bound to state the fact that the development of my own views has been influenced by him only to a very slight degree. I did not make the acquaintance of his books until much later, when my convictions concerning all essential problems had already assumed definitive shape; in the seventies and eighties Fechner was little known and generally misjudged as an author. Among the philosophers who exercised a decisive influence on my own thought in its formative period Lotze occupies a much more significant position. . . . As to Fechner, I regretfully count it among the numerous missed opportunities of my life that I never tried to get in touch with him either by correspondence or in the form of personal intercourse.[31]

Along with Lotze, Kant's writings also naturally had a great influence on Paulsen's philosophy. After Paulsen finished his military service in 1873, he began rereading works of Kant which he had routinely studied in school.

---

* Fechner's psychophysical researches involved him in experiments of the same kind as Helmholtz's work on acoustics. For Fechner, however, harmony represented a higher relation of psychic and physiological states. "Indeed, I feel that the experience of harmony and melody, which undoubtedly have a higher character than single tones, is based on the ratios of the vibrations that themselves underlie the separate sensations, and that these ratios can change only in exact relationship to the manner in which the single tones are sounded together or follow one another. Thus, harmony and melody suggest to me only a higher relation, and not one lacking a special relationship of dependency between the higher mental sphere and its physical basis." Gustav Fechner, *Elements of Psychophysics,* trans. Helmut Adler (New York: Holt, Rinehart and Winston, 1966), 1:13. Fechner wrote to his friend, Helmholtz, in 1869 disagreeing with the latter's theory of overtones. See Königsberger, *Hermann von Helmholtz,* pp. 226–228.

And now at last my mind was opened to the meaning of Kant's philosophy. I saw how the German philosopher, setting out from Wolff's metaphysics, gradually approached the standpoint of Hume; in his writings published during the sixties one can follow this movement step by step. And then I saw him changing front, as if with a sudden jolt, in the dissertation of 1770. It seems as if he had suddenly seen an abyss yawning in front of him—the abyss of skepticism—and had started back and clutched at the position that the a priori elements of perceiving (space and time) and of reasoning (the categories) put us in reach of a priori knowledge: the former of the *mundus sensibilis,* and the latter of the *mundus intelligibilis.* And that remained the permanent font of Kant's philosophy: the rescue of knowledge founded on pure reason—or in other words: the rescue of philosophy as a priori knowledge—from David Hume's all-devouring skepticism. Then, as I read the *Critique of Pure Reason,* the scales fell from my eyes. It was quite plain: what Kant really wanted to prove was not that "the things-in-themselves are unknowable," as I had hitherto imagined with the result that his whole argumentation seemed curiously distorted, but rather that "pure" knowledge (that is, knowledge based on pure reason) is possible, and that this provides a foundation for "pure" morality, and in the last resort for a *Weltanschauung* or general philosophy based on pure reason.[32]

Consequently, Paulsen's *Einleitung in die Philosophie* (1892) began with Kant's hypothesis that we are only conscious of mental states. But Paulsen quickly proceeded to contradict Kant by affirming that this consciousness *does* constitute a knowledge of the *Ding-an-sich,* because the latter is the soul as practical reality, known by its will. To qualify as a thing-in-itself, the will therefore had to be redefined. Instead of conceiving of it—as Kant or Fichte had—in terms of rational desire, Paulsen denied that the will was conscious intelligence. But neither could it be unconscious and irrational desires. Instead, it was an instinct to live: *Zielstrebigkeit,* purposive impulse, theology without design.*

By the early years of the twentieth century, Friedrich Paulsen had attained some stature in German pedagogy. His emphasis on the will and on the ethical fiber of education accorded with the new German state's conscious rise to international prominence. Some even accused Paulsen of having written his widely-read history of higher education

---

* According to Paulsen, the will did have its own ends, but it could not reason about means. See Friedrich Paulsen, *Introduction to Philosophy,* trans. Frank Thilly (New York: Henry Holt and Company, 1906), p. 218. Paulsen took the term, *Zielstrebigkeit,* from K. E. von Baer's *Studien aus dem Gebiet der Naturwissenschaften* (1876), which attacked the "teleophobia" of modern natural science and sought to demonstrate the inevitability of a teleological view of the organic world.

to satisfy both Bismarck and the Center Party, for which the Prussian Education Act of 1902 was partly an appeasment by von Bülow.[33] Besides being an historian of education, Paulsen was well known as the author of the *System der Ethik*. The aim of this book, Paulsen said, was to make of ethics an analytically constructed system, the necessity of which would be determined by its causal connections.

It seems to me to be an indisputable fact that ethics resembles the natural sciences, rather than mathematics, in its method. It does not deduce and demonstrate propositions from concepts, but discovers the relations which exist between facts, and which may be established by experience. . . . The correctness of the rule is proved by the causal connection; and causal connections are ascertained by experience alone.[34]

It is easy to estimate the effect of such a statement on the many Chinese students then enrolled in German universities. If ethics were determined by the inductive study of experience, then "irrational" cultural sanctions like Confucian virtues did not deserve the same label. One such student, Ts'ai Yuan-p'ei (then pursuing psychology and aesthetics at Leipzig), was interested enough by Paulsen's book to wish to translate it into Chinese. The translation appeared in print in China in 1913 under the title *Lun-li-hsueh yuan-li* (characteristically, *yuan-li* is better translated as "origins" than as "system"), and was widely read by intellectuals. Impressed by Paulsen's theories, Yang Ch'ang-chi even assigned the text to his pupils. Mao Tse-tung read it avidly.

PART FOUR

Necessity

For the purpose of attaining freedom in society, man must use social science to understand and change society and carry out social revolution. For the purpose of attaining freedom in the world of nature, man must use natural science to understand, conquer, and change nature and then attain freedom from nature.

Mao Tse-tung, "Speech at the Inaugural Meeting of the Natural Science Research Society of the Border Region" (February 5, 1940).

14

Socialism

The copy of Paulsen's *System der Ethik* which Mao Tse-tung read at the First Normal School contains 12,100 characters of Mao's personal comments.* Scholars who have considered the question of influence have attributed some of Mao's voluntarism to the inspiration of Paulsen, since the *System* frequently exalts individual will.[1]

The nature of the highest good is in reality not determined by the intellect, but by the will. The individual has an idea of the conduct of his individual life, a life-ideal, the realization of which he feels to be his true function as well as the highest goal of his desires. It is really not the intellect from which this idea springs, although it appears in the form of an idea; its excellence cannot be proved to the reason; it is nothing but the reflection of the innermost essence and the will of the individual himself in ideation. If other individuals have different ideals, I cannot prove to them the inadequacy of their ideals either by logical demonstrations or by empirical causal investigations. I may, perhaps, make them feel the value of my idea by the mere revelation and description of it; indeed, I may convince them that mine has greater value than theirs, and thus win them over to mine. Nevertheless, it is not the understanding, but the will which impels them to decide in its

* *System* was the textbook which Yang Ch'ang-chi assigned during Mao's last two years at the school. Mao's own copy was kept by a classmate and later perused by Li Jui. The marginal notes were so copious and tiny that it often required a magnifying glass to read them. Especially annotated were chapters 4, 5, and 6. Many of the marginal comments referred to Chinese historical incidents or such figures as Mo-tzu, Mencius, T'an Ssu-t'ung, and Wang Fu-chih. In many instances Mao simply noted his assent or dissent with specific statements; for example, "I do not feel that this theory is after all entirely satisfactory." See Li Jui, *Mao Tse-tung* (Peking: Chung-kuo ch'ing-nien ch'u-pan she, 1957), p. 47.

favor. The intellect as such knows absolutely nothing of values, it distinguishes between the true and the false, the real and the unreal, but not between the good and the bad.[2]

What Paulsen offered Mao Tse-tung was a rational justification for placing the will over the intellect. Since the turn of the century, Chinese students had been searching for a positive expression of their negative conviction that traditional society had doomed the nation. They were unfettered by the passion of Tsou Jung's (1885–1905) *Revolutionary Army,* Chang Chi's (1882–1947) anarchism, Wang Ching-wei's (1883–1944) populist terrorism. But these were less intellectual redefinitions than passionate convictions, destructive yearnings. With Paulsen the intellect itself was systematically—and, of course, intellectually—demeaned. His explanation seemed to prove that social relations (the regulation of which had been a Confucian calling since Chou times) were neither decided by the intellect nor a meek acceptance of existing social forces; rather they were determined by the force of the individual will. As sheer ego was liberated in this manner, Mao discovered the self—still of, but not determined by, nature. As he wrote in the margin of *System der Ethik:* "Although we are determined by nature, we are also a part of nature. Hence, if nature has the power to determine us, we also have the power to determine nature." [3] The self had stood at the center of orthodox Confucian philosophy. Yet its cultivation was its taming, its domestication, and, metaphysically, the task of bringing it into accord with nature. Even Wang Fu-chih's vitalism, which partly denied Chu Hsi's ontology, rested on the sage's knowledge of cosmic determination.

The *ch'ien's* knowing with ease is just its vigor [*ch'ien,* which can also mean constancy]. The *k'un's* being capable with simplicity is just its according [*shun,* which can also mean to yield]. If there is vigor, then it can be enlarged. If there is according, then it can be prolonged. If it can be enlarged, then it is the worthy man's virtue. If it can be prolonged, then it is the worthy man's venture. Prolonging and enlarging are [the result of] the worthy man's exerting his vigor and accord. Ease and simplicity are the Tao of Heaven and Earth; they are not in man's capacity. To know to the very extreme is to exert man's Tao. To know to the very utmost is to accord with and wait upon Heaven.[4]

But out of Paulsen came the notion that the self was will, strengthened by resisting rather than accepting nature. Beside one section of the *System* which defined culture as human resistance, Mao commented:

"The river issues from T'ung-kuan [that is, the passes separating Shensi from the Central Plain]. Because there is the resistance of Mount T'ai-hua, the river's strength increases its current." [5] Force was enhanced by its opposition; effort was determined by its challenge.

The Neo-Confucian self was looked *into* as a receptacle of cosmic spirit, cultivated from without. But with this twentieth-century liberation of the individual will, the nurturing of the self was from within, while Mao's spiritual expansion was directed outward. "I must myself [wrote Mao] completely develop the capacity of my own body and spirit. Worshipping the spirit, how can one not worship the self since the self is spirit. Outside of this what other spirit is there?" [6] The spirit's receptacle, the body, was cultivated as the machine of the will. Or, as Paulsen quoted Emerson: "The first requisite of a gentleman is *to be a good* animal." [7] Paulsen's *System* thus devoted an entire chapter to hygiene, physical training, and "the bodily life," attacking customs which deprecated manual labor and repeatedly stressing the importance of physical training for the survival of the species. To illustrate this natural struggle, Paulsen cited Sir John Lubbock's study of insects: "A species of ants which were once warlike and vigorous conquered and made slaves of another species. They became so accustomed to be waited upon that they were finally absolutely unable to help themselves; they could not even feed themselves, the slaves pushing the food into the masters' mouths. . . . Does this not sound like a satirical fable on good society?" [8] Fortunately, said Paulsen, "with the rise of the military spirit among the Prussian people," Germany was overcoming this danger. *Turnen*—gymnastic exercises—had been in vogue since the turn of the century.[9] The German species would certainly survive.

The struggle for survival was not unfamiliar to Mao Tse-tung. The analogy to ants had even been used by Wang Fu-chih in his famous tract, the *Huang shu* (Yellow Book), which argued for the separate preservation of each race. "Now, even ants have a ruler who leads their anthills. Were other [insects like] the red *pi* and flying *wei* to encroach upon his gates, then [the ruling ant] would have to assemble his race (*tsu*) to bite and kill them, driving them far from his mound so that there would be no more conflict between mixed [species]. Hence, whoever would lead the ants must be able to protect them." [10] But Wang's text had only tried to spell out the responsibilities of a ruler to his people. It had not, like Paulsen's book, provided Mao with the notion that a social organism survived by according with historical stages of growth. Preservation, in short, was a matter of adaptation. As Mao marginally

noted in Paulsen: "Tradition can stifle what is new; the old can over-
whelm what is new. When this happens, man will lose his ability to
adapt himself to a new age and in the end this organic body in history
will perish. China is now in such a state." [11] For, as Mao wrote in "On
Physical Education," it was crucial that the individual recognize the
outer laws governing the self. By sharpening the physical senses, one
could better observe the outside world, which was mastered by "har-
monizing your emotions" with it.[12] Therefore, Mao's reading of Paulsen
both enhanced his awareness of the social character of those external
laws and replaced harmony with a theory of mutual resistance. The self
might still be in accord with the natural principles of an assertive, striving cosmos, but the individual was bound to resist social realities like
capitalism—a system which Mao mentioned for the first time in his
Paulsen notes. "We must develop our physical and mental capacities to
the fullest extent. . . . Wherever there is repression of the individual,
wherever there are acts contrary to the nature of the individual, there
can be no greater crime. That is why our country's three bonds (san-
kang) must go, and constitute, with religion, capitalists, and autocracy
the four evil demons of the empire." [13] Paulsen's *System der Ethik*
categorized these social evils as mere customs (*Sitten*) or instincts:

[Moral philosophy] is confronted with a naturalistic, unscientific, traditional
morality. Just as bodily life was originally governed by instincts and blind
habits, without physiology, so the entire human life, especially social life,
was originally governed without science, by a kind of moral instinct. These
moral instincts of peoples are called *customs*. . . . Is the truth really incapable of proof, can moral philosophy do nothing but collect and arrange
these absolute commands and prohibitions? To say so is to deprive it of its
character as a science, for science does not consist in taking inventories, but
in the discovery and proof of truths.[14]

Thus it instilled a sense of confidence in humanity's ability to reorder
society. Nor—despite the primacy of individual will—was this merely
a matter of subjective choice. Moral law was "not the product of caprice, not the arbitrary command of a transcendent despot or of an
uncontrollable 'inner voice.' " [15] Morality was the expression "of an
immanent law of human life" which could be conceived (thought Paulsen) by Kantian synthesis. A society's proscription of falsehood, for
example, might only express the uniform behavior of its members. But
that would replace logic with consensus, making universal values relative and moral law a simple description of what is. On the contrary,

argued Paulsen, a moral law has to be universally valid, because society could not otherwise exist. There could be no culture based on false-hood, "not because falsehood *ought* not to be, but because it *cannot* be a universal mode of conduct. Falsehood can occur only as an exception. . . . The causal law forms the basis of the practical rule." [16]

Paulsen's confidence in the mind's ability to devise viable social principles relieved Mao Tse-tung of some of his fears that the destruction of tradition would undo society altogether. "In the past," Mao marginally noted, "I worried over the coming destruction of our country, but now I know that fear was unnecessary. I have no doubt that the political system, the characteristics of our people, and the society will change." [17] But, concerned as he was with both the discovery and invention of historical tendencies, Mao remained confused about "the ways in which the changes can be successfully brought about." [18] For, in this ideological phase, Mao was still confined to Liang's metaphor of destruction/construction.

I incline to believe that a reconstruction is needed. Let destruction play the role of a mother in giving birth to a new country. The great revolutions of other countries in the past centuries swept away the old and brought forth the new. They were the great changes which resurrected the dead and reconstructed the decayed.[19]

Furthermore, Mao's conceptualization of particular and universal relationships was indiscrete. In some ways it even resembled K'ang Yu-wei's prescientific vision of Taoist or Buddhist universal relativities, which—from a metaphysical point of view—created an identity of indiscernibilities.

I say: the concept is reality; the finite is the infinite; the temporal is the intemporal; imagination is thought; I am the universe; life is death; death is life; the present is the past and the future; the past and the future are the present; the small is the great; the yin is the yang; the high is the low; the impure is the pure; the thick is the thin; the substance is the words; that which is multiple is one; that which is changing is eternal.[20]

However, Mao differed from K'ang by virtue of acquiring the empiricist notion of actuality in his reading of the *System der Ethik*. When his marginal comments declared that "If the subjective and objective are both satisfied then we later call it good," or that "I must take practice of the greatest good as my duty," he was expressing the ontological impossibility of abstracting moral values from actuality.[21] "When I com-

ment critically on history saying that so-and-so is good and so-and-so
is bad, this indicates the actuality (*shih-shih*) of a person's good or bad.
Apart from actuality there is no good or evil. Therefore, to think of
preserving one's fame for a millennium is foolish. It is also foolish to
delight in others' preserving one's name." [22] This was an important, although still incomplete, departure from Yang Ch'ang-chi's teachings.
Yang had insisted upon the actual effectiveness of will, but he preserved
the notion of a transmittable pneuma as the personal imprint of a
chün-tzu upon history. Mao now was to replace the idea of a singular
individual bequeathing his reputation to mankind with the concept of
an individual's connection to actuality or events. The latter endured
along with the person, instead of name or person surviving alone. The
spirit of will was only an illusion.

The spirit and matter which together form my life are experience (*ching-
yen*) in the world. I must devote my strength to the actual. Such an action
[is] this objective arrangement of real events which have been exhaustively
executed. [Such] a thought [is] this subjective arrangement of real events
which have been exhaustively realized (*shih-hsien*). I am only obliged to
what is subjectively and objectively actual to myself. I am generally not
obliged to what is not my own objective and subjective actuality.[23]

There was no reality apart from objective actuality and subjective experience, because action and thought were both realized in real events.
Paulsen's theory of will therefore suggested that the union of these two
freed man from traditional social trammels, as well as enabling him to
transcend the division between subject and object. But that left two
important questions still unanswered. First, if the individual's action in
society must accord with universal laws of human progress, how are
these laws to be determined? And, second, if the subject was to be
realized in the object, how then could the self define society in such a
way as to struggle with—not against—it?

For Mao Tse-tung, the first question was partly answered in politically reactive terms. "When we began our revolution," he told members
of a work conference of the Party Center during the Cultural Revolution,
"we had contact not with Marxism–Leninism, but with opportunism.
When [I was] young, I had not even read the *Communist Manifesto*." [24]
In this formulation, at least, his revolutionary position in the class struggle enrolled him in the "school for brigands" mentioned earlier. "For
myself, I had all sorts of non-Marxist ideas before, and it was only later
that I embraced Marxism. I learned a little Marxism from books and

so made an initial remolding of my ideas, but it was mainly through taking part in the class struggle over the years that I came to be remolded. And I must continue to learn if I am to make further progress, or otherwise I shall lag behind." [25] But while action can precede ideology, the creation of political consciousness depends upon a true dialectic of theory and practice. Action cannot be thoughtless; the intention to revolt has to be given theoretical revolutionary form.

Mao Tse-tung learned the neologism, "socialism" (*she-hui chu-i*), before political engagement. During his military service in 1911, he became a devoted reader of the Ch'ang-sha daily, *Hsiang-chiang jih-pao* (Hsiang River Daily). "Socialism was discussed in it and in these columns I first learned the term. I also discussed socialism, really social reformism, with other students and soldiers. I read some pamphlets written by Chiang K'ang-hu about socialism and its principles." [26] Chiang K'ang-hu, who taught Chinese at the University of California at Berkeley from 1913 to 1920, was the first person who publicly avowed socialism in China. [27] Born in 1883 into a prestigious Kiangsi family and precociously literate in the classics, he became a Japanese-language student in the government Foreign Language Institute (*T'ung-wen hsueh-she*) at the age of fourteen. After studying in Japan, he returned to China as a protégé of the governor-general of Chihli, Yuan Shih-k'ai (1860–1916), who made him the chief compiler of the Pei-yang editorial bureau. Chiang was soon appointed a Japanese-language teacher at the imperial university (later renamed Peking University) in the capital. During his tenure there he also founded several women's normal schools. Indeed, feminism occupied a central position in the theory of socialism which Chiang developed after traveling to Japan again in 1907. After meeting socialists like Kōtoku Shūsui (1871–1911), Katayama Sen (1860–1933), and Sakai Toshihiko (1870–1933), Chiang began to study Henry George's writings. A visit to Europe in 1909–1910, when he attended the Brussels Congress of the Second International as an unofficial Chinese representative, put him in touch with the Parisian anarchist circle led by Wu Chih-hui (1867–1953), who edited *Hsin Shih-chi* (*Siècle nouveau*). In fact, it was that journal which published Chiang's first two articles on radical social theory under the nom de plume of Hsu An-ch'eng. The first, on "Non-familism," likened family life to serving a prison sentence. Marriage—it asserted—was not a sacred institution but rather a simple social custom designed to domesticate man's animal sexuality. [28] The second piece attempted, like so many writings of the time, to reconcile self-assertion with social harmony. To Chiang, the phrase "from each according to his abilities, to each according to his needs" conflicted with his assumption that man's natural drives were a love of luxury and a desire for self-aggrandizement. He argued, therefore, that one must begin by recognizing human competitiveness and then go on to design social institutions based on free enterprise. His own device was educational. Each citizen should be educated at public expense until he was prepared to assume his place in the social struggle by earning a livelihood. The individual would then amass as much wealth as his personal ambition dictated. Society need not artificially inhibit its fitter citizens, because when they died their wealth would be confiscated by the state to educate the next generation.* Public education had the additional benefit of weakening the traditional family by removing the child's dependence upon his parents' financial support. For, like Yang Ch'ang-chi, Chiang K'ang-hu believed that the family system inhibited individual initiative. What he added to the attack on primary social units was Great Harmony utopianism.

Before a person has attained adulthood, he receives the benevolent attention of society (*kung-kung she-hui*); then, when he dies, he returns what he has acquired in order to repay [that benevolence]. Consequently, he does not alone love his relatives, nor alone father his own son. This is not far from what is called the *Ta-t'ung* (Great Harmony) . . . and it fits extremely well with the principle of survival of the fittest [literally, competitive evolution].[29]

Chiang elaborated the connection between social welfare and antifamilism in another essay written that summer which singled out three causes for humanity's tragic condition: political oppression, religious enslavement, and familial tyranny. The last was undoubtedly the most fundamental, especially insofar as the institution of inheritance perpetuated unearned social inequalities. That is, financial inequality was tol-

---

* Because there are indications in Chiang's first article (which purported to be sent in by an anonymous writer who was simply passing on the words of the recently deceased Mr. Hsu) that he had been, or was, in London around this time, one wonders whether or not this theory of state confiscation of bequeathed property was influenced by contemporary English politics. Lloyd George's death-duties budget was announced on April 29, 1909—sixteen days before Chiang's second article appeared. To be sure, death-duties did not figure as prominently as the surcharge on the unearned incremental value of property, which certainly did suggest Henry George's influence. The deviser of the budget, Philip Snowden, was of course a socialist.

erable (because natural) as long as it resulted from an individual's own effort. But if one possessed property thanks to parental effort, then the system was obviously unfair. Furthermore, the family itself was the social base of political oppression and religious enslavement. Destruction of the foundation would also remove those other two causes of unhappiness, allowing complete human self-realization along with the opportunity for increased economic productivity.* Consequently, anyone in search of liberty and equality "must first destroy (*p'o*) the family." [30]

"Hsü An-ch'eng" had closed his second article with an appeal for a great convocation to discuss the implementation of nonfamilism. After returning to China in order—ironically—to observe the conventional mourning period for his father's death, Chiang K'ang-hu seized the opportunity for such a public forum. Asked to deliver a public lecture in Hangchow on June 1, 1911, Chiang employed the occasion to explain the meaning of socialism—a doctrine never before publicly discussed in China. Although the word socialism (*she-hui chu-i*), explained Chiang, was borrowed from Japanese, the concept was culturally universal, since the broad goal of socialism "was simply the demand that mankind share happiness and good fortune by overcoming the discrepancies of economic inequality." [31] Thus, there were as many different political forms (constitutionalism, republicanism, anarchism, and so on) of socialism as there were means (mass education, political fiat, revolutionary terrorism) to realize it. Chiang's speech, which was given before the fall of the Ch'ing, stressed the compatibility of socialism and constitutional monarchy. "Let us reflect that a decade ago under autocracy, the bulk of the population was shocked at what they considered to be the strange notions of those advocating the establishment of a constitution, and that now it is not only discussed in every town and village; it is actually being implemented by the dynasty. We shall see the same phenomenon a decade hence with socialism." [32] Education was therefore to be the gradual means of transition to socialism. At this point, in fact, education stood *for* socialism, because it liberated the

---

* Economic scholars of contemporary China have recently stressed the similarity between Maoism and capitalistic entrepreneurship: the encouragement of technological innovation, self-sacrifice for future reward, and so forth. There is certainly a capitalist bias in Marxian thought as such, but these early Chinese antecedents of modern Maoism suggest that the parallel between Samuel Smiles and the *Quotations* of Mao Tse-tung can be stretched back to the very earliest of Chinese socialists.

individual from familial ascription and created "socially uniform elements": sons became men, "chaste mothers and virtuous widows" became "worldly individuals" or citizens.*

As mild as it was, Chiang's speech aroused official displeasure. Had it not been for Chiang's bureaucratic connections, he would have been arrested and tried for heretical thinking. But, protected by friends in the government, he continued to lecture under the auspices of the Woman's Progressive Society (*Hsi-yin kung-hui*), addressing a group of four hundred in Shanghai on September 2, 1911. Although education was still the keynote, he now emphasized the differences between regular and socialist forms of education. Because the latter used public lectures, study groups, and mass media in place of the textbook or classroom, it opened education to all; the underprivileged could improve themselves without having to give up their normal occupations. Consequently, he believed the task at hand was to emulate the West by forming socialist education groups (*she-hui chiao-yü t'uan*).[33] Fifty members of Chiang's audience were enthused enough by his presentation to form such a group immediately, creating a nucleus from which the Chinese Socialist Party would emerge the following year. In the meantime, Chiang continued to publicize socialism in the pages of the *Socialist Star,* which he had founded on July 10, 1911, in a Shanghai hotel room. Declaring that "socialism is the most prevalent doctrine of the twentieth century and this magazine is the very first socialist one in China," its editor held no single and exclusive socialist doctrine. Rather, wrote Chiang, we must come to learn all forms and then select from among them those which suit us best. Research or study was the order of the day.[34]

And study it would be for Mao Tse-tung during the next six years. Of course, Mao's introduction to socialism by way of Chiang K'ang-hu was somewhat abortive. The intervening years, as we have seen, were devoted primarily to the study of Social Darwinism, classical Chinese philosophy, and German idealism. Not until 1917–1918 would Mao again be exposed to socialist theory. Then, however, political involvement would radically shape his reaction. The first crucial period of exposure seems to have fallen between September of 1918 and February

---

* The similarity between this idea of Chiang's and some of Yang Ch'ang-chi's theories hardly needs to be emphasized for the reader. During these early years of Mao Tse-tung's intellectual development, the transition from one influence to the next was both consistent and gradual, because the core ideas of individualism, liberation from familial tyranny, and realization of the self in the nation were shared by so many writers.

of 1919, when Mao worked as an assistant in the Peking University library. The job, which he owed to Yang Ch'ang-chi's influence, was quite menial. He did get to see future May Fourth luminaries like Fu Ssu-nien or Lo Chia-lun in the library's reading room, but they scarcely noticed him. Very much on his own, then, Mao began to explore radical social theory, developing a deep interest in anarchism.

My interest in politics continued to increase and my mind turned more and more radical. I have told you of the background for this but just now I was still confused, looking for a road, as we say. I read some pamphlets on anarchy and was much influenced by them. There was a student named Chu Hsun-pei who used to visit me. I often discussed anarchism and its possibilities in China. At that time I favored many of its proposals.[35]

From pamphlets Mao moved on to some of the works of Mikhail Bakunin (1814–1876) and Peter Kropotkin (1842–1921), and even contemplated founding his own anarchist group. At the same time he fell under the influence of his library director, Li Ta-chao (1889–1927), who did much in those years to popularize Marxism among Peking University intellectuals. Consequently, when Mao returned to Ch'ang-sha to teach in a primary school during the spring of 1919, he was able to give a public lecture on the nature of Marxism and the Russian Revolution.[36]

The May Fourth movement of 1919 swept up Mao along with every other young urban intellectual of the time. During that summer he even edited a journal of his own, the *Hsiang River Review* (*Hsiang-chiang p'ing-lun*), which published one of Mao's first important political essays, "The Great Union of the Popular Masses."[37] That particular essay clearly indicated, though, that Mao was still in a pre-Marxist and populist phase. Reformist education, destruction and construction, and industrialization were all brushed aside in favor of a single theme. China was so decadent that nothing less than totally fundamental change would suffice. The agent of that change was to be a great union of the popular masses. This union—truly a mystique for Mao—would succeed by the collective strength of numbers alone. "Why is the great union of the popular masses so terribly effective? Because the popular masses in any country are much more numerous than the aristocracy, the capitalists, and the other powerful people in a single country."[38] The class character of this alliance was quite imprecise. Many "small unions" of peasants, workers, students, and women would be organized around pre-Marxist (that is, evaluative rather than normative) issues: a landlord's treatment of peasants, the level of a worker's wages, and so forth.

Mao's populist essay accurately reflected the character of social ferment during the heady summer of 1919. Students were for the first time addressing urban workers at street-corner rallies; in many cities merchants cooperated fully with the most radical young intellectuals in the anti-Japanese boycott; a mass populist union seemed certain to awaken the nation and usher in a new age at last. Locally, this meant allying to oust the Hunanese warlord, Chang Ching-yao (who closed down the *Hsiang River Review* after "The Great Union of the Popular Masses" appeared). Mao became so deeply involved in petition campaigns and public demonstrations that he was selected by the provincial leaders of the movement to go to Peking during January of 1920 in search of national support. By his own account, this participation articulated his own revolutionary consciousness. "From this time on I became more and more convinced that only mass political power secured through mass action could guarantee the realization of dynamic reforms." [39]

This second visit to Peking also provided an occasion for Mao Tse-tung to learn more about Marxism.

During my second visit to Peking I had read much about the events in Russia, had eagerly sought out what little Communist literature was then available in Chinese. Three books especially deeply carved my mind and built up in me a faith in Marxism from which once I had accepted it as the correct interpretation of history I did not afterward waver. These books were the *Communist Manifesto* translated by Ch'en Wang-tao and the first Marxist book ever published in Chinese; *Class Struggle* by Kautsky; and the *History of Socialism* by Kirkup. By the summer of 1920 I had become in theory and to some extent in action a Marxist, and from this time on I considered myself a Marxist. [40]

One can easily imagine the impact which the *Communist Manifesto* must have had on Mao at the time. Its stirring and almost poetic combination of economic determinism and popular will not only made a necessity of revolution; the *Manifesto* provided a new way to conceive of past and present. "The history of all hitherto existing society is the history of class struggle." [41]

Class struggle, too, was the theme of Karl Kautsky's (1854–1938) book, which was slightly more familiar to Mao because it contained themes to which he had already grown accustomed. Like Liang Ch'i-ch'ao, for example, Kautsky identified modern capitalism with the accumulation of economic power by single trusts or syndicates. But unlike Liang, he did not believe that the destruction of preexisting economic forms (handicrafts production or small businesses) could be justified in terms of construction or progress. Since capitalism only existed thanks to the expropriation of small production, "a revolution as bloody as any in history," [42] Kautsky revealed a certain nostalgia for communal and precapitalist economic units. To be sure, Kautsky was insisting that capitalism, not socialism, expropriated the small farmers' property partly because he wished to gain their allegiance for the German Social Democratic movement. Furthermore, he took care to point out that he had no intention of reviving the communal past in a socialist future. But by repeatedly telling his readers that commodity production had destroyed cooperative forms of social life, he presented capitalism as the force which had destroyed both *Gemeinschaft* and the economic individuality of the producing household. This must have seemed novel to Mao, because so many of the writers he had read previously were opposed to economic individualism and the nuclear family. Kautsky, on the other hand, explained that during the precapitalist stage of history, production had been conducted within units like the family and had depended on one's personal qualities. Such individuality was sacrificed in the modern labor force. Socialism was not designed to destroy the family; the working conditions of capitalism already had done so. In fact, socialism would preserve the family unit by emancipating women from the "servitude of the house." Each individual would become "mistress of herself, the equal of man . . . [and] quickly put an end to all prostitution, legal as well as illegal. For the first time in history monogamy will become a real rather than a fictitious institution." [43] For, the essence of capitalism was dehumanization: the dissolution of independent and self-sufficient units into a proletarianized mass of toilers for whom individuality was impossible. Even intellectuals were no more than "educated proletarians."

Since those days the development of higher education has made immense progress. The number of institutions of learning has increased wonderfully, and in a still larger degree, the number of pupils. In the meantime, the bottom has been knocked out of small production. The small property holder knows today no other way of keeping his sons from sinking into the proletariat than sending them to college; and he does this if his means will at all allow.[44]

Once out of college, the intellectual faced the same kind of overstocked labor market as the manual worker, so that "the time is near when the bulk of these proletarians will be distinguished from the others only by their pretensions." [45]

Although Mao Tse-tung probably felt a sympathetic twinge when he read lines like those, the conclusions of Kautsky's Erfurt Program must have puzzled him. *Class Struggle*, unlike the *Manifesto*, did not call for revolution. In fact, the paradox of German Social Democracy was this combination of the notion of economically determined class struggle and political reformism. Kautsky did argue that the social reforms of the ruling classes were only designed to prevent revolution, and he did try to show his readers that despite the "irresistible and inevitable" trend of history, revolution would not take place by itself. But he also argued that such a revolution need not be quick or bloody.

Such a revolution may assume many forms, according to the circumstances under which it takes place. It is by no means necessary that it be accompanied with violence and bloodshed. There are instances in history when the ruling classes were either so exceptionally clear-sighted or so particularly weak and cowardly that they submitted to the inevitable and voluntarily abdicated. Neither is it necessary that the social revolution be decided at one blow; such probably was never the case. Revolutions prepare themselves by years or decades of economic and political struggle; they are accomplished amidst constant ups and downs sustained by the conflicting classes and parties; not infrequently they are interrupted by long periods of reaction.[46]

Because socialism was an ongoing movement rather than a blueprint of the future, Kautsky underscored the importance of rejecting static utopias, manufactured in advance of the socialist stage of production.

In this matter as little as any other, is socialist society likely to move by leaps and bounds, or start all over anew; it will go on from the point at which capitalist society ceases. . . . We must not think of the socialist society as something rigid and uniform, but rather as an organism, constantly developing, rich in possibilities of change, an organism that is to develop naturally from increasing division of labor, commercial exchange, and the dominance of society by science and art.[47]

This "natural" development was—in Kautsky's eyes—a discovery of the great intellectual revolution of the nineteenth century. Marx and Engels' insight had enabled them to realize that history was determined "by an economic development which progresses irresistibly, obedient to certain underlying laws and not to anyone's wishes or whims." [48] Of course, even though thinkers could discover such trends, "they can never themselves determine the course of social evolution." [49]

A new social form does not come into existence through the activity of certain especially gifted men. No man or group of men can conceive of a plan, convince people by degrees of its utility, and, when they have acquired the requisite power, undertake the construction of a social edifice according to their plan. All social forms have been the result of long and fluctuating struggles. [50]

Still, the individual was not entirely unimportant. His character could deeply influence even a class movement.

Everyone who is active in society affects it to a greater or lesser extent. A few individuals, especially prominent through their capacity or social position, may exercise great influence upon the whole nation. Some may promote the development of society by enlightening the people, organizing the revolutionary forces and causing them to act with vigor and precision; others may retard social development for many years by turning their powers in the opposite direction. [51]

Because of this, the revolutionary "camp of the exploited" might harbor reactionary elements and counterrevolutionary factions. A socialist order was no exception. If anything, it evolved even more rapidly than other kinds of societies. To avoid falling out of step, revolutionary leaders would have to pay the closest attention to contemporary developments and adapt political forms accordingly.

Never yet in the history of mankind has it happened that a revolutionary party was able to foresee, let alone determine, the forms of the new social order which it strove to usher in. The cause of progress gained much if it could as much as ascertain the tendencies that led to such a new social order, to the end that its political activity could be a conscious, and not merely an instinctive one. No more can be demanded of the Socialist Party. [52]

The impress of Kautsky's book, then, was that the socialist future could not be preconceived like a dreamer's utopia. It was to be enacted, not designed; and when it finally did come about, it would not be free from the mutations that characterize all societies. Nor would it be free from the factional dissonance of other economic and social systems. Individuals would rise and fall, leaders come and go. The important thing was to determine—through the laws of social development that Marx and Engels had discovered—the trend of society at any given moment and to adapt quickly to it.

The same emphasis on socialism as a "thing in movement" rather than "an abstract system" was to be found in the other study which Mao read in 1920: Thomas Kirkup's *History of Socialism*. Like the book's Chinese translator, Chiang K'ang-hu, Kirkup (1844–1912) believed that socialism's political forms were transitory functions of its social essence, which itself underwent continuous transformations. Socialism was not "wedded to any stereotyped set of formulas, whether of Marx or any other, but [was] rooted in reality, and while molding facts, it must adapt itself to them." [53] Kirkup stressed flexibility and instrumentality for three reasons. First, he was concerned by socialism's tendency "to degenerate into a stiff and barren orthodoxy which sought to solve all problems by narrow and half-digested theories." [54] Second, he believed, like Kautsky, that to organize a new society before it was realized "would require fifty Montesquieu's." [55] Finally, Kirkup simply wondered how a doctrine conceived in one setting, the European continent, could be transported unchanged to countries such as England or America. Although this may suggest that Kirkup had a rather sophisticated theory of national praxis, he was in fact merely reflecting some of the assumptions of the time about national character. A Scotsman trained for the Presbyterian ministry, he had come to socialism late. Internationalist in theory, he was often parochial in practice, so that his history of socialism frequently attributed differences in social theory to national or cultural provenance (for example, Marx's "rabbinical exactitude," Adam Smith's Scotch common sense, and so forth).[56] But all was not relative; Kirkup certainly did prefer some forms of socialism to others. He felt, for example, that utopian socialists like Saint-Simon and Fourier "had an excessive faith in the possibility for human progress and perfectibility." This was because "they knew little of the true laws of social evolution . . . which Darwinism has brought out so clearly." [57] Yet even as Kirkup dismissed human perfectibility by taking the laws of Social Darwinism for granted, he believed—like Huxley—that competition (the essence of capitalism) ought to be socially restrained. However, he by no means intended to oppose Darwinism with socialism. In fact, the former's laws, which were "the dominating tendencies of social evolution," gave socialism its "true meaning." [58] Because the means of production tended to be concentrated in ever larger (capitalist) enterprises, there grew another (socialist) need for collective or cooperative association to restore economic control to the workers. It is obvious, then, that although Kirkup was trying very hard to inject an evolutionary necessity into socialism, he actually made it a kind of reaction to the prevalent notion of the survival of the fittest. That is, the capitalistic arbitration of a supposedly free market was more logically consistent with Social Darwinism than cooperative forms of social and economic organization.

The same contradiction (or, at least, ambiguity) existed in Kirkup's prescription for social improvement. As he described social development in evolutionary terms, Kirkup repeatedly emphasized that socialism could not be mechanically forced upon humanity. Revolutionary violence was an entirely insufficient lever of change if it ran counter "to the fundamental laws of human nature or the great prevailing tendencies of social evolution." [59] But if those fundamental laws were Spencerian, assuming struggle and competition, then how could they be reconciled with Kirkup's belief in another human tendency toward association?

One mode of reconciliation was spiritual. Not only was the scope of socialism to be compared to that of the Protestant Reformation; Kirkup also called for an organic conjunction between external circumstances and the "inward moral spirit." Life may well be a struggle, represented in its latest form by competitive capitalism, but social progress (as distinct from social evolution) must take other ethical aspects of humanity into consideration so long as they do not absolutely contradict Darwinism. If, for instance, we define man's striving for ethical perfection as a form of struggle per se, then—by legerdemain—we can include it under the broad rubric of evolution while actually opposing the two.

Progress chiefly and supremely consists in the growing control of ethical principle over all the forms of selfishness, egotism, unscrupulousness, and cruelty called for by such struggle. In other words, progress mainly consists in the growing supremacy of law, order, and morality over the excess of the self-regarding principle in which the individual struggle has its root.[60]

No more satisfying was Kirkup's effort to identify the other tendency of mankind toward sociality with evolution. For, the same device was used once again. Because men struggled to create larger and larger social units, moving from tribe to nation-state to humanity, their continuing "readiness to associate for common ends" was ultimately not supposed to conflict with competitive drives to survive.[61] Endeavor, in short, was consistently confused with struggle. His impulse, therefore, was to combine historical necessity and human will. Kirkup respected

Marx for describing "a revolution determined by the natural laws of social evolution . . . independent of the will and purpose of individual man," but he characteristically feared that the German often leaned too far in the direction of fatalism.[62] Fortunately, this was sometimes counterbalanced by documents like the *Communist Manifesto,* which expressed "his strong assertion of the revolutionary will." [63]

Kirkup's wish to reconcile natural and artificial developments, "human evolution" and "civilized progress," was a source of continual ambivalence. He deeply admired Proudhon for believing "that through the ethical progress of men government should become unnecessary," [64] and he praised Bakunin's insistence that man obey only laws of nature instead of submitting to laws imposed by an external authority. But because anarchism assumed that all government was evil and that industry could be carried on without organization, Kirkup thought it to contain a fatal flaw. In short, while he shared the ideal of anarchism (every man a law unto himself), he could not believe that Bakunin's program—the destruction of external authority by every available means[65]—would realize that state. Anarchism was but one of two socialist stereotypes. One, traced back to Saint-Simon, was the "principle of authority, of centralization" in the state. The other, represented by anarchism but going back to Fourier, preferred "local and individual freedom," the *phalange* or commune. The best example of the latter was Robert Owen's ideal of small, self-sufficient communities with public kitchens, communal nurseries, and so forth. Such a unit, "while mainly agricultural . . . should possess all the best machinery; it should offer every variety of employment and should as far as possible be self-contained," uniting the "advantage of town and country life." [66] But for all his admiration, Kirkup felt that the commune need not be selected over the state; "in a well ordered community there would be no real opposition of the two." [67]

It is not easy to weigh the impact of Thomas Kirkup's eclectic, if intellectually flaccid, survey of contemporary socialist theories upon Mao Tse-tung. Certain institutional devices which Mao later favored, like the self-sufficient commune linking city and countryside, may have been inspired by Kirkup's presentation. The Scotsman's ethical fervor, his desire to combine historical laws and human will, may also have persisted in Mao's thought. But what Kirkup, Kautsky, and Marx really offered Mao Tse-tung was a new intellectual currency with which to conceive of human development in economic terms. Chiang K'ang-hu or Yang Ch'ang-chi's attacks on familism were thus placed in a uni-

versal context. Every society evolved from communal and then feudal
stages of production to the fragmented and proletarianized world of
modern capitalism. China, not yet at that stage, would have its own
primary social units dissolve, giving way eventually to more inclusive *collectives*
collectivities based upon the socialist principle of association. Withal,
Mao retained the original impulse of the May Fourth generation to free
the individual will. For there was no elaborate distinction between the
free will of philosophers like Friedrich Paulsen and the partial determinism of socialists like Kirkup. Both idealists and materialists were
profoundly influenced by Social Darwinism, and hence remained aware
of the potential conflict between the survival of the fittest and ethical
advance. The two might be partly reconciled in the general struggle of
humanity toward collective freedom, but the philosophical contradiction
remained. Mao, as we shall see, could have resolved the theoretical
dilemma by means of one variant of Hegelianism. As a revolutionary,
though, he either laid it aside or solved the matter in practice. For,
whether from reading Paulsen and Kautsky, or by becoming a political
activist (the two coming very close to coincidence), Mao realized his
will in the actuality of struggle. Action was all the easier once he believed—as Kautsky and Kirkup had often pointed out—that man did
not need to have a complete blueprint of the future because revolution
was as much transition as achievement, as much concrete movement as
static abstraction.

15

Marxism

"The battlefield," as Mao Tse-tung said in 1965, "is a school." [1] By then—the time of the Cultural Revolution—he had grown dubious of formal learning. "I am suspicious of this university education. It takes a total of sixteen, seventeen, or twenty years for one to reach the university from primary school, and in this period one never has a chance to look at the five kinds of cereals, to look at how the workers do their work, how the peasants till their fields, and how traders do business." [2] Too much of higher education involved useless abstractions, whereas specific concepts provided better descriptions of the world. A small child, he said admiringly:

. . . learns some concepts. "Dog" is a big concept, while "black dog" and "yellow dog" are smaller concepts. The yellow dog in his home is a concrete object. "Man" is a concept which leaves out many things. It makes no distinction between men and women, between adults and children, between Chinese and non-Chinese, and between revolutionary people and counter-revolutionary people. [3]

Thus, truly creative people were those whose youthful minds had not been cluttered with empty words.

To date no highest graduate of the Hanlin Academy was outstanding. . . . All *chin-shih* and Hanlin [bachelors] lacked success. T'ai-tsu and Ch'eng-tsu were the only two successful emperors of the Ming Dynasty. One was illiterate and the other was able to read not many characters. Later when the intellectuals came into power under the reign of Chia-ching the country was poorly run. Too much education is harmful and one with too much education cannot be a good emperor. . . . Examinations at present are like tackling enemies, not the people. . . . They are nothing but a method of testing official stereotyped writing. I disapprove of them and advocate wholesale transformation.[4]

Since ancient times, those who created new ideas and new academic schools of thought were always "young people without much learning." [5] Confucius was only twenty-three years old when he began formulating his system, and Shakyamuni was only nineteen. "What learning did Jesus have? . . . In history it is always those with less learning who overthrow those with more learning." Heroes of invention (creators, not mere intellectuals) were always young: Marx writing the *Communist Manifesto* at age thirty, Chang Ping-lin, Ben Franklin, K'ang Yu-wei, Liu Shih-p'ei, Wang Pi, Li Shih-min, Liang Ch'i-ch'ao, and so forth.[6] Rote learning and examinations either stifled originality or taught the impractical. One learned by doing, not by memorizing, so that school work was largely a waste of time.[7]

The school years are too long, courses too many, and the method of teaching is by injection instead of through the imagination. The method of examination is to treat candidates as enemies and ambush them. . . . Generally speaking, the intellectuals specializing in engineering are better, because they are in touch with reality. Scientists, pure scientists, are worse, but they are still better than those who specialize in art subjects. [Liberal] art subjects are completely detached from reality. Students of history, philosophy, and economics have no concern with studying reality; they are the most ignorant of things of this world. . . . Of course, we have learnt a little Marxism–Leninism, but Marxism–Leninism alone won't do. [We] must study Chinese problems, starting from the characteristics and facts of China. . . . Philosophy is book philosophy. What is the use of philosophy if it is not learnt from society, from the masses, and from nature? It can be composed only of vague ideas.[8]

One had to learn by doing, step by step, spending—as Mao put it in 1964—twenty-eight years from the foundation of the Chinese Communist Party to the liberation of the whole country in order to forge a set of policies suitable to the revolution.[9] In that sense, Mao's Marxism was really a matter of practice.

During the summer of 1920—after Kirkup, Kautsky, and the *Manifesto*—Mao had become convinced that Marxism was the correct revolutionary theory to guide his action. The following year he became a member of the Chinese Communist Party. Moving into labor organization, he led a coal miners' strike in the autumn of 1922, and by the next summer had been elected to the Party's Central Committee. The United Front engaged him in liaison work, so that by 1925 he was serving as deputy chief of the Kuomintang Propaganda Bureau, preparing to mobilize the peasant movement which he actively led in Hunan during 1926. Throughout the edgy months of collaboration late that year and early in 1927, Mao continued to cooperate with the Kuomintang. In fact, his ties were not completely severed until the Autumn Harvest Uprising of 1927, when he barely escaped arrest by fleeing to an isolated mountain base at Chingkangshan in the Kiangsi–Hunan borderlands. There he helped found a soviet, initiating a new period in the history of the Communist Party which would last until the Long March ended in 1935, after he and his comrades reached the relative sanctuary of the northwest.

The writings of Mao Tse-tung extant from this period are primarily and most masterfully concerned with political strategy; secondarily with Marxist theory as such. In fact, his "Analysis of All the Classes in Chinese Society" (January–February, 1926) demonstrated a confused and hesitant grasp of Marxian class analysis. Pieces from 1927, however, were much more confident, expressing his growing awareness of the importance of peasant uprisings as an actual consequence of rural revolution in Hunan and south central China during that year. The most famous statement was his report on the peasant movement in Hunan —perhaps "a-Marxist" in its neglect of the proletariat, but quite Leninist in its conception of political struggle as the key to economic conflict.[10] Even more specific were his communications and reports dating from the Kiangsi soviet period. The task at hand was to formulate a strategy of protracted warfare and of military mobilization of the peasants, a tactic of guerrilla engagements, and an analysis of the precise economic structure of the countryside around him. Finally, there were the speeches and writings from the period of the second United Front, beginning in 1935. Then his key ideological concept (influenced by Lenin and Stalin and given fullest expression in Mao's "On People's Democratic Dictatorship" of 1949) was the idea of a four-class bloc (workers, peasants, petty bourgeoisie, and national bourgeoisie) allying to conduct a "new democratic revolution" under the democratic dictatorship of the proletariat.[11]

From 1920 on, Mao was constantly exposed to several sorts of influences, none of them especially theoretical: the actual military and political situation (which led him to devise his own, most effective theory of guerrilla warfare), a loose Marxist–Leninist interpretation of the social forces active in the Chinese Revolution, and a series of quite specific strategic pronouncements (often cast, incidentally, in the same "wave" images he so favored) from Party Central and the Soviet Union. He, at the same time, became quite habile at envisaging and formulating the many different stages of revolution in Marxist–Leninist terms. But it was not until the Long March was over that Mao, for the first time in fifteen years, had the opportunity to study the basic classics of Marxism. Indeed, the two years from late 1935 to September of 1937 represented the second great abstract or theoretical phase of his intellectual development.

One reason for this spate of reading was that he now had access to works not available earlier. Most of the major works on Marxism were not translated until the Yenan period (1935–1945): the writings of leading Soviet philosophers like Abram Deborin, Mark B. Mitin or Mark M. Rosental, as well as such classic texts (which Mao cited) as Engels' *Anti-Dühring* and *Ludwig Feuerbach,* Marx's *Theses on Feuerbach,* and Lenin's *Materialism and Empirio-criticism* and *Philosophical Notebooks.* This is not to say that serious Marxist works were not written or published in China before 1935. Li Ta's *She-hui hsueh ta-kang* (An Outline of Socialist Theory), as well as Li Chi's *Ma-k'o-ssu chuan* (Biography of Marx) and *Chung-kuo she-hui shih lun-chan p'i-p'an* (A Criticism of the Polemic on the History of Chinese Society) were all books of considerable sophistication. But not until 1936 did some of the issues they raised become publicly current in Chinese Marxist circles. That year there began a philosophical debate, within and without the Chinese Communist Party, that was then compared with earlier polemics in the Soviet Union between Abram Deborin's idealists and the mechanists loosely identified with Nikolai Bukharin.[12]

Deborin (1881–   ), the Russian philosopher who had led the attack in 1924 against Georg Lukacs, battled for seven years during the 1920s to maintain "that the law of the unity of opposites must be made the basis of theoretical physicists."[13] Deborin's opponents, "vulgar materialists" and "scientific mechanists" like Skvortsov-Stepanov (1870–1928), had argued for scientific positivism. Just as the proletariat's dictatorship defeated the blind force of capitalism, so should science expel the dregs of irrational Hegelianism from the socialist republics. As in any quarrel (Marxian or Confucian) where canonicity is at stake, much of the debate was exegetical, arguing over Engels' intent in the *Dialectics of Nature* (just published then in 1925). The mechanists insisted that Engels had by the end of his life realized the error of reading philosophy into the natural sciences.* Deborin rebutted that Engels had consistently and correctly maintained the inseparability of the philosophy of dialectical materialism and scientific theory. Not only was there no such thing as a science free from value-laden philosophical assumptions; if Soviet scientists tried to maintain the autonomy of "pure" research by divorcing it from philosophy, the integrity of the Marxist dialectic would be shattered and an actually more pernicious philosophy of positivism put in its place. As Engels' notes to the *Dialectics of Nature* put it:

Natural scientists believe that they free themselves from philosophy by ignoring it or abusing it. They cannot, however, make any headway without thought, and for thought they need thought determinations. But they take these categories unreflectingly from the common consciousness of so-called educated persons, which is dominated by the relics of long obsolete philosophies. . . . Hence they are no less in bondage to philosophy, but unfortunately in most cases to the worst philosophy, and those who abuse philosophy most are slaves to precisely the worst vulgarized relics of the worst philosophers.[14]

Furthermore, argued the Deborinists, the Marxist theory of the identity of opposites supposed the two contradictory elements to be of unequal strength, whereas the mechanists stressed the equilibrium of opposites. Because that made movement or change depend on an external disequilibrium, their mechanism, like that of the eighteenth century, denied the internality of a true dialectic.

Deborin's cause was momentarily won when the Society of Militant Materialists and Dialecticians which he controlled agreed with the Stalinists that the mechanists' theories (which denied Deborin's belief that contradiction and struggle characterized all forms of being) lent credence to Bukharin's "right-wing deviationist" arguments that the party should not intensify the class struggle. The mechanists were shortly condemned in public at the April 1929 meeting of the All-Union Conference of Marxist–Leninist Research Institutes.

* The mechanists could hardly base their brief on the early Engels, who, for example, wrote to Marx in 1873 from London: "Dear Moor: In bed this morning the following dialectical ideas on the natural sciences came into my head: the subject matter of natural science—matter in motion, bodies. Bodies cannot be separated from motion . . ." His excitement over the idea was matched only by his fear of plagiarism. The letter ends: "If you people believe that there is something in this thing, then don't talk about it, so that no lousy Britisher may steal it on me; getting it into shape will take a long time yet." Engels to Marx, May 30, 1873, in Karl Marx and Friedrich Engels, *Selected Correspondence* (Moscow: Foreign Languages Publishing House, n.d.) pp. 342-343.

But Deborinism did not reign for long. Its hegemony was challenged by 1930, when the same kind of attack was launched on Deborin as he had led on the mechanists. Because of the Hegelian cast of his thought, he was accused of idealism and hence associated with Trotskyism. In December of that year, Stalin appeared at a meeting of the party cell of the Institute of Red Professors, then the center of Deborin's opposition led by three Party men (not "just" scholars): Mitin, Pavel Yudin, and Vasili Raltsevich. There Stalin mentioned Deborin's "Menshevizing idealism" and thus virtually commanded his downfall.

Deborinism's strength was its weakness. As it challenged the ideological autonomy of science, it was a yeoman of party control over the country's research institutes. But as it sought to make science and philosophy as one, affirming the dialectic's validity for every form of investigation, it fell too easily into what could appear to be dogmatic idealism. That was *too* philosophical, too much at odds with the practical resolutions of the Sixteenth Party Congress. Mitin, Yudin, and Raltsevich's attack on Deborinism, which was printed in *Pravda* on June 7, 1930, made just that point. "Reality is confronting theory with tremendous problems. It is necessary to start at once with the preparation and theoretical generalization of these problems on the basis of Marxist–Leninist methodology. Instead we notice that theory is lagging considerably behind." [15] Deborin, therefore, was supposed to be maliciously divorcing philosophy from the practical problems of the country.

To protect himself from being labeled a Trotskyist, Deborin engaged in public self-criticism. Recanting before the Institute of Philosophy in 1933, he urged his followers to abandon their principles:

Our fundamental mistake lay in separating theory and practice. I must admit that for a long time I did not understand the causation, because, after all, I was constantly speaking of practice as the criterion of truth. . . . The essence of that matter was that we failed to establish a connection between our theoretical and methodological investigations and the concrete tasks of socialist construction, that we separated theory from life.[16]

Shortly thereafter Deborinism simply became a term of abuse for philosophical revisionists who favored pure theory at the expense of revolutionary practice. As this definition was transferred to the Chinese Communist context, the label of "Deborinism" was affixed to thinkers like Yeh Ch'ing, who actually did not share Deborin's views.

Yeh Ch'ing (Jen Cho-hsuan, 1896–   ) had joined the French

Communist Party while studying abroad in 1920.[17] An able organizer, he was by 1923 chief secretary of the Paris branch of the Chinese Communist Party. Expelled from France two years later for organizing demonstrations, he studied in the Soviet Union before returning to China in 1926 where he became a leader of the Communist underground in Ch'ang-sha. Arrested by Nationalist authorities, Yeh shortly renounced the Communist Party and joined the Kuomintang as a propaganda expert—a function which he has exercised up to the present. This was hardly then the volte-face it seems now. The Kuomintang was still an intellectually radical party in the early 1930s. In fact, many respectably left-wing intellectuals clustered around Yeh, who established a bookstore in Shanghai which specialized in the translation of "scientific materialists" like Heraclitus, Condillac, Planck, Eddington, Einstein, Plekhanov, and Deborin. Also associated with Yeh was the journal, *Erh-shih shih-chi* (Twentieth Century), in which Yeh Ch'ing publicized ideas soon to type him in the eyes of his contemporaries as a Deborinist. In 1934 these theories were presented in a book—*Che-hsueh tao ho-ch'u ch'ü* (Where Is Philosophy Going?)—which argued that philosophy, obeying the same evolutionary laws as religion, was in the process of perishing while dialectical materialism—a science of pure thought reflecting industrial society—arose. Dialectical materialism, his *Che-hsueh wen-t'i* (Philosophical Problems) insisted in 1936, was a synthesis of Feuerbach's materialism and Hegel's idealism, compressed into a scientific system of thought which spelled an end to the history of philosophy.

Yeh Ch'ing's Communist adversaries in Yenan—Ai Ssu ch'i (1910–1966) and Ch'en Po-ta (1904–   )—immediately responded that the supposed union of materialism and idealism in Marxism was nonsense. Furthermore, to ignore the problem of false consciousness by considering dialectical materialism a pure science beyond history was to overlook the social basis of all thought.[18]

So far, there was a clear distinction between Yeh Ch'ing's Deborinism and the historical materialism of his opponents. But categories began blurring when Ch'en Po-ta and Ai Ssu-ch'i blamed Yeh for supposing an equality of contradictions between two unequal things. Confusing this with Deborin's "unity of opposites," they were actually accusing him of a mechanist error. Moreover, many Communists, like Mao himself, were often just as Deborinist as Yeh Ch'ing, strongly identifying dialectical materialism with science. Mao wrote in 1938 that: "The history of science furnishes man with proof of the material nature of the world and of the fact that it is governed by laws and helps man to see the futility of the illusions of religion and idealism and to arrive at materialist conclusions." [19] In fact, Mao was later constantly to seek the single scientific law of being that could sustain all aspects of revolutionary theory. He argued during the Hangchow Conference that Stalin's four dialectical laws should really be reduced to one basic truth, the law of contradiction and the unity of opposites. "Quality and quantity, affirmation and negation, phenomenon and essence, content and form, necessity and freedom, possibility and reality, etcetera, are all unity of opposites." [20] And when he could, he warmly welcomed news of any scientific discoveries or physical theories which lent credence to his monism. He was especially excited by the work of the Japanese physicist, Sakata Shiyouchi,* who has argued publicly in Peking that elementary particles are a "mistaken concept." These subatomic particles discovered in recent years by experimental physicists were—he claimed—erroneously thought to be the origin of matter. In Sakata's view, "elementary particles are a single, material, differentiated, and limitless category which make up the natural order." [21] So, instead of breaking matter down into elementary and indivisible units, Sakata preferred to believe in an inclusive class of material force which combined and divided by internal opposition or contradiction. There was nothing in the universe without opposition, nothing that could not be divided as one into two. Behind all being was the universal dialectic, confirmed by science's own advances.

As Mao Tse-tung sought to impress Sakata's Leninist model on Chinese physics—"In atomic physics, we can get by with the Sakata model. We do not have to start with the Bohr theory of the Danish school. If you studied in this way, you could spend ten years at it and never graduate. Sakata always used dialectics. Why do you people not do the same?" [22]—he would seem guilty of the very Deborinist tendencies which his famous essay "On Contradiction" attacked years earlier.†

---

* Sakata teaches at the University of Nagoya. He is best known as the author of *Kagaku to heiwa no sozo* [Science and the Creation of Peace] (Tokyo: Iwanami, 1963), 370 pp. The last portion of the book includes a diary of his trip to a peace conference in Peking in 1956.

† To be sure, he may also have meant the mistake of believing in an equality of opposites, which—as we have seen—was actually the mechanists' position. There may be a connection as well between his attack on Deborinism and his struggle with the Trotskyists in Yenan, because Deborin was linked in the Soviet Union with Trotsky's idealism. For an account of the extent of Trotskyist influence in China during the Yenan period, see Richard C. Kagan, "Ch'en Tuhsiu," Ph.D. diss. (University of Pennsylvania, 1969).

But by then Deborinism was such a loosely conceived notion that it probably represented nothing more than the mechanical application of abstract Marxist theory to a concrete historical situation. In that regard Yeh Ch'ing certainly did seem a consistent Deborinist, since he promoted Marxist dialectics from methodology to economic science. Given the precisely opposite tendency in Mao, as well as some of the theoretical embarrassments such an economic science suffered in the Chinese context, it is no wonder that Mao Tse-tung was obliged to explain his own doctrine of actuality.

This was not just a matter of academic philosophical controversy. All those patriotic intellectuals who had joined the party during the early years of the Sino–Japanese War (1937–1945) had to realize that the arrow of Marxist theory which they so lovingly stroked was useless without a real revolutionary target. Consequently, one of the major goals of the party rectification movement during the early 1940s was to convince these new recruits that they were actually less learned than the workers and peasants they hoped to lead. Mao therefore insisted that there existed only two kinds of true knowledge: that of man's struggle to produce and that of class struggle. Natural science and social science were simply the respective "crystallizations" of these two kinds of knowledge. Because book knowledge (theory generalized from the experience of predecessors engaged in struggle) by itself was "inverted, backward, [and] one-sided," students had to verify theories for themselves if they wanted to be more than "half intellectuals." Verification was not an easy task. In fact, insisted Mao, the greater the difficulty, the closer the truth. Put most vividly, it was easier to read a book than to slaughter a pig, because "a book placed on a desk can neither run nor squeal." *

Such hyperbole certainly helped destroy traditional attitudes of intellectual veneration, but it also placed Mao in a slightly embarrassing position vis-à-vis Marx (no butcher he!). In fact, Mao had to take special pains to portray Marx as a whole intellectual on the basis of his

* To be fair to Mao, we should suppose that the difficulty of slaughtering an animal was not the complexity of the task but rather the degree of concrete emotional involvement. He would stress therefore the difference between passively turning a book's pages and actively butchering a squealing swine. Part of his design was to teach bookish theorists to wage revolution, which—in the words of Mao's report on the Hunan peasant movement—"is not the same as inviting people to dinner or writing an essay or painting a picture or embroidering a flower." From even the crudest epistemological point of view, however, Mao here deliberately confused learning *how* to do something with *why* it was to be done at all.

participation in the revolutionary movement and of his research into commodity production ("a reality which was all inclusive").[23] But Mao's original intention was not to disesteem Marx. Rather, he wished to temper the universal theory of Marxism with the specific practice of revolution in China. By the late 1930s, in fact, Mao's growing hegemony within the party was becoming identified with the sinification of Marxism. As he attained this stature, however, he may also have felt it necessary to emulate Lenin and Stalin by making a universal theoretical contribution of his own to Marxism. At least, that is how some scholars have explained why his three major theoretical works—"On Practice," "On Contradiction," and "On Dialectical Materialism"—were authored during this period.

The three essays were actually parts of a single whole. After intensely studying the Marxist classics during the summer of 1936 in Yenan, Mao began lecturing on dialectical materialism that winter to members of the party and army. These *Lecture Notes on Dialectical Materialism* (*Pien-cheng-fa wei-wu-lun chiang-shou t'i-kang*) were probably not as theoretically sophisticated as the final versions published under their individual titles in the 1950s. However, the piece "On Practice," which was ostensibly designed to counteract the wave of doctrinaire idealism then sweeping the party, was apparently much the same in both 1937 and 1950 versions.*

"On Practice" begins by praising Marxism for its belief in the historical progress of human knowledge.[24] Because Marxism realizes that there are lower and higher levels of knowledge, depending upon the stage of social advance, it alone of philosophical doctrines is a true science. The certainty of its—and man's—discoveries, however, can

---

* The dating, and the level of philosophical content, of these pieces has aroused a good deal of scholarly controversy. Much of Mao's piece "On Dialectical Materialism" was drawn from Mitin's article on that topic in the *Soviet Encyclopedia,* as well as from Mitin's longer work on *Dialectical Materialism* (Moscow, 1933) which was partially translated in Ai Ssu-ch'i's *Che-hsueh hsuan-chi* [Selected Readings in Philosophy] (Shanghai, 1939). See: Karl August Wittfogel and C. R. Chao, "Some Remarks on Mao's Handling of Concepts and Problems of Dialectics," *Studies in Soviet Thought,* 3: 251–277. Some scholars, like Arthur A. Cohen (*The Communism of Mao Tse-tung,* Chicago: University of Chicago Press, 1964), have also argued that whatever was written in 1936–1937 hardly resembled the pieces published after 1950. In fact, it has even been suggested that the later pieces were composed after the Civil War was over. Stuart R. Schram, however, came across a 1938 manuscript which proves that all three pieces were indeed written in the late 1930s and form part of the lecture series mentioned above. See Stuart R. Schram, *The Political Thought of Mao Tse-tung,* rev. ed. (New York: Praeger, 1969), pp. 85–89.

only be verified when man achieves in the process of social practice the results which he anticipated. At the very start of his discourse, therefore, Mao departs from Marx and Engels by explicitly distinguishing between verifying (*cheng-shih*) and realizing. Success—from the point of view of knowledge—is the measure of correctness of any view as verified in social practice, which must accommodate itself to objective necessity: "If man wants to achieve success in his work, that is, to achieve the anticipated results, he must make his thoughts correspond to the laws of the objective world." Consequently, Mao's practice is more of a guideline to successful action than traditional Marxist praxis. Like parts of the *Quotations,* "On Practice" tells us how to get things done. Because failure is the mother of success, practice is a way of correcting or rectifying (*kai-cheng*) our thoughts so they will correspond with the objective laws of reality. That is why, says Mao, dialectical materialism has such a unique theory of practice. By cautioning us not to depend on our subjective feelings instead of objective results, dialectical materialism creates the concept of social practice (*she-hui shih-chien*) as the sole "criterion of truth."

To prove this claim, Mao Tse-tung proceeds, without ontological discussion, first to posit matter and then to describe cognition. In the process of practice man at first sees only the phenomenal aspects (*hsien-hsiang fang-mien*) of things as emotion reacts to sensation. During this perceptual stage we have no more than a rough sense of the external relations between things. However, the repetition of social practice produces a sudden change in the mind, giving birth to concepts that deal with much more than mere external relations between phenomena. So far as concepts regard the essence, totality, and internal connections of things, they take on an independent life of their own in the mind, interacting to create independent judgment. "Proceeding further and employing the method of judgment and inference, we can then draw conclusions that conform with logic." This, rather than a priori cognition, was truly "rational knowledge."

The movement from conceptual to rational knowledge was, as Mao explained in a later essay ("Where Do Correct Ideas Come from?"), a dramatic leap forward by means of practice. "Man's knowledge makes another leap through the test of practice. This leap is more important than the previous one [that is, the leap from perceptual to conceptual knowledge]. For it is this leap alone that can prove the correctness or incorrectness of the first leap in cognition." [25] Once attained, such rational knowledge did not represent an immediate and absolute truth. It was merely part of a spiraling movement toward truth that rose ever higher, each gyre closer than the one before, but never—it would seem —reaching absolute reality. Thus, there was no absolute identity between thought and reality. Even though influenced by Lenin's *Materialism and Empirio-criticism,* Mao did not apparently accept the law of identity (A equals A). He seemed instead closer to Engels, whose law of the development of contradictions (A equals A only if it is non-A) described objective reality dialectically. Because A could simultaneously equal both A and non-A (the absolute precondition of A), opposites existed in complementarity. Pushed to an extreme—their quality transformed by quantity—these opposites changed each into the other.[26] The same sense of dialectical change probably inspired Mao's own distinction between perceptual knowledge (which only perceives the outer relationships among things) and rational knowledge (which arises from concepts that can rearrange relationships). Lenin had believed knowledge to emerge progressively and gradually from ignorance—not as a reflection of reality but as a process in which the subject participated by moving from a perception of the concrete to the abstract, from subjective idea to objective truth.[27] For Mao, however, knowledge was moving not just toward abstract laws, but to a stage of consciousness in which the subject could perceive the conflict between things, their "inner contradictions." Perceptual knowledge and rational knowledge differed because the former dealt only with the external relations of things, while the latter understood their "internal contradictions" (*nei-tsai ti mao-tun*).

In order to reflect the essence (contradiction) of things in his own mind, man must create a system of concepts by rebuilding the data of perceptions. Kant's critical logic had supposed data to be arranged by a necessary order of categories external to the human mind. Mao made man, as subject, the sole source of those categories. Because that would lead to subjectivism, even idealism, Mao concluded that this "reconstructed knowledge" (*kai-tsao-kuo ti jen-shih*) was based, in the final analysis, on practice which—we might add—objectified the self. Consequently, even though Mao's method was dialectical, his final construction of knowledge was monistic. Although this could easily be a reflection of Hegel's *Logic,* I believe Mao Tse-tung was more likely influenced by the Chinese philosopher, Wang Yang-ming, who rejected earlier dualisms. Mao did not acknowledge Wang's inspiration, but his essay "On Dialectical Materialism" particularly emphasized the harmful consequence of epistemological duality:

When men think, they must use concepts. This can easily cause our knowledge to be split into two aspects: reality, which is of an individual and particular character; and concepts, which are of a general nature. . . . Originally, the particular and the general are inseparably linked; once separated, they depart from objective truth. . . . Pre-Marxist materialism (mechanistic materialism) did not stress the thought process in the development of knowledge, but regarded thought merely as the object of action, as the mirror that reflects nature. . . . Only dialectical materialism correctly shows the role of thought, and at the same time points out the limitation imposed upon thought by matter. It points out that thought arises from social practice and at the same time actively shapes practice.[28]

Consequently, practice meant subjectively participating in objective reality. "If you want to know the taste of a pear, you must change the pear by eating it yourself."

The fallacy that to acquire a sensation one must alter its source (does one change the sun in order to see it?) was quickly passed over in "On Practice," as Mao shifted his philosophical demonstration from things to events, identifying participation with Lenin's theory of the stage of consciousness. As the proletariat came to understand the essence of capitalism by fighting it, or as the May Fourth generation (in contrast to the indiscriminately xenophobic Taiping Rebels or Boxers) arrived at a rational knowledge of imperialism by opposing it, men grew through practice to know their own historical task and thereby changed from members of a "class in itself" (*tzu-tsai chieh-chi*) to being part of a "class for itself" (*tzu-wei chieh-chi*). Theory did not spring from the heads of observers. Mao's disdain for nondoing philosophers was vividly expressed in "On New Democracy," where he quoted Marx's famous line, "The philosophers have only interpreted the world in various ways; the point, however, is to change it." [29] Theory sprang instead from doers like Engels and Lenin, who had "personally participated in the practical struggle to change reality" through class struggle.

Mao Tse-tung's conception of knowledge may be partly explained by his personal history. As a receptor of revolutionary theory which he sinified, Mao tended to neglect the genesis of theories: how Marx and Engels derived the theory of materialistic socialism in the first place, or how Lenin hammered out the vanguard theory of the party. Ideas, as a force in themselves, were quite absent from his analysis, whereas they did figure in Marx's writing. When Marx told Sorge that utopianism "*before* the era of materialistically critical socialism concealed the latter within itself in embryo," he meant to show that utopian socialism after the event of materialism was "silly, stale, and reactionary." [30] But that statement—like the *Manifesto*—also acknowledged the importance of those utopian theories to the early development of communism. Mao could neither appreciate nor explain such an influence within the strict limits of his theory of practice. For, the true knowledge he described occurred only when inner relationships were verified in practice. Because the final proof of rational knowledge was its operational efficacy, its importance as theory was strictly to guide action (*chih-tao hsing-tung*).

> Knowledge starts with practice, reaches the theoretical planes via practice, and then has to return to practice. The active function of knowledge not only manifests itself in the active leap from perceptual knowledge to rational knowledge, but also—and this is the more important—in the leap (*fei-yueh*) from rational knowledge to revolutionary practice. . . . This is the process of testing and developing theory, the continuation of the whole process of knowledge.[31]

Knowledge was not merely cognition. To *be* knowledge, it had to be continuous: carried out to its fullest. This continuity, rather than being a projection of intent (that is, the creation of a self-fulfilling reality), was the entire realization of a process that began in cognition and was wholly completed in action. For, "the problem of whether theory corresponds to objective reality" simply could not be solved in the rational stage of knowledge alone. The only way to "solve it completely" was to "redirect rational knowledge to social practice, to apply theory to practice and see whether it can achieve the anticipated results."

Was the final result, then, absolutely necessary truth? Mao Tse-tung seemed to return to Lenin's *Materialism and Empirio-criticism* when he said:

> The Marxist recognizes that in the absolute, total process of the development of the universe, the development of each concrete process is relative; hence, in the great stream of absolute truth, man's knowledge of the concrete process at each given stage of development is only relatively true. The sum total of innumerable relative truths is the absolute truth.[32]

But he was in fact closer to Engels than to Lenin, who believed in an absolute truth which was the sum of all known relative truths. Because Mao referred to the latter as "innumerable," he projected the absoluteness of reality into an unknowable future, implying—as did Marx's first thesis on Feuerbach—that there never could be a sacred or absolute final truth. Thus, perhaps without ever having read the *Dialectics of*

Nature, Mao would have agreed with Engels' contention that the only universal truth was that of motion. His skepticism about either a priori knowledge or the ability of ideas to survive the flow of time therefore turned him to practice: truth in the sense of continual becoming, rational knowledge in correspondence with the eternal flux of the objective process (*k'o-kuan kuo-ch'eng*). "The process of change in the objective world will never end, nor will man's knowledge of truth through practice. Marxism–Leninism has in no way summed up all knowledge of truth, but is ceaselessly opening up, through practice, the road to the knowledge of truth." [33] Because Marxism–Leninism was just a pathway to the ultimate truth of universal change, then it alone was not eternally valid.

Of course, Marx and Engels did not themselves claim to have discovered a timeless and permanent essence of humanity. Human nature was only its history, *die Geschichte der Menschheit;* and they continuously refused even to reduce history exclusively to economic necessity. Engels reminded Bloch that, in the materialist conception of history, production was only *ultimately* the determining factor of change.

More than this neither Marx nor I have ever asserted. Hence if somebody twists this into saying that the economic element is the *only* determining one, he transforms that proposition into a meaningless, abstract, senseless phrase. The economic situation is the basis, but the various elements of the superstructure . . . also exercise their influence upon the course of the historical struggles and in many cases preponderate in determining their *form.* [34]

And Marx advocated an even more general doctrine of change in the *Poverty of Philosophy:*

The same men who establish their social relations in conformity with their material productivity, produce also principles, ideas, and categories, in conformity with their social relations. Thus these ideas, these categories, are as little eternal as the relations they express. They are *historical and transitory products.* There is a continual movement of growth in productive forces, of destruction in social relations, of formation in ideas; the only immutable thing is the abstraction of movement—*mors immortalis.* [35]

Clearly, Mao did not refute Marx when he wrote of change. The difference between them seemed rather to be that the founder, having admitted change, generalized laws from history for the sake of governing social process. Mao believed in those laws; they provided him with assurance. But he was less interested in deriving them than in guiding human society through revolutionary change by showing men how to make and remake themselves and their environment by the dialectical "unity of knowing and doing" (*chih hsing t'ung-i*). In many ways the self was thus more important to Mao than to Marx. For, as Paulsen's writings helped liberate Mao's revolutionary ego, so Marx's laws enabled Mao to fulfill his self by subjectifying them.

Since that may overstate the difference, let me try to pose it in a slightly different way. Marx's theory of praxis stated that the only genuine questions were those which human action could solve. The rest should be regarded as merely scholastic issues of no real import. In his own way, Marx was solving the *Ding-an-sich* dilemma by placing his confidence in social reality. Mao Tse-tung (at least as the author of "On Practice") did not worry about things-in-themselves at all. As knowledge was participation in the changing of the objective world, the unity of the two proceeded by analytic stages: outer world/sensations/ external relations quantified/participation/qualitative leap to inferences/rational knowledge knows real world behind objects, namely inner contradictions/consciousness/mastery of world and self, namely remolding. Knowledge *is* remolding. This, Mao's so-called voluntarism, depended upon the productive relationship between mind and nature as they moved according to the same dialectic principles.

These principles, if not absolutely universal, were at the very least scientifically valid. In "On Dialectical Materialism," Mao described the history of philosophy as a struggle between the two armies of idealism and materialism.[36] Idealism, like any philosophical theory, was the product of a particular class: in this case the doctrine of a society ruled by intellectuals who worshipped their own idealist thinking and denigrated the material labor of their worker-subjects. Both idealism and materialism were therefore weapons in the class struggle, and the battle between them would rage as long as classes continued to exist. Idealism would not be argued away; it would abruptly cease to exist when the distinction between manual and intellectual labor was erased.

That Mao could make such statements, that he could recognize philosophy to be a class product, was in itself proof to him of the scientific character of dialectical materialism. This was because Mao Tse-tung conceived of what really were two different levels, even two different directions, of ideology: the relative (looking toward) and the absolute (looking from). In its formation, ideology seems only relative. A process is described: idealist philosophy gives way to materialism, class conquers class, ideas change with the times. Yet by describing this relative transformation, one also objectified the phenomenon of class consciousness, deriving absolute principles or laws of analysis from a material and dialectic perception of being. Or, less tortuously: if thought is the product of class relations, then (relative) idealist thought is (absolutely) described in materialist terms. Thus, the victory of the one school of thought over the other was the victory of material force over spirit, of rational technology over irrational religion. The birth of materialism was midwifed by the conquest of nature which is man's liberation from superstition. Only primitive man, helpless prey of nature's forces, had to rely on the illusion of guiding spirits to which he falsely believed himself to be wedded. "But in the long-range process of production, man came into contact with surrounding nature, acted upon nature, changed nature, and created things to eat, to live in, and to use, and adapted nature in the interests of man and caused man to believe that matter has an objective existence." [37]

As scientific truth is dialectical, its absolute essence concerns struggle, a law which "does not depend upon subjective human will." [38] In other less philosophically guarded pronouncements, Mao could even insist that, "Struggle is absolute, while unity is relative." [39] Science itself was struggle—a conviction permeating many of Mao's major theoretical pronouncements since 1956. The chairman's 1958 draft on work methods of the Central Committee, for example, stated:

The law of unity of opposites, the law of quantitative change and qualitative change, and the law of affirmation and negation forever and universally exist. But the nature of struggle and revolution is different from the past; it is not a class struggle, but a struggle between the advanced and the backward among the people, a struggle between advanced and backward science and technology. The transition from socialism to communism is a struggle, a revolution. With the advent of the communist era, there will also be many, many stages of development, and the relationship between this stage and that stage is inevitably a relationship leading from quantitative change to qualitative change. All kinds of mutation and leap are a kind of revolution and must go through struggle. [40]

Everything that Mao learned of life—theoretical or practical—bore out that truth: all is struggle. K'ang Yu-wei could hardly bear the notion of natural strife; Mao Tse-tung's entire structure of thought and action was based upon it.

In this strict sense, Mao's Marxism was just another variation of Social Darwinism: if not a teleology, then at least a scientific theodicy. Marx, on the other hand, had used Darwin to abolish teleology by confirming the endogeneity of class struggle. "Darwin's book is very important and serves me as a natural–scientific basis for the class struggle in history. One has to put up with the crude English method of development, of course. Despite all deficiencies, not only is the deathblow dealt here for the first time to 'teleology' in the natural sciences but its rational meaning is empirically explained." [41] Even Engels, who was much more enthusiastic about the theory of evolution, agreed that it best served as a solvent of teleology.[42] But for Mao, Darwinism preceded Marxism; it constituted the prime scientific discovery of his youth. A philosophy like Marx's was therefore scientific to the degree that it recognized the inevitability of struggle. In fact, the teleology Marx had thought to see erased still existed for Mao in science. If scientific advance defined progress, then human history was all at once man's conquest of nature, class struggle, and the history of science itself. The more those progressed "on all three fronts," wrote Mao, the more capable would man be of "consolidating" materialist philosophy.[43] Therefore, despite his instrumentalization of Marxism–Leninism, Mao also used it like a scientistic template to structure all reality. The various parts of that structure retained their coherence thanks to one invariable principle—call it struggle, contradiction, or the dialectic—which explained all phenomena. Yet this dialectic, lacking the absolute and dichotomous categories of German logic, tended to become a uniform and monistic principle which, like T'an Ssu-t'ung's *jen,* was as much sentiment as idea. The dialectic, in fact, lay pragmatically between subject and object, perceiver and perceived, actor and action. Consequently, "On Practice" lived up to its title. To succeed, a man's thoughts must correspond to the objective patterns or laws which his own success proved to exist. And, since Mao Tse-tung did not believe in cognitive absolute laws, failure was even better than success at revealing those principles.[44] For only when man by practice pushed events to the very brink of failure was he certain that he could and must turn away to search for yet another path toward truth.

16

Wang Yang-ming:
The Parallel Tradition
of Practice

Any Chinese-educated reader coming to the last line of Mao Tse-tung's essay "On Practice" thinks of Wang Yang-ming. Mao's phrase *chih-hsing t'ung-i* instantly recalls Wang's *chih-hsing ho-i,* the two equally meaning the unity of knowledge and action. Even to a twentieth-century audience the identification would not be esoteric, for Wang Yang-ming's slogan occupied an important niche in Chinese revolutionary thought. Sun Yat-sen and Chiang Kai-shek both pondered the relationship between thought and action as Wang had described it; and Mao cannot but have been influenced by the greatest theoretician of practice in Chinese history.*

* Mao was definitely exposed to some of these philosophical ideas while a student in Ch'ang-sha, where he studied the seventeenth-century scholars of "practical learning." Yen Yuan, whom Mao cited in his own writings, was perhaps the most adamant of these philosophers of practice, emphasizing the inadequacy of book learning:

Take, for example, one who desires to know music. Even if he reads a musical score hundreds of times, and discusses, asks, thinks, and sifts scores of times, he cannot know music at all. He simply has to strike and blow musical instruments, sing with his own voice, dance with his own body, and go through all these himself before he knows what music really is. Those who know music this way know it perfectly. This is what is meant by "When things are *ko* [investigated, reached], true knowledge is extended." The word *ko* is the same as that in the expression, "*Ko* (subdue and kill) fierce animals with one's own hands."

Yen Yuan, *Ssu-shu cheng-wu* [Corrections of Wrong Interpretations of the Four

Not long before the year 1524, Wang Yang-ming wrote about his philosophy to a friend named Ku T'ung-chiao (1476–1545). One part of this letter became such a famous example of Wang's concern for mankind that it was later published as a separate essay, entitled "Pulling up the Root and Stopping up the Source." It begins as Wang tells of his fear that men are degenerating into animals and barbarians. Perhaps only a sage can save humanity at this point. Indeed, that would be a sage's highest obligation, because his prime characteristic is the ability to form one body with all things.

The mind of a sage regards Heaven, Earth, and all things as one body. He looks upon all people of the world, whether inside or outside his family, or whether far or near, but all with blood and breath, as his brothers and children. He wants to secure, preserve, educate, and nourish all of them so as to fulfill his desire of forming one body with all things.[1]

Once, during the Three Dynasties, all men were akin to the sage; and until their minds became "obstructed by selfishness and blocked by material desires,"[2] they lived in a harmonious society of people who did "not have different opinions, nor did families have different practices."[3] Prospering by a refined division of labor, each person knew his proper place, and "there was no pursuit after the knowledge of seeing and hearing to confuse them, no memorization and recitation to hinder them, no writing of flowery compositions to indulge in, and no chasing after success and profit."[4] Although differentiated, the community was still an integrated organism.

There was no distinction between the self and the other, or between the self and things. It is like the body of a person. The eyes see, the ears hear, the hands hold, and the feet walk, all fulfilling the function of the body. The eyes are not ashamed of their not being able to hear. When the ears hear

Books], 1:2b, cited and translated in Wing-tsit Chan, *A Source Book in Chinese Philosophy* (Princeton: Princeton University Press, 1963), p. 708. Mao's school notebooks contained other references to the three Wei's of Ning-tu: Wei Li (1629–1695), Wei Chi-jui (1620–1677), and Wei Hsi (1624–1681). See Li Jui, *Mao Tse-tung* (Peking: Chung-kuo ch'ing-nien ch'u pan-she, 1957), p. 38. The preface to Wei Hsi's works "explains what he meant by useful learning, that is to say, learning which is the result of clear reasoning and which can be put to practical use. Knowledge which cannot be so applied is, according to Wei Hsi, no knowledge at all." Arthur Hummel, *Eminent Chinese of the Ch'ing Period* (Washington, D.C.: Government Printing Office, 1943), pp. 847–848. Finally, other instances of both Wang Yang-ming and Wang Fu-chih's influence on Mao have been singled out in Fung Yu-lan, "Mao Tse-tung et la philosophie chinoise," *La Pensée,* 55:79–87.

something, the eyes will direct their attention to it. The feet are not ashamed that they are not able to grasp. When a hand feels for something, the feet will move forward. For the original material force feels and is present in the entire body, and the blood and veins function smoothly.[5]

Somehow—for, Wang did not have a satisfactory explanation of degeneration—the "kingly way" was stopped up, and the weeds of self-seeking and profit suddenly obstructed the Tao of the sage. People ceased to be contented limbs of the body politic. As they coveted the virtues* of others, even the doorway to Confucianism was blocked. Different schools of interpretation arose; fripperies and formalisms— textual criticism, memorization, flowery writing—developed. "Students of the world found themselves in a theater where a hundred plays were being presented, as it were," so that "the poison of the doctrine of success and profit has infected the innermost recesses of man's mind and has become his second nature." [6]

Wang Yang-ming's ideal society may appear in some of the assumptions of Chinese Marxists: personal interests are egoistic, socially destructive, and characteristically poisonous; the ideal society functions through members united in a single body; intellectual learning for its own sake is a stylish waste of time. However, Wang Yang-ming's ideal society mattered less for its political absence than its intellectual presence, which inspired his sagelike mission. Men's minds might be poisoned, but "fortunately, the Principle of Nature is inherent in the human mind and can never be destroyed and the intelligence of innate knowledge shines through eternity without variation." [7] His doctrine of mind, declared Wang, could save society, if "heroic scholars" would ponder it long enough to recover their own "original minds."

Wang's own "original mind" had not been recovered with ease.[8] The son of Wang Hua, minister of personnel in Nanking, he was born in 1472 in Yü-yao, just southeast of Hangchow in Chekiang. At first interested in military studies, then in Buddhist and Taoist self-cultivation, he finally acquired the metropolitan degree in 1499. Wang's brilliant ideas on strategy against the Mongols soon made a name for him in the capital—a reputation enhanced even further in 1504 when the examination questions he posed to the candidates of Shantung province revealed his broad learning and acute intelligence. In another era such a promising young official might have been satisfied to live up to his peers' esteem. But these were not placid years. Wang's intense desire

---

* "Virtue" in this context resembles its meaning in Plato's *Republic* as the condition of a thing which allows it to perform well its proper function.

to understand himself, combined with the challenges imposed on his integrity by political turmoil, impelled him toward fundamental philosophical invention. In 1505, for instance, a new emperor (Wu-tsung) acceded to the throne and promptly fell under the domination of the most notorious eunuch in Ming history, Liu Chin. After purging three hundred civil officials who opposed him, Liu installed allies of his own in most official posts and went on to enrich himself and his followers at the expense of the state. (When his wealth was later confiscated it was said to amount to 2,400,000 pieces of gold and 25,791,800 ounces of silver.) Forced to choose between sycophancy and resistance, Wang Yang-ming elected in 1506 to participate in the opposition to Liu. For this he was sentenced to be flogged forty strokes (a punishment which could sometimes be capital, depending upon the recipient's health— Wang fell unconscious at the thirtieth) and ordered to serve as head of the relay system at Lung-ch'ang in Kweichow.

By the spring of 1508, Wang found himself in the malarial mountains of southwestern China serving as a menial postal official, surrounded by Miao aborigines and quite convinced that he would not physically survive the exile. He faced the prospect of extinction, of nothingness, with profound despair until the night he experienced a moment of revelation—an illumination as important to Chinese philosophy as Pascal's fall from the carriage was to French thought. But let us have the *nien-p'u* (chronological biography) of Wang Yang-ming speak for itself:

Third Year [of Cheng-te, that is, 1508]. The Teacher was 37 sui [that is, 36 years old]: at Lung-ch'ang.

Spring: reaches Lung-ch'ang.
The Teacher began to apprehend *ko-wu* and *chih-chih.**

Lung-ch'ang is in the midst of the dense brambles† and myriad mountains of northwestern Kweichow. Vipers, goblins, noxious poisons, and malarial miasmas abound there. Barbarians [speak] a shrike-tongued chatter. Outlaws from the Central Land [of China] are the only ones who can communicate with them. Formerly they had no dwellings and [it was Wang Yang-ming who] first taught them the custom of erecting wood-frame abodes.

At this time [Liu] Chin's hatred had not yet abated. [Wang] himself calculated that success and failure, honor and disgrace, could all be transcended;

---

* These terms will be explained below.
† This phrase has come to mean "a place of detention."

and thought only of life and death. His consciousness had not yet altered, and so he made [himself] a sarcophagus, and took an oath before it, saying, "I will await my fate, and that is all." Day and night he dwelt in uprightness, clearing his gloom in order to seek the oneness of tranquility. This he prolonged, flushing his breast.*

As all of his retainers had fallen ill he himself cut firewood and fetched water, making rice gruel to feed them. Moreover, since he feared that they would dwell on their grief, he sang odes to them. As they were still joyless, he chanted *Yueh* melodies, mixing [the songs] with jokes until they were able to begin to forget their desperate plight [amid] barbarians and disease.

Since he reflected that the sages had occupied this [kind of desperate position as well without losing self-control], what kind of Tao had they? In the middle of the night he abruptly had a great awakening (*ta-wu*) to the meaning of *ko-wu* and *chih-chih*. It was as though a voice spoke from within. He unconsciously cried out and jumped up, startling awake all his retainers. He had begun to realize that the Tao of the sages is that my own nature (*hsing*) is sufficient unto itself. Hitherto, he had been mistaken in seeking principles in things. Now he tacitly recalled the words of the Five Classics as proof.[9]

The proof he sought was to be found in the original text of the *Ta hsueh* (The Great Learning, or, as Chu Hsi interpreted it, Learning for Adults) from the *Li chi* (Record of rites). The original text had been slightly altered by Chu Hsi to become one of the famous "Four Books," which were the staple of doctrinaire learning during the Ming dynasty. In it occurred the two phrases which Wang had pondered during his Lung-Ch'ang exile: *ko-wu* and *chih-chih*. The altered *Ta hsueh* reads:

The ancients who wished to illustrate illustrious virtue throughout the kingdom first ordered well their own states. Wishing to order well their states, they first regulated their families. Wishing to regulate their families, they first cultivated their persons. Wishing to cultivate their persons, they first rectified their hearts. Wishing to rectify their hearts, they first sought to be sincere in their thoughts. Wishing to be sincere in their thoughts, they first

---

* This refers to Taoist meditation. *Ching,* tranquility, was the form of Neo-Confucian meditation widely practiced in the Ming under Taoist influence. See Liu Ts'un-yuan, "Taoist Self-Cultivation in Ming Thought," in Wm. Theodore de Bary, ed., *Self and Society in Ming Thought* (New York: Columbia University Press, 1970), pp. 291–330. These techniques of meditation were practiced by Chan Jo-shui (1466–1560), Wang Yang-ming's friend, who was a disciple of Ch'en Hsien-chang (1428–1500). I believe that the "flushing in the breast" (or mind, *hsiung-chung shuai-shuai*) refers to Ch'en's practice of "washing the mind" (*hsi-hsin*) in order to preserve its quiescence through sustained effort. See Jen Yu-wen, "Ch'en Hsien-chang's Philosophy," in de Bary, *Self and Society,* p. 78.

extended to the utmost their knowledge. Such extension of knowledge (*chih-chih*) lay in the investigation of things (*ko-wu*).[10]

The original text in the *Li chi* appended two more phrases to this section: "This is called knowing the root (*pen*). This is called the perfecting of knowledge."

What Chu Hsi had done was to pull those two sentences out of context and insert them later in the *Ta hsueh* as the commentary of Tseng-tzu, Confucius' disciple. Without those two phrases, the portion quoted just above made the foundation of self-cultivation the "investigation of things" or *ko-wu*. All Confucianists agreed that good governance depended upon cultivation of the self. Chu Hsi specifically believed that the latter was a series of stages of refinement, beginning with the awareness that the "heart" or mind—the metaphysical portion of the self—was the master of the body. Normally quiescent, it could be aroused by sensations to send out activities or thoughts in the form of volition or will (*i*): "that which is sent out by the mind" (*hsin chih so fa*).[11] Refinement of the self therefore depended upon making that will sincere by extending one's knowledge through the investigation of things. As Chu explained it in his commentary to the *Ta hsueh:*

If we wish to carry out knowledge to the utmost, we must investigate the principles of all things we come into contact with, for the intelligent mind of man is certainly formed to know, and there is not a single thing in which its principles do not inhere. But so long as all principles are not investigated, man's knowledge is incomplete. On this account, the Learning for Adults [namely Great Learning], at the outset of its lessons, instructs the learner, in regard to all things in the world, to proceed from what knowledge he has of their principles, and pursue his investigation of them, until he reaches the extreme point. After exerting himself in this way for a long time, he will suddenly find himself possessed of a wide and far-reaching penetration. Then, the qualities of all things, whether external or internal, the subtle or the coarse, will all be apprehended, and the mind, in its entire substance and its relations to things, will be perfectly intelligent. This is called the investigation of things. This is called the perfection of knowledge.[12]

However, Chu Hsi's interpretation disturbed many philosophers, because it subsumed the cultivation of the inner heaven-given self under the laborious "investigation" of outer objects. As Chu Hsi urged men to search for the principles of being in external things in order to better illuminate the self, he seemed to separate the personal subject from the world of objects. This was no Cartesian divorce, to be sure; for, was the self not united by those principles to the greater Being of all nature? But it still offended those accustomed to Taoistic modes of immersion in uninterrupted Being. Perhaps they did not fully understand Chu Hsi's entire system of thought, because if T'ang Chün-i—the twentieth-century philosopher—is right, Chu Hsi did devote a great deal of attention to the inner quietistic mind.* Nevertheless he appeared, in contrast with other philosophers, to be splitting the ego from nature.

Opposed to Chu Hsi's School of Principle (*li-hsueh*) was Lu Hsiang-shan's (1139–1193) School of Mind (*hsin-hsueh*), which tended to reject the doctrine of external investigation. Once Lu's pupil, Li Po-min, asked his teacher to explain how things should be investigated. Lu responded: "Investigate the principle of things." Po-min said: "The myriad things under heaven are extremely multitudinous; how, then, can we investigate all of them exhaustively?" The teacher replied: "The myriad things are already complete in us. It is only necessary to apprehend their principle." [13] And, in a letter to another disciple, Lu wrote:

How can this principle not exist in us? If we cause our will not to waver, then it [that is, principle] will daily become clearer and brighter, like a stream which daily grows more luxuriant. If one seeks to infuse it [that is, this principle into oneself] from without, this is to choke oneself off from its source and cut oneself off from its origin.[14]

Lu did not distinguish between inner and outer mind because the universe itself comprised our *hsin,* there being only one original mind which we must attain by combatting our individual egoisms. Although this is a form of idealism, it should not be misunderstood as a Neo-Platonic

---

* In a recent article—"The Development of the Concept of Moral Mind from Wang Yang-ming to Wang Chi," in Wm. Theodore de Bary, ed., *Self and Society in Ming Thought* (New York: Columbia University Press, 1970), pp. 93–120—T'ang argued that Chu Hsi's analysis of the mind was structured at two different levels. Psychologically, it dwelt in the realm of matter (*ch'i*) and therefore responded to external impressions with feelings. Ontologically, it contained heaven's principles on its own, though these were not necessarily self-consciously realized. These two states, ontological and psychological, were expressed in Chu Hsi's epistemology by the distinction between not yet expressed (*wei-fa*) and already expressed (*i-fa*) moments of, respectively, quiescence and activity. Therefore, says T'ang, Chu Hsi makes an axiological distinction between the mind at the highest level of realization (namely, attaining the Tao of heaven), at the medium and most commonly human, and at the lowest level in which mind sinks into its own selfish desires. The cultivation of the mind depends therefore on both level and function. In terms of the latter, the not yet expressed mind is to be cultivated by *han-yang* or self-nourishment; and the expressed portion by the investigation of things.

mysticism which believed outer objects to be mere manifestations of real essences projected by the original mind.[15] Instead, the *hsin* represented for Lu Hsiang-shan both man's rational and affective nature. Thus, his idealism unified matter and principle, function and substance, instead of allowing them to become separated as in Chu Hsi's thought.

When Wang Yang-ming engaged in meditation at Lung-ch'ang, he was pursuing the quiescence of the School of Mind. However, he had neither intuitively found that state nor resolved the difficulty which Chu Hsi's doctrine of "investigation" posed for it, before his moment of revelation which amounted to the certain conviction that the highest good—heavenly principle—existed within the mind and was accessible to it without immediate reference to external things. It was an underlying principle, not a category; a state in which the mind dwelt, not a categorical imperative.

Abiding in the highest good is to manifesting character and loving people as the carpenter's square and compass are to the square and circle, or rule and measure to length, or balances and scales to weight. . . . People fail to realize that the highest good is in their minds and seek it outside. As they believe that everything or every event has its own definite principle, they search for the highest good in individual things. Consequently, the mind becomes fragmentary. . . . Once it is realized that the highest good is in the mind and does not depend on any search outside, then the mind will have definite direction and there will be no danger of its becoming fragmentary.[16]

As a twenty-year-old, Wang had once tried to realize Chu Hsi's doctrine of investigation by spending seven days gazing at a grove of bamboos—laboriously seeking Being's principle in those plants. According to his *nien-p'u,* he believed that: "A blade of grass or a tree was each imbued with the extreme principle. In the official residence [of his father in Peking] were many bamboos, and so he thought to take the bamboos and investigate them. He reflected deeply on their principle but got nothing. Subsequently he fell sick." [17] Years later, long after the Lung-ch'ang illumination, Wang explained the incident to his disciples. The experiment had begun with a friend of his named Ch'ien, who had succumbed to exhaustion after three days of forced meditation on the bamboos.

At first I said that it was because his energy and strength were insufficient. Therefore I myself went to try to investigate to the utmost. From morning till night, I was unable to find the principles of the bamboos. On the sev-

enth day I also became sick because I thought too hard. In consequence
we sighed to each other and said that it was impossible to be a sage or
worthy, for we do not have the tremendous energy to investigate things that
they have. After I had lived among the barbarians for [almost] three years,
I understood what all this meant and realized that there is really nothing in
the things in the world to investigate, that the effort to investigate things is
only to be carried out in and with reference to one's body and mind, and
that if one firmly believes that everyone can become a sage, one will naturally be able to take up the task of investigating things. This idea, gentlemen, I must convey to you.[18]

The Lung-ch'ang experience was therefore Wang's discovery after years
of effort that he had been searching for his selfhood in the wrong place.
The simple truth that principles were not external to the mind was a
conviction that gave joyous relief. Simply know thyself, he urged thereafter; look *into* your own mind and you will find there the nature which
heaven has bestowed upon all of us. Do not confuse this with Taoist
meditation: the empty quest for one's original mind. Instead, consciously search within for the *principle* of Being which, while identical
with, actually creates the temporal manifestations of all cosmic principles.

He who only seeks his original mind and consequently neglects the principles of things is one who has lost his original mind. For the principles of
things are not external to the mind. . . . The substance of the mind is
nature, and nature is identical with principle. Consequently, as there is the
mind of filial piety toward parents, there is the principle of filial piety. As
there is the mind of loyalty toward the ruler, there is the principle of loyalty.
If there is no mind of loyalty, there will be no principle of loyalty.[19]

Because Wang was, after all, a Confucianist who had rejected Buddhism for its inattention to familial obligations, he was bound to a degree of orthodoxy that would not permit him to abandon the sanction
of the classics. His illumination at Lung-ch'ang had personally convinced him that the orthodox Neo-Confucian theory of *ko-wu* was
wrong. But how was he to square that belief with the passage in the
Ta hsueh which Chu Hsi had used to justify his doctrine of investigation? The proof—the sanction for his vision—which the *nien-p'u* men-
tions came when he reflected on Chu Hsi's rearrangement of the text. By
going back to the original text, which he now declared the correct one,[20]
Wang saw that the passage in question now ended with "the perfecting
[or extension, that is, *chih*] of knowledge," in place of the "investigation

of things." Suddenly the entire sequence of cultivation was dramatically reversed for him. Chu Hsi's version had been a regression:

From rectification of the heart or mind (*last act*)
to sincerity of thought or will (*preceding act*)
to extension of knowledge (*preceding act*)
to the investigation of things (*starting point*).

As soon as Wang realized that the original passage ended with a summing up, he made of it a progression:

From rectification of the mind (*first act*)
to sincerity of will (*succeeding act*)
to extension of knowledge (*succeeding act*)
to the investigation of things (*last act*).

The *Li chi's* meaning must have recognized the importance of beginning within oneself and then moving outward.

The task of the *Great Learning* consists in manifesting the clear character. To manifest the clear character is none other than to make the will sincere, and the task of making the will sincere is none other than the investigation of things and the extension of knowledge. If one regards the sincerity of the will as the basis and from there proceeds to the task of the investigation of things and the extension of knowledge, only then can the task have a solution. Even doing good and removing evil are nothing but the work of the sincerity of the will. But according to Chu Hsi's new arrangement the first step is to investigate the principles of things to the utmost. In that case one will be drifting and be at a loss and there will not be any solution at all.[21]

Now there was only one more definition Wang would have to make to reconcile the canon with his belief. The original text did unambiguously promote the "investigation of things." But why, in the end, investigate the principles in things if they are already in one's mind? Wang was inspired to semantically transform the *ko*, or investigation, into a willful act of realization. This was permitted him by other denotations of that word.

The fundamental meaning of *ko* is "to attain to." Even Chu Hsi's phrase included the notion alluded to in his discussion of the *Changes*: a knowledge of heaven puts the sage on a kind of par with the cosmos. *Ko yü kao t'ien*, for instance, means to be equal to heaven-on-high, deriving that sense from *ko chih t'ien ming*, to attain to the knowledge of heaven. As Chu Hsi himself conceived of knowledge as a form of power, Wang Yang-ming made that concept even more purposive—not only by emphasizing will as the function of knowledge, but also by taking *ko* in another one of its meanings: to pattern or correct (as in *ko-hsin,* to regulate the mind).

The word *ko* in *ko-wu* is the same as the *ko* in Mencius' saying that "A great man rectified (*ko*) the ruler's mind." It means to eliminate what is incorrect in the mind so as to preserve the correctness of an original substance. Wherever the will is, the incorrectness must be eliminated so correctness may be preserved. In other words, in all places and at all times the Principle of Nature must be preserved. This is the investigation of principles to the utmost.[22]

As Wang so redefined the "investigation of things," he also thought to discover the true meaning of *chih-chih* (knowing to the utmost): the extension or realization of knowledge in action.

The necessity of the *Great Learning* is making the will sincere and that is all. The effort (*kung*) of making the will sincere is the rectification (*ko*) of objects, and that is all. The norm (*chi*) of making the will sincere is resting in the highest excellence. The pattern (*tse*) of resting in the highest excellence is the extension of knowledge and that is all.[23]

Wang Yang-ming's doctrine of self-realization prized independent judgment. Although he sought classical sanction, he was quick to insist that his own sense of right and wrong mattered most in the end.

If words are examined in the mind and found to be wrong, although they have come from the mouth of Confucius, I dare not accept them as correct. How much less those from people inferior to Confucius! If words are examined in the mind and found to be correct, although they have come from the mouth of ordinary people, I dare not regard them as wrong. How much less those of Confucius! [24]

This daring prerogative, which burst through all of his writings, gave tremendous force to his teachings—especially since they spread in a time when men so heavily felt the weight of their distant past. What capacity had any of them for creativity with so much so far behind them? How could any really hope to emulate the accomplishments of Confucius, or more than foolishly dream of becoming a sage? Wang's own youthful disappointment in his lack of energy, his sheer inability to imitate the concentration of the sages, disappeared after the euphoric self-discovery at Lung-ch'ang; and he tried hard to transmit that same sense of self-possibility to all who would listen.

The sages are sages simply because their minds are purely imbued with the heavenly principle without being muddled by human desires. It is just as pure gold is pure merely because its fineness is sufficient, being untarnished by brass or lead. When a man reaches [the point of] being purely imbued with the heavenly principle, then he is a sage. When gold reaches [the point of] being sufficient in fineness, then it is pure. Thus, the talents of the sages are as much of uneven volume as the quantity of gold is of differing weight. Yao and Shun are like a mass of gold which weighs ten thousand *i.* Wen wang [ancestor of the Chou] and Confucius, nine thousand *i;* Yü [founder of the Hsia], T'ang [founder of the Shang] and Wu wang [first ruler of the Chou], seven or eight thousand *i;* and Po I [minister of Shun] and I Yin [minister of T'ang] like four or five thousand *i.* Though their talent differed, their pure adherence to the heavenly principle was the same, and they can all be called sages; just as though gold may differ in weight, all can be called pure as the quality is equally pure. . . . Therefore, even common men can become sages if they are willing to study so as to make their minds purely imbued with the heavenly principle.[25]

That is what is meant when it is said that anyone can become a Yao or a Shun. Pity those who still believed that they had to have the total capacities of a sage—the learning, the knowledge, the concentration—*before* enlightenment. Such poor souls would futilely spend the rest of their lives poring over books and scrutinizing institutions in the hope of educing sagehood, when the principle was already accessible just within them. If the hallmark of Sung philosophy had been its hope of directly approaching the sages of the past via their writings, then Ming thought, under Wang's influence, was distinguished by its belief in the possibility of discovering sagehood in the self, directly accessible to those who would let the mind create itself.

Wang Yang-ming's sage was not a superhuman creature beyond mortal attainment. In fact, it was his closeness to average men that defined him best. As Wang described him, he was a being whose mind encompassed all creatures, and for whom "the highest good is the ultimate principle of manifesting character and loving people." [26] That last quality—loving the people, *ch'in min*—also differentiated Wang's hero from Chu Hsi's sage. This difference hung upon the textual interpretation of a single character in the *Great Learning.* Chu Hsi had declared the Ch'eng brothers right for believing that the word *ch'in* (relatives; affection, to love; self, to attend in person) really stood for *hsin* (to renovate); and that the phrase *ch'in min* in the *Great Learning* actually signified that the sage who had once manifested character (*ming-ming te*—illustrated [his own] illustrious nature [by self-cultivation]) would effect a similar transformation in others by renovating the people (*hsin min*).²⁷ Since that placed the sage above normal men, his obligation to extend himself *down* to them was an elitist mission of paternalism.* By declaring that anyone could be a sage, Wang Yangming was trying to shorten the distance between the enlightened and those who had not yet "manifested character." He was especially conscious of the danger of paternal condescension. Such an egoism deluded the seeker of sagehood, who could easily confuse true knowledge with intellectual arrogance. The seeker should begin by opening himself to all men, combining the manifesting of character with the special tasks it entailed. In that sense there was no before-and-after change. One did not begin with cultivation and only after success begin to renovate others. "Loving people" and "manifesting character" went hand in hand. Action and knowledge accompanied each other.

For its time this was a bold and egalitarian doctrine of humaneness which invigorated Confucianism as it spread among humbler strata of fifteenth- and sixteenth-century Chinese society. (In fact, Ku Yen-wu's seventeenth-century elitism can be seen in part as a reaction to the populist appeals of some of Wang's many disciples.) Yet, despite the size of Wang's following, most of his students found it quite hard to acquire the same degree of confidence in the self that their master per-

* This Neo-Confucian image of the sage (*sheng-jen*) corresponds to that of the superior man (*chün-tzu*) in later New Text thought. Perhaps the common element, at least so far as the *chün-tzu* was the center of K'ang Yu-wei's philosophy, was the Buddhist influence. K'ang, as we have seen, at first saw himself as a Bodhisattva who had attained enlightenment and was obliged to help the still-benighted. The figure of the sage in Ch'eng-Chu Confucianism also looked to that inspiration. See Denis Twitchett, "The Fan Clan's Charitable Estate, 1050–1760," in David Nivison and Arthur Wright, eds., *Confucianism in Action* (Stanford: Stanford University Press, 1957), pp. 97–133. There are interesting social suggestions as well. Although the eleventh century saw the establishment of the examination gentry as the dominant social elite, the upper classes retained a characteristically aristocratic attitude toward their inferiors. The spread of education during the Ming blurred the distinction between the *shih* and commoners. However, as that trend increased in the Ch'ing, and especially in the nineteenth century as so many bought degrees, we might suppose that some—seeking claims to distinction—would conceive of an aristocracy of the mind. Juan Yuan's circle would be just such a group. K'ang Yu-wei himself came from a family which had just risen in the world. But so had many others, so that it was not sufficient to merely boast a degree as such. Once again, the "true" gentleman would look down on the rest of society, mixing deprecation with paternalistic obligation.

sonally demonstrated to them. A man of action who had forged his philosophy under dire emotional stress, Wang realized the trouble others who lacked his strength of mind might have in combining meditative intuition and worldly principles. The difficulties stemmed less from the logic of his idealism than from the tendency of his students to allow meditation or reflection on the original substance of the mind to divert them from the task of realizing knowledge through the secular mission of rectification. It was to combat this tendency that Wang reiterated the theme of the unity of knowledge and action.[28]

To Wang the essence of the Confucian creed was action. How could one possibly conceive of knowledge divorced from practice? Some might believe that the opening line (*hsueh erh shih hsi chih*) of the *Analects* meant "learning with a constant perseverance"; but in Wang's view the proper signification was "under the circumstances of learning one is constantly practicing (*hsi*)." His meaning was more subtle than it seems; for, Wang believed that one simply cannot know anything unless it is done, unless it simultaneously inspires action. When Ku Tung-ch'iao insisted that he had to know what the task was before he could perform it, Wang said: "A man must have the desire for food before he knows the food. This desire to eat is the will; it is already the beginning of action." [29] The will concretized or objectified knowledge into things.

The mind is the master of the body, and the pure intelligence and clear consciousness of the mind are the innate or original knowledge. When this innate knowledge which is pure intelligence and clear consciousness is influenced by things and events and responds to them with activity, it is called the will. With knowledge, there will be the will. Without knowledge, there will be no will. Is knowledge not the substance of the will? For the will to function, there must be the thing in which it is to function, and the thing is an event. When the will functions in the service of parents, then serving parents is a thing. . . . Wherever the will is applied there cannot be nothing. Where this is a particular will, there is a particular thing corresponding to it, and where there is no particular will, there will be no particular thing corresponding to it. Is a thing, then, not the function of the will? [30]

Although Wang Yang-ming began with idea (innate knowledge), he avoided ideation by making volition the response of consciousness to outer objects. Volition or will was then the function of knowledge and in rational action created a thing as its own particular function.

To be sure, Wang's things were really events, not objects. But that was the only way he could preserve the unity of knowledge and action without falling to either side of the narrow epistemological promontory he occupied. On the one side was Buddhist subjectivism, which declared external things a projection of the mind. On the other was Chu Hsi's rationalism, which empirically assumed the existence of outer things and made enlightenment the prize for investigating the cosmic principles imbedded within them. Because he thought the consequences of Buddhism were far more harmful than Ch'eng-Chu Confucianism, Wang steadfastly decried the temptation of assuming that the outer world was not real. But if knowing objects was then not their ideational creation, Wang could only retain his union of self and nature by transforming knowing from a reception of principle into its projection—an idea expressed by his definition of *chih-chih* as the extension of knowledge. Even after the Lung-ch'ang revelation, however, Wang continued to distinguish the substance of mind from its active functioning. It was true that the cultivation of moral action refined the substance of mind, but for a long time to come he would not conceive of the necessary and absolute identity of mental substance and function. That connection became apparent to him in the same way he realized the meaning of *ko-wu* and *chih-chih:* as an existential conviction required to carry him through another great personal political crisis.

In 1510 Wang Yang-ming was brought back from exile in Lung-ch'ang to serve as the magistrate of Lu-ling district (modern Chi-an) in the more civilized region of Kiangsi. In the autumn of that year, the eunuch Liu Chin died, and Wang's administrative talents were thereafter permitted to flourish. A string of successful assignments in the Ministry of Justice and the Ministry of Personnel culminated with his appointment in 1514 as chief minister of the Court of State Ceremonial in Nanking. Two years later, after government forces had repeatedly failed to pacify a spreading peasant rebellion in Fukien and Kiangsi, Wang was recommended because of his command of military strategy for the post of grand coordinator, elevated to the rank of censor, and placed in charge of the suppression campaign. His pacification of the two provinces was masterful. By 1518 he had perfected his *hsiang-yueh* (village covenant) system and brought relative order back to those troubled areas.

The next year the army garrison at Foochow mutinied. On his way there to quell the revolt, Wang suddenly received news that Prince Ning (earlier a supporter of Liu Chin), who was based at Nan-ch'ang in Kiangsi, was marching on Nanking with sixty thousand troops to usurp the throne. Wang did not hesitate to return to Kiangsi and capture the enemy base, forcing Prince Ning to turn back to Nan-ch'ang to try to recover his headquarters. After four days of fighting, Wang Yang-ming defeated and captured Prince Ning.

This victory should have produced great rewards for Wang. Instead, it provoked a grave crisis for him and his followers. When the prince had begun his march on Nanking, Emperor Wu-tsung (who reigned from 1506 to 1521) had been urged by his flattering courtiers to personally lead the imperial columns mustered against the usurper. Wang's lightning success now deprived Wu-tsung of that glorious opportunity; and his courtiers, in turn, resented Wang Yang-ming's disregard for the court's sensibilities (he could at least have had the decency to await the emperor's arrival before delivering the coup de grâce!). Soon, capital rumormongers were heard to say that Wang had conspired with Prince Ning to revolt in the first place. As evidence, they reminded the emperor that Wang and the prince had exchanged envoys *before* the coup was launched. Actually, Wang had been trying to dissuade the prince from his rash act, but to many this seemed proof of treason. In fact, until 1521, when Emperor Wu-tsung died, Wang Yang-ming's fate was quite uncertain. The innuendo could not be dispelled; and he, a loyal minister, was not even allowed to communicate with his emperor. Because hundreds, even thousands, of lives hung in the balance, the crisis was even more frightening for him than the Lung-ch'ang exile. As Wang was once again thrown back on the resources of his own conscience, he endured his anxiety by constructing the final element of his philosophic system: *liang-chih* or original-good knowing.[31]

In the early months of 1521, Wang wrote his disciple, Tsou Ch'ienchih (1491–1562), that:

I have recently come to believe that the three words, "extend the original-good knowing" (*chih liang-chih*), are truly the pure and uncorrupted dharma-eye* of the disciples of the sage [Confucius]. Last year I still had not quite dispelled my doubts. But now, owing to many recent events, [I am convinced that] this original-good knowing alone is absolutely complete and sufficient [in itself]. It is like controlling a boat by getting its helm. In calm and shallow waters, everything is up to the will. But supposing one runs into a squall and adverse seas; the tiller remains in the hand so that one can avoid the peril of drowning.[32]

* *Cheng-fa yen-ts'ang*, which Buddhists regard as the same as *ch'ing-ching fa-yen* or the *Parisuddhi* (free from evil) dharma-eye of the bodhisattva. Wang's use of this term elevates the *liang-chih* beyond good and evil, which posed difficulties I discuss later.

The term *liang-chih* occurred in *Mencius:* "The ability possessed by men without having been acquired by learning is intuitive ability (*liang-neng*), and the knowledge possessed by them without the exercise of thought is their intuitive knowledge (*liang-chih*)." [33] As Wang redefined it in his "Inquiry on the *Great Learning*":

This innate knowledge of the good is what Mencius meant when he said, "The sense of right and wrong is common to all men." The sense of right and wrong requires no deliberation to know, nor does it depend on learning to function. This is why it is called innate knowledge. It is my nature endowed by heaven, the original substance of my mind, naturally intelligent, shining, clear, and understanding. Whenever a thought or a wish arises, my mind's faculty of innate knowledge itself is always conscious of it. Whether it is good or evil, my mind's innate knowing faculty also knows it. It has nothing to do with others. [34]

Thus, his *liang-chih* existed above mere thought. Instead of being a superego socially conditioned to morality by *li* (propriety), Wang's *liang-chih* expressed his Mencian faith in man's essential goodness and distilled the heavenly principle within us. A thought might be correct or deviant, but the *liang-chih* (the faculty of knowing the good or evil of those thoughts) provided the moral guidance that made it unnecessary to look outside the self, to the judgment of others or the writings of the sages, for direction. Where Wang had formerly written of devoting the self to principle, he now substituted the formula: "The *liang-chih* of my mind is precisely what is called heavenly principle." [35]

Would it therefore be detached from sensory knowledge? Not in the least. "*Liang-chih* does not exist owing to the senses nor [does it] separate itself from the senses." [36] It is not pure reason or abstract schemata transcendent to the world of things. It *knows* on a higher plane than our senses know, but it only knows what our volition (*i-nien*) wills by judging the morality of concrete events. "Truly this [*liang-chih*] is a touchstone to test gold, a compass needle to point the way." [37] The unity of knowledge and action is consequently guaranteed in the higher knowing of *liang-chih,* for truly to know is to extend one's innate knowledge by judging those concrete events.

Now, when one sets out to extend his innate knowledge to the utmost, does this mean something illusory, hazy, in a vacuum, and unreal? No, it means something real. Therefore, the extension of knowledge must consist in the investigation of things. A thing is an event. For every emanation of the will there must be an event corresponding to it. The event to which the will is directed is a thing. To investigate it is to rectify. It is to rectify that which is incorrect so it can return to its original correctness.[38]

By identifying *liang-chih* with heavenly principle, Wang defined innate knowledge as both the act of moral intuition and the principle of that intuition.[39] This, as T'ang Chün-i brilliantly points out, was the essential point of Wang Yang-ming's philosophy as well as its major claim to originality. It permitted Wang an existential monism that still employed the ontological dualism of Chu Hsi. That is, Wang kept substance (*t'i*) and function (*yung*) as logical categories so that he could regard the mind's substance functionally while explaining the mind's function substantially.[40]

The great appeal of *liang-chih* to Ming Neo-Confucianists was its monism: the immersion of mind in being. The certainty of its existence came from the thinker's sense of personal totality, which was an intuition in the end immune to critical analysis. If the forte of Kantian logic was its brilliant acuity and fine sensitivity to categorical distinctions—adamantine and diamond-sharp in their polished facets—then the force of Neo-Confucian thought was its adumbrations of meaning, its suggestive shadows. Naturally, there is both more and less to the difference than a contrast between, say, chiaroscuro and a misty Sung landscape, and we should not make too Pascalian a distinction between some archetypically European *esprit de géometrie* opposed to the Orient's *esprit de finesse*. Is there that much less clarity in Wang's "original-good knowing" than in Karl Jaspers' *Existenz*?

When *Existenz* understands itself, it is not like my understanding of another, nor the sort of understanding whose contents can be abstracted from the person understanding, nor a sort of looking at; rather it is an origin which itself first arises in its own self-clarification. It is not like sharing in something else, but is at once the understanding and the being of what is understood.[41]

And for that matter, were Chu Hsi's antithetical categories—movement and repose (*tung/ching*), not expressed and already expressed (*wei-fa/i-fa*), substance and function (*t'i/yung*)—not concerned with hard certitudes?

At least a few of Wang Yang-ming's own students were interested enough in these logical categories to ask him how they specifically related to his doctrine of the mind. Wang had explained that:

The mind is without movement and repose. To speak of its repose [designates] its substance. To speak of its movement [designates] its function. Therefore, the learning of a superior man does not divide movement and repose. In his repose, he is constantly stable and is never [possessed by] existence. Thus, he is constantly tranquil. Constantly reacting and constantly tranquil, his movement and his repose both consist of [moral] devotion to the self. This is called "accumulating righteousness." As righteousness is accumulated, he thus can be without regret. This is called "stability in movement and stability in repose." The mind is as one, and that is all. Repose is its substance. Now, were we to seek the foundation of repose, this would disturb its substance. Movement is its function. Now, were we to be apprehensive of its acting with ease, this would destroy its function. Consequently a mind searching for repose is precisely in movement, and a mind hating movement is precisely in repose.[42]

Because he wanted his disciples to be composed in action yet not fall prey to the quietistic pursuit of substance for its own sake, Wang stubbornly denied the distinction between *wei-fa* (not expressed) and *i-fa* (already expressed) to students who argued that mental acts were certainly "expressed." "The meaning of the 'unexpressed' is simply *liang-chih*. Being without before and after, inner and outer, it is wholly a single substance." [43] For, breaking down states of mental activity into epistemological categories meant fragmenting the unity of the *liang-chih*. Wang might privately believe in the logical distinction between *wei-fa* and *i-fa,* but he would refuse to admit that aloud for fear of distracting his students' existential purpose. "If I say that there is an 'unexpressed' and an 'already expressed' then my listeners will just as before fall into the outlook of later literati." [44]

As he guarded the principle of moral intuition (thought and action) from ontological distinction (thought or action), Wang revealed his concern that the doctrine of mind might turn into a justification for inaction. If all the sage had to do was bring himself into accord with the Way, then how was that different from Taoist cultivation? Ch'eng-Chu Confucianism at least used the separation of spirit and matter to enforce aspiration away from self-indulgence toward higher being. Or, to put it another way, Chu Hsi's mission to renovate the people was a more definite call to action than Wang's loving them, which might be mistaken for an appeal to emotion, to merely expressionist feelings. In order to free the conscience, Wang had made the mind complete unto itself. But that independence could have dangerous consequences, because anyone's mind could serve as its own moral judge. Wang, who had expressed such deep faith in the natural ability of men to know the good, could not help but pessimistically realize that men whose will had not been tested were often prone to the illusion of self-mastery divorced from any moral principles whatsoever. Yet to avow categorical imperatives or external absolutes meant breaking the unity of mind, so that Wang could only hope to give the conscience a chance to test itself by making an imperative of action as such. This meant stressing the impossibility of knowing anything without doing it. To Ku Tung-ch'iao he said:

Study, inquiry, thinking, sifting, and practice are all ways of learning. No one really learns anything without carrying it into action. . . . To learn archery, one must hold out the bow, fix the arrow to the string, draw the bow and take aim. To learn writing, one must lay out the paper, take the brush, hold the inkwell, and dip the brush into the ink. In all the world, nothing can be considered learning that does not involve action. Thus the very beginning of learning is already action.[45]

Indeed, effort should be praised for its own sake. When one of his students confessed that he felt obliged at times to forsake effort to reflect, Wang told him: "Throughout his life, a man's effort to learn aims only at this one thing. From youth to old age and from morning to evening, whether anything happens or not, he works only at this one thing. And that is: 'Always be doing something.' "[46]

"Doing something" helped integrate mind with action; true knowledge (which corresponded to Mao's urging to complete acts once begun rather than to Marx's praxis) was fulfillment in action. When a disciple argued that he might know how his parents *should be* filially served without necessarily doing so, Wang responded:

The knowledge and action you refer to are already separated by selfish desires and are no longer knowledge and action in their original substance. There have never been people who know but do not act. . . . They must have actually practiced filial piety and brotherly respect before they can be said to know them. . . . Or take one's knowledge of pain. Only after one has experienced pain can one know pain.[47]

In other words, selfishness explained why people could make a moral judgment without necessarily following it. The *liang-chih* was common to all men, even thieves. If it were entirely extended, a person would spontaneously act in harmony with his naturally good self. Evil appeared when one betrayed the intuitive judgment of the *liang-chih* by following egoistic desires. And because it was so easy to fall into the habit of selfishness, which was the one barrier to a natural union of knowledge and action, one should begin with the sense of effort to overcome the gap between knowledge and action.

The flaw in this explanation was that although each act of perception, each quantum of knowledge, was supposed to engender *spontaneous* action, it did not. Whether illusion or not, a son really could conceive of filial piety without actually practicing it. Therefore, Wang's philosophy was sometimes more hortatory than demonstrative. *He* knew that the original mind is capable of moral intuition. The question was how to formulate it in such a way as to convince his students. As a moralist, he stood in the front rank of Chinese thinkers. As a metaphysician, he faltered at the moment of his philosophy's transmission to his disciples.

17

Wang Yang-ming: Existential Commitment

Late in the fall of 1527—the last year of his life—Wang Yang-ming was recalled from retirement to subdue a rebellion in Kwangsi. The day before his departure from home, his two most ardent disciples—Wang Chi (1498–1583) and Ch'ien Te-hung (1496–1574)—met to discuss their master's teachings. According to the generally accepted account of the meeting, Wang Chi argued that when Wang Yang-ming said that *liang-chih,* the original substance of the mind, was beyond good or evil, he was implying that no such distinction existed in the will because it was impossible to separate the mind's functions from its original substance.

If we say that the substance of the mind is without good and without evil; then, the will is also without good and without evil, knowing is also without good and without evil, and things are also without good and without evil. If we say that the will possesses good and evil, then after all there will still exist good and evil inherent to the mind's substance.[1]

Ch'ien Te-hung had to agree that the mind's substance could not possess evil, since it had been endowed by heaven, the supreme good. But the mind could also be tarnished by bad habits, so men must work at removing selfishness to recover their original purity. "If originally there were no good and evil, there would be no point in discussing [the necessity of] effort (*kung-fu*)." [2]

That evening the two disciples met with Wang Yang-ming on T'ien-ch'üan bridge and asked him to reconcile their difference of opinions. Wang answered that both were correct, just as there were two different types of people in the world. Although the first kind, "men of sharp intelligence" (*li-ken chih jen*), were rarely found, they existed in enough numbers to prove that a person could consciously apprehend the original substance of the mind without laboriously cultivating the will.

Men of sharp intelligence attain revelation directly from their original source. The original substance of men's minds is at first brilliantly clear, and without obstructions (*wu chih*). It is at first that equilibrium of the "not-yet expressed" (*wei-fa*). As soon as men of sharp intelligence have apprehended the original substance, this is precisely their effort, which at once penetrates others, their selves, inner and outer, altogether.[3]

But most people were of a secondary sort (*ch'i-tz'u*), "who cannot prevent habits dwelling on their minds, darkening the original substance." [4] Such a person would first have to be taught how to remove evil from the will before being able to proceed toward the apprehension of the mind's substance.

[Since most] people's minds are [ruled by] habits, if we do not teach them to exert concrete effort to do good and remove evil in their innate knowledge, then they will merely think of original substance suspended in a void. Nothing that they do will in any way be authentic and they will do no more than nourish and realize a [mind of] vacuous quietude.[5]

After reminding Wang Chi and Ch'ien Te-hung of his four basic principles ("The substance of the mind is without good and without evil; the activity of the will possesses good and evil; innate knowledge (*liang-chih*) is knowing good and knowing evil; to rectify things (*ko-wu*) is to do good and remove evil." [6]), Wang Yang-ming urged them each to use the other's method. Since Wang Chi's ideas were best suited for "men of sharp intelligence," and Ch'ien Te-hung's for average people, their teachings would then be complementary. "If you mutually take [each other's interpretation] in practice, then average men—superior ones, inferior ones—can all be led into the Tao." [7]

By admitting that there were two different roads to enlightenment, Wang Yang-ming's T'ien-ch'üan conversation fissioned his school of thought. This was partly because different aspects of the doctrine of mind appealed to different people. Years later, Wang Chi admitted to his own disciples that: "Although none of us codisciples would dare to abandon the basic theory of *liang-chih,* it is still unavoidable that each would determine its meaning by mixing together that which most approximated his particular nature." [8] Furthermore, the T'ien-ch'üan dialogue was reported in conflicting ways. The account used here is taken from Wang Chi's writings and does not mention statements which appear in other sources suggesting that Wang Yang-ming tried to qualify Wang Chi's interpretation. For example, Wang Yang-ming's *nien-p'u* reported that Wang Chi questioned the use of the four basic principles once the original substance had penetrated all things. Wang Yang-ming was supposed to have answered:

These [basic principles] are the thoroughgoing enlightenment of superior and inferior [faculties]. From the very beginning of learning to the attainment of sagehood, there is only this effort. By using this at the beginning of learning there is a methodological entry [into enlightenment]. Though sagehood be attained, it is [still] thoroughly and inexhaustively explored. When Yao and Shun exerted pure effort, it was no more than this. [9]

And Ch'ien Te-hung's version had Wang warn his two disciples: "If each of you holds on to one side, right here you will err in handling properly the different types of man and each in his own way will fail to understand fully the substance of the Way." [10]

Above all, the distinction between "men of sharp intelligence" and those of a secondary mentality (which Wang Chi styled *tun-ken*, ordinary intelligence) posed an elitist temptation for Wang Chi, whose account of the T'ien-ch'üan meeting significantly divided his teacher's doctrine into esoteric and exoteric wings.

The doctrine of our master, Yang-ming, focusses on the *liang-chih*. Nevertheless, when he spoke to his disciples, he taught the Four Axioms. Hsiu-shan [that is, Ch'ien Te-hung] asserts that those were the master's definitive rules, which could not be changed at all. But Lung-ch'i [that is, Wang Chi] says that the master teaches according to circumstances and that these [Four Axioms] are no more than a provisional rule which does not deserve to be regarded as definitive. For, the original substance and activity, what is manifested and what is secret, are nothing more than the same vitality. Mind, thought, knowledge, and object are no more than the same action. If we have understood that the mind is a mind without good or evil, then thought will be a thought without good or evil, knowledge will be a knowledge without good or evil, and the object will be an object without good or evil. . . . The nature which heaven has given us is supremely good without any mixture of evil. . . . If there is good or evil [in the mind], then the thought is disturbed by the object; and then we no longer have the natural flowing of the mind but rather a halt in the forethought of good and of evil. That which flows entirely naturally from nature is a movement without movement.[11]

Consequently, Wang Chi's disciples came to believe that the four basic principles were designed for the less gifted. They, luckier souls, would pursue the higher doctrine of the original substance free of good and evil.

Wang Chi's group was only one of at least three separate schools of Wang Yang-ming's thought which formed soon after his death. Considered most orthodox was Ch'ien Te-hung's, especially opposed to quietists among the master's disciples.

My former teacher [Wang Yang-ming] said, "The substance of the mind is without good and without evil." Shuang-chiang [that is, Nieh Pao, see below] then declared that since the *liang-chih* is originally without good and evil and is the substance of the not-yet expressed (*wei-fa*) state of tranquility, then all one has to do is cultivate this and things (*wu*) will rectify (*ko*) themselves. Now to follow the sway of sensations and objects, and only afterward add the effort of rectifying things is to delude substance for the sake of exploring function—muddying the source to purify the current, so that effort (*kung-fu*) has already fallen to become a second[-ranking] obligation.[12]

Ch'ien did not deny the inner mind. In fact, he prized it so much that he felt it should be kept inviolate. But in his view quietism was a misnomer, because the cultivation of original substance disturbed the very tranquility it sought to achieve; and, by extending effort into the *liang-chih,* ended by obscuring it.

This mind [of ours] comes from nonbeing and initial equilibrium. It is originally static. Though there be one thousand thoughts and one hundred concerns, they are only the divine working of nature: one thousand sensations and one hundred impressions [which is the mind reacting to external nature]. Coming from its source, original substance is constantly tranquil. It is only because I myself have [ordinary] knowledge [of the external world] that there is manifested [love of] success and profit, lust and desire, [differing] capacities, and the senses: all of which make our wills obstinate, creating sensational knowledge along with irresolution and disturbances in the self while the utmost good and the original substance are lost. One must entirely let go of the mind [created by] these habits by beginning to believe in acquiring what is fundamentally one's own nature, which is originally like this [pure mind]. Though the sage be in the midst of helter-skelter and conflict, he can still point to his unmoving true substance: this is *liang-*

chih. Though myriad emotions run helter-skelter, yet [his intuitive sense of] good and evil are not obscured. Though masses [of entities] wish to conflict, yet brightness is in his soul. This is [innate] knowledge. Utmost change without shape, utmost divinity without trace: that is the substance of *liang-chih.* In the equilibrium of the extreme void there is no being in which it dwells [solely]. For, if it had a [single] dwelling place, then that would hinder the extreme void. In people's sensations and impressions there is no time in which it does not exist, yet it has no single moment of cessation. For, if it ceased [that is, if there were a before and after, a *wei-fa* and an *i-fa,* of innate knowledge] then that would obstruct pure spirit. That is why when rage and delight, fear and grief, are each manifested in being, the mind cannot acquire its own rectitude. For, the effort [to attain] the correct mind does not lie in searching elsewhere, but only in making the will sincere. Substance occupies the bright and thoroughgoing [enlightenment] of the original substance; it rests in the utmost good, and that is all.[13]

In sum, Ch'ien sharply divided the mind in two. Pure or essential mind was static nonbeing. Active or existential mind was the product of being: a cluster of sensations created by external objects. Because those sensations were invariably aroused by (selfish) desires, the would-be sage must rectify his sensations—curb those desires—to gain access to pure mind. The quietists erred by treating pure mind as an object of cultivation per se. As *liang-chih* was the principle of heaven within pure mind (shared by all, owned by none) its attribute of universality was easily destroyed by selfishly focussing one's active mind on it for its own sake.

Although Ch'ien Te-hung seemed to be saying that essence was unknowable, he did not mean, like Kant, that it was impervious to analytic reason. His argument rather melded ethics and epistemology. Will (selfish emotion) could sully universal mind with *particularness* by—in terms of Western logic—rendering it contingent. From this Ch'ien could have concluded that emotions (the sum of ordinary knowledge) should be eschewed altogether. But remembering Wang Yang-ming's plea for action, he rejected the quietists and taught his followers to bring the outer mind into consonance with *liang-chih* by making their wills sincere, by stripping themselves of selfishness. In a sense, then, meditation was the height of selfishness, for it "muddied the source."

To remove evil one must exhaust one's fundamental intelligence [in effort]. To do good one cannot occupy one's being [by empty meditation]. This is the principle of rectifying things (*ko-wu*). Therefore, it is not the study of how to investigate the ultimate and original substance which rests in the utmost good. If the motive [behind] good and evil—which, indulged in,

[can] destroy one's life—is sought in nonexhaustion [of effort, that is, quietist meditation], then this obscures one's fundamental intelligence and harms one's incipient life, muddying the source and discriminating the emotions at their current's issue. Such is to regard the knowledge of good and evil as the extreme of knowledge, while not knowing that the substance of *liang-chih* originally was without distinctions between good and evil.[14]

And so, while keeping the precious inner mind free from discrimination, the moral man should observe the proper direction of effort from fundamental intelligence (*ken,* the purposive faculty of *liang-chih*) outward to the will.

By dividing will and thought so widely, Ch'ien Te-hung satisfied neither those wishing to probe more deeply the inner sanctum of mind nor those mainly attracted to Wang Yang-ming's philosophy by its monism. Ch'ien's doctrine of effort was based upon such a dread (*chieh-chü*) of doing evil that it threatened to disturb the mind in search of tranquility. If sagely equilibrium were indeed the goal, why not cultivate that state directly? Or, if the Ch'eng-Chu dichotomy between spirit and matter offended, how could Ch'ien's ambivalence toward nature and his shakier interpretation of being refine the ambiguities of his teacher's thought?

Understandably, many students of Wang Yang-ming's thought found the quietism of Nieh Pao (1487–1563) more congenial than Ch'ien's teachings. Nieh had not been a formal disciple during Wang Yang-ming's lifetime. Later, however, when Nieh Pao was prefect of Soochow, he secured his discipleship by worshipping Wang's manes in the presence of Ch'ien Te-hung.[15]

Unlike Ch'ien, Nieh pursued an extremely active bureaucratic career, eventually becoming minister of war and tutor to the heir apparent.* In fact, he developed his own interpretation of Wang Yang-ming Confucianism while jailed during one of the bureaucratic intrigues of the time. As Huang Tsung-hsi's *Ming-ju hsueh-an* described it:

The teacher [continued to] study in jail and at leisure prolonged his spiritual meditation [literally, meditation on the ultimate]. Suddenly he saw that this mind [of ours] is true substance, lucid and brilliant, encompassing all the myriad things. He then spoke out in joy, "This is the equilibrium of the

* It would be interesting to see if there were any relationship in the early sixteenth century between the meditative school and bureaucratic involvement. An hypothesis worth testing would be that men out of office were more adamant about effort, while working bureaucrats sought privacy in quietism—feeling no need to preach what they actually practiced.

not-yet expressed (*wei-fa*). Guard it without losing it, and all the principles of the world will issue forth from it." [16]

As was true of so many Confucian philosophers, Nieh Pao's teachings were largely *post facto* expressions to others of his own religious conviction. These explanations were designed to show the unenlightened how meditation upon the original substance of the mind helped one attain the same illumination of universal principles that he had experienced.

Although Nieh owed much to Wang Yang-ming's idealistic monism, he was so inspired by Taoism that he broke the unity between thought and action. Like Wang Chi, Nieh believed that the master's philosophy was cast at two levels. *Ko-wu* was only for those mired in the world of selfish emotions and unable to directly attain the pure substance of mind. Because such people mistakenly confused the activities of *liang-chih* (filial piety, loyalty, and so on) with *liang-chih* itself, Nieh urged his own followers to distinguish between *liang-chih* as principle and as faculty, focussing on substance rather than function.

The original tranquility of the *liang-chih* responds to beings and subsequently there is [ordinary] knowledge. Knowledge is its manifestation; and [such] knowledge should not be confusedly taken as the *liang-chih* [itself] by forgetting that from which it comes. The mind dominates within. As it reacts to the outer [world of objects] there is subsequently an outer [world of objects]. The outer is its shadow.[17]

In other words, Nieh either failed to grasp or refused to accept the essence of Wang's monism: *liang-chih* as *both* functioning substance and substantive function. As Nieh veered toward ideation, therefore, the usual questions of being were raised. Were there outer objects after all?

This may seem to be identical to Bishop Berkeley's dilemma two centuries later, but the difficulties it posed for Nieh's friends and students were more strictly phenomenological. For instance, the ostensible quietist Lo Hung-hsien (1504–1567) found it difficult to reconcile Nieh Pao's abiding in pure mind with Wang Yang-ming's dynamic interpretation of *liang-chih* as a purposive mental force. In his preface to Nieh's *K'un-pien lu* (A Record of Anxious Argumentation), Lo Hung-hsien wrote:

For, from the point of view of *liang-chih*, there can be no distinction between [expressed] action and not-yet expressed action. From the point of view of why this knowledge can be [innately] good, there is indeed a [state of] not-yet expressed [consciousness] which dominates it in the center [of the mind]. Otherwise, should [the *liang-chih*] be extended to what is not good, then having manifested itself it would not know [how] to return [to its original state]. As my [mind] is temporarily at rest, it also has [a consciousness] of self-examination, just as it also has [a faculty] of self-domination. Nothing is more active than the mind, and thus even the sage [treats] it as dangerous. If there is nothing which dominates, [the mind] will act as it is swayed by sensations [of external objects]. This is like riding a horse with the bit escaped from the hand. How else can one acquire the medium degree of speed which one seeks of this obstinately galloping steed? [18]

Thus, although Lo clearly affirmed Nieh's defense of pure mind, the very proof he cited—the need for a dominating inner self—ultimately cracked its metaphysical integrity. By emphasizing the mind's function, Lo soon found himself asking whether Nieh's observation of the silent substance of the "not-yet expressed" might not be illusion. And what were the implications of Nieh's statement that the outer world was a mere shadow of the inner? Besides, there was the ethical danger of regarding silence as a state in itself. By sealing it away from our reaction to external things, Nieh risked destroying Wang Yang-ming's unity of the mind. [19]

To retain the transcendence of mind, quietists like Nieh Pao sharply distinguished that sanctum of tranquility from ordinary sensational knowledge. As *chih* (extension) was dropped from *chih liang-chih* (the extension of innate knowledge), and *ko-wu* relegated to an inferior place, the unity of knowledge and action was shattered. It was this tendency that Wang Chi, founder of the third great school, most deplored.

Wang Chi in translation sometimes appears to be the kind of quietist he opposed. This is because of the connotations in English of *wu:* nothing.* For example, he once approvingly quoted Wang Yang-ming as saying: "If one can realize the original substance in which there is neither good nor evil, one will know what absolute nothing [*wu*] is. And then all will, knowledge, and things will emerge from nothing. Once this is done, it settles everything." [20] But his "nothing" was not passive nonbeing. The very phrases quoted above were followed by these lines:

* Wing-tsit Chan has written: "There is nothing wrong in rendering *wu* as a negative. However, in some cases it has to be interpreted. For example, *wu-hsin* is not just 'no mind' but 'no deliberate mind of one's own,' and *wu-wei* is not simply 'inaction' but 'taking no unnatural action,' or in Buddhist usage, 'not produced from causes.'" See Wing-tsit Chan *A Source Book in Chinese Philosophy* (Princeton: Princeton University Press, 1963), p. 796.

"Effort is substance. This truth is simple and direct." [21] *Wu* could therefore be associated with energy and creativity. In fact, at the very heart of Sung Neo-Confucianism was the concept of generation from nothing, from *wu*. Chou Tun-i's (1017–1073) famous explanation of the diagram of the great ultimate begins, "The nonultimate (*wu-chi*) and also the great ultimate (*t'ai-chi*): the great ultimate moves and engenders *yang*. Its movement reaches its limit and is tranquil (*ching*); tranquil, it generates *yin*." [22] Beginning with nothing, movement operates the cosmic rhythms that create all beings: out of nonbeing to being. And the sage, paragon for all, creates the tranquility of *wu* in himself to approximate—to attain—that same state of creativity, of incipient activity (*chi*): "The state when movement [has started] but not yet taken shape, in between being and nothingness (*wu*)." [23] Chou's contemporary, the famous philosopher Chang Tsai (1020–1077), made the same connection between the sage and another form of nothingness: *hsu* or vacuity.*

The great *hsu* has no form; it is the original substance of material force (*ch'i*). Its collection and dispersion are transient** forms of the transformation [of being]. [Human] nature at its source is utterly tranquil and without sensations. Consciousness and knowledge exist as transient sensations of contact with [outer] beings. Only he who can exhaustively [develop] his nature can unify the transient sensations and transient forms with nonsensation and nonform.[24]

This was the state which Wang Chi wished to reach. To succeed did mean retaining one's detachment from being, for the secret key (*hsuan-chi*) of the universe could not be consciously grasped. As the activating, creating force (*sheng-chi*) behind all things, this key could only be held

---

* Wing-tsit Chan explains *hsu* (vacuous) as a Taoist term used by the Neo-Confucianists: "As a description of a state of mind, it means absolute peacefulness and purity of mind and freedom from worry and selfish desires and not to be disturbed by incoming impressions or to allow what is already in the mind to disturb what is coming into the mind. . . . *Hsu* also means profound and deep continuum in which there is not obstruction. It is not to be equated with the Buddhist term *k'ung* (empty)." See *Source Book,* p. 788.

** *K'o:* a traveler or guest. Wing-tsit Chan translates *k'o-hsing* (my "transient forms") as "objectification" (*Source Book,* p. 501). I follow Wang Fu-chih's explanation of the term: "The sun and moon rising and setting, the four seasons' alternating, creatures' living and dying: along with wind and rain, dew and thunder, they avail themselves of opportunities [literally, time] to arise and opportunities to rest. As one, [they each] transit (*k'o*) forms. 'Transit' means to come and go." Wang Fu-chih, annotator, *Chang-tzu Cheng-meng chu* [An Annotation of Master Chang's *Correcting Youthful Ignorance*] (Peking: Ku-chi ch'u-pan she, 1956), p. 3.

by a sage if his acts were natural and spontaneous, free of selfish desires and cerebral forethought.

Naturally, Wang Chi believed that Ch'ien Te-hung was far too attached to his own sensations to so qualify. But he also felt that the quietists, deep in the Taoist and Buddhist pitfall of cultivating the *illusion* of original substance, were just as strongly attached to their own selves as Ch'ien. Nieh Pao and Ch'ien Te-hung should both learn to train the self in *actual* life by making effort the substance, by transforming being into nothingness.[25]

Takehiko Okada has characterized Wang Chi as an existentialist.[26] Wang's confidence in spontaneity does recall some forms of European existentialism to anyone versed in both philosophical traditions. In fact, the quote just above from Chang Tsai—especially the last sentence—suggests the resemblance between Neo-Confucianism *in toto* and phenomenology.* Think, for example, of the motive behind Edmund Husserl's (1859–1938) creation of a vocabulary of phenomenology: to describe human existence without obscuring preconceptions. Martin Heidegger (1889–   ) employed that same vocabulary to distinguish between substantial being (*das Seiende*) and functional being (*das Sein*). There should be, he said, no separation between man and being, no detachment from existence. Man *is* being-in-the-world. If he opens himself naturally to the field of being (*Dasein*), he will thereby know himself and Other. In fact—said Heidegger—the essence of phenomenology is present even in its etymology. Just as the Greek root of the word is *phaos* (light), so true knowledge is enlightenment *from* nature *to* man's basically nonanalytic sense of truth. Playing our own Heideggerian word games, we might even argue that phenomenology best translates Ch'eng Hao's term for enlightenment: *ming-chüeh tzu-jan,* bright perception of the natural.[27]

However deeply this comparison underscores the common humanity of man, Chinese or European, we should not be misled into placing Neo-Confucianism squarely alongside phenomenology as an equivalent philosophical development. European existentialism can be accounted for in

* That might even suggest a rather farfetched reason for the late Ming affinity between Confucian literati and European Jesuits. Both believed in the unity of essence and existence, as far as the orthodoxy of their respective sects was concerned. While the Dominicans (who of course provoked the Rites Controversy) believed in Saint Thomas' (1225–1274?) judgment that man could not be his own essence, the Jesuits were told by their great theologian, Francis Suarez, that Duns Scotus (1265–1305) was closer to the truth in declaring that existence and essence were identical. Just as God's essence was his basic attribute, so man made himself what he wanted to be.

many ways, some of which might appear analogous to Chinese intellectual history; but as a reaction to the rationalists' denial of the medieval faith in nature's entire intelligibility, it is uniquely Western. For, the price of enshrining reason was the skepticism of sensibility. As Kepler had defined the *real* world to be mathematical harmony instead of mere impressions, so did Galileo differentiate primary "knowledge" of the absolute mathematical world from secondary "opinions" about the subjective sensible world. Newton, going even further, dismissed Kepler's a priori certainty of innate ideas and only claimed truth for what was deduced from phenomena: Aristotelian forms, Cartesian minds, were merely hypotheses, unsuited for scientific philosophy. As E. A. Burtt so vividly put it:

The gloriously romantic universe of Dante and Milton, that set no bounds to the imagination of man as it played over space and time, had now been swept away. Space was identified with the realm of geometry, time with the continuity of number. The world that people had thought themselves living in—a world rich with color and sound, redolent with fragrance, filled with gladness, love and beauty, speaking everywhere of purposive harmony and creative ideals—was crowded now into minute corners in the brains of scattered organic beings. The really important world outside was a world hard, cold, colorless, silent, and dead; a world of quantity, a world of mathematically computable motions in mechanical regularity. The world of qualities as immediately perceived by man became just a curious and quite minor effect of that infinite machine beyond. In Newton the Cartesian metaphysics, ambiguously interpreted and stripped of its distinctive claim for serious philosophical consideration, finally overthrew Aristotelianism and became the predominant world view of modern times.[28]

And eventually man's ability to see into that cold world of quantity was even called into question. Werner Heisenberg's (1901–   ) principle of indeterminacy (formulated in 1927), or Niels Bohr's (1885–1962) principle of complementarity which ambiguously defined the electron as both wave and particle, or Kurt Gödel's (1906–   ) demonstration in 1931 that mathematical truth cannot be identified with derivability from any particular set of axioms and therefore lacks self-subsistent reality—all of these discoveries in the early twentieth century lengthened the gap between man the *ego* and nature the *alter*.

Sixteenth-century Chinese "existentialists" may have been as intent as Heidegger on overcoming the separation between mind and being, but they would have shared none of the later Western doubts about the determinacy of mind. Their universe was completely intelligible. More than that, it was morally purposive, "good." Wang Yang-ming never dreamed of asking Ivan Karamazov's questions; he would have never demanded to know how heaven could permit a Liu Chin to appear. Yet, it was just those kinds of questions which associated post-Enlightenment existentialism with its Western origins. Whether stemming from St. Paul's placement of faith over and (if need be) against reason and Tertullian's choice of the absurd (*credo ut intelligam*),* or from the Protestant refusal to accept nature, the crisis theology of a Kierkegaard invoked the necessity of human will as mind encountered self in desperate Either/Or choices.

There was no such militant passion in the thought of a Wang Chi, nor in the substratum of Neo-Confucianism which he inherited. Heidegger has toyed with the word-root of "virtue" in the West: *virs,* a military ardor to dominate. Although *te* (virtue) may have meant in Shang times "to go out," "to send out a military expedition," by the time Han lexicographers glossed it in the *Kuang-ya* it was associated in men's minds with another *te* (to obtain) and exemplified by *te-hsin* (to obtain the mind): entirely civil control of others and the self.[29] Once again we must emphasize the Chinese wish to bring the self into accord with nature; for, even so will-conscious a philosopher as Wang Yang-ming himself said:

The Way is nature and is also destiny. It is complete in itself. Nothing can be added to or substracted from it, and it requires no touching up. What need is there for the sage to regulate and restrict? To do so would imply that nature is not perfect. . . . When heaven has conferred something on man, that which is conferred is called man's nature. When man acts in accord with his nature, that nature becomes the Way. And when man cultivates the Way and learns, the Way becomes education. To be in accord with his nature is the task of a sincere man. . . . As the sage acts in accord with his nature, the Way obtains. . . . Only with the cultivation of the Way can one avoid violating the Way and restore the original substance of his nature. When that point is reached, his Way will be the same as that in accord with which the sage acts.[30]

While this belief was high testimony to the fundamental optimism of post-Sung thought, it also dispelled the need for piety and therefore for demonstration in action. Without piety, without an externally defined

---

* "And the Son of God died; it is by all means to be believed, because it is absurd. And he was buried and rose again; the fact is certain because it is impossible." *De Carne Christi,* cited in William Barrett, *Irrational Man: A Study in Existential Philosophy* (Garden City, N.Y.: Doubleday Anchor, 1962), pp. 94–95.

asceticism, Wang Yang-ming's emphasis on effort was bound to attenuate within his school as time passed. Masters could speak out of the conviction of personal crisis, but they left no transcendent conditions for disciples to follow. Many, like Wang Chi, realized how likely it would be for his own successors to confuse natural with selfish desires and so mistake the original substance;[31] and Lo Hung-hsien was to say of the scholars of the 1560s: "All day long one talks of the inner self without speaking about moral effort and as soon as moral effort is as much as mentioned it is considered a heresy. If Wang Yang-ming came back to life he surely would wrinkle his brow." [32]

Only Wang Yang-ming's continuing personal presence—the ethical revelation and commitment which he exemplified—could have made a difference.* For, the dualism he had sought to overcome between self and object, or between cognition and action, was really in the end a conflict between action and inaction. Consequently, his doctrine of the unity of knowing and doing, which was designed to illuminate the existential path of sagehood rather than resolve ontological difficulties, was quite different from the Marxian theory of practice. Marx's first thesis on Feuerbach attacked the simple cause-and-effect relationship of materialist philosophy for being unable to explain perception or to account for human thinking.[33]

The chief defect of all materialism up to now (including Feuerbach's) is, that the object, reality, what we apprehend through our senses, is understood only in the form of the *object* or *contemplation;* but not as *sensuous human activity,* as *practice;* not subjectively. Hence in opposition to materialism the *active* side was developed abstractly by idealism—which of course does not know real sensuous activity as such. Feuerbach wants sensuous objects, really distinguished from the objects of thought: but he does not understand human activity itself as *objective* activity. Hence, in *The Essence of Christianity,* he sees only the theoretical attitude as the true human attitude, while practice is understood and established only in its "dirty Jew" appearance. He therefore does not comprehend the significance of "revolutionary," of "practical–critical" activity.[34]

The materialists, however sound their instinct to begin with an objective empirical supposition, had to use the logical agreement between cause and effect to avoid crassness (thoughts to the brain like bile to

---

* That is why the *nien-p'u* (chronological biography) was such an important part of any philosopher's remains. It served to extend the master's presence beyond death. To return to an earlier metaphor: person (thinking) mattered more than *persona* (thought).

the liver); but the agreement still failed to solve the sequential problem of causation. Were ideas effects of things, or vice versa?

Idealism, on the other hand, provided real insight into subjectivity and perception. Kant had been the first to analyze the relationship between the act and content of consciousness; but because his idealism rested on the belief that the truth of any idea was its coherence with other ideas, he had—in Marx's eyes—failed to establish correspondence with empirical fact, as symbolized by the unknowable *Ding-an-sich*. Naturally, Hegel had gone much further by reconstituting object and subject as an interaction between matter and mind. However, if one refused to accept the idealist premise of causative consciousness, then he would have to ask the same question posed to the materialists. Which really came first in the correspondence? Were ideas made of material? Was material formed from ideas?

Having set the conundrum in this manner, Marx solved it for himself with the touchstone of praxis. As the second thesis on Feuerbach put it:

The question whether objective truth is an attribute of human thought—is not a theoretical but a *practical* question. Man must prove the truth, that is, the reality and power, the "this-sidedness" of his thinking in practice. The dispute over the reality or nonreality of thinking that is isolated from practice is a purely *scholastic question*.[35]

Marx's method of solution has been succinctly analyzed by Sidney Hook in *From Hegel to Marx*.

When Marx says that any dispute about the truth or falsity of a judgment which is isolated from Praxis is a scholastic question, he is saying that such questions cannot be answered in principle, that in short, they are not genuine questions at all. The truth of *any* theory depends upon whether or not the actual consequences which flow from the Praxis initiated to test the theory are such that they realize the predicted consequences. In other words, for Marx all genuine questions are scientifically determinable even though for a variety of reasons we may never know the answer to some of them. Since all judgments are hypotheses, the expectations which enter into the process of discovering the truth about them are not the personal and private expectations of the individual thinker but the public and verifiable expectations which logically flow from the hypotheses entertained. What a man wants to believe is relevant only to *what* he believes, but not to its truth. There is no will to believe in Marx but a will to action in order to test belief and get additional grounds for further action if necessary.[36]

Despite the Maoist bridge between them, the distance separating Marx and Wang Yang-ming's theories of practice—at least insofar as they responded to differing philosophic inquiries—was apparently quite vast. Wang's form of praxis was not devised as a logical solution to the problem of truth. It was designed to prevent the seeker of good from becoming so infatuated with abstract principles of being that he overlooked the need for worldly action. Men had lost the Way precisely because philosophers had been content to know *in vacuo*. Yet as Wang condemned knowledge for its own sake as mere idle speculation, he too was declaring that the aim of philosophy was human improvement. What really distinguished him from Marx in this regard was the danger he hoped to avoid. Marx's praxis was directed against the bleak mundanity of materialism which left no room for human consciousness. Wang's unity of knowledge and action opposed the delusion of subjectively knowing morality without ever practicing it. By insisting that the *liang-chih* judged the morality of concrete acts which the volition willed, Wang made knowledge contingent upon events. Marx, on the other hand, put cognition before action and tried to mediate the familiar Western philosophical dualism between abstract theory and concrete praxis with his dialectic. Wang Yang-ming's instrument of resolution was an equally abiding monism, a practice which encompassed the entire cosmos and urged men to change things in order to know them. If only others could be engaged in action, the will would be freed from abstract knowledge.

Mao Tse-tung apparently wedded these two traditions of practice in a way that enabled him to ignore the problem of false consciousness altogether. Philosophical metaphors are certainly not the only way of describing his particular revolutionary consciousness, but they do suggest that Mao's need to act depended upon finding some new way of his own to relate personal will to historical universals.

PART FIVE

History and Will

Do not stop half way and do not ever go backward. There is no way behind you.

> Mao Tse-tung, "Progress" (June 21, 1967).

Wind will not cease even if trees want to rest.

> Mao Tse-tung, "The Objective Existence of Class Struggle" (June 2, 1966).

18

Neo-Hegelianism

It was Yang Ch'ang-chi, his philosophy teacher, who introduced Mao Tse-tung to the Neo-Hegelianism of Thomas Hill Green (1836–1882). Yang's course in ethics was summed up in *A Critique of Western Ethical Theories*,[1] which—very much like a class syllabus—cogently exposed his students to Western moral philosophy.

Yang began with asceticism (*chin-yü chu-i*), comparable in some respects to the then unpopular Neo-Confucian concept of subduing the self (*k'o-chi*). Originating with the Stoics, asceticism was expressed with the greatest refinement by Immanuel Kant, who made rationalism the essence of human nature and morality an expression of its control over desires. Although Yang admired Kantianism, he felt that it opposed the natural human desire for gratification. After all, Schiller's poetry had shown how contrary Kant's pure moralism was to the human grain; without wants, men even lacked an incentive for action.

Hedonism (*k'uai-le chu-i*) was next presented, starting from Aristippus and Epicurus, and ending in three contemporary schools of thought. First was the selfish individualism of Hobbes, Machiavelli, and Nietzsche—realistic but ultimately antisocial. Second came Bentham or Mill's utilitarianism. Social calculus was intellectually appealing, but because Yang viewed the "greatest good of the greatest number" as simply an aggregate of the desires of individual egos, he could not consider that slogan a universal principle of social morality. Finally there was a third school, represented by Spencer and Darwin, whose evolutionary theories recognized desire as a basic attribute of human nature, biologically necessary to its survival. Like Huxley, however, Yang believed that competitive drives and selfish desires conflicted with many of the ethical ideals of civilization, such as providing for the welfare of the disadvantaged. Furthermore, the hedonism underlying evolutionary theory favored immediate gratification at the expense of long-term social benefits. This was a fatal contradiction, argued Yang, because the survival of a species was a collective end which often forced individual members to sacrifice their own interests. Something—morality (*tao-te*)—was capable of inspiring acts which destroyed the mortal self. Biological drives could not alone explain "the willingness of a man to sacrifice himself for the sake of higher motives." [2]

Consequently, Yang's presentation of Western ethics depicted a polar conflict between moral self-control and natural self-interest. This primary contradiction of all modern thought was, however, resolved by a third major school of philosophy: the doctrine of self-realization (*tzu-wo shih-hsien chu-i*). Stemming from Aristotle's entelechy, shaped by the idealism of Kant, Fichte, and Hegel, self-realization had reached its highest point in the Neo-Hegelian dialectic of two Englishmen, Francis Herbert Bradley (1846–1924) and T. H. Green.[3]

The English idealists did not actually think of themselves as "Neo-Hegelians." Bradley insisted in 1883, for example, that his greatest debt was to Lotze rather than to Hegel.

For Hegel himself, assuredly I think him a great philosopher; but I never would have called myself an Hegelian, partly because I can not say that I have mastered his system, and partly because I could not accept what seems his main principle, or at least part of that principle.* I have no wish to conceal how much I owe to his writings, but I will leave it to those who can judge better than myself, to fix the limits within which I have followed him. As for the "Hegelian School" which exists in our reviews, I know no one who has met with it anywhere else.[4]

Apart from metaphysical disagreement, the major reason for Bradley and other British idealists to disassociate themselves from Hegel was his identification with the German enshrinement of the state. In fact, the novelty of their idealism—especially as it appeared in the writings of T. H. Green—was the fusion of liberal reformism with an ardent faith

---

* Bradley could not accept what he viewed as Hegel's excess of relativity, that is, that we can only know the relations between positives and negatives as expressed in the theory of contradiction. According to Bradley's analysis of the logic of contradiction, the Hegelian assertion that A = b + not-b, is to break down the fact A into needlessly disparate elements. However, Bradley did not refute contradiction altogether. See F. H. Bradley, *The Principles of Logic* (London: Kegan Paul, Trench, 1883), pp. 135–149.

in the dialectical advance of freedom via the state. For, most English-men had connected idealism with individual sacrifice to the state à la Carlyle or Coleridge. At the time, however, traditional liberalism, which was classically concerned with the social interests of free individuals under a laissez-faire state, failed to meet what seemed to many an ob-vious need for social welfare legislation. For that reason Green's apothe-osis of freedom through the state injected a fresh vigor into Victorian reformism, making him "one of the saviors of Liberalism" at Oxford.[5]

Green was novel because, while doubting Hegel's free individual realized in the state, he did believe that freedom was attained with the help of the state. He managed this by distinguishing man's metaphysical progress toward absolute moral freedom from actual political freedom. The former, although hoped for, was not yet realized. The latter could at least serve the present as each individual's reason persuaded him to accept the surrounding system of social relations as a necessary guide to his own self-development. Thus, there were two levels of freedom: the total self-realization of consciousness toward which man constantly progresses, and the realization that the common good and one's own good were identical. The second might not attain the level of moral ideal, but it at least moved man toward it. Consequently, freedom was not just the obliteration of obstacles to individuality, but the removing of hindrances to morality as well. A rigid libertarian notion of license might allow a dipsomaniac to follow his desire to drink himself to death, whereas Green's concept of freedom would have the state forbid the alcoholic his poison. Individual will must be adjusted to laws which rationally determine where self-satisfaction is to be sought; the state must exert its positive function.

The liberal roots of British idealism helped it resist the German embodiment of idea in government. But its entelechy, its consciousness of the individual striving for self-realization, was consonant with the spirit of Hegel's system. Therefore, in the sense that Marcuse gives Hegel's *Logic,* men like Bradley or Green certainly should be called Neo-Hegelians.

Every particular existent is essentially different from what it could be if its potentialities were realized. The potentialities are given in its notion. The existent would have true being if its potentialities were fulfilled and if there were, therefore, an identity between its existence and its notion. The differ-ence between the reality and the potentiality is the starting point of the dialectical process that applies to every concept in Hegel's *Logic.* Finite things are "negative"—and this is a defining characteristic of them; they never are what they can and ought to be. They always exist in a state that does not fully express their potentialities as realized. The finite thing has as its essence "this absolute unrest," this striving "not to be what it is." [6]

Their writings are permeated with that same "absolute unrest."

The philosophical foundation of British idealism was best laid by Bradley's study of logic. Declaring the usual empirical distinction between idea and sensation logically irrelevant, Bradley instead stressed the difference between idea and fact in order to eventually unite the two. Although idea possessed existence and content, its symbolic significance made it stand for something else, so that it lost a part of its self-existence. But it gained at the same time universal meaning as a component of judgment. Because "judgment proper is the act which refers an ideal content (recognized as such) to a reality beyond the act," [7] even a partial judgment reflects a superior reality because the act has qualified the real world. Therefore, the truth of a judgment is *more* than idea. It is in itself a new fact.

The ideal content is the logical idea, the meaning as just defined. It is recognized as such, when we know that, by itself, it is not a fact but a wandering adjective. In the act of assertion we transfer this adjective to, and unite it with, a real substantive. And we preserve it at the same time, that the relation thus set up is neither made by the act, nor merely holds within it or by right of it, but is real both independent of and beyond it.[8]

Affirmative judgment, in other words, possesses a quality of the real; and as Bradley coolly demonstrated this, his proof was more impregnable to attack than the *sollen* exposition of the Neo-Kantians. For, the principle of his argument was to separate sensation and judgment, and confer logical or factual existence upon ideas arranged in new relationships by the act of judgment itself. In these terms an idea which is not yet judged may be a strong impression passing into sensation, but it is less *real* than even an idea which has been judged negatively. This was not to say that impressions lacked reality; Bradley was no ideationist. What he did want to show was that as man had developed ideas into symbols of things, he had mistakenly thought them to be mere figments.

That the thing as it is, and as it appears in perception, are not the same thing, is, we all are aware, a very late afterthought. But it is equally an afterthought, though not equally late, that there is any kind of difference between ideas and impressions. For a more primitive mind a thing is or it is not, is a fact or is nothing. . . . And hence for this mind ideas never could be symbols. They are facts because they *are*.[9]

Instead, by pushing logic as far as possible, we realize that ideas-as-symbols make possible the act of judgment which can still predicate an idea while admitting it is nothing more than an appearance.

The image is not a symbol or idea. It is itself a fact, or else the facts eject it. The real, as it appears to us in perception, connects the ideal suggestion with itself, or simply expels it from the world of reality. But judgment is the act which, while it recognizes the idea as appearance, nevertheless goes on to predicate it.[10]

Bradley only seemed to be on the same track as Kant. In truth he could not accept Kant's synthetic categories, because he believed that analysis and synthesis were ultimately identical. "Analysis is the synthesis of the whole which it divides and synthesis the analysis of the whole which it constructs." [11] By breaking up the confused whole, analysis makes the relations between elements more and more abstract; and the laws demonstrated by these relations are syntheses in turn. Synthesis, on the other hand, works down from first principles to individual facts which, although constructively unified, are unconsciously analyzed all along the way. Thus, neither logical method is solely adequate for entire understanding: analysis treats a datum defined by external relations as though it had no unity with the real; synthesis seeks to create a complete whole without incorporating the full range of a being's contingency.

In the end, Bradley's own skill at logical demolition forced him to conclude that logic itself was a necessarily limited law of reasoning whose truths were finite. "Starting from particular perceptions of sense, there is no way of going to universal truths by a process of demonstration perfectly exact, and in all its steps theoretically accurate." [12] But despite this confession, he—and this characterized all the English idealists—held on to the deep, though vague, conviction that the totality of experience was meant to be this way. The mind was simply not intended to ratiocinate the icy purity of Kant's architectonics. Beyond logic was a poetic splendor of being, a higher and perhaps even irrational reality, which we must still strain to reach with the imperfect tools of reason at our command.

A lingering scruple still forbids us to believe that reality can ever be purely rational. It may come from a failure in my metaphysics, or from a weakness of the flesh which continues to blind me, but the notion that existence could be the same as understanding strikes as cold and ghostlike as the dreariest materialism. That the glory of this world in the end is appearance leaves the world more glorious, if we feel it is a show of some fuller splendor; but the sensuous curtain is a deception and a cheat, if it hides some colorless movement of atoms, some spectral woof of impalpable abstractions, or unearthly ballet of bloodless categories. Though dragged to such conclusions we can not embrace them. Our principles may be true, but they are not reality.[13]

The ideal instrument to pierce the curtain of abstractions between us and existence would be a way of thinking which holds for the entirety of reality a system of differences immanent in each difference, so that by analyzing any single element we are able to produce the system's totality.

Then, the elements knowing themselves in the whole and so self-conscious in one another, and the whole so finding in its recognized self-development the unmixed enjoyment of its completed nature, nothing alien or foreign would trouble the harmony. It would all have vanished in that perfected activity which is the rest of the absolute.[14]

What would that way of thinking be? Bradley could have fallen back on Hegel's Speculative Reason. Instead, he answered that there must be something in our reasoning to account for our very awareness of its absence. It could not be logic, because analysis and synthesis both lack the ability to have a subject appropriate a possible predicate if that predicate is left alone, if other predicates are excluded. How, logically, can one say X *may be* Y? Might not the logical impossibility of that statement be the root of reasoning? And if so, might not its negativeness (I must because I cannot otherwise) be stated positively: I must *so* because I will *somehow?* This metaphysical emotion, this self-development of reason, had to be the essence of mind; for, "The striving for perfection, the desire of the mind for an infinite totality, is indeed the impulse which moves our intellect to appropriate everything from which it is not forced off." [15]

A decade after the *Logic* had ended on so haunting a note, Bradley's *Appearance and Reality* reprised the theme. Here the ultimate fact for Bradley was the unbreakable unity between perceiver and perceived as expressed in the totality of experience: the *implicit* containment of all our rationally explicit differentiations. Now, judgment—the key to his *Logic*—was admitted to be finite. In order to be absolutely true, a single judgment would have to harmonize with all others; but we already know that since nature is only an appearance within the reality of experience, a manifestation of the Absolute, then totality is beyond any single judgment. The Absolute might form the subject of our judgment, but it would still not represent the entire sum of finite judgments. Nor could the Absolute simply stand alone: a self-conscious mind. For, the Absolute must be perfect, without any degrees of truth or reality (predicates only in the world of appearance), transcending the distinctions of phenomena. Were the Absolute to exist under either of the former circumstances, it would be conditioned by relations (as judgment's subject, external ones; as conscious in itself, internal ones); and, as the *Logic* had demonstrated, reality had to be nonrelational, requiring nothing beyond itself.

Therefore, even though we know—we feel—the Absolute to be there behind it all, its transcendence is inexplicable. We can show its existence by negative proof (that is, there is no form of the finite which overthrows this principle of the Absolute), to be sure, but its perfect truth cannot be fully attained. However, this did not oblige us to reject judgment altogether. Its insufficiency was only relative.

Our judgments, in a word, can never reach as far as perfect truth, and must be content merely to enjoy more or less of *validity*. I do not simply mean by this term that, for working purposes, our judgments are admissible and will pass. I mean that less or more they actually possess the character and type of absolute truth and reality. They can take the place of the Real to various extents, because containing in themselves less or more of its nature. They are its representatives, worse or better, in proportion as they present us with truth affected by greater or less derangement.[16]

Arguing for an absolute system of total experience which is reality, Bradley had to admit that, taken as it appears, nothing finite is real. But simply because the finite *is,* it does partake of absolute reality in some form. Was there a Kantian antinomy lurking somewhere behind the thing-in-itself? Bradley refused to take that way out, and propounded in its place a doctrine of relative truths. All finite truth is relative; but although the Absolute can never appear, this relativity exists by degrees insofar as the finite imports into its own core of being a mass of foreign connections with total experience. According to the *Principles of Logic,* this import would distract the unity of the finite's substance, and so impel growth. Consequently, his doctrine of relative truths was taken to show the capacity of finite being to grow into harmony with the whole of its external elements (the Absolute) and so demonstrate its concrete universality. "By growth the element becomes, more and more, a consistent individual, containing in itself its own nature; and it forms, more and more, a whole inclusive of discrepancies and reducing them to system." [17] Thus, "To possess more the character of reality, and to contain within oneself a greater amount of the real, are two expressions for the same thing." [18] The Absolute is preserved, and the finite substantiated, by positing a chain of higher and higher truths in harmony toward which the individual, the concrete universal, must try to ascend.

Like Bradley, Bernard Bosanquet (1848–1923) owed much to Lotze's doctrine that logic was the clue to reality. Bosanquet even edited and translated Lotze's *Logic and Metaphysics,* after being influenced at Balliol by T. H. Green to turn toward moral philosophy. And, like Lotze, he evinced in his own histories of art the belief that aesthetics reconciled the a priori and a posteriori through a logic of coherence for which the harmony of color was as valid as a syllogism. But Bosanquet went on to refine that perception of truth or reality in the whole with Hegel's spirit of noncontradiction.

What is, is by determinate self-maintenance. There is no meaning in "it is" apart from "it is what it is," . . . but in as far as "is" affirms a certain determinate self-maintenance and "is not" affirms a different one, or the character of otherness in general, so far to attach the two as predicates to the same point of being is to allege that in its self-maintenance it fails to maintain itself. . . . The universal is just that character of experience which overcomes the "is not" by reducing it to an element harmonious with and corroborative of the "is." It is "the self in the other." [19]

For him, the key to this reconciliation was Bradley's "concrete universal." As the individual was a true type of universality, the value of a world or a cosmos was that every member was distinct, contributing to the unity of the whole thanks to the peculiarities of its own distinctness. "The ultimate principle, we may say, is sameness in the other." [20]

Bosanquet thus deplored the "centrifugal illusions" of other philosophies. William James' abnegation, his belief that philosophy was an abstraction alien to real life, obstructed the penetrative imagination. Other thinkers who believed in "dangerous immediates" like "fact, life, and self" pessimistically severed the connection between real existence and the principle of perfection. Those who isolated endeavor and function "fail[ed] to catch the heartbeat of the Absolute in our actual world." [21] What really mattered to philosophers was centrality, the "sane and central experience" which would take as its standard "what man recognizes as value when his life is fullest" in order to nurture a logical *and* sympathetic insight into being.[22] The conservation of particular minds—the detached individual—destroyed the web of experience, the continuity which each man should feel as "a trustee for the whole world." [23]

In his own way, then, Bosanquet was trying to overcome the post-Enlightenment rift between subject and object by transforming logic into an instrument of self-transcendence. Like Hegel, he believed that good belonged to an entire world together, not just to its individual members. The world was thus "a place of soul-making" where the value of particularities was each one's contribution to the whole.[24] This was neither Fechner's panpsychism (which Bosanquet critically classified with Leibniz's monadism as a reduction of the complementariness of mind and nature to a homogenous mass)[25] nor Lockean individualism.

In a word, then, we hold that no ideal of freedom lies in the direction of isolating the self from the world. Freedom lies in the direction toward unity and coherence; and all that becomes one with the self is capable of contributing (even through apparent contradiction and the effort which it stimulates) to this satisfaction of the inherent logical tendency.[26]

At times Bradley and Bosanquet's concrete universality vividly resembles the monism of Wang Yang-ming Confucianism. When Bosanquet tells us that life and mind are the appearance of an omnipotential principle, and that "the strength of the principle lies in what may be called its emptiness," [27] one can begin to appreciate the impact of English idealism on some modern Chinese thinkers. The same impulse to retain the self immersed in the total experience of being must have seemed familiar to philosophers like Shu Yu-chung, who came to English idealism with a Chinese metaphysical background.* But the familiarity was an identification of the moment, and their monism an eclectic selection of recipes from entirely different cuisines. For, as we have already seen, Wang Yang-ming's defense of the integrity of experience against Ch'eng-Chu dualism was hardly parallel to the Neo-Hegelian rejection of Kant's *Ding-an-sich.* True comparability existed only in the reconciliation of these diverse traditions, as when Ho Lin[28] married Wang Yang-ming *to* Hegel in search of an Oriental–Occidental

---

* Shu, in his metaphysical work *Shuo hsin* (On the Mind, 1943), acknowledged the influence of Bradley and Bosanquet on the development of his own subjective idealism in which mind was substance (noumenon) and experience was phenomenon. "It is aesthetic experience which is the meeting place between spirit and matter. . . . Each forgets itself: the subject and the object are made one." Cited and translated in O. J. Brière, *Fifty Years of Chinese Philosophy, 1898–1948,* trans. Laurence G. Thompson (New York: Praeger, 1965), p. 73.

syncretism for common Oriental–Occidental predicaments. One such predicament was a consequence of scientific materialism—a development as distressing to some Chinese as it was to those Victorian idealists.

Although the Victorians came long after Newton had dismembered Milton's God, Lyell and Darwin's discoveries delivered a shocking coup de grâce. By placing man in an organic nature subject to Newtonian motion, and by bringing the innumerable species of the world into a single system mechanically determined by natural selection, Darwinism gravely insulted human dignity. After all, though Descartes had separated man and nature, he did so to the greater glory of the rational ego. Lyell and Darwin made man merely native to nature—an advanced primate—so that many of the contradictions of Victorian culture (especially its late-flourishing romanticism) seemed to express a sense that the world had been divided into two spheres: a practical realm of quantity and a subjective realm of moral and aesthetic experience. Indeed, it was the yearning for harmony between these two spheres that conditioned the philosophies of idealists like Bosanquet wishing to restore consciousness to the order of nature. As the British novelist Charles Kingsley put it: "Men found that now they have got rid of an interfering God—a master-magician, as I call it—they have to choose between the absolute empire of accident and a living, immanent, everworking God.[29]

The demise of the master-magician did not so disturb Chinese intellectuals, because their own teachers had not depended upon such a craftsman to explain the universe. But Darwinism certainly did weaken their faith in a benign universe, threatening to sever the connection between social and cosmic relations. Some philosophers, like Ts'ai Yuan-p'ei (the translator of Paulsen), thought to find a substitute for the universal force of good in Neo-Kantian aesthetics. In his *Che-hsueh ta-kang* (An Outline of Philosophy), Ts'ai wrote:

Now, since aesthetic feeling is an expression of concrete life, and since all that is contingent on what is called sensation, reason, morality, and religion occupies a portion of the content of life, then it (that is, what is contingent) is synthesized in the content of aesthetic feeling, which also affirms its (that is, what is contingent) which[-ness]. Yet the aesthetic concept does not initially lose its independent value because of this. What is proclaimed by voluntarism is that morality is actually the very center of one's own life, while the ultimate meaning of morality is its expression as the thought of religion. The traces of its advance are all genuinely confused among the generalizations of science. The ideal of philosophy is both generalization and ideal, each of which adjoins the abstract. Now, the aesthetic concept completes them both with its own concreteness, allowing one to possess in one's own consciousness what is called a serene and untroubled world view.[30]

Others either tried to ignore the implacable competition of Social Darwinism, or searched for more hopeful formulas of human development. Li Shih-tseng, for instance, adopted Kropotkin's theory of a survival instinct of mutual aid. Less biological and more politically conservative was Liang Shu-ming's contention that the spirit of the Orient was opposed to materialistic strife. Like Liang Ch'i-ch'ao, Liang Shu-ming may have felt the need for cultural superiority to the West, but he was also rejecting the mechanism of competition. Thus, the philosophers most akin to the English idealists were the syncretists of the 1920s—Hsiung Shih-li, Chang Chün-mai, and so forth—who argued that life expressed a cosmic moral conscience reflecting man's free will, not the survival of the fittest. Combining elements from Wang Yang-ming, Buddhism, Bergson, Fichte, Kant, and Hegel, the syncretists tried to unite man with the soul of the world, although this was sometimes at the expense of the force of personal will. Spiritual consciousness might be represented by will, but the sum of the relatively gentle idealism of a Bradley or Bosanquet, plus Neo-Confucian monism or Buddhist ideation, was a metaphysic which blurred the singular individual. We would therefore not expect revolutionary thought to have been influenced by this particular form of idealism. In fact, it was not Bradley but T. H. Green who appealed to Mao Tse-tung; and Green was characteristically much more concerned with *becoming* than other English idealists.

Green's lectures as Whyte Professor of Moral Philosophy at Oxford formed the substance of the posthumously published *Prolegomena to Ethics*. Those lectures began with the same assertion Bradley made: to ask "What is man?" is to ask "What is experience?" because experience is that of which we are conscious. The only things which we can declare incontrovertibly to exist are the facts of consciousness. Kant's *Ding-an-sich* is inadmissible because, were phenomena to be effects of the thing-in-itself, then the latter *qua* cause would itself be just as much a phenomenon. No, insisted Green to his students; if we are to reason about the nature of being, then we must begin with mental functions. Of course, it is true that those functions could be conditioned by matter; but because the constituents of matter belong to the world of experience, they can neither create nor account for the principle of consciousness which made the world possible in the first place.[31] And why was that principle necessary? Because nature itself exists in our sense perception as a consciousness of change, and logic tells us that such a consciousness cannot be produced by experience (the process of change) or previous changes. Ergo, consciousness itself cannot be a result of nature.[32]

Because Green assumed a unity of perception (the consciousness of change), his starting point was more markedly Kantian than either Bradley or Bosanquet's. His reliance on the ideality of critical logic (which, of course, also came from his study of Hegel) showed up as well in Green's discussion of ontology, which commenced with the often used distinction between real ideas and mere ideas. Real ideas are true because they correspond to a comprehensible reality which is obedient to systematic laws of relationship. Although we may only be capable of conceptualizing that intelligible system of relations *ideally,* the very act of conceptualization proves the system's existence as an ideal reality, and consequently assumes some noncontingent principle to make the relationships possible at all. For, that possibility could not exist if the principle were determined by the relationships themselves.

If these relations really exist, there is a real unity of the manifold, a real multiplicity of that which is one. But a plurality of things cannot of themselves unite in one relation, nor can a single thing of itself bring itself into a multitude of relations. . . . There must, then, be something other than the manifold things themselves, which combines them without effacing their severalty.[33]

In other words, the unity of relations and our knowledge of it have a common origin in a nonnatural and spiritual principle: a "self-distinguishing consciousness," unconditioned by the relations it sets up between phenomena, and consequently outside of space and time. It is to this consciousness, which we call God, that the world really is.[34]

Although human consciousness is an expression of this eternal consciousness, it is finite and cannot attain the divine knowledge of the universe as it (the universe) is. But as man's consciousness gradually grows aware of consciousness itself * as an eternal order, it can know the universe as it becomes. Green explained the necessity for this growth, this becoming, quite simply. When consciousness distinguished itself from impressions, it also differentiated itself from its wants and therefore acquired a motive to satisfy them: the will.[35]

* This, of course, was remarkably close to Chu Hsi's discourse on *ch'ien* in the *Book of Changes.*

Will then is equally and indistinguishably desire and thought—not however *mere* desire or *mere* thought, if by that is meant desire or thought as they might exist in a being that was not self-distinguishing and self-seeking, or as they may occur to a man independently of any action of himself; but desire and thought as they are involved in the direction of a self-distinguishing and self-seeking subject to the realization of an idea.[36]

In sum, by identifying itself as the motive of realization, consciousness rationally and freely determines itself. For, the will is not an independent faculty of the mind. "The will is simply the man . . . the expression of the man as he at the time is. . . . In willing he carries with him, so to speak, his whole self to the realization of the given idea." [37] Freedom is entelechy; the moral ideal of man is to willfully realize his capabilities for self-consciousness, for self-objectification.

Of course, man does not know to what state those capabilities will finally lead him, but he does realize that their development will be an improvement. Indeed development *is* improvement. Infinite process as such, unrelated to an end, would not be development at all.

If the history of mankind were simply a history of events, of which each determines the next following, and so on in endless series, there would be no progress or development in it. As we cannot sum an infinite series, there would be nothing in the history of mankind, so conceived, to satisfy that demand for unity of the manifold in relation to an end, which alone leads us to read the idea of development into the course of human affairs. If there is a progress in the history of men it must be toward an end consisting in a state of being which is not itself a series in time, but is both comprehended eternally in the eternal mind and is intrinsically, or in itself, eternal.[38]

Green directed this teleology toward man *in* society. Each human self is not an abstraction. Influenced by its interests in others, it cannot be wholly satisfied until conscious that other men are also satisfied. "The man cannot contemplate himself as in a better state, or on the way to the best, without contemplating others, not merely as a means to that better state, but as sharing it with him." [39] Therefore, man must seek the development of all humanity and not just the development of his own self.

Green's *Prolegomena* contained a familiarly Hegelian contradiction between the spontaneous unfolding of the individual will and this commitment to the interests of others, or even to the state at large. The contradiction gave his philosophy its great political appeal, as he made of it a simple paradox in the *Principles of Political Obligation*. There

Green's argument for freeing the will from external constraint was as eloquent as in the *Prolegomena*.

Any direct enforcement of the outward conduct which ought to flow from social interests, by means of threatened penalties—and a law requiring such conduct necessarily implies penalties for disobedience to it—does interfere with the spontaneous action of those interests, and consequently checks the growth of the capacity which is the condition of the beneficial exercise of rights.[40]

In fact, a will of which man is not conscious as belonging to himself simply cannot be. To ask the individual from which it issues if he has power over it is like asking if he is something besides himself. "Thus the question whether a man, having power to act according to his will, or being free to act, has also power over his will, or is free to will, has just the same impropriety that Locke points out in the question whether the will is free." [41]

But Green was obliged at the same time to admit that the will was bound to an object which shaped it. He recognized this metaphysical tension as a Pauline paradox: fulfillment in necessity through "righteousness."

To the [free] man thus delivered, as St. Paul conceives him, we might also apply phraseology like Kant's. "He is free because conscious of himself as the author of the law which he obeys." He is no longer a servant but a son. He is conscious of union with God, whose will as an external law he before sought in vain to obey, but whose "righteousness is fulfilled" in him now that he "walks after the spirit." [42]

This loving gift of the self to necessity corresponded precisely to Hegel's highest stage of thought. Speculative-Reason "expressly rises above and absorbs such oppositions, as that between subjective and objective, which the understanding cannot master." Speculation "means very much the same as what, in special connection with religious consciousness and religious truth, used to be called mysticism." [43] Here, as much as anywhere, Hegelianism revealed its affinities with the Pauline faith to overcome contradiction—a sense which Marxist thought, despite its materialism, still conveys.

Green tried to demonstrate that the contradiction was only a paradox by proving that when man wills something he makes it his own.

The right way out of the difficulty (of reconciling will and constraint) lies in the discernment that the question whether a man is free to will, or has power over the determinations of his will, is a question to which there is no answer, because it is asked in inappropriate terms; in terms that imply some agency beyond the will which determines what the will shall be . . . and that as to this agency it may be asked whether it does or does not lie in the man himself. In truth there is no such agency beyond the will and determining how the will shall be determined; not in the man, for the will *is* the self-conscious man; not elsewhere than in the man, not outside him, for the self-conscious man has no outside. He is not a body in space with other bodies elsewhere in space acting upon it and determining its motions. The self-conscious man is determined by objects, which in order to be objects must already be in consciousness, and in order to be *his* objects, the objects which determine him, must already have been made his own.[44]

This creed could be dramatically iconoclastic. Because the will is practical reason and does not take customs (unrationalized restraint) for granted, it attains its autonomy by directing itself toward ideal objects of its own making. Institutions are the creations of the practical reason of an earlier age. To accept them uncritically in one's own age would merely be adjustment instead of freedom.* Furthermore, "there can be no real determination of the will by reason unless both reason and will are operating in one and the same person," [45] so that each member of a society must be made to forge it rationally. Only then is the freedom of the entire society guaranteed, as society forces the individual to be free through its own institutions. "The value then of the institutions of civil life lies in their operation as giving reality to these capacities of will and reason, and enabling them to be really exercised." [46] The parallel with Maoism is absolutely striking.

To sum up, because man is always his own object in willing, the will is necessarily free. Indeed, *free will* is the pleonasm, *free freedom*.[47] The nature of that freedom can differ, however, according to the kind of object with which a man identifies himself. Because freedom means a consciousness of authorship on the part of he who wills an outcome, freedom is less the protection of the individual than his realization in the object willed: community. And the ideal community, in turn, possesses institutions that require men consciously and rationally to will "I" and "others" (always maintaining Bradley's "concrete universality") into one system of relations for the sake of their own freedom.

Lest his political society be confused with Rousseau's, Green insisted

---

* The connection here between practical reason and freedom is much clearer than in Friedrich Paulsen's *System der Ethik.* In the latter, will was glorified on the one hand, and reason's ability to analyze *Sitten* (customs) on the other. T. H. Green (who was introduced to Mao Tse-tung after Paulsen) reconciled the two.

that there could exist no sovereign power in conflict with the primary demands of human consciousness. However, Green misunderstood Rousseau to believe that the state was an aggregation of individuals under sovereign power which defended their rights as they might exist in a state of nature. Although Green actually veered toward Rousseau's concept of artificial human nature by emphasizing the unique nature of social rights, he thought to distinguish his concept of freedom from the French philosopher's by stating that rights belong to men as:

> . . . members of a society in which each recognizes the other as an origina-tor of action in the same sense in which he is conscious of being so himself . . . and thus regards the free exercise of his own powers as dependent upon his allowing an equally free exercise of his powers to every other member of the society. . . . [Rights] attach to the individual, but only as a member of a society of free agents. A right then to act unsocially . . . is a con-tradiction.[48]

Even counterrights against a particular society must be founded on a relation to social well-being, for "all virtues are really social." [49]

Naturally, Green could not fail to see the resemblance of his concept of freedom to Hegel's. As we have seen, Hegel held freedom to be the condition in which the will was determined by an object adequate to itself. Green insisted that he could not blandly accept Hegel's assertion that because the objects which the state presents to man are the perfect expression of his reason, he is entirely free.[50] But it was not difficult to derive that conclusion from Green's own premises. My own convic-tion is that his Neo-Hegelian conception of freedom could only retain self-determination by finding the object of will in movement: to be free, one must will *change*. Consequently, Green had to suppose a common human struggle in order for freedom to continue to exist in society. "The activities by which a society of men really free is established . . . in rough outline . . . are those by which men in mutual helpfulness conquer and adapt nature, and overcome the influences which would make them victims of chance and accident, of brute force and animal passion." [51] At least this was the construction which Yang Ch'ang-chi placed upon Green's philosophical system: "This realization of the char-acter (*jen-ko*) of each man can only be completed in the life of a so-ciety." [52] Self-development was social development. And so, said Yang, we should combine Green's ideal of self-realization with a doctrine of social responsibility, and—like Wang Yang-ming—develop the world to develop the self.

However similar this is to Maoism, I cannot with certainty say just how much of Green's philosophy was absorbed by Mao Tse-tung during his student days in Ch'ang-sha. One could hesitantly work out an ideological calculus for Mao by listing the metaphysical integers from what we know of his early studies and the intellectual influences to which he was exposed. From Wang Yang-ming there certainly came a conviction that thought was to be expressed in action. From Paulsen and the Neo-Kantians came the assurance that reason created social forms, liberating the self from customs. From K'ang Yu-wei, Yen Fu, and the Darwinists came the notion of objective and universal laws of science which proved evolutionary change. From Wang Fu-chih came the intuition that change operated within matter, through its own internal relations. And from T. H. Green came not only the intense glorification of will, nor just the civil society of a Rousseau, but the depiction of political society as an instrument of individual realization. State/society, reintegrated, would force the individual to be free; for no single man could be free until all were. And the very struggle to attain that against human and natural opponents would both define will and elicit the kind of common effort that might prevent the state from becoming the static monolith—reason incarnate—represented by Hegel's thought.

Perhaps these suppositions only prove the obvious: Mao and others of his generation were disposed by native and foreign metaphysics to recognize in Marxism a philosophy of history which united their aspirations with possibility. Of course, as historians look back through the fact of China's communist revolution, they unavoidably miss other contingencies. Marxism–Leninism was just one of many political philosophies current among that generation, and its doctrinal superiority to anarchism or syndicalism was no inevitable matter. Nonetheless, its appeal seems so obvious, so necessary, once we stop to consider how all of those integers cried out for realization in a life of the one Idea. To be sure, those who regard Marxism–Leninism as an imported revelation in its own right would dismiss these other factors and probably declare the elements in Maoism which reflected Green or Wang Fu-chih's influence to have existed in Marx to begin with. Are we overexplicating, overstraining those hazy early influences for ideas which Mao Tse-tung could just as well have gotten from, say, Engels? Was Green's notion of the will so unique? Engels once wrote to Bloch:

History is made in such a way that the final result always arises from conflicts between many individual wills, of which each in turn has been made what it is by a host of particular conditions of life. . . . For what each individual wills is obstructed by everyone else, and what emerges is something that no one willed. Thus history has proceeded hitherto in the manner of a natural process and is essentially subject to the same laws of motion. But from the fact that the wills of individuals . . . do not attain what they want, but are merged into an aggregate mean, a common resultant, it must not be concluded that they are equal to zero. On the contrary, each contributes to the resultant and is to this extent included in it.[53]

Mao's definition of will and history could have come from this and other clippings of the testament of Marxian thought. But if only for one reason—the *idea* of freedom—Mao does look to other sources. Think of Marx's hatred for the Hegelian tyranny of idea over man. Think of his contempt for Proudhon's philosophy, of which he wrote to Annenkov: "In short it is not history but old Hegelian junk, it is not profane history—a history of man—but sacred history—a history of ideas. From his point of view man is only the instrument of which the idea or the eternal reason makes use in order to unfold itself." [54] Will only existed in history, process was only purposive where:

The social categories of the material continuum are involved. . . . *Social* movement very definitely involves reference to volition. . . . The point of departure is human need. . . . The process of social development has no ends to realize which are not the ends willed by men. But those ends are not realized merely because they are willed by men. *What* is willed must be continuous with a discovered situation which is not willed but accepted. *When* it is willed must be determined by objective possibilities in the situation.[55]

Although we must realize that this note of necessity in Marx's writings added the final element to Mao's thought (permitting all the other factors to combine in the crucible of revolution), we must also remember that those earlier reflections allowed Mao a commitment to continuous and unending historical change which was far more extreme than Marx's own.

19

Contradictions

There is a passage in Mao Tse-tung's classic essay "On Contradiction" (*Mao-tun lun*) which states, "If there were no contradictions in the party and no ideological struggles to resolve them, the party's life would come to an end." [1] By that standard any who doubted the vigor of the Chinese Communist Party should have been reassured. As Mao himself said in 1959: "The thirty-nine year history of our party has been such an experience: when one opposed the right, the 'left' was bound to emerge; and when one opposed the 'left,' the right was bound to emerge. This is inevitable." [2] And later he added, before a plenary session of the Central Committee: ". . . we have factions within our party. That has always been the case. It is normal." [3] Or, more picturesquely in 1968: "Except in the deserts, at every place of human habitation there is the left, the center, and the right. This will continue to be so ten thousand years hence." [4] By the time of the Cultural Revolution, a special slogan ("Struggle-Criticism-Transformation") had even been formulated to direct the stages of such factional strife and to invite criticism from outside the party.[5] Party members themselves were then bluntly told by Mao that struggle and turmoil were salutary. "Do not be afraid to make trouble," he advised them. "The more trouble you make and the longer you make it the better. Confusion and trouble are always noteworthy. It can clear things up." [6]

Mao's instinct for struggle was no surprise. We have seen how frequently he insisted that conflict was an absolute law of nature. Strongly influenced by Lenin,* Mao believed that dialectics was the study of

---

* Arthur Cohen has taken pains to point out how derivative was Mao Tse-tung's theory of contradiction. Mao's major premise, that the basic cause of de-

struggle or contradiction in the essence of objects. According to Mao's *Mao-tun lun,* the Han philosopher Tung Chung-shu had distorted reality when he said: *T'ien pu pien, tao i pu pien* ("Heaven does not change, nor does the Way change"). Instead there was nothing but change or development, and dialectical materialists correctly realized that "the development of things should be seen as their internal and necessary self-movement": the contradictions within things, not their interaction with outer objects.[7] Mao's philosophical proof for this was logically vague. Declaring that being was matter in motion (*wu-chih yun-tung*), he made its essence the specific contradiction particular to its form of motion. Of this form of motion there were two modes or states: relative rest and conspicuous change. Even in a state of relative rest, a thing underwent minute quantitative change. As it accumulated, as that quantitative change reached a culminating point (*tsui kao tien*), its unity dissolved and it qualitatively transformed into its opposite through a change now conspicuous to the observer.[8]

Thus, Mao's theory of contradiction was both a theory of the laws of natural development and an epistemology which could be divided into five distinct steps.[9]

1. Axiom: Every thing contains one or more contradictions within it.
2. Contradictions, existing as complementary sets, form a single universal and necessary unity *within* things. Contradictions *between* things (each thing being a unified contradiction to begin with) exist contingently when two contradictory things complement each other in a new and third contradictory unity.

---

velopment was the contradiction within a thing, was the same as Lenin's "development as a unity of opposites." His supposedly original distinction between antagonistic and nonantagonistic contradictions—argued Cohen—had been made by Russian Marxists in the 1930s. Even his revision of Marx (productive forces can become dependent upon the superstructure) was stated by Stalin's ghostwriters in *Dialectical and Historical Materialism.* Because that book was published in 1938, Cohen argued that Mao did not really author a complete version of "On Contradiction" in 1937, as claimed, but rather put it in final shape just before its publication in *Jen-min jih-pao* on April 1, 1952. See Arthur A. Cohen, *The Communism of Mao Tse-tung* (Chicago & London: The University of Chicago Press, 1964), pp. 16–22. Stuart R. Schram, however, has shown in *The Political Thought of Mao Tse-tung* that "On Contradiction" was written in its original form before Mao read Stalin. He did agree, though, that the version which I have used here has been refined considerably. Finally, Vsevolod Holubnychy's article—"Mao Tse-tung's Materialistic Dialectics" *China Quarterly,* 19:3–37—has tried to prove that Mao's theory of nonantagonistic contradictions was certainly not taken either from Stalin or Lenin.

3. Contradictions are universal, but appear as concrete particularities. Therefore the universal *category* of contradiction does not imply a qualitative identity between things.
4. Axiom: The unity of opposites is an uneven relationship between a principal and secondary contradiction, namely: New Contradiction = Principal Contradiction + Secondary Contradiction
5. The tendency of the development of any contradiction can be determined by observing certain conditions: the movement from relative rest to conspicuous change, and the culmination of quantitative change in qualitative change, which dissolves the unity.

The only absolute constant was change. "We often speak of 'the new superseding the old' (*hsin ch'en fa hsieh*). The suppression of the old by the new is a general, eternal, and inviolable law of the universe." [10] The dialectical law of the identity of opposites showed the manner of that change by explaining that a "thing" was actually a contradiction, of which each element was the condition (*t'iao-chien*) for its opposite's existence. By that same law, these opposites ended by transforming each into the other. To build the dictatorship of the proletariat meant preparing the conditions for its disappearance; "To establish and build the Communist Party is in fact to prepare the conditions for the elimination of the Communist Party and all political parties." [11] As Mao thus defined simple sequence as opposites transforming into each other, he revealed the joint inspiration for this notion by adjoining two quotes: a Chinese aphorism, "things that oppose each other also complement each other" (*hsiang-fan, hsiang-ch'eng*); and Lenin's "There *is* an absolute *in the* relative." [12] At the same time he differed from both. Lacking the balance of *yin* and *yang,* his "unity of opposites" was not the same as the polarity of the *Book of Changes.* Lacking Hegelian categories like *Aufhebung* and stressing the inward complementarity of opposites, Mao's "unity of opposites" was not identical with Lenin's dialectic.[13] However, a major portion of "On Contradiction" was devoted to the Hegelian notion of "concrete universality." As "it is precisely in the particularity (*t'e-shu hsing*) of contradiction that the universality (*p'u-pien hsing*) of contradiction resides," [14] then "in identity there is struggle, in particularity there is universality, and in individuality there is generality." [15] But the ontological complexities of this theory were barely explored in *Mao-tun lun,* which was really a treatise on materialistic epistemology (gnoseology). Mao merely pointed out that

because the "range of things" was so vast and their development unlimited, "what is universal in one context becomes particular in another." [16] It was not clear what determined context, because he seemed
to mean that an idiographic contradiction particular to one historical
stage (for example, the conflict in capitalist society between the character of production and the private ownership of its means) was of
nomothetic significance to someone like Marx who could derive its
universal significance. Working from observation toward actuality, Mao
also argued, less skillfully than in "On Practice," that contradiction was
a case of the general (*kung-hsing*) being invested in the individual
(*ko-hsing*). Since the individual case was temporary and relative, the
general was the true absolute: contradiction as such. "To deny contradiction," therefore, "is to deny everything." [17]

Apparently content with his quantitative/qualitative explanation,
Mao did not really explain how dialectic change necessarily occurred.
There were many examples in "On Contradiction," drawn from history
to illustrate opposites transforming into each other, but how those
changes took place was not actually explained. One stage simply succeeded the next, like a before-and-after still photograph without intermediate motion. "The old unity with its constituent opposites yields to
a new unity with its constituent opposites, whereupon a new process
emerges to replace the old.[18] Or, returning to the theme of "On Practice," Mao pointed out that after knowledge has gone from the particular to the general it must move back to the particular again because
"cognition always moves in cycles (*hsun-huan*) . . . and each cycle
advances human knowledge a step higher." [19] Directed against the
Deborinist dogmatists within the party, this prescription may have been
an accurate description of how knowledge actually did evolve; but why
always "a step higher"? Where was the necessary development connecting one cycle to the next? Although Mao assumed purposive change
for the better, he ostensibly abhorred inner principles of either a Neo-
Confucian or Aristotelian form of potentiality. Without those, being
would have to be determined by external conditions. "Why can human
beings give birth only to human beings and not to anything else? The
sole reason is that the identity of opposites exists only in necessary given
conditions (*i-ting ti pi-yao ti t'iao-chien*)." [20] This made poor biological
sense, but it certainly was a reasonable explanation of history.

History, too, was a better example of Mao's famous distinction between the principal and minor aspects of a contradiction. In fact, official

philosophers in China usually praised this concept for its utility during the revolution.

Comrade Mao Tse-tung led the Chinese revolution to today's enormous victory precisely because during each phase of the revolution he was skilled in adapting and seizing the principal contradiction and the principal aspect of the contradiction, proceeding to grasp the particularity of contradiction and its inseparability from the method of dialectical materialism.[21]

Consequently, the theory of the aspects of a contradiction did less to explain being than it did to distinguish precise stages of change. As Mao described it, the contradiction of a thing (itself a unity of opposites) could become intensified or stimulated (*chi-hua*) to the point of changing the unity.[22] Because most processes, most situations, most "things" (here situations would be more appropriate) did not consist of one contradiction alone, one could only understand the change by singling out the principal contradiction (*chu-yao ti mao-tun*) which determined all the others. "There is no doubt at all that at every stage in the development of a process, there is only one principal contradiction which plays the leading role." [23] And because every contradiction consisted of two aspects (*fang-mien*) as well, it was also crucial to know which of these was principal. For, as situations proceeded, a once-principal aspect might come to be determined by its opposite. Mao used this variation to argue that the superstructure could become a determining force in a society.

When the superstructure (politics, culture, and so on) obstructs the development of the economic base, political and cultural changes become principal and decisive. Are we going against materialism when we say this? No. The reason is that while we recognize that in the general development of history the material determines the mental and social being determines social consciousness, we also—and indeed must—recognize the reaction of mental on material things.[24]

Just as Mao's examples of contradiction were mainly culled from recent Chinese history, so did he personally demonstrate that mental effort— "will"—could determine a revolution.

By design, "On Contradiction" also enabled doctrinal flexibility. As Mao Tse-tung urged concrete practice, he emphasized that qualitatively different contradictions called for qualitatively different methods of resolution. While a contradiction between proletariat and bourgeoisie would be solved by revolution, "contradiction within the Communist Party is resolved by the method of criticism and self-criticism." [25] This distinction and its political implications were spelled out during the Cultural Revolution in the resolutions of the Eleventh Plenum:

A strict distinction . . . between the two different types of contradictions: those among the people and those between ourselves and the enemy. Contradictions among the people must not be made into contradictions between ourselves and the enemy; nor must contradictions between ourselves and the enemy be regarded as those among the people. . . . The method to be used in debates is to present the facts, reason things out, and persuade through reasoning. Any method of forcing a minority holding different views to submit is impermissible. The minority should be protected, because sometimes the truth is with the minority. . . . When there is a debate, it should be conducted by reasoning, not by coercion or force.[26]

The proper selection of method was another reason for accurately assessing the relation between the two aspects of the contradiction, "the specific position each aspect occupies." [27] By discovering which was principal, revolutionaries could push aside the confusion of minor contradictions to reach the core of a situation. At the same time, they would become more tactically responsive, because the moment one redefined a contradiction by selecting a newly dominant aspect, every other element in the relationship changed. For this reason Mao Tse-tung's theory of contradiction was slightly different from Engels' or Lenin's. They had developed the doctrine of the unity of opposites and of quantitative/qualitative change in order to prove that no principle of mind was constant. Engels' attack on Dühring for his monistic moralism, for his belief in constituent principles, was intended to vindicate materialism. "What he [that is, Dühring] is dealing with are therefore *principles,* formal principles derived from *thought* and not from the external world, which are to be applied to Nature and the realm of man, and to which therefore Nature and the realm of man have to conform." [28] Mao was not as concerned with exposing idealism and the false independence of moral values because he tacitly assumed norms which Engels would have excoriated. Indeed, Mao was not so much against unalterable principles of good and evil as opposed to unalterable formulas (*pu k'o kai-pien ti kung-shih*) for diagnosing situations.*

---

* Mao Tse-tung, *Mao-tun lun* [On Contradiction], in *Mao Tse-tung hsuan-chi* [Selected Works of Mao Tse-tung] (Peking, Jen-min ch'u-pan she, 1969), 1:286. This is still within the Leninist tradition. Georg Lukacs once pointed out that the Leninist corollary of the Marxist dialectical recognition that "although men make

Mao's formula to avoid unalterable formulas was the recognition of antagonism within contradictions. Even contradictions between classes were not always open struggles; only after developing to the state of antagonism (*tui-k'ang*) would revolutionary struggle break out. But there was no hard and fast rule for this process. Because the nature of a contradiction depended upon circumstances, it might at one time be absolute or antagonistic, yet later change into its opposite, a nonantagonistic contradiction. Therefore, good Marxists should define the circumstances of any given contradiction with great care, and refrain from dogmatic conflict where gradual transformation into the unity of opposites was called for. Of course, this also meant that the converse was true. Normally nonantagonistic contradictions, such as those within the Communist Party itself, could as well be defined as antagonistic.

. . . so long as classes exist, contradictions between correct and incorrect ideas in the Communist Party are reflections within the party of class contradictions. At first, with regard to certain issues, such contradictions may not manifest themselves as antagonistic. But with the development of class struggle, they may grow and become antagonistic. The history of the Communist Party of the Soviet Union shows us that the contradictions between the correct thinking of Lenin and Stalin and the fallacious thinking of Trotsky, Bukharin, and others did not at first manifest themselves in an antagonistic form, but that later they did develop into antagonism. There are similar cases in the history of the Chinese Communist Party.[29]

Of those, the most outstanding was the Great Proletarian Cultural Revolution, which lasted from 1965 to 1969.

---

their own history they cannot do so in circumstances chosen by themselves," is a rejection of left wing radicalism opposed to compromise. "For Lenin," wrote Lukacs, "compromise is only possible in dialectical interaction with strict adherence to the principles and method of Marxism; it always indicates the next realistic step toward the realization of Marx's theory." Georg Lukacs, *Lenin: A Study on the Unity of His Thought,* trans. Nicholas Jacobs (London: NLB, 1970), p. 83.

20

To Embrace the Moon

The Great Proletarian Cultural Revolution—in Mao's words, "a nationwide civil war without guns" [1]—had manifold causes. The simplest and most immediate was Mao's personal effort to regain the power he had yielded to other leaders like Liu Shao-ch'i and Teng Hsiao-p'ing* after the Lushan plenum. Mao's retirement from the "first front" of leadership had been his way of appeasing criticism of his Great Leap policies as well as paving the way for political succession after his death.

Why divide [leadership] into the first and second fronts? First because [my] health is poor, and second because of the lesson of the Soviet Union. Malenkov was immature. He had not held power before Stalin's death. Every time he drank to [Stalin's] health he laid it on thick. So I wanted to have their prestige established before I died. [2]

Then, since I was in the second front, I did not take charge of daily work. Many things were done by others and their prestige was thus cultivated, so that when I met with God, the state would not be thrown into great convulsions. Everybody approved this view of mine. [3]

As Mao's personal power retrenched, his *persona* was exalted as though it were already posthumous. For, it was really only after 1959 that the so-called Mao cult took deep root. Ironically, the more his thought was glorified the less of a ruling role he played, so that like

* Teng Hsiao-p'ing, then general secretary of the Central Committee of the Chinese Communist Party, was vilified during the Cultural Revolution as "the other leading person taking the capitalist road," which ranked him closely alongside Liu Shao-ch'i, "China's Khrushchev."

some cloistered emperor, he was gradually excluded from important decisions. He later claimed to have wanted it that way, but his tone was grieved and acrimonious: too much had been taken away from him.

> Comrade T'ao Chu* says that power has fallen to the hands of subordinates. But I deliberately let it fall that way. However, they have now set up independent kingdoms. There were many things about which they did not consult with me. . . . These things should have been discussed by the Central Committee and decisions taken on them. Teng Hsiao-p'ing never consulted with me. He has never consulted with me about anything since 1949.[4]

The new party leadership, Mao argued, had proved insufficient. Important policies were only carried out with half a heart—especially if they disturbed party bureaucrats. Put to the test of the mass line, the new leadership was found wanting.[5] Party rectification would have to come from without; Mao would personally have to reoccupy the "first front."

Party rectification by means of a mass line was not a new departure for Mao. As early as 1928 he had stressed its importance as a way of preventing the development of dictatorial tendencies.[6] Indeed, the orthodox theory of democratic centralism paid more than lip service to that principle. But there was a difference between a Leninist dialectic of party vanguard and masses and the Maoist mass line. The former was approximated by figures like Liu Shao-ch'i, who forged party lines by democratic consultation with the masses and then executed the new policies via central organization. This theory, particularly as elaborated in Liu Shao-ch'i's "On the Party," was certainly not opposed to a mass line. But in "coming from the masses and going to the masses," the more orthodox Leninist wing of the party was convinced both that some mass views could be incorrect and that it alone truly understood the people's long-term interests.[7] Mao did not disagree with that contention altogether; even during the Cultural Revolution he avowed that party members were, by virtue of their affiliation, more conscious of the proletariat than the proletariat itself.[8] But he at the same time underscored the party's entire derivation of legitimacy from the people at large. "Our power—who gives it to us? The working class gives it to

---

* T'ao Chu, fourth-ranking in the Communist hierarchy as of June 1966, was to be attacked by Red Guard wall posters in Canton in October; named a counterrevolutionary by Cultural Revolution leaders in Peking on January 4, 1967; and arrested on January 25 by Maoist rebels who had taken over the public security apparatus. See Ezra Vogel, *Canton under Communism: Programs and Politics in a Provincial Capital, 1949–1963* (Cambridge: Harvard University Press, 1969), pp. 325–329.

us and the masses of laboring people who comprise over ninety percent of the population give it to us. We represent the proletariat and the masses, and have overthrown the enemies of the people. The people therefore support us." [9] Perhaps because China's economic stage did not pose the specter of a labor aristocracy, Mao did not share Lenin's ambivalence toward a people which could so easily undergo a process of *embourgeoisement* and therefore required a separate party vanguard. As the party was a simple representative of the people, any barrier between it and the masses was a sign that the party—bereft of legitimacy —was in error. But Mao was not only convinced that exposure of party members to mass criticism would prevent political lithification; he also believed that the mass line best aroused and channeled collective social enthusiasm, unifying the proletariat's energies by removing the barrier that separated cadres and masses.

What began as a question of emphasis soon became a policy dispute in many different sectors. Economically, for example, the Leninist wing of the party favored state planning and coordination over the Maoist reliance on less differentiated and more decentralized fulfillment of quotas through popular spontaneity and moral incentives. These distinctions sharpened by cycles. After the mass line was criticized during the Eighth Party Congress (1956) for being too disruptive once the state was settled and the civil war over, it was enthusiastically renewed as part of the Great Leap Forward. Mao's "opening wide" policy (March 1957) urged "all people to express their opinions freely, so that they dare to speak, dare to criticize, and dare to debate." [10] But after the Great Leap, party leadership was once again vaunted. On September 28, 1959, Liu Lan-t'ao (the alternate secretary of the Central Committee's secretariat) announced:

The Chinese Communist Party constitutes the vanguard of the working class and the supreme form of class organization of the working class of China. It is composed of the most progressive, outstanding, courageous, and communism-conscious elements. It is the sacred duty of our Communists to fulfill the great socialist and communist aims in China. Marxism–Leninism is our guide in all categories of our work. Under the leadership of the Central Committee headed by Comrade Mao Tse-tung, our party has firmly adhered to the policy of combining Marxism–Leninism with the realities of the Chinese Revolution.[11]

All revolutionary organizations—"be they governments, armed forces, [or] people's organizations"—would be placed under the unified leadership of party committees. Within three years, though, the pendulum swung back as Mao criticized the party for only pretending to follow a policy of democratic centralism. Truly to carry out democratic centralism might mean the demotion of some cadres, but what difference should that make? "Comrades," he said in 1962, "we are revolutionaries. If we have truly committed 'mistakes,' and such mistakes are harmful to the party cause and the interests of the people, we should solicit the views of the masses of the people." [12] How could they forget that the key to a dictatorship of the proletariat was the proper combination of democracy and centralism—its own unity of opposites?

It is necessary to create a political phase in which there is centralism as well as democracy, discipline as well as freedom, unified will as well as ease of mind and liveliness for the individual. . . . Difficulties cannot be overcome without democracy. Of course it also won't do to have no centralism. But without democracy there is no centralism.[13]

By 1965, when the party numbered twenty million members, Mao placed even more emphasis on the inadequacy of leadership and the importance of relying on the masses.

Politics must follow the mass line. It will not do to rely on leaders alone. How can the leaders do so much? The leaders can cope with only a fraction of everything, good and bad. Consequently, everybody must be mobilized to share the responsibility, to speak up, to encourage other people, and to criticize other people. . . . Democracy means allowing the masses to manage their own affairs. . . . Our politics is mass politics. Democratic rule is the rule of all, not the rule of a few. . . . Nothing can be done well if it depends entirely on the leader, not on the leadership of the party. [We] must rely on the party and [our] comrades to deal with matters, not on a solitary leader.[14]

The original mass line having failed, cadres now had to be forcefully reminded not to distance themselves from the masses. It had been too easy in the past to stand up in public and cry *mea culpa* for the sin of bureaucratism, and then casually return to the evil habits of the past. Formulaic renunciations would not do this time. Mao bluntly told members of the Central Committee in 1966: "If relying on yourself to confess your errors does not work, you should resign from your office. You should live and die as Communist Party members. The life of sitting on sofas and using electric fans will not do." [15]

Was it not after all in the party's best interests to be reinvigorated? Without fresh blood, Mao argued in 1968, the organism would sicken.

A human being has arteries and veins and his heart makes the blood circulate. He breathes through the lungs, exhaling carbon dioxide and inhaling oxygen afresh, that is, getting rid of the waste and letting in the fresh. A proletarian party must also get rid of the waste and let in the fresh, for only in this way can it be full of vigor. Without eliminating waste and getting fresh blood the party has no vigor.[16]

Mao Tse-tung's crescendo of concern reflected his growing conviction over the years that the party was too self-interested to function anymore as an instrument of leadership for mass campaigns. There was another institution at hand in the form of the People's Liberation Army, which after 1960 took a leading role in propaganda work. But its increasing influence was a consequence rather than an agent of the Cultural Revolution. Instead of depending on organization at all, Mao's ultimate conception of the mass line would be realized by society as such: "emancipation of the masses by the masses" and the "mobilization of the masses from below." [17]

The Cultural Revolution* was an ideological paradox: a class war within the superstructure of public opinion.[18] Some elements of it therefore appeared artificial: the designation of bureaucrats as a class, or the obvious attempt to re-create a revolutionary experience for the successor generation. But there were genuine social causes—causes whose existence Mao had especially sensed among China's youth. Their alienation (in the sense of powerlessness, of the individual's expectation that his behavior cannot determine the occurrence of the goals he desires) stemmed from the growing awareness of a new "class" division within society. Those youths advantaged by primary education or family background could more or less routinely enter higher educational institutes. But most were of peasant background, and not equipped to compete with, say, the progeny of party officials living in the capital. On June 6, 1966, for instance, students at Peking's First Girls' Middle High School wrote Mao, urging that the traditional entrance examinations (now controlled by "reactionary elements") be replaced with an "ideological diploma" granted by the masses, so that no student would receive higher

---

* The concept, "cultural revolution" (*wen-hua ko-ming*), was coined in "On New Democracy" (1940) when Mao Tse-tung so styled the May Fourth Movement. Later in 1964 when the attack had begun on "feudal" traces in Peking opera, the playwright, Ts'ao Yü, published an article entitled "A Great Cultural Revolution." The full phrase, "Great Proletarian Cultural Revolution" (*wu-ch'an chieh-chi wen-hua ta ko-ming*), finally made its appearance in a newspaper editorial on June 1, 1966. See H. C. Chuang, *The Great Proletarian Cultural Revolution* (Berkeley: Center for Chinese Studies, 1967), pp. 3–5.

education without first working among the people.[19] Otherwise—the petition implied—there would emerge an official elite resembling the "new class" of the Soviet Union. To be sure, the criteria of vertical mobility were universalistic. But were examination scores and technical expertise better standards than class background or doctrinal redness? At the same time, even those who had succeeded in acquiring a higher degree were discontent. Once graduated, many were selected by district committees for "rustification": semivoluntary residence away from the excitement of the great cities, or perhaps even colonization of the distant frontier provinces which had once been places of political exile under the Ch'ing.

Characteristically urban, the Cultural Revolution was therefore a movement of the deprived: students unable to find urban jobs and asked to emigrate to the hinterland or frontier, menial laborers envious of more highly paid state employees, demobilized soldiers resentful of regular party cadres, local party members who had lost out to bosses sent in from outside their area, and so forth.* These were the stalwarts of the most radical Red Guard groups which answered the summons of Peking's Cultural Revolution Group under Chiang Ch'ing, Mao's wife, to "bombard" local party headquarters, municipal bureaus and military garrisons. The Cultural Revolution offered them an opportunity to recover momentary control over their future by choosing new leaders, organizing new political centers, attaining new positions of personal enhancement. But the place of adolescents in the Cultural Revolution

---

* Ezra Vogel, *Canton under Communism*, pp. 321-349. A similar study of the Cultural Revolution in Shanghai by Lynn White, III makes the point more strongly. Noting the simple demographic problem (a death rate declining faster than the birth rate) in cities like Shanghai, he carefully examined the kinds of discontent that preceded the Cultural Revolution. Lower-ranking cadres, calling for inner-party democracy, attended rallies attacking the "bourgeois" line of their party chiefs. Workers hostile to "bourgeois" students criticized management and welfare trade unions which granted superior housing or better vacations to others singled out for their superior performance or higher skills. Students in schools divided into those whose parents were wealthy or influential and those whose parents held lower positions. Above all, students were resentful of the role of lane committees and intermediate leaders who selected them for rustification to Sinkiang. There was, for example, a sharp rise in the rate at which youth were sent to Sinkiang in June of 1966, just before the Cultural Revolution began to accelerate in Shanghai. Lynn White, III, "Shanghai's Polity in Cultural Revolution," (Hong Kong: University of Hong Kong, Center of Asian Studies, n.d.). Michael Oksenberg has also emphasized the career frustrations of youth in Communist China in "The Institutionalization of the Chinese Communist Revolution: The Ladder of Success on the Eve of the Cultural Revolution," *China Quarterly*, 36:61-92.

should not be narrowly interpreted in terms of selfish interest alone.
Mao, searching for allies outside the established order, turned to that
population group both because the young had not yet acquired rooted
social interests and because they possessed the greatest and most optimistic faith in his revolutionary authority.

In order to transform student attacks on educational authorities into
a mass movement, Mao had to bypass party cadres at intermediate
levels. There were three means of doing this. First, he encouraged the
replacement of party work teams (which had been ordered to channel
protest in the schools in the first place) with delegates from what would
become the Cultural Revolution Group led by his wife, Chiang Ch'ing.
Second, party propaganda cadres were replaced by members of the
People's Liberation Army. Finally, Mao contrived to communicate directly with the masses by means of big-character posters (*ta-tzu pao*)
plastered on the walls of Chinese cities.

During the Great Leap period, Mao had regarded the big-character
poster as a "useful new weapon" to arouse the masses.* By the spring
of 1966, it had become a major medium of communication among
students in Peking. Mao greeted this phenomenon enthusiastically on
July 21 of that year.

Nieh Yuan-tzu's big-character poster of May 25 is the declaration of the
Chinese Paris Commune of the sixties of the twentieth century; its significance far surpasses that of the Paris Commune. It is beyond our ability to
write this kind of big-character poster. Who [in the past] suppressed student
movements? Only the northern warlords. It is anti-Marxist for the Communist Party to be afraid of student movements. We trust the masses and
must be their pupils before becoming their teachers. The great Cultural Revolution is a world-shaking event which [tries us out to see] whether we can
or cannot, dare or dare not pass the test. . . . You will have to direct the
revolution toward yourselves, ignite it, and fan it up. Will you do that? It
will burn you! [20]

As he urged that the word "fear" be replaced with "dare," Mao seemed
perfectly willing to sap the party's authority altogether and define its

* Mao Tse-tung, "Introducing a Cooperative" (April 15, 1958), in *Selected
Readings from the Works of Mao Tse-tung* (Peking: Foreign Languages Press,
1967), pp. 403–404. It was then, in 1958, that Mao also referred to the poem
by Kung Tzu-chen (the early nineteenth-century thinker who greatly influenced
the Kung-yang school) which was later to become a slogan of the Cultural
Revolution.

> Only in wind and thunder can a country show its vitality,
> Alas the ten thousand horses are all muted!

struggles as a form of class conflict. The Cultural Revolution thus departed dramatically from the rectification movement of the 1940s, when Mao had declared that even "intraparty sectarianism" hindered the unification of the party.[21] Even later, as he maintained the continuous contradiction under socialism between productive forces and the relations of production, he did not publicly doubt that the class war had been won within China.[22] But by 1966, he had come to define the Russian party conflicts of 1938 as class struggle, and the basic contradiction of the Cultural Revolution as being between the proletariat and the bourgeoisie.[23]

To shape that class struggle, Mao Tse-tung penned his own big-character poster, "Bombard the Bourgeois Headquarters," on August 5, 1966. Accusing "some leading comrades" of "adopting the reactionary stand of the bourgeoisie," he exclaimed that they had "enforced a bourgeois dictatorship and struck down the surging movement of the Great Cultural Revolution of the proletariat. . . . How poisonous!"[24] The poster was nevertheless a politically vague proclamation, leaving precise implementation up to individuals. That was because clear directives detailing an organizational division of labor would have empowered specific and entrenched groups to act. It was exactly those groups, of course, which were managed by the party.

At the time, Mao Tse-tung seemed contritely surprised by the effect of his big-character poster. On October 24, 1966, he explained to the Central Committee: "Nobody had thought, and I had not expected, that a single big-character poster, a Red Guard, and one big exchange of revolutionary experiences would create such turmoil in various provinces and cities. The students have made some mistakes too, but it is mainly we lords and squires who made the mistakes."[25] And the following day, in a confused committee session, he actually confessed to having done something "disastrously wrong" in approving the big-character poster by Nieh Yuan-tzu,* in writing a letter to the middle school attached to Tsinghua University, and in penning his own big-character poster.

* Nieh Yuan-tzu was secretary of the Chinese Communist Party branch in the department of philosophy at Peking University where she held the post of lecturer. In 1964 she was accused by Lu P'ing, president of Peking University, of being an antiparty element. In May of 1966 Nieh and six others put up a wall poster exposing the relationship between Lu and P'eng Chen. It was this poster which was so highly praised by Mao Tse-tung and which signaled the beginning of the Red Guard movement at the university. By April 1969, Nieh Yuan-tzu had become an alternate member of the Ninth Central Committee of the Chinese Communist Party.

The time was very short; all these things were done in June, July, August, September, and October—in less than five months. Our comrades could not be blamed for failing to understand these things sufficiently. The time was very short, but the situation developed so rapidly as to surprise me. The broadcast of the big-character poster of Peking University stirred up the whole country. Before the letter to the Red Guards was sent out, Red Guards in the whole country were mobilized and went on charging—charging with such force as to amaze you. I myself had caused this big trouble and I cannot blame you if you have complaints against me.[26]

However, by blaming himself he was also pointedly attesting to his own ability to arouse the masses, and even—at another level—suggesting the necessity for a *deus ex machina* within his own theoretical framework of contradiction. Mao's *mao-tun* (contradictions) were designed to keep the mobile of history internal to the dialectic. However, they actually had no logical mechanism for moving from quantitative to qualitative change, or for pushing a nonantagonistic contradiction to its antagonistic stage. To prevent otherwise successively unpatterned complementarities, some externality had to intervene, if only to choose when to force an antagonism to its moment of confrontation. Mao Tse-tung's "On Contradiction," therefore, was a construction of change which he actually followed, because it implicitly called for a helmsman of acumen to drive potential conflict relationships to their conclusion in struggle.

The decisiveness of Mao Tse-tung's intervention was repeatedly proved during the Cultural Revolution. One Cantonese Red Guard described the steps of that process as follows. His senior middle school was aroused to activity after May 16, 1966, when it received news of the Central Committee's condemnation of Lo Jui-ch'ing. Realizing that this justified mass criticism of local party members, the school principal dutifully had his party committee single out a few of the older teachers as targets. But within a month, the publication of a *People's Daily* editorial ("Sweep out All Monsters and Ghosts," June 1), the appearance of Nieh Yuan-tzu's big-character poster attacking Peking educational officials (June 2), and the announcement that the Peking party committee had been entirely reorganized (June 4) frightened the principal into denouncing seven more teachers. The students, however, were already growing suspicious of the school's party committee's intentions, and so went directly to the provincial committee, which responded by dispatching work teams.

Yet the provincial party authorities, too, soon lost the students' confidence. The work teams were willing enough to denounce the school committee, but felt they had to refuse the students' request to attack local powerholders at an all-school meeting. "By July 20," recalled the Cantonese Red Guard, "things had become really boring. All we did was say the same things day after day. We seemed to be making no progress at all," especially because the "Cultural Revolution Preparatory Committee" formed by the work teams contained the same old school leadership of Communist Youth League members.[27] Ennui was accompanied by rumors in Canton that work teams were being denounced elsewhere in China. Those rumors were confirmed on August 6, when the students were summoned to a meeting to hear recordings of speeches by Liu Shao-ch'i, Chou En-lai, and Teng Hsiao-p'ing asking the work teams to withdraw. As the famous sixteen-point Resolutions of the Eleventh Plenum soon made clear, the leadership could not stand on the sanctity of the party alone.*

In certain schools, units, and work teams of the Cultural Revolution, some of the persons in charge have organized counterattacks against the masses who put up big-character posters against them. These people have even advanced such slogans as: opposition to the leaders of a unit or a work team means opposition to the party's Central Committee, means opposition to the party and socialism, means counterrevolution. . . . This is absolutely impermissible.[28]

* The Eleventh Plenum of the Eighth Central Committee of the CCP was convened in Peking from August 1–August 12, 1966. Mao, who introduced Red Guards into the meeting itself, carried the day by securing the adoption, on August 8, of the famous sixteen points: (1) the Great Proletarian Cultural Revolution was a new stage in the socialist revolution; (2) despite "twists and turns," the workers, peasants, soldiers, revolutionary intellectuals, and cadres would continue to advance; (3) the masses would be boldly aroused and daring placed above all other feelings; (4) the masses would be educated in the movement itself; (5) it was necessary to distinguish carefully between enemies and friends; (6) similarly, there should be a distinction between contradictions among the people and those between the people and their enemies; (7) it was important to guard against those who were inclined to call the revolutionary masses counterrevolutionaries; (8) cadres were to be divided into categories of "good," "comparatively good," and so on, according to their acceptance of the mass line; (9) the new mass organizations should be firmly approved; (10) education must be reformed to serve proletarian politics; (11) people would be criticized by name in the press only after clearance by the respective party committees; (12) most scientists and technicians were loyal citizens; (13) the Great Proletarian Cultural Revolution should be combined with the Socialist Education movement in the countryside; (14) production should be stimulated; (15) both the Cultural Revolution and the Socialist Education movement were to be carried out under the instructions of the military commission of the Central Committee and the general political department of the army; (16) Mao Tse-tung's thought was the ultimate guide to action in the Cultural Revolution.

By August 22, 1966, the Cantonese students were ready to form their own Red Guards, aided by a Tsinghua University student who had participated in the Peking movement. This final step completed the destruction of party authority. On August 23, the Red Guards convened a meeting which was also attended by skittish representatives from the provincial party committee. The assembly soon became acrimonious, and the Red Guard leaders suddenly ordered the party delegates to leave the hall. When provincial representatives meekly trooped out, they were "destroyed in the eyes" of the students present.

We had already lost the better part of our confidence in them and this incident completed the process. We knew that it wasn't even necessary to consult or advise anymore. We could do essentially as we pleased as long as we remained in step with the central Cultural Revolution Group. . . . We now thought of the party as consisting of a core represented in the central Cultural Revolution Group and of ourselves as being in direct communication with it. The term "party" had taken on a different meaning for us. It seemed to be the central leaders only and especially Mao Tse-tung. We Red Guards saw ourselves as taking orders directly from him.[29]

This kind of experience, repeated across China, soon exacerbated the struggle beyond normal control. What was to prevent one Red Guard unit from claiming to be closer to Mao's orders than another? Mao could arouse the masses personally, as he did when he appeared with Lin Piao before a million individuals at T'ien-an-men Square on August 18, 1966. But he also had to find some way of mediating between the multitude of different groups which responded to his personal appeal but were beyond his direct reach. For, these transitory forms of political activity resembled clique behavior under imperial regimes. Noncorporate groups formed around local leaders or on particular issues and engaged in factional struggle. Although their organizational diffuseness and dependence served Mao, as factions had served earlier rulers, they differed because struggle was now declared legitimate. As a consequence, Red Guard groups were created in tandem: "Red Flag" versus "East Wind." Conflict was the sole key to their existence, so that Proudhonian communalism could only occur in a state of continuing crisis as groups defined themselves in struggle. The pace of the Cultural Revolution therefore followed a seesaw motion with periods of relative calm succeeded almost overnight by extreme disorder. Mao's own predilections seemed to vary. "In my opinion, we should let the chaos go on for a few months," he declared in August of 1966.[30]

But by March of 1968, he would be urging the masses to "resolutely overcome lack of discipline or even, in many places, anarchy." [31] This ambivalence was especially visible in his attitudes about the establishment of Paris-style communes.

In the context of the Cultural Revolution, the Paris Commune (*Pa-li kung-she*) was at first a model for new mass organizations. The ninth of the Eleventh Plenum's sixteen resolutions stated that:

Many new things have begun to emerge in the great proletarian Cultural Revolution. The cultural revolutionary groups, committees, and other organizational forms created by the masses in many schools and units are something new and of great historic importance. . . . These . . . are excellent new forms of organization whereby under the leadership of the Communist Party the masses are educating themselves. They are an excellent bridge to keep our party in close contact with the masses. They are organs of power of the proletarian Cultural Revolution . . . and should not be temporary . . . but permanent, standing mass organizations . . . suitable not only for colleges, schools, and government and other organizations, but generally also for factories, mines, other enterprises, urban districts, and villages. It is necessary to institute a system of general elections, like that of the Paris Commune, for electing members to the cultural revolutionary groups and committees and delegates to the cultural revolutionary congresses. The lists of candidates should be put forward by the revolutionary masses after full discussion. . . . The masses are entitled at any time to criticize members of the cultural revolutionary groups and committees and delegates elected to the cultural revolutionary congresses. If these members or delegates prove incompetent, they can be replaced through election or recalled by the masses after discussion.[32]

More classically, the Paris Commune was also viewed as an illustration of the proletariat seizing power by creating new organs to replace the old state ones it had smashed. This was Marx's notion of the breaking of "the modern state power," as well as Engels' idea of *Gemeinwesen*.[33]

The whole talk about the state should be dropped, especially since the commune, which was no longer a state in the proper sense of the word. . . . With the introduction of the socialist order of society the state will of itself dissolve and disappear. As, therefore, the "state" is only a transitory institution which is being used in the struggle, in the revolution, in order to hold down one's adversaries by force, it is pure nonsense to talk of a "free people's state"; so long as the proletariat still *uses* the state, it does not use it in the interests of freedom but in order to hold down its adversaries, and as soon as it becomes possible to speak of freedom, the state as such ceases to exist. We would therefore propose to replace the word "state" everywhere by the word *Gemeinwesen* [community], a good old German word, which can very well represent the French word commune.[34]

As interpreted by Lenin, Engels' "most important theoretical statement" meant that a majority of the population—*Gemeinwesen* (the total system of communities) instead of *Gemeinde* (a single commune) —replaced the bourgeois state.[35] The Paris Commune further embodied the idea of preventing a restoration of bourgeois control: Engels' "hold down" was actually *niederzuhalten,* holding back from restoration.[36] Thus, over time, the Commune not only represented a revolutionary and armed seizure of state power; it also symbolized the proletariat's retention of power in socialist societies whose governments threatened to become bourgeois dictatorships. This, at least, was *Red Flag*'s interpretation of the Paris Commune in March of 1966, as a demonstration of the way direct-recall elections kept proletarian state organs from being transformed into the masters of society.[37]

These were the implications which Ch'en Po-ta had in mind early in 1967, when he proposed that the people of Peking follow the example of the Paris Commune and seize power on a city-wide basis. By February 6 a Shanghai People's Commune had been formed, and a week later its counterpart was announced in Peking. But both were extremely short-lived, and municipal elections were never held. After conferring personally with the Shanghai Commune leaders, Mao made his disapproval known—ostensibly because he did not wish to rename the People's Republic.[38] Nomenclature was probably only an excuse for his opposition. Mao had always favored local particularity to encourage initiative and meet specific conditions, but—as he said in 1956 of the rural commune system—"we need unity as well as particularity." [39] Municipal communes, on the other hand, suggested the dangers of localism, which had already appeared in some places in China as part of the Cultural Revolution. Cantonese guerrillas had again taken to the hills against extraprovincials, and Shanghai workers demonstrated strong feelings against outsiders.[40] Communalism would have been a much more articulated and legitimized form of this putative regionalism. Furthermore, the Paris Commune movement expressed—as did the entire Red Guard movement itself—such an egalitarianism as to abolish state organization altogether. As Mao noted:

The Shanghai People's Council offices submitted a command to the premier of the state council in which they asked for the elimination of all the chiefs. This is extreme anarchy; it is most reactionary. Now they do not wish to refer to anyone as the chief of such and such; they call them orderlies or attendants. In reality this is just a matter of appearances. Actually, there always have to be chiefs.[41]

By the time the Shanghai Commune was established, Mao Tse-tung had already asked the army to step in and "support the left" by guiding the formation of revolutionary committees throughout China.

The demise of the eighteen-day-old Shanghai Commune did not obliterate the Paris model altogether, but its meaning changed significantly. Instead of being a plebiscitarian fusion of state and society, it became a symbol of Mao's own willingness to support a mass movement which might occasionally err but was instinctively correct in its revolutionary spontaneity. The Paris Commune analogy also likened Mao to Marx— a connection which Mao had made over a decade earlier during the Lushan plenum[42] and which was renewed in the spring of 1971.

Marx, the great teacher of the proletariat, highly valued the revolutionary initiative of the masses of the people and set a civilian example of the correct attitude to adopt toward the revolutionary mass movement. In the autumn of 1870, prior to the founding of the Paris Commune, Marx pointed out that the conditions were not right for an uprising by the French workers, but when the proletariat of Paris did rise in revolt with heaven-storming revolutionary heroism in March 1871, Marx, regarding himself as a participant, promptly and firmly supported and helped this proletarian revolution. Although he perceived the mistakes of the commune and foresaw its defeat, Marx considered the air of revolution the most glorious exploit of the French working class.[43]

Like Marx, Mao had been faced with the revolutionary's ultimate choice: ". . . to march at the head of the masses and lead them? To trail behind them, gesticulating and criticizing? Or to stand in their way and oppose them?" [44]

Obviously, Mao would march in the vanguard. But however firm his own commands, the procession still required monitors. That is, Mao's technique of inspiring relatively undefined conflict between factions and then pressing for complementarity ("unity, criticism and self-criticism, unity")[45] demanded some form of direct local mediation which was simply beyond any single man's ability. How could the chairman personally decide each and every case of struggle in provinces thousands of miles from the capital? Some chain of command had to be used; some form of local authority had to be sanctioned to judge for him. Because the party could not be employed, Mao turned instead to the army.

The politicization of the People's Liberation Army was neither abrupt nor—given its role during World War II—novel. Mao's request in 1958 that cadres serve a month of each year as privates, the defeat of Marshal P'eng Teh-huai in 1959, the dismissal of Lo Jui-ch'ing, and Mao's "May Seventh Instruction" (which instructed Lin Piao to follow the Yenan model by turning the army into a "big school") in 1966 [46] all committed a consistently deprofessionalized PLA to the national social struggle. Lin Piao's "Four Firsts" (October of 1960) placed living ideas over bookish theory, ideology over routine, political work over other duties, and men over weapons. [47] And so by 1963, the soldier Lei Feng was being hailed as a model for the entire nation, and hundreds of thousands of army propaganda workers were deeply involved in the Socialist Education campaign. After February of 1966, in fact, the PLA conducted its own internal cultural revolution under the aegis of Chiang Ch'ing, who helped Lin Piao replace Lo Jui-ch'ing's "bourgeois military line" (weapons and techniques first) with Chairman Mao's "proletarian" one (militia and politics first). [48]

This task was all the more urgent because it was rapidly becoming apparent that however ostensibly "noninvolved" the army was in local struggles, it actually had replaced the party as the sole remaining organ of central authority. Because in many areas the PLA exercised *de facto* rule—intervening to support one side or another if public security was badly threatened—Mao decided on January 27, 1967, that the army could no longer stay aloof. [49] Urged at first by Mao to support the left, the PLA did not always acquiesce. In July of that year, the Wuhan regional command came close to mutiny, and it was apparent that many other military commanders preferred to support workers and party members rather than Red Guard detachments. At the same time, though, the army was coming to play such an important role in the formation of the "three-way alliance" leadership of the new revolutionary committees that it was obviously one of the basic pillars of Mao's rule, representing a gradual return to order after the apogee of the Cultural Revolution. [50] Indeed, army personnel dominated the party itself: by 1969, 40 percent of the members of the Central Committee were ranking military leaders. Of course, the army's separate command structure—however useful to Mao during the high tide of the Cultural Revolution—could become threatening later. In 1971 it would be necessary to shunt aside Lin Piao, Huang Yung-sheng, and other important military figures in order to place the PLA "under the direct command of Chairman Mao." [51]

The Chinese Communist Party, too, was redefined during the aftermath of the Cultural Revolution. In spite of the attacks on its membership (70 percent of those belonging to the Central Committee were either dismissed or subjected to mass criticism during this time), the party was not entirely discredited owing to the two ways in which Mao Tse-tung defined the conflict. First, Maoists were careful to limit their attacks on the party to the "headquarters" within it which housed the "handful" of "agents of the bourgeoisie." * Second, ideal party members were distinguished from the bloodsucking "class" of "bourgeois" bureaucrats who lacked revolutionary spirit and stood in "sharp opposition to the working class and poor and lower-middle peasants." [52] "Proletarian" leadership was equated with any single cadre's willingness to face the masses and accept their criticism.† Naturally this definition of class consciousness stripped the party of ideological defenses, but it also provided a way for individual members to redeem themselves. Rectification was, after all, a moral affair. "We must believe," Mao declared in 1968, "that more than 90 percent of our cadres are good or comparatively good. The majority of those who have made mistakes can be reformed." [53] Furthermore, there existed in the May Seventh Cadre

---

* There had been throughout the entire historical period of socialism—declared a *Hung-ch'i* editorial in the summer of 1967—a continual struggle between the proletariat and the bourgeoisie. Of course, since the accession of the dictatorship of the proletariat and the socialist transformation of the means of production, it had become impossible for capitalists to restore the old order alone. They needed help from the agents of the bourgeoisie in party and state organs: that "handful of top party persons in authority taking the capitalist road." This handful constituted the "hidden headquarters of the bourgeoisie," so that within the party itself there was taking place a struggle between the bourgeois and proletarian "headquarters." Victory could not be won by the latter alone. Consequently, Chairman Mao had decided that the agents of the bourgeoisie would not be defeated by being dismissed from office or by being punished with strict organizational methods. Rather, he had followed a revolutionary line "by boldly mobilizing the masses" who were "armed with Mao Tse-tung's thought." *Hung-ch'i* editorial No. 13, "Completely Smash the Bourgeois Headquarters," *Peking Review*, 33:6–9.

† The Resolutions of the Eleventh Plenum divided leadership into four categories of descending order. First were those party leaders who dared "to stand in the van of the movement" and "arouse the masses boldly" by advocating big-character posters and public debates. Second were the cadres who "lagged" behind the masses, "putting fear above everything else" and falling back on party routine. The third category consisted of leaders farther along the scale of fear (and therefore of distance from the masses) but still capable of being pardoned if they would accept mass criticism. Finally there were those who had actually taken the capitalist road and were "extremely afraid of being exposed by the masses." Jerome Ch'en, *Mao Papers* (London: Oxford University Press, 1970), pp. 119–120.

Schools—which were modeled on self-supporting communes—an institutional device for the rehabilitation of tens of thousands of officials through manual labor.* At the same time, the party itself could be reconsolidated and its membership reformed thanks to the revolutionary committees which had replaced it during the Cultural Revolution.

As revolutionary committees slowly formed throughout China (by March of 1971, three hundred-odd county-level and fourteen provincial-level committees had been announced), former party cadres elected to them were asked to form a "party consolidation leading group." These groups solicited the opinions of other committee men and women about prospective members for what was to be a reformed party. Ideally the party would be rebuilt from the bottom up with mass participation. "Rebuilding is necessary. Every branch needs reorganization by the masses. It must be done through the masses. Not only a few party members but also the masses outside the party should attend meetings and discussions. If there are individuals who really cannot do as required, they should be persuaded to quit." [54]

In practice, however, party remnants (*petits bourgeois* on the right) sometimes claimed consolidation to be their own business, and had to be reminded that their reconstruction was taking place "in the midst of the masses . . . with their participation and not merely a few party members." [55] Conversely, "anarchists" or "bourgeois factionalists on the left" were just as often—in the words of one newspaper editorial— "infatuated with sectarianism and mountain-stronghold mentality, . . . infected with anarchism and ultrademocracy," by believing in "no centers at all" of authority. They had to be reminded in turn that the party was still regarded as "the highest form of organization" of the working class, and that its Central Committee under Chairman Mao was "the whole center of leadership for the whole party, the whole army, and the people throughout the country." [56] The latter theme became even more pronounced as time went on, so that by the spring of 1971 the party's

---

* By the summer of 1971, 90,000 cadres had attended these schools, both reducing the number of bureaucrats in office as well as providing an opportunity for *lao-tung kai-tsao* (reform through labor). This was clearly a continuation of the *hsia-fang* (sent down) movement, which was first elaborated by Teng Hsiao-p'ing in 1956 as a method of despatching personnel to lower levels in order to prevent bureaucratization. Praised by Mao in "On the Correct Handling of Contradictions" (February 1957), *hsia-fang* was widely applied throughout that year. By the winter of 1957, 810,000 cadres had been "sent down" for labor reform. On the eve of the Cultural Revolution, *hsia-fang* was developed still further as "rustification": *shang-shan hsia-hsiang* (to go up to the mountains and down to the countryside). T. A. Hsia, *A Terminological Study of the "Hsia-fang" Movement* (Berkeley: Center for Chinese Studies, 1963), pp. 20–24.

primacy within the revolutionary committees was not to be questioned at all.

First: the party committee must strengthen its leadership over the revolutionary committee. The party committee must make the decisions on major questions. It should not let things run their own course nor should it monopolize all activities.

Second: the revolutionary committee must establish a clear idea of accepting the leadership of the party committee and consciously accept the party committee's leadership in exercising power and carrying out its work.[57]

But by its new definition, the party was functionally no more than an instrument of Chairman Mao's leadership.

Resolutely maintaining and strengthening the leadership of the party is the fundamental guarantee that the work of party consolidation and party-building will advance triumphantly along Chairman Mao's party-building line. . . . The leadership of the party is the leadership of Chairman Mao, the leadership of Mao Tse-tung thought and the leadership of Chairman Mao's proletarian revolutionary line. . . . Party power is the core of political power; it is "the power of all powers," as the masses put it. Party power must be firmly in the hands of Marxist–Leninists loyal to Chairman Mao before the gains in party consolidation and party-building can be consolidated, the implementation of Chairman Mao's proletarian revolutionary line guaranteed and the dictatorship of the proletariat strengthened.[58]

In this post-Cultural Revolution formula, Mao ruled as his own *troika:* the person of Chairman Mao, the *persona* of Mao Tse-tung's thought, and the personification of his populist line—all of which together embodied the dictatorship of the proletariat.

After 1959 Mao's person had been ignored in favor of the *persona,* but those who glorified his thought in order to abstract the chairman out of power fell when his actual person recovered its prominence. Their successors—Ch'en Po-ta and Lin Piao—ruled until 1969, when their increasingly exclusive identification with Mao's person conflicted with the mass line which he personified. The signal of Lin Piao's demise in September of 1971, was the assertion by *Hung-ch'i* that there was no such thing as a naturally superior man destined to lead the masses—a rebuke conveyed by quoting Chairman Mao! "The people and the people alone are the motive force in the making of world history. . . . When we say that Marxism is correct, it is certainly not because Marx was a prophet but because his theory had been proved correct in our practice and in our struggle." [59] In the final analysis, nobody—military leader, Maoist acolyte, or party secretary—could stand against the historical union of Mao and the people. After the Cultural Revolution, the Communist Party would once again be strengthened as "the core of leadership of the whole Chinese people." But this was only because it ruled "in accordance with Chairman Mao's thinking"; this was only because it had become conscious of its role as a vanguard by means of struggle, of Mao's thought, and of its "faith in the masses." [60]

How different this was from Lenin's Bolsheviks, at once producer and product of the revolutionary mass movement.[61] Opposed to Kautsky (for whom organization was the precondition of revolutionary action), and to Rosa Luxemburg (who reversed that order), Lenin conceived of the party as a vanguard transforming the unconscious spontaneity of the masses into a fully conscious theory of revolution. For Lenin, the party had to exist apart from the masses, because without that separation there could be no dialectical movement to and fro. Mao, on the other hand, came to believe that the vanguard simply issued from the people by means of struggle—a struggle shaped by his leadership rather than by autonomous class consciousness. "The conscious class ideology of the proletariat does not come spontaneously or mature automatically from plain class feeling. It can only be the result of study or the re-molding of our world outlook with Marxism–Leninism–Mao Tse-tung thought." [62]

Equating that last hyphenated phrase (Mao's *persona*) with Gramsci's Modern Prince, we see that Mao "takes the place, in the conscience, of the divinity or of the categorical imperative, and becomes the basis of a modern laicism, of a complete laicization of the whole of life and of all customary relations." [63] But where was teleology without a divinity or categorical imperative in the first place? Indeed, the Cultural Revolution (in contrast to the Great Leap Forward, which promised a thousand years of utopian happiness after three years of sacrifice) stressed postponement: struggle goes on forever.[64] From personal revolutionary experience, from reading Kautsky, from Yang Ch'ang-chi's lectures on will and efficacy, Mao Tse-tung learned to think of socialism as becoming rather than as being. But did not such a momentist theory of practice leave the future in doubt? Gramsci once remarked that any serious movement supposed "that every act is a stage in a complex process which has already begun and which will end." [65] It was precisely that sense of continuity, even without end, which distinguished Mao's theory of revolution from those of most other Marxists. He could be orthodox enough about the disappearance of parties and the state: "When a man reaches old age, he will die; the same is true of a party. When classes disappear, all instruments of class struggle—parties and the state machinery—will lose their function, cease to be necessary, therefore gradually wither away and end their historical mission; and human society will move to a higher stage." [66] But those words were written in 1949. By 1956 ongoing history had superseded the end of class conflict.

Parties are things brought forth in history. Nothing in the world is not brought forth in history. This is the first point. The second point is that anything which has been brought forth in history must also disappear in history. The Communist Party has been brought forth in history, and because of this, it is bound to disappear one day. [67]

And, because "modern history is continually divided into two," because "it is a history of continuous struggle," [68] the Cultural Revolution was only one among many. "There may be another revolution several years from now," Mao told the Central Committee in 1969, [69] so that the new party constitution of the Ninth National Congress (April 1, 1969) formalized the idea that "continued revolution" would characterize the historical period of socialist society. [70] Always, change was the only permanence, the only certain constant. In fact, this motion was so ever-present, this change so ongoing, that revolutionary man must hasten to keep pace with it. Mao's interest in the changing aspects of contradiction and the lesson he drew from his own history alerted him to the constant succession of historical stages. Thinking of Hu Shih or Ch'en Tu-hsiu, men who began well but ended as counterrevolutionaries, he remarked: "We must draw our lesson from history. We cannot become easygoing." [71] It was as though revolution was its own master, pulling men forward, demanding constant readjustment from them. Time moves so swiftly; the present makes new demands. Speaking of comrades who had been cloistered or imprisoned during the height of the Cultural Revolution, Mao warned those who were about to rehabilitate them that, "It is necessary to teach them history, the history of two years of the Great Cultural Revolution so that they may be gradually awakened to the present." [72]

Certainly, Mao believed that man made his own history, that he projected his image on events, making himself through them.

I advocate the theory of uninterrupted revolution. You must not think that this is Trotsky's theory of uninterrupted revolution. In making revolution, it should be like striking the iron when it is hot, one revolution to be followed by another, and the revolution must advance without interruption. As the Hunanese would say: "Straw sandals have no shape, but they look more and more like sandals as one knits on." [73]

But he was always conscious of history's own necessity. During the great debates in 1959 over the achievements of the Great Leap, for example, he called for synchronism with history, for consonance and accord with its moments of change. Yet that still issued from his own faith that history was revolution and therefore will. Without this optimism how could one be a revolutionary?

Sun Yat-sen said: "Where it is in keeping with the reasons of heaven, commensurate with the sentiments of man, adapted to the tide of the world, and geared to the needs of human emotions, and where it is done resolutely by men of foresight and vision, it will surely succeed." This appraisal is a correct one. . . . The ideology of pessimism is one that corrodes the party and the people, and it runs counter to the will of the proletariat and the poor people. It is also contrary to Marxism–Leninism.[74]

Mao Tse-tung explained his theory of necessity in a more formal way when he reported to the Central Committee in 1966.

Freedom is the knowing of necessity and the transformation of the objective world. Only on the basis of knowing necessity can there be free activities for people. This is the dialectical law of freedom and necessity. What is called necessity is the law of objective existence. . . . The question of knowing the objective world: the leap of one's objective knowledge from the realm of necessity to the realm of freedom follows a process. I saw [that] our Communist Party of China had a very difficult time during the period of democratic revolution, but it successfully learned the law of the Chinese Revolution. The object of this historical condition is to lead comrades to comprehend such a thing: the knowledge of socialist construction necessarily follows a process and necessarily proceeds from practice, from knowing this unknown realm of necessity—socialism—to the gradual overcoming of thoughtlessness, from knowing the objective law and hence acquiring freedom and registering a leap in understanding to the realm of freedom.[75]

Here, we might say, was the Hegelian notion of freedom in necessity. But was Mao truly echoing Hegel's logical notion of reciprocity between substance and effect, of freedom being in and of the same cause? For Hegel, man was genuinely free when he acknowledged his dependence upon absolute idea.

The criminal, when punished, may look upon his punishment as a restriction of his freedom. Really the punishment is not foreign constraint to which he is subjected, but the manifestation of his own act: and if he recognizes this, he ranks in that way as a free man. In short, man is most independent when he knows himself to be determined by the absolute idea throughout. It was the consciousness of this, and this attitude of mind, which Spinoza called the *Amor intellectualis Dei.*[76]

But Mao ignored idea and placed the cause of change within things, somewhat like Wang Fu-chih. External agents, whether ideas or things, were abolished. Interaction *between* things was *within* things—a form of struggle which was neither Hobbesian conflict nor utilitarian enmeshment. Unlike the Western social scientists who observed him, Mao did not regard organized strife as the drive of institutions to maintain themselves. Institutions existed within the larger entity—which was no absolute idea, but rather the political society encompassed by his vision of the people. Even though the party at times appeared to be outside this circle, in his world view its contradiction with the people kept the two within the unity of opposition—a perfectly valid concept for a revolutionary who had not arisen from a corporate political tradition.

For this reason Mao Tse-tung and Hegel enjoyed quite different political visions. Under its *Geist,* Hegel's state summed up the individual attachments of its subjects. Like a magnet attracting filings, the state drew them together into a new disposition. But Hegel's image of the state—which was so congenial to a Frederick William the Third or a Freiherr von Stein—would have puzzled a Ch'ing monarch and his ministers. Assuming the qualified charge of heaven, Chinese rulers neither monopolized divine right nor dared to make the state (was there such a word in Chinese?) independent of the entire *kuo.* The smallest disturbance in the empire—"all-under-heaven"—could theoretically affect government. Embodied but not incorporated, the Chinese state was not separate enough to be a magnet. The emperor's task was virtuous projection, not political attraction: an obligation to extend the fields of moral force in order to change others *in loco.* He ruled best who connected his sagely self with the transformations of heaven, earth, and man. The *Doctrine of the Mean* reads:

Only the person of the greatest sincerity under heaven can separate and plait the great warp of [all] under heaven. [Only he] can establish the great root [of human virtues] of [all] under heaven and know the transforming and nurturing [operations] of heaven and earth. Does this person possess any being beyond which he himself depends? Utterly genuine his human-kindness, profound his depths, vast his heaven-ness! [77]

Would it illuminate the contrast between Hegel and Mao Tse-tung to suggest that Mao replaced the old order's heavenly principles with Marxism's internal laws by which he too could separate and plait history?* At least it would remind us of Mao's dialectic in "On Practice" between perceiver and perceived, and point out that his perceiver's ability to know history tacitly demanded a kind of virtue, a kind of revolutionary sincerity, that morally judged the dialectic. Karl Marx (although guilty of it himself at times) would have scorned such piety. "Communists," Marx said, "do not preach morality. They make no moral demands upon people such as 'Love one another' or 'Do not be egoistic.' " [70] But the *Quotations of Chairman Mao* was filled with such demands. As a moral philosopher, therefore, Mao Tse-tung was more deeply touched by certain strains of Chinese thought than of European; although, of course, it was the combination of both that really formed his world view.

Let us, for instance, sketchily conceive of the history of European philosophy as the problem of knowing the absolute. Kant accepted its inaccessibility and synthesized a system of values whereby reason willed its own ends. Fichte apotheosized that reason into spirit. Hegel erased the antinomy with absolute idea and the dialectic. Marxism overcame the abstraction altogether—the absolute which continued to haunt it—by praxis. In Chinese thought an equally central theme would not have been so exclusively ontological. Its history would not be primarily concerned with the gap between essence and existence, but instead with the divorce of moral principle from material change. The Ch'eng-Chu school bequeathed a dualism between spirit and matter. However, the separation was not explicit enough to drive men into ascetic self-strife either for or against spiritual laws. Rather, they were urged to accord themselves "with ease." Wang Yang-ming's solution was personally satisfying if metaphysically uneasy; and Wang Fu-chih—one among many post-idealist Confucianists—reacted with a tentative materialism, seeing the motor within energy, while positing moral force devoid of rational intent. K'ang Yu-wei or T'an Ssu-t'ung identified that force with the normative value of *jen,* but injected it into history without the mecha-

* If Mao Tse-tung were to be told that in his own way he fits the *Chung-yung's* definition of a great ruler, he would probably scoff, just as the reader might do well to jeer at someone who suggests that Mao is Confucius in a Sun Yat-sen jacket. But I do not at all mean to say that here we have an emperor in disguise. Instead, what I hope to have shown at times in this study is the cultural complexity of the modes and motives of Mao's thought. Sometimes, as here, I can only suggest that his vision of himself was framed by barely realized traditional assumptions.

nism to effect change. Hegelianism and Marxism–Leninism provided the final element of necessity. However, the ultimate meld retained Neo-Confucianism's monistic identification of purposive change from within with moral good. Change *as such* was good. And that, I would venture, brings us back to Mao Tse-tung.

Although change is good, it may not be kind. Against Hegel's abstract notion of freedom in necessity, let me pose Chuang-tzu, Mao's favorite Taoist sage:

Once we have gotten our physiques we await extinction without running away. As the physique makes contacts with all creation it moves like a rushing steed, and nobody can halt it. Isn't it sad? Always hard at work on this or that, it never sees what is accomplished. Weak and sickly, it does not understand toward what it is moving. Can we fail to lament it? What advantage is there in saying that it is better than death? [79]

Mao Tse-tung ruminated elliptically on that same necessary mortality to Ch'en Po-ta and K'ang Sheng in 1965.

What has indivisible ties in this world? Some ties must inevitably be severed. Those not negated are to be negated. Affirmation and negation . . . affirmation . . . each link in the development of things is affirmed and then negated. A slave society will negate the primitive society, but affirm the feudal society. . . . How to synthesize? . . . Briefly, one eats the other, and one overthrows the other. One class is eradicated and another emerges; one society is eradicated and another arises. . . . If someone else does not do the eliminating, you do it yourself. Why must man die? This is a natural law. The life of trees is longer. Some even live several thousand years. How can we manage without death? . . . I approve of Chuang-tzu's method. After his wife dies, he beats on a pan and sings. When someone dies, we must hold a rally to celebrate the victory of dialectics. Dialectical life is a continual procession toward its opposite. Ultimately mankind will also arrive at an end. Theologians say that the final day is a sad one, but we say that the death of mankind is the transition to something even more advanced. Marx starts from a necessary kingdom to a free kingdom. Freedom is understanding the inevitable. This is not all. We have only talked about half of it. I will not mention it any further. Understanding by itself is freedom, freedom being the understanding and transformation of the inevitable. . . . Chuang-tzu also said that one day's sayings cannot be "exhausted" in five thousand generations. This is the truth.[80]

Mortal man completes this eternal process by understanding it. Marx challenged the divine by having man make himself. Mao had no such creator to contest. Ultimately more humanistic, he placed man squarely in the center of being, fulfilling himself by completing nature. And, because man's own struggle was the principle of the universe, anything was possible, nothing could not be done.

This brings us back one last time to the great enigma of "On Contradiction": Mao's belief that there *is* purposive change, yet his apparent inability to explain it without recourse to external principle. The problem was a classical one for Marxists, of course; but Mao solved it without having to make a Jansenist wager. History, the cosmic universal, moves its own way. Men die, nations disappear, civilizations perish; for that is history's right. Within universal history, though, there are smaller histories, stages of progress. Any who know how to analyze the moment can accord with it, move at the right time, emerge supreme. Mao's own writings were thus filled with the buoyant imagery of stages. The revolution will be won for the moment because the time is ripe, because history *now* is on our side. But when Mao reflected on cosmic history, he realized that man is pitted against time and change. There is consolation if one will accept change as such, because then— unafraid to give up permanence—man will realize that even momentary setbacks (the negations of current positives) will be set back in turn.

We must also recognize the possibility of the restoration of reactionary classes. . . . [but] even to head in the opposite direction may not be too important, because a negation of negation may come about, thereby leading in the opposite direction again later on. If the generation of our sons should espouse revisionism and head in the opposite direction which, although called socialism, would actually be capitalism, then our grandsons will definitely stage an uprising to overthrow their parents because of mass disaffection.[81]

Yet the acceptance of change, of history, is no passive act. Like a mountain to be moved, this greater history is a resistance with meaning, existing to define man's purpose. The purpose is not absurd; man is not Sisyphus forever rolling that stone up the hill, because he does not stand alone. He marches with others. Unlike Chuang-tzu's poor soul, Mao could see himself in others. When he won the civil war he said, "Our past work is only the first step in a long march of ten thousand *li*."[82] And although many may fall by the wayside, they—like Mao himself—will know what the will of the people has already accomplished; they will know what remains to be done.

Revisiting his old guerrilla lair at Chingkangshan in 1965, Mao wrote:

> Wind and thunder rumbled;
> Banners unfurled;
> The realm was made stable.
> Thirty-eight years have elapsed
> Like a snap of the fingers.
> Reach the ninth heaven high to embrace the moon
> Or the five oceans deep to capture a turtle: either is possible.
> Return to merriment and triumphant songs.
> Under this heaven nothing is difficult,
> If only there is the will to ascend.[83]

To stay even with history, to will *against* it, is to accept it while understanding the need to face it. By finding an opposite force to confront, Mao knew himself as victorious revolutionary against overwhelming odds and as sage chairman conscious of historical development. Fichte may have been right: the self has to know its own opposite, whether it be death for life or the consciousness of history's erosion of individual man's temporal remains. The confidence of current history's laws enables accordance; but the urge to define the self creates a necessity for, adds a fundamental purpose to, what must be a contest with cosmic flux. Mao put it very well in discussing "identity" (*t'ung-i hsing*) in "On Contradiction":

The fact is that no contradictory aspect can exist in isolation. Without its opposite aspect, each loses the condition for its existence. . . . Without facility, there would be no difficulty; without difficulty, there would be no facility. . . . Without the bourgeoisie there would be no proletariat; without the proletariat, there would be no bourgeoisie.[84]

Without will there would be no history. And without history, no will at all.[85]

Appendix:
Ku Yen-wu on Pure
Discussion (Ch'ing-i)

Ku Yen-wu explained the meaning of "pure discussion"—sometimes translated as "public opinion"—with a characteristically etymological analysis.*

The wise kings of antiquity set official regulations for the feudal princes, and extended punishments as warnings to those of [noble] rank in order to rectify the hundred princes [of the feudal order]. They also established rural scholars and local schools for this [same purpose]. They preserved "pure discussion" in the *chou* (districts) and *li* (counties) in order to assist the implementation of punishments. In the Former and Latter Han periods (206 B.C.–A.D. 220), when this system was observed, the *hsiang* (village) recommended [local notables] and the *li* (counties) selected [from among them for actual appointment to office].† First, the [candidate's behavior]

* Ku Yen-wu, *Jih-chih lu* [Record of Daily Learning] (Taipei: Kuo-hsueh chipen ts'ung-shu, n.d.), 3 *shang:* 47.

† This refers to the *hsiao-lien* (filial and incorruptible) system of the Han period, when locales were allowed to recommend their worthies for office. Hsu Chou-yun ("The Changing Relationship between Local Society and the Central Political Power in Former Han: 206 B.C.–A.D. 8," *Comparative Studies in Society and History,* 7.4:354–370) has shown that the *hsiao-lien* system made it possible for the local magnates of eastern China (especially in Shantung) to recover from the harshness of Han Wu-ti's rule (140–85 B.C.)—when military governors tried to crush this local elite—by reforging ties with the central government and especially by forming bureaucratic contacts with the scholarly cliques of the National Academy.

through life had to be examined. If a single blemish was [revealed by] "pure discussion," then he was not eligible for the rest of his life. Consequently, superior men harbored a dread of punishment, and mean men retained the custom of being ashamed of a [bad] character. By demarcating the society through instructions to inferiors, those [ruling] above did not [have to] be severe [in applying punishments]. By settling [conflicts] through discussion in the villages, the people did not have to rebel. . . . Then, when Sung Wu-ti* usurped the throne, he proclaimed that the rebellious *hsiang* (villages) were [actually] engaging in "pure discussion." . . . Thereafter all [rebels and usurpers] encountered extraordinary clemency. . . . The "Small Refinement" was abolished and the Central Kingdom thereby lessened. Customs became decadent and rebellious strife was realized. As a result, the vileness of village chatter was so annoying that an imperial mandate was required to dissipate it. But is this not otherwise the undeviating Way of the three [sage] dynasties [of antiquity]? [The Tao] could still reside in this populace even though we fear the people's loquaciousness. For, it is as though a day appeared when customs changed. "I hear that below there is an unmarried man who therefore should be employed, for he has controlled the Three Evils. Because of no talent, [there was] an assignment and a conferral." Even though the two [sage] Emperors [Yao and Shun] selected good officials and eliminated bad ones [by their own sense of virtue], they still never failed to make inquiries among the rustics, thereby using elevated criticism to aid officials in the Ministry of Punishments. This is entering into the village [to seek] criticism in order to sustain the realm. If once again the gathering of intelligence is made cardinal, the monarch's rule cannot be depreciated.

Ku's historical researches thus showed that what was by the Ming and Ch'ing a synonym for the "right" of dissent had originally been no right at all. *Ch'ing-i* was rather an imperial institution which was designed to select bureaucrats so as to unite the throne and local villages, bypassing the feudal aristocracy which originally stood between them.

In fact, the mistaken identification of *ch'ing-i* as the "right" of local notables to judge rulers was a consequence of the usurpation of an imperial pretender, Sung Wu-ti, who tried to turn it into an instrument of demagogic rule. The Mandate, Ku clearly implied, is given by heaven. To reverse the conferral of sovereignty and seek legitimacy in populist dissent was a distortion of *ch'ing-i*. Indeed, Sung Wu-ti's act historically terminated the virtuous claims of those engaging in pure discussion.

* Sung Wu-ti was the imperial name of Liu Yü, who served as a *t'ai-shou* under the Eastern Chin emperor, An-ti (397–418). Liu Yü usurped the throne and justified his act by declaring that the previous ruler's ministers had been evil and corrupt, as witnessed by the *ch'ing-i* or pure discussion of scholars who dared oppose them. Liu reigned from 420–422, and his dynasty, the Liu Sung, continued for another fifty-seven years before expiring.

But if pure discussion was at one time enlightened enough to help the emperor govern, then the people must have inherently possessed some degree of virtue *(te)* in the first place. How could Ku alienate it from them?

The first clue to this puzzle was Ku's use of the phrase, Small Refinement *(Hsiao ya)*. Large Refinement *(Ta ya)* is the titled portion of the *Book of Odes* containing court⁄songs. The Small Refinement is the folk song section, and here suggests Arcady, when the very simplicity of village life expressed its virtue, especially because *ya,* refinement, was also glossed as rectitude or to be correct *(cheng)*. However, as Chou Nan's *Kuan chü hsü* (Preface to the Opening Words of the Odes) explains: "To be *ya* is to be correct, and refers to the instrument of extinction or promotion of a monarch's rule. Governance has both large and small [forms of rectitude]. Therefore, there is both a large *ya* and a small *ya*." * Village *ya* was only "small," perhaps even in its pristine state before customs changed already depending on the higher virtue of the ruler. But because village virtue was at least instrumental to the emperor's rule, might it not still be the final *locus* of sovereignty?

Ku Yen-wu answers that in the section beginning, "I have heard that below. . . ." This is a quotation from the last part of the Canon of Yao in the *Shang shu* (Book of Documents), where the sage-Emperor Yao plans to resign the throne. Looking for a virtuous successor, he tells his court:

"Point out some one among the illustrious, or set forth from among the poor and mean." All [in the court] said to the emperor, "There is an unmarried man among the lower people, called Shun of Yü." The emperor said, "Yes, I have heard of him. What is his character?" His Eminence [the Minister] said, "He is the son of a blind man. His father was obstinately unprincipled, his [step-] mother was insincere, his [half brother] Hsiang was arrogant. He has been able, however, by his filial piety to live in harmony with them, and to lead them gradually to self-government, so that they no longer proceed to great wickedness." The Emperor said, "I will try him." †

Hence, the Three Evils mentioned in Ku's original text were an explicit reference to the paradigmatic Shun, chosen to rule China for his sage-like ability to lead his unprincipled relatives to self-government. For,

---

* This gloss is given in Morohashi Tetsuji, *Dai Kan-wa jiten* [The Great Chinese-Japanese Dictionary] (Tokyo: Taishūkan shoten, 1957–1960), entry 41973.

† *Shang shu* (Book of Documents), 1.3:12. I have relied on James Legge's translation: *The Chinese Classics,* 3.1:26.

the people are not otherwise naturally good. An exceptional and quasi-divine figure like Shun was needed to "set forth the beauty of the five cardinal duties" of Confucian social relationships to the common people.*

Ku Yen-wu's perception of the source of *te* (the virtue of sovereignty) was etched even more sharply in the subsequent phrase of that discussion: "Because of no talent, [there was] an assignment and a conferral" (*pu ts'ai so i t'ou pi*). The three key words here are talent (*ts'ai*), conferral (*pi*), and assignment (*t'ou*). *Ts'ai* actually meant more than talent or to be talented. In the *Mencius,* for instance, it was almost an animus: an essential capacity conferred by heaven on men as part of their original natures (*pen hsing*). The meaning of conferral (*pi*) can be derived from its *locus classicus* which is also, naturally, the *Shang shu* (the opening of the Books of Chou):

In the thirtieth year, the king went to inquire of the Viscount of Ch'i, and said to him, "Oh! Viscount of Ch'i, Heaven, unseen has given their constitution to mankind, aiding [also] the harmonious development of it in their various conditions. I do not know how their proper virtues in their various relations should be brought forth in due order." . . . The Viscount of Ch'i thereupon replied, "I have heard that of old time Kuan dammed up the inundated waters, and thereby threw into disorder the arrangement of the five elements. God was thereby aroused to anger, and did not confer (*pi*) upon him the great Plan with its nine Divisions, whereby the proper virtues of the various relations were left to go to ruin. Kuan was then kept a prisoner till his death, and Yü rose up to continue his undertaking." †

Pi was therefore the conferral by heaven of a plan for rule which enabled the monarch to fulfill its mandate. Because there were no natural relations derived from society as such, it was only heaven who could confer that proper ordering by using the ruler as its instrument. As orthodox commentaries of this passage have remarked, heaven first established the *ch'ang tao* (unvarying way), which was transmitted down to the people (*hsia min*).

What of *t'ou* (assignment)? The *locus classicus* is once again part of the *Shang shu* in the famous Great Announcement by the Duke of Chou that he must fulfill the charge of heaven to overthrow the Shang dynasty (traditionally 1766–1123 B.C.). When his ministers warned him of the military hardships his own subjects would suffer, the Duke responded:

* *Shang shu,* 1.2:2. Legge, 3.1:31.
† *Shang shu,* 4.1:1–2. Legge, 3.1:320, 323.

"I, in my youth, think also continually of the hardships, and say, Alas! these senseless movements will deplorably afflict widowers and widows! But I am the servant of Heaven, which has assigned (*t'ou*) me this great task, and laid this hard duty on my person." * *T'ou* thus meant heaven's assignment of a charge to rule the empire. This divine obligation was more compelling than a lord's responsibility to his subjects and therefore denied them any ultimate sense of sovereignty. Finally, Ku Yen-wu's laconic phrase ("because of no talent there was an assignment and a conferral") described both the people's loss of primal virtue (Small Refinement) as "customs changed," as well as the alternation of dynasties when one ruler (all the more central to heaven's scheme now that popular virtue had waned) lost his "talent" and saw heaven confer his charge on someone else. The legitimacy of any single emperor's rule might be judged, arbitrated, even challenged. Its ultimate legitimization could not.

* *Shang shu,* 5.7:8. Legge, 3.1:368–369.

Abbreviations Used in Footnotes

CB	American Consulate General, Hong Kong, *Current Background*.
CGS	*Che Guevara Speaks: Selected Speeches and Writings* (New York: Merit Publishers, 1967).
CLG	*Chinese Law and Government*.
JCMP	Jerome Ch'en, *Mao Papers: Anthology and Bibliography* (London: Oxford University Press, 1970).
JMJP	*Jen-min jih-pao* [People's Daily].
JPRS	United States Department of Commerce, Joint Publications Research Service, 49826 (February 12, 1970), "Translations on Communist China." Joint Publications Research Service issues other than No. 49826 will be followed by their serial number.
LJMTT	Li Jui, *Mao Tse-tung t'ung-chih ti ch'u-ch'i ko-ming huo-tung* [The Early Revolutionary Activities of Comrade Mao Tse-tung] (Peking: Chung-kuo ch'ing-nien ch'u-pan she, 1957).
MA	"Mao's Autobiography," recounted in Edgar Snow, *Red Star over China* (New York: Grove Press, 1961), pp. 121–188.
MCHST	Mao Tse-tung, *Mao chu-hsi shih-tz'u* [The Poetry of Chairman Mao] (Peking: Jen-min wen-hsueh ch'u-pan she, 1963).

PR	*Peking Review.*
SRMTT	Mao Tse-tung, *Selected Readings from the Works of Mao Tse-tung* (Peking: Foreign Languages Press, 1967).
SSMTT	Stuart R. Schram, *Mao Tse-tung,* rev. ed. (Baltimore: Penguin Books, 1967).
SSPT	Stuart R. Schram, *The Political Thought of Mao Tse-tung* (New York: Praeger, 1969).
SW	Mao Tse-tung, *Selected Works,* 4 vols. (Peking: Foreign Languages Press, 1960–1965).
WHPF	Chien Po-tsan, et al., eds., *Wu-hsu pien-fa* [The Reform of Wu-hsu (1898)] Shanghai: Shen-chou kuo-kuang she, 1955).

Notes

CHAPTER ONE

1. Noriyuki Tokuda, "Mao Tse-tung's Ideological Cohesion with the Party and the Revolutionary Movement, 1935–1945" (Paper delivered at the Conference on Ideology and Politics in Contemporary China, Santa Fe, N.M., August 1971).

2. Mao Tse-tung, "Report to the Second Plenary Session of the Seventh Central Committee for the Communist Party of China" (March 5, 1949), in SW, 4:374.

3. Mao Tse-tung, "On the Correct Handling of Contradictions Among the People," reprinted by *China Pictorial* (Peking, 1967), p. 29. Mao's animus against bureaucracy continued to develop over the course of the republic's evolution. By 1967, he had come up with twenty characteristics of bureaucracy: divorce from reality and the masses, conceit and complacency, routinism, egoistic overlordism, dishonesty, irresponsibility, negligence, deceit, stupidity and confusion ("They are rotten sensualists; they glut themselves for days on end; they are not diligent at all, they are inconstant and they are ignorant. This is the stupid, useless bureaucracy"), laziness, Parkinsonian proliferation ("Government offices grow bigger and bigger"), red-tape formalism, particularism ("One person becomes an official and his entire family benefits; one person reaches nirvana and all his close associates rise up to heaven"), love of luxury, selfishness, squabbling, disunion, sectarianism, factionalism, degeneracy, and "erroneous tendencies and reaction." See Mao Tse-tung, "Chairman Mao Discusses Twenty Manifestations of Bureaucracy" (early 1967), translated in JPRS, 90:40–43.

4. Mao Tse-tung is cited by Lin Piao in "Report to the Ninth National Congress of the Communist Party of China," PR, 18:16–35.

5. Cited in Richard H. Solomon, "One Party and 'One Hundred Schools': Leadership, Lethargy, or *Luan*?" *Current Scene*, 7.19–20:6; also see SSMTT, p. 286.

6. Mao Tse-tung, "On the Correct Handling of Contradictions Among the People," pp. 21–22.

7. Lin Piao, "Report to the Ninth National Congress."

8. Mao Tse-tung, "Get Rid of the Baggage and Start Up the Machinery" (April 12, 1944), in SRMTT, p. 250; also see T. A. Hsia, *A Terminological Study of the "Hsia-fang" Movement* (Berkeley: Center for Chinese Studies, 1963), p. 14.

Kuo Mo-jo's study is entitled *Chia-shen san-pai nien chi* [The Three-hundredth Anniversary of *Chia-shen* (1644)] (Peking: Jen-min ch'u-pan she, 1954).

9. LJMTT, pp. 3–4.

10. Mao Tse-tung, "Speech at the Lushan Conference" (July 23, 1959), in CLG, 1.4:28.

11. LJMTT, pp. 4–5.

12. Lo Kuan-chung, *Romance of the Three Kingdoms,* trans. C. H. Brewitt-Taylor (Shanghai: Kelly and Walsh, 1929), p. 1.

13. *How the Soviet Revisionists Carry Out All-round Restoration of Capitalism in the USSR* (Peking: Foreign Languages Press, 1968), pp. 46–50.

14. Mao Tse-tung, "Bombard the Bourgeois Headquarters" (August 5, 1966), in PR, 33:9.

15. Mao Tse-tung, "Talk at Enlarged Work Conference" (January 30, 1962), in JCMP, p. 39; also see JPRS, 50792:58; and CB, 891:67.

16. Mao Tse-tung, "Speech at the Tenth Plenary Session of the Eighth Central Committee" (September 1962), cited in Lin Piao, "Report to the Ninth National Congress."

17. Lin Piao, "Report to the Ninth National Congress."

18. This phrase is from the "Twenty-Three Article Document" prepared under Mao's guidance. The work conference is referred to in Lin Piao, "Report to the Ninth National Congress." The quotation is taken from Mao, "Bombard the Bourgeois Headquarters."

19. Mao, "Bombard the Bourgeois Headquarters."

20. *Ibid.*

21. Mao Tse-tung, "Speech at the Tenth Plenum" (1962), in JCMP, p. 136; also see SSPT, p. 367; PR, 10.23:17; and CLG, 1.4:92.

22. *Ta hsueh* [The Great Learning], in *The Four Books,* trans. James Legge (Taipei: Wen-hua shu-chü, 1960), p. 1.

23. Wang Shou-jen (Yang-ming), *Wang Wen-ch'eng kung ch'üan-chi* [The Complete Works of Wang, Duke Wen-ch'eng] (Shanghai: Commercial Press, 1934), 1.7:96. This is the entire text of the *Nan-kan hsiang-yueh* [The Southern Kiangsi Village Covenant], which is also translated in Wang Yang-ming, *Instructions for Practical Living and Other Neo-Confucian Writings,* trans. Wing-tsit Chan (New York: Columbia University Press, 1963), pp. 298–306.

24. Wang, *Wang Wen-ch'eng kung ch'üan-chi,* 1.7:94.

25. The best succinct discussion in English of the *hsiang-yueh* system is given by Kung-chuan Hsiao in *Rural China: Imperial China in the Nineteenth Century* (Seattle: University of Washington Press, 1967), pp. 184–191. A more elaborate explanation, giving the texts of the various edicts, is provided by James Legge's articles on "Imperial Confucianism" in *The China Review, or Notes and Queries on the Far East,* 6:147–158, 223–235, 299–310, 363–374.

25a. Hsiao, *Rural China,* p. 189.

25b. *Ibid.*

26. James R. Townsend, *Political Participation in Communist China* (Berkeley: University of California Press, 1969), p. 183.

27. *Ibid.,* p. 182.

28. H. C. Chuang, *The Little Red Book and Current Chinese Language* (Berkeley: Center for Chinese Studies, 1968), pp. 7–8.

29. *Ibid.,* p. 44.

30. *Quotations from Chairman Mao Tse-tung,* edited and with an introductory essay by Stuart R. Schram (New York: Bantam Books, 1967), p. 81.

31. *Ibid.,* p. 102.

32. *Ibid.,* p. 105.

33. *Ibid.,* p. 106.

34. *Ibid.*, p. 107.

35. Mao Tse-tung, "Attributes of the Peoples of the World" (January 10, 1966), in JCMP, p. 132.

36. Mao Tse-tung, "Think Hard" (September 1, 1967), in JCMP, p. 145.

37. Mao Tse-tung, "Reform in Learning," in *Mao's China: Party Reform Documents, 1942-1944*, ed. Boyd Compton (Seattle: University of Washington Press, 1952), p. 24.

38. *Quotations from Chairman Mao Tse-tung*, p. 68.

39. *Ibid.*, p. 59.

40. *Ibid.*, p. 2.

41. *Ibid.*, p. 131.

42. *Ibid.*, p. 166.

43. *Ibid.*, p. 155.

44. H. C. Chuang, *The Great Proletarian Cultural Revolution* (Berkeley: Center for Chinese Studies, 1967), pp. 10–11.

45. *Quotations from Chairman Mao Tse-tung*, p. 2. In 1958 Mao said: "If we do not scorn the old systems and the reactionary production relationships, what are we to do? If we have no faith in socialism and communism, in what do we have faith?" Mao Tse-tung, "Speech at the Ch'eng-tu Conference" (March 22, 1958), in JPRS, 90:50–51.

46. Mao Tse-tung, "Violent Struggles" (September 5, 1966), in JCMP, p. 130; also see CB, 885:6.

47. Mao, "On the Correct Handling of Contradictions," pp. 23–24.

48. Stuart Schram's introductory essay in *Quotations from Chairman Mao Tse-tung*, p. xix.

49. In 1939, Mao Tse-tung said: "In the last analysis, all the truths of Marxism can be summed up in one sentence: 'To rebel is justified.' " Mao Tse-tung, "Talk at Meeting of All Circles in Yenan Celebrating the Sixtieth Birthday of Stalin" (December 21, 1939), in CB, 891:10; also see SSPT, pp. 427–428; and PR, 12.39:7.

50. Mao Tse-tung, "Talk at Meeting of All Circles"; also see Chuang, *Great Proletarian Cultural Revolution*, p. 14.

51. Lin Piao, "Report to the Ninth National Congress."

52. This is a line from one of Mao's poems entitled "Reply to Comrade Kuo Mo-jo" (January 9, 1963), in *Ten More Poems of Mao Tse-tung* (Hong Kong: Eastern Horizon Press, 1967), pp. 14–15.

53. Cited and translated in Joan Robinson, *The Cultural Revolution in China* (Baltimore: Penguin Books, 1969), pp. 115–116.

54. Mao Tse-tung, "To the Masses of the Great Proletarian Cultural Revolution" (August 19, 1966), in JCMP, p. 127; also see SSPT, p. 369. According to Schram, this is a statement which was made at the first Red Guard rally on August 18, 1966, and published by JMJP on the following day. CB, 892:43 attributes the same statement to an article in JMJP (November 12, 1966), entitled "Chairman Mao Is Always in the Midst of the Masses."

55. For an exciting discussion of this problem, see Stuart R. Schram, "The Party in Chinese Communist Ideology," *China Quarterly*, 38:1–26.

56. Mao Tse-tung, "The Resolutions of the Eleventh Plenum" (August 1966), in JCMP, pp. 117–118; also see PR, 33:6.

57. Mao Tse-tung, "Conversation with Premier Chou" (1967), in JCMP, p. 49.

58. Mao Tse-tung, "Uninterrupted Revolution" (May 18, 1967), in JCMP, p. 139; also see SSPT, p. 370; and PR, 39:8. The statement is quoted in a JMJP editorial dated May 23, 1967: "Beacon Light for the Great Proletarian Cultural Revolution in Commemoration of the Twenty-fifth Anniversary of the Publication of the 'Talks at the Yenan Forum on Literature and Art.' "

59. Mao Tse-tung, "The Chinese and World Revolutions" (April 15, 1969), in JCMP, p. 159; also see PR, 39:8.

60. Robinson, *Cultural Revolution,* pp. 45–46.

CHAPTER TWO

1. This is Snow's paraphrase of the conversation. His notes were checked by Mao's aides before being released. The interview was published in the *Washington Post,* February 14, 1965.

2. Ku Ah-tao (a female peasant, fifty-three years old, illiterate, who was noted for addressing many meetings in her county in Kiangsu), "Down with Anyone Who Opposes Chairman Mao!" in PR, 33:15–17.

3. For such an example of the emperor's ecumenical claims, see the illustration of Ch'ien-lung's apotheosis as Buddha. Harold L. Kahn, *Monarchy in the Emperor's Eyes* (Cambridge: Harvard University Press, 1971), p. 185.

4. H. C. Chuang, *The Great Proletarian Cultural Revolution* (Berkeley: Center for Chinese Studies, 1967), pp. 30–37. The word for talisman here is *fa-pao,* a word which originally referred to the sutras and later in popular fiction came to mean a magical weapon which could crush entire armies.

5. "Speech at Enlarged Meeting of Central Committee Political Bureau," in JPRS, 90:78. Neither author nor date is given. I would guess the former to be Lin Piao and assume the latter to be during the Cultural Revolution.

6. Hannah Arendt, *The Human Condition* (New York: Doubleday Anchor Books, 1959), pp. 163–164.

7. T. A. Hsia, *A Terminological Study of the "Hsia-fang" Movement* (Berkeley: Center for Chinese Studies, 1963), pp. 25–31, 52. The connotation here is one of deep penetration, of a forceful, aggressive act of plunging directly into society at large, expressed as well by the even stronger image of "striking roots" (*chia-ken,* in which *chia* means to prick or pierce).

8. Mao Tse-tung, "Talk at Enlarged Work Conference" (January 30, 1962), in JCMP, pp. 36–39; also see JPRS, 50792:40–43; and CB, 891:65–67.

9. Mao Tse-tung, "His Wish" (July 29, 1966), in JCMP, p. 115; also see the JMJP editorial of July 29, 1966: "Be a Pupil of the Masses before Becoming Their Teacher."

10. *Ibid.,* p. 38.

11. Mao Tse-tung, "Four Instructions at a Standing Committee Meeting [of the Politburo]" (1967), in JCMP, p. 151.

12. Editorial, JMJP (October 30, 1970), cited and translated in *China Quarterly,* 45:199–200.

13. *Ibid.*

14. "Forum of Leading Cadres in Chang-chun, Kirin Province" (October 26, 1970), radio broadcast, cited and translated in *China Quarterly,* 45:202–203.

15. *Ibid.*

16. *Ibid.*

17. For a discussion of the influence of these models on the revolutionaries of 1911, see Mary Backus Rankin, *Early Chinese Revolutionaries* (Cambridge: Harvard University Press, 1971), p. 39; John Lust, "Les sociétés secrètes, les mouvements populaires et la révolution de 1911," in Jean Chesneaux, ed., *Mouvements populaires et sociétés secrètes en Chine aux XIXe et XXe siècles* (Paris: François Maspero, 1970), pp. 360–392.

18. This evolution is subtly analyzed in J. R. Levenson, *Revolution and Cosmopolitanism* (Berkeley: University of California Press, 1971).

19. T. A. Hsia, *Metaphor, Myth, Ritual, and the People's Commune* (Berkeley: Center for Chinese Studies, 1961), p. 25. During the Yenan period, Mao had

already stressed the importance of singling out labor heroes as models of attitudes, both for other members of the party and for the masses at large. Mao Tse-tung, "Ts'ai-yung hsin ti tsu-chih hsing-shih yü kung-tso fang-shih" [Selecting and Using the New Organizational Forms and Working Methods], *Chieh-fang jih-pao* [Liberation Daily] (September 5, 1944), p. 1.

20. Chuang, *Great Proletarian Cultural Revolution,* p. 28.

21. *A Model for Revolutionary Youth* (Peking: Foreign Languages Press, 1970), p. 32.

22. *Ibid.,* p. 25.

23. *Ibid.,* p. 28.

24. This is an excerpt from the diary of another hero, Li Chuan-chou, *Wu-hsien chung yü Mao chu-hsi te hao tang-yuan—Li Chuan-chou* [Li Chuan-chou— A Good Party Member Infinitely Loyal to Chairman Mao] (Shanghai: n.p., 1970), p. 24.

CHAPTER THREE

1. Nikolai Lenin, "How the State Makes the Transition to Communism," *The State in Revolution,* appendix to Karl Marx, *Critique of the Gotha Programme* (New York: International Publishers, 1938); also see Lenin, "The Dictatorship of the Proletariat in Communism," *Notebook,* in *ibid.,* pp. 55–59.

2. Mao Tse-tung, "Leadership and Democracy" (January 1, 1967), in JCMP, p. 133; also see CB, 885:12, which contains the first part of this quote but not the reference to democracy. The statement also appears in the JMJP editorial of January 1, 1967: "Carry the Great Proletarian Cultural Revolution through to the End."

3. Rosa Luxemburg, *The Russian Revolution* (Ann Arbor: University of Michigan Press, 1970), p. 72.

4. Mao Tse-tung, "Notes on Comrade Ch'en Cheng-jen's Report on His 'Squatting Point' " (January 29, 1965), in JCMP, p. 100; also see JPRS, 23; and CB, 891:49.

5. Mao Tse-tung, "Comment on the Second Group of Materials on the Hu Feng Antiparty Clique" (1955), in JCMP, p. 53; also see CB, 891:20.

6. Mao Tse-tung, "Form of Revolutionary Organization" (October 19, 1967), in JCMP, p. 147; also see JMJP editorial of October 1, 1967.

7. For an enlightening discussion of this difference, see George Lichtheim, *Marxism: An Historical and Critical Study* (New York: Praeger, 1967), pp. 47–50.

8. Karl Marx and Friedrich Engels, *The German Ideology,* pts. I and II (New York: International Publishers, 1947), p. 5.

9. *Ibid.,* p. 13.

10. *Ibid.,* p. 15.

11. *Ibid.,* p. 19.

12. G. W. F. Hegel, *Erstes Systemprogramm des deutschen Idealismus,* translated in Lichtheim, *Marxism,* p. 36.

13. Karl Marx, *Early Writings,* trans. T. B. Bottomore (New York: McGraw-Hill, 1964), p. 26.

14. *Ibid.,* p. 16.

15. Marx, *Gotha,* p. 116.

16. Cheng Kuan-ying, *Sheng-shih wei-yen* [Words of Warning in a Seemingly Prosperous Age] (Taipei: Hsueh-sheng shu-chü, 1965), 2:29, 99. For the emphasis on *kung,* see especially 2:36, 93.

17. John Wilson Lewis, *Leadership in Communist China* (Ithaca: Cornell University Press, 1966), p. 57.

18. Mao Tse-tung, "Closing Speech at the Eleventh Plenum of the Central Committee" (August 12, 1966), in JCMP, pp. 34–35. However, Liu Shao-ch'i was singled out as the leader of a private faction: "the number one faction in power within the party taking the capitalist road" (*tang-nei t'ou-hao tsou tzu-pen chu-i tao-lu te tang-ch'üan p'ai*). What mattered in the context of the accusation was *tzu-pen chu-i* (capitalism).

19. Mao Tse-tung, "Youth" (September 26, 1966), in JCMP, p. 131.

20. Cited and translated in James R. Townsend, *Political Participation in Communist China* (Berkeley: University of California Press, 1969), p. 68.

21. JMJP (October 9, 1958), cited and translated in Townsend, *Political Participation*, pp. 182–183. This refers to the attitude of the peasantry with respect to the communes.

22. Cited and translated in H. C. Chuang, *Evening Chats at Yenshan, or The Case of Teng T'o* (Berkeley: Center for Chinese Studies, 1970), p. 1.

23. Mao Tse-tung, "Opening Address to the Chinese People's Political Consultative Conference, Third Meeting" (October 23, 1951), in JMJP (October 24, 1951), p. 1.

24. Chou En-lai, "On the Question of Intellectuals" (January 14, 1956), in John K. Fairbank and Robert R. Bowie, *Communist China: 1955–1959* (Cambridge: Harvard University Press, 1962), p. 129.

25. Richard H. Solomon, "One Party and 'One Hundred Schools': Leadership, Lethargy, or *Luan*?" *Current Scene*, 7.19–20:10.

26. Cited and translated in *ibid.*, p. 15.

27. This interpretation is based on Solomon, "One Party."

28. Mao Tse-tung, "Comments on 'How a Marxist Should Correctly Deal with Revolutionary Mass Movements'" (August 15, 1959), in CLG, 1.4:71. This edition of the journal contains the so-called "in camera statements of Mao Tse-tung."

29. Mao Tse-tung, "Speech at the Lushan Conference" (July 23, 1959), in CLG, 1.4:36.

30. *Ibid.*, 1.4:28.

31. *Ibid.*, 1.4:35.

32. *Ibid.*

33. Mao Tse-tung, "Speech at the Eighth Plenary Session of the Eighth Central Committee" (August 2, 1959), in CLG, 1.4:61–62.

34. Mao Tse-tung, "Concerning Mei Ch'eng's *'Ch'i-fa'*" (August 2, 1969), in CLG, 1.4:57–58. The illness metaphor had occurred to him before—for example, see "On Ten Major Relationships" (April 1956), in CB, 892:32.

35. Mao Tse-tung, "Letter to Chang Wen-t'ien" (August 2, 1959), in CLG, 1.4:54. Chang had been secretary-general of the party in the 1930s and dropped out of sight after serving as acting minister of foreign affairs from November of 1956 to February of 1957.

36. LJMTT, p. 8.

37. Liang Ch'i-ch'ao, "Hsin-min shuo" [Discussing the New People], *Hsin-min ts'ung-pao* [The New People Magazine], 11:1–14. This was an ongoing editorial, published in each issue.

38. Mao Tse-tung, "In Opposition to Party Formalism" (February 8, 1942), in Boyd Compton, *Mao's China: Party Reform Documents, 1942–1944* (Seattle: University of Washington Press, 1952), p. 37.

39. Mao Tse-tung, "Reform in Learning," in Compton, *Mao's China*, pp. 31–32.

40. Mao Tse-tung, "Talk at Enlarged Work Conference" (1962), in JCMP, p. 39; also see JMJP (August 21, 1967).

41. *Ibid.*, p. 35.

42. Mao Tse-tung, "Mistakes" (August 21, 1967), in JCMP, p. 144.

43. Mao Tse-tung, "Comment on the Report Concerning the Dissolution of the Wu-wei *Hsien* Mess Halls" (August 10, 1959), in CLG, 1.4:68.

44. Mao Tse-tung, "The Origin of Machine Guns and Mortars" (August 16, 1959), in CLG, 1.4:73–74.

45. Marx, *The German Ideology,* p. 20.

46. Karl Marx, *Capital* (Chicago: Kerr, 1906), 1:198.

47. Karl Marx and Friedrich Engels, *The Communist Manifesto,* in Karl Marx, *Selected Works* (Moscow: Marx–Engels–Lenin Institute, 1933), 1.6:543–544.

48. Marx, *The German Ideology,* p. 39.

49. Mao, "Eighth Plenary Session," pp. 62–63.

50. Mao Tse-tung, "Hai Jui and P'eng Teh-huai" (May 29, 1967), in JCMP, p. 140; also see the "Circular of the Central Committee of the Chinese Communist Party" (May 16, 1966), in JCMP, pp. 106–107; and PR, 21:6–7.

51. Chuang, *Evening Chats,* p. 9.

52. "P'eng Teh-huai's Testimony: Record of Interrogation on P'eng Teh-huai in Custody" (December 28, 1966–January 5, 1967), in *The Case of P'eng Teh-huai, 1959–1968* (Hong Kong: Union Research Institute, 1968).

53. Chuang, *Evening Chats,* p. 21.

54. Hsiao Ch'ien, Li Hsiu-lin, Tung Hsin-min, and Fang Ko-li, "Teng T'o: Big Conspirator against the Party and Socialism" (May 18, 1966), in CB, 792:47.

55. Chu Li-chang. "Po-k'ai mi-wu k'an 'ch'ing kuan' " [Dispersing the Fog to Take a Clear Look at "the Pure Official"], in *Wu-han p'i-p'an ch'üan chi* [A Complete Collection of the Judgment of Wu Han] (Hong Kong: O.K. News Agency, n.d.), p. 46.

56. Mao Tse-tung, "Give Serious Attention to the Discussion of the Film 'The Life of Wu Hsun' " (May 20, 1951), in CB, 891:15.

57. Mao Tse-tung, "Talk at the National Representative Conference of the Communist Party of China" (March 1955), in CB, 891:18.

58. Yao Wen-yuan, "On the New Historical Play 'Dismissal of Hai Jui' " (November 30, 1965), in CB, 783:4.

CHAPTER FOUR

1. Jean-Jacques Rousseau, *The Social Contract,* trans. Henry J. Tozer (London: George Allen & Unwin, 1924), pp. 123–124.

2. Mao Tse-tung, "Combat Liberalism" (September 7, 1937), in SW, 2:31–33.

3. Mao Tse-tung, "The Center's Instruction on Learning from Each Other and Overcoming Complacency and Conceit" (December 13, 1963), in JCMP, pp. 87–89; also see CB, 892:15–17.

4. JMJP (January 2, 1966), p. 2; cited and translated in H. P. Chuang, *The Great Proletarian Cultural Revolution* (Berkeley: Center for Chinese Studies, 1967), p. 39.

5. Mao Tse-tung, "Combat Selfishness and Criticize Revisionism" (November 6, 1967), in JCMP, p. 149; also see JMJP (November 6, 1967), p. 2.

6. Rousseau, *The Social Contract,* p. 180.

7. *Ibid.,* p. 113.

8. I am here presenting only one of many explanations for the theory of divine right and the origin of sovereignty in European thought. Although I do not necessarily believe that the English school of interpretation (cf. John Neville Figgis, *The Divine Right of Kings,* 2nd ed., Cambridge: Cambridge University Press, 1922) is solely correct and certainly do accept the explanations preferred by Otto Gierke and Fritz Stern, I am relying more upon the former for the sake of comparison with the Chinese case.

9. This discussion owes much to Ernest Barker's introduction to Otto Gierke, *Natural Law and the Theory of Society, 1500–1800* (Boston: Beacon Press, 1960).

10. Hiram Haydn, *The Counter-Renaissance* (New York: Harcourt, Brace & World, 1950), p. 152.

11. Rousseau, *The Social Contract,* pp. 134–135.

12. Mao Tse-tung, "The Foolish Old Man Who Removed the Mountains" (June 11, 1945), in SW, 3:322.

13. Mao Tse-tung, "Reshape the World" (January 12, 1968), in JCMP, p. 151; also see JMJP (January 12, 1968), p. 1.

14. Mao Tse-tung, "On the Correct Handling of Contradictions Among the People," reprinted by *China Pictorial* (Peking, 1967), p. 16.

15. T. A. Hsia, *Metaphor, Myth, Ritual, and the People's Commune* (Berkeley: Center for Chinese Studies, 1961), p. 10.

16. Kuan-tzu, "Emperor versus His Officers," in Liang Ch'i-ch'ao, *History of Chinese Political Thought During the Early Tsin Period* (Taipei: Ch'eng-wen Publishing Company, 1968), p. 116.

17. *Ibid.,* pp. 123–124.

18. Han Fei-tzu, "On Five Sources of Trouble," in Liang, *Chinese Political Thought,* pp. 128–129.

19. Han Fei-tzu, "The Codification of Law," in Liang, *Chinese Political Thought,* p. 114.

20. Kuan-tzu, "On the Sanctity of Orders," in Liang, *Chinese Political Thought,* p. 132.

21. *Yin Wen,* in Liang, *Chinese Political Thought,* p. 118.

22. *Ta hsueh* [The Great Learning], commentary of Tseng, 1:1.

23. *Chung yung* [Doctrine of the Mean], 20:11.

24. Han Fei-tzu, "Misgivings on Circumstances," in Liang, *Chinese Political Thought,* pp. 117–119.

25. Shun Tao, in Liang, *Chinese Political Thought,* p. 115.

26. Han Fei-tzu, "Misgivings," in Liang, *Chinese Political Thought,* p. 116.

27. *Mencius,* V, 1.5:4.

28. *Ibid.,* V, 1.5:5.

29. *Shang shu,* V, 1.2:7, in James Legge, *The Chinese Classics* (Hong Kong: Hong Kong University Press, 1970), p. 292.

30. *Ibid.,* V, 1.1:11, in Legge, *The Chinese Classics,* p. 288.

31. *Mencius,* I, 2.6:2–3.

32. Tung Chung-shu, *Ch'un-ch'iu fan-lu chu* [Luxuriant Gems of the *Spring and Autumn,* Annotated], Huang Ch'ing ching-chieh edition (Taipei: World Book, n.d.), p. 254.

33. *Ibid.,* pp. 294–295.

34. *Ibid.,* pp. 75–76.

35. *Ibid.,* pp. 151–152.

36. *Ibid.,* p. 152.

37. Ch'eng I and Ch'eng Hao, *Erh Ch'eng yü-lu* [Quotations from the Two Ch'eng's] (Shanghai: Commercial Press, 1936), 1:9. This is from Ch'eng Hao.

38. *Ibid.,* 1:26.

39. Chu Hsi, *I Shu,* in Wing-tsit Chan, *A Source Book in Chinese Philosophy* (Princeton: Princeton University Press, 1963), pp. 627–628.

40. Cited in E. G. Pulleyblank, "Chinese Historical Criticism: Liu Chih-chi and Ssu-ma Kuang," in *Historians of China and Japan,* eds. W. G. Beasley and E. G. Pulleyblank (London: Oxford, 1961), pp. 153–154.

41. Stuart R. Schram, *The Political Thought of Mao Tse-tung* (New York: Praeger, 1963), p. 11. For an instance of citation, see Mao Ze-dong, *Une Étude*

de l'éducation physique, trans. Stuart R. Schram (Paris, La Haye: Mouton, 1962), p. 24.

42. Julian H. Franklin, ed., *Constitutionalism and Resistance in the Sixteenth Century: Three Treatises by Hotman, Beza, and Mornay* (New York: Pegasus, 1969), pp. 19–20.

43. *Ibid.,* pp. 30–39.

44. I have been aided in this particular interpretation of Bodin by reading Samuel P. Huntington, *Political Order in Changing Societies* (New Haven: Yale University Press, 1968), pp. 98–107.

45. Frederic Wakeman, Jr., "Localism and Loyalism during the Ch'ing Conquest of Chiang-nan: The Siege of Chiang-yin" (Paper delivered at the Conference on Local Control and Social Protest during the Ch'ing Period, Honolulu, June 1971), pp. 34–37.

46. Liang Ch'i-ch'ao, "Min-yueh lun chü-tzu Lu-so chih hsueh-shuo" [The Theory of the Social Contract of the Great Man, Rousseau], *Hsin-min ts'ung-pao* [The New People Magazine], 11:15–26. According to LJMT, pp. 8–9, Mao read and reread this issue of the journal.

47. Liang Ch'i-ch'ao, "Min-yuch," p. 22.

48. *Ibid.,* p. 25.

49. *Ibid.,* p. 26.

50. *Ibid.*

CHAPTER FIVE

1. For example, Karl Korsch has left an unpublished essay on Maoism. As Fred Halliday notes, "Mao Tse-tung's emphasis on revolutionary ideas as concrete forces has some analogy to Korsch's theses on ideological struggle." Fred Halliday, introduction to Karl Korsch, *Marxism and Philosophy,* trans. Fred Halliday (London: NLB, 1970), p. 22.

2. Georg Lukacs, *History and Class Consciousness: Studies in Marxist Dialectics,* trans. Rodney Livingstone (Cambridge: MIT Press, 1971), preface to the 1967 edition, p. xiii.

3. *Ibid.,* p. xviii.

4. Many of the points here have been made in Alvin W. Gouldner, "History and Class Consciousness," review of Georg Lukacs, *History and Class Consciousness,* in *New York Times Book Review* (July 18, 1971), pp. 4–5, 14–15.

5. Lukacs, *History and Class Consciousness,* preface to the 1922 edition, p. xxiv.

6. G. H. R. Parkinson, "Introduction," in *Georg Lukacs: The Man, His Work and His Ideas,* ed. G. H. R. Parkinson (New York: Vintage Books, 1970), pp. 9–10.

7. Lukacs, *History and Class Consciousness,* p. 13.

8. Gouldner, "History and Class Consciousness."

9. Antonio Gramsci, *The Modern Prince and Other Writings* (New York: International Publishers, 1957), p. 137.

10. *Ibid.,* p. 135.

11. *Ibid.,* p. 137.

12. *Ibid.,* p. 138.

13. John M. Cammett, *Antonio Gramsci and the Origins of Italian Communism* (Stanford: Stanford University Press, 1967), pp. 210–211.

14. *Ibid.,* p. 195.

15. Gramsci, *Prince,* pp. 90–92.

16. Mao Tse-tung, "Report of an Investigation into the Peasant Movement in Hunan" (March 1927), in SW, 1:46.

17. Roxane Witke, "Mao Tse-tung, Women, and Suicide in the May 4th Era," *China Quarterly,* 31:128–147.

18. Mao Tse-tung, "Oppose Book Worship" (May 1939), in SRMTT, p. 35.

19. Mao Tse-tung, "Reform in Learning, the Party, and Literature" (February 1, 1942), in Boyd Compton, *Mao's China: Party Reform Documents, 1942–1944* (Seattle: University of Washington Press, 1952), pp. 12–13.

20. *Ibid.,* p. 14.

21. Mao Tse-tung, "Speech at Opening of the Party School in Yenan" in *ibid.,* pp. 21–22.

22. Mao Tse-tung, "Rectify the Party's Style of Work" (February 1, 1942), in SW, 3:40.

23. Frederick Engels, *Herr Eugen Dühring's Revolution in Science (Anti-Dühring),* trans. Emile Burns (New York: International Publishers, 1939), p. 131.

24. *Ibid.,* p. 147.

25. *Ibid.,* p. 344.

26. *Ibid.,* p. 305.

27. *Ibid.,* p. 345.

28. Che Guevara, "Ideology of the Cuban Revolution" (October 8, 1960), in CGS, p. 18.

29. *Ibid.,* pp. 20–21.

30. Che Guevara, "Farewell Letter to His Parents" in CGS, pp. 142–143.

31. Antonio Gramsci, cited in Alastair Davidson, *Antonio Gramsci: The Man and His Ideas* (Sydney: Australian New Left Review Publication, 1968), p. ii.

32. Georg Lukacs, *Lenin: A Study on the Unity of His Thought,* trans. Nicholas Jacobs (London: NLB, 1970), p. 31.

33. Parkinson, "Introduction," in *Georg Lukacs,* p. 12.

34. Lukacs, *History and Class Consciousness,* p. 19.

35. Lukacs, *Lenin,* p. 9.

36. *Ibid.,* p. 11 (italics mine).

37. *Ibid.,* p. 13.

38. *Ibid.,* p. 43.

39. *Ibid.,* p. 48.

40. *Ibid.*

41. *Ibid.,* p. 101.

41a. Martin Evan Jay, "The Frankfurt School: An Intellectual History of the Institut für Sozialforschung, 1923–1950" (Ph.D. diss., Harvard University, 1971).

42. Gouldner, "History and Class Consciousness."

43. *Gespräche mit Georg Lukacs,* p. 45, cited in Istvan Meszaros, "Lukacs' Concept of Dialectic," in Parkinson, *Georg Lukacs,* p. 54.

44. This point is developed in Leszek Kolakowski, "Intellectuals against Intellect" (Paper delivered at the Conference on Intellectuals, Jerusalem, March 1971).

45. Michel Simon, et al., *Lénine: la philosophie et la culture* (Paris: Editions Sociales, 1957), p. 27.

46. Gouldner, "History and Class Consciousness."

47. George Lichtheim, "The Concept of Ideology," in George Lichtheim, *The Concept of Ideology and Other Essays* (New York: Vintage, 1967), pp. 18–21.

48. Lucien Goldmann, *The Hidden God: A Study of Tragic Vision in the Pensées of Pascal and the Tragedies of Racine,* trans. Philip Thody (London: Routledge and Kegan Paul, 1964), p. 308.

49. *Ibid.,* pp. 308–309. Sensitive to the popularity and influence of his own *History and Class Consciousness* on French existentialism, Lukacs later pointed

out that because Hegel had identified alienation with every form of objectification, Hegelian Marxism seemed very close indeed to bourgeois existentialism.
Thinkers like Heidegger "sublimate a critique of society into a purely philosophical problem, that is, . . . convert an essentially social alienation into an eternal
'condition humaine'." Lukacs, *History and Class Consciousness*, p. xxiv.

50. Cited in George Lichtheim, "From Pascal to Marx," in Lichtheim, *Concept*, p. 278.

51. Louis Althusser, "Sur la dialectique matérialiste (de l'inégalité des ori-
gens)," *La Pensée*, 110:10.

52. *Ibid.*

53. Louis Althusser, "From *Capital* to Marx's Philosophy," in Louis Althusser
and Etienne Balibar, *Reading Capital* (Paris: François Maspero, 1968), pp. 24–
28.

54. Althusser, "Sur la dialectique," p. 14.

55. *Ibid.*, p. 16.

56. *Ibid.*, p. 18.

57. CGS, pp. 121–138.

58. *Ibid.*, p. 124.

59. *Ibid.*, p. 126.

60. *Ibid.*, p. 127.

61. *Ibid.*, p. 128.

62. *Ibid.*, p. 129.

63. *Ibid.*, p. 137.

64. *Ibid.*, p. 129.

65. *Ibid.*, pp. 123–124.

CHAPTER SIX

1. Chu Hsi, cited in Moss Roberts, "Double Judgments in the *Spring and
Autumn*, Kung Yang: The Reign of Duke Yin," in *Nothing Concealed: Essays
in Honor of Liu Yü-yun*, ed. Frederic Wakeman (Taipei: Chinese Materials and
Research Aids Service Center, 1971), pp. 28–29.

2. *Wen-yen*, cited and translated in Hellmut Wilhelm, *Change: Eight Lectures
on the I Ching*, trans. Cary F. Baynes (New York: Harper Torchbooks, 1964),
p. 52.

3. Ch'eng I, *I Ch'eng chuan* [Ch'eng's Commentary on the *Changes*] (Taipei:
Shih-chieh shu-chü, n.d.), 1:6.

4. Wilhelm, *Change*, p. 56.

5. Ch'eng I, *I Ch'eng chuan*, 1:8.

6. *Ibid.*, *hsu* [addendum], pp. 1–2.

7. Chu Hsi, *I pen i* [The Fundamental Meaning of the *Changes*] (Taipei: Shih-
chieh shu-chü, n.d.), 3:56.

8. *Ibid.* Later references to Chu Hsi's gloss in this section are from this same
passage unless otherwise noted.

9. K'ung Ying-ta, *Chou-i cheng-i* [The Rectified Meaning of the Chou
Changes], Ssu-pu pei-yao edition (Taipei: Chung-hua shu-chü, 1966), 7:2b. This
particular version of K'ung's recension based on Wang Pi's commentaries (originally written in A.D. 638) was prepared by Juan Yuan's *Hsueh-hai t'ang*. It was
probably the most current text of the late Ch'ing period, although it was strongly
attacked by members of the school of Han Learning in the early eighteenth
century.

10. *Ibid.*, 7:3a.

11. Chu Hsi, *I pen i*, 3:56.

12. Pico della Mirandola, "Oratio de Dignitate hominis," in Nikolaus Lobko-wicz, *Theory and Practice: History of a Concept from Aristotle to Marx* (Notre Dame, Ind.: University of Notre Dame Press, 1967), p. 135.

13. Nicholas of Cusa, *De Conjecturis*, in Ernst Cassirer, *Individuo e cosmo* (Firenze: La Nuova Italia editrice, 1935), p. 141.

14. Cited in Wilhelm, *Change*, p. 32.

15. Joseph Needham, "Human Laws and Laws of Nature in China and the West (II)," *Journal of the History of Ideas*, 12.2:216–217.

16. *Ibid.*, p. 218.

17. Derk Bodde, "Evidence for 'Laws of Nature' in Chinese Thought," *Harvard Journal of Asiatic Studies*, 20.3–4:709–727.

18. I have not had an opportunity to read Willard Peterson's important work on Fang I-chih, which he completed as a doctoral dissertation for Harvard University.

19. For a brilliant analysis of this perception, see Benjamin Schwartz, *In Search of Wealth and Power: Yen Fu and the West* (Cambridge: Harvard University Press, 1964).

20. LJMTT, pp. 29–30. The magazine was called *Ch'uan-shan hsueh-pao* [The Ch'uan-shan Journal] and was devoted to—in the words of its opening editorial by Liu Jen-hsi—"grieving over the Chinese republic." Its contents were largely limited to republications with detailed commentaries of Wang Fu-chih's works. Li Jui describes it as a magazine of the "national essence" sort. It went through two periods of publication. The first was from August 1915 until August 1927, making a total of eight issues. The second period of publication was from 1932 to 1937, consisting of fourteen issues. The study society was a major center of resistance to Yuan Shih-k'ai's attempt to make himself emperor. According to Stuart Schram, there is a complete run of this journal in the Tōyō Bunko.

21. *Ibid.*, pp. 12, 16.

22. Jerome Ch'en, *Mao and the Chinese Revolution* (London: Oxford University Press, 1965), pp. 12, 24, 48.

23. Wang Fu-chih, *Chou-i nei chuan* [Inner Commentary on the *Book of Changes*], *Ch'uan-shan i-shu* [Bequeathed Writings of (Wang) Ch'uan-shan], 3:36a, in *A Source Book in Chinese Philosophy*, trans. Wing-tsit Chan (Princeton: Princeton University Press, 1963), pp. 698–699.

24. Wang Fu-chih, *Shang-shu yin-i* [Elaboration on the Meanings of the *Book of History*], *Ch'uan-shan i-shu*, 3:6a, in *ibid.*, p. 699.

25. Karl Marx, "Sixth Thesis on Feuerbach," in Frederick Engels, *Ludwig Feuerbach and the Outcome of Classical German Philosophy* (New York: International Publishers, 1941), pp. 83–84.

26. Wang Fu-chih, *Chou-i wai-chuan* [Outer Commentary on the *Book of Changes*], 5:25, in Chan, *Source Book*, p. 695.

27. Karl Korsch, *Marxism and Philosophy*, trans. Fred Halliday (London: NLB, 1970), p. 116.

28. *Ibid.*, p. 117.

29. Leszek Kolakowski, *Toward a Marxist Humanism: Essays on the Left Today*, trans. Jane Zielonko Peel (New York: Grove Press, 1968), p. 12.

30. "Yuan Tan," MCHST, p. 7.

31. H. C. Chuang, *The Great Proletarian Cultural Revolution* (Berkeley: Center for Chinese Studies, 1967), pp. 7–10.

32. T. A. Hsia, *Metaphor, Myth, Ritual, and the People's Commune* (Berkeley: Center for Chinese Studies, 1961), p. 31.

33. Chuang, *Great Proletarian Cultural Revolution*, pp. 17–19.

34. *Ibid.*, p. 23.

35. *Ibid.,* p. 24.
36. Mao Tse-tung, "Shih-liu tzu ling" (1935), in MCHST, pp. 16–17.
37. Mao Tse-tung, "K'un-lun" (1935), in MCHST, pp. 19–20.
38. Mao Tse-tung, "Winter Clouds" (December 20, 1962), in *Ten More Poems of Mao Tse-tung* (Hong Kong: Eastern Horizon Press, 1967), pp. 18–19.
39. Mao Tse-tung, "Ode to the Plum Blossom" (December 1961), in *Ten More Poems,* pp. 16–17 (my translation).
40. This poem is given in Chinese in *ibid.,* p. 30.
41. Mao Tse-tung, "Ch'ung yang" (1929), in MCHST, p. 6.
42. Mao Tse-tung, "Fan ti-i tz'u ta 'Wei chiao' " [August the First Great Encirclement] (1931), in MCHST, pp. 10–11.
43. Mao Tse-tung, "Reply to Comrade Kuo Mo-jo" (January 9, 1963) in *Ten More Poems,* pp. 14–15.
44. Mao Tse-tung, "Ts'ung Ho-chou hsiang Ch'ang-sha" [From Ho-chou to Ch'ang-sha] (1930), in MCHST, p. 9.
45. Wang Fu-chih, *Sung-lun* [An Essay on the Sung Dynasty], Ssu-pu pei-yao edition (Taipei: Chung-hua shu-chü, 1966), 10:15a.
46. Mao Tse-tung, "Report of an Investigation into the Peasant Movement in Hunan" (March 1927), in SW, 1:21–23.
47. Mao Tse-tung, "Yellow Crane Tower" (1927), translated in Jerome Ch'en, *Mao and the Chinese Revolution,* p. 322.
48. Mao Tse-tung, "Tidal Waves of Revolution" (July 26, 1966), in JCMP, p. 114. This is taken from the JMJP editorial of July 26, 1966: "Follow Chairman Mao and Advance in the Teeth of Great Storms and Waves."
49. Mao Tse-tung, "Talk at the Work Conference of the Center" (October 25, 1966), in JCMP, p. 44; also see CLG, 1.1:11; and CB, 891:77.
50. Mao Tse-tung, "Ch'ang-sha" (1927), in MCHST, pp. 1–2.
51. Mao Tse-tung, "Revolution and Productive Force" (August 3, 1967), in JCMP, p. 143. This is taken from a *Liberation Army Daily* editorial of August 3, 1967, reproduced in JMJP (August 3, 1967), p. 7.
52. In the words of the "Resolutions of the Eleventh Plenum" (August, 1966), in JCMP, pp. 125–126: "The Great Proletarian Cultural Revolution is a powerful motive force for the development of the social productive forces in our country." This also appears in PR, 33:11.
53. Mao Tse-tung, "Bombard the Bourgeois Headquarters" (August 5, 1966), in PR, 33:9.
54. Mao Tse-tung, "Reply to Comrade Kuo Mo-jo," pp. 20–23.
55. Mao Tse-tung, "Introducing Cooperatives" (1958), in SRMTT, p. 403.

CHAPTER SEVEN

1. MA, p. 127.
2. *Ibid.,* p. 128.
3. H. C. Chuang, *The Little Red Book and Current Chinese Language* (Berkeley: Center for Chinese Studies, 1968), p. 39.
4. LJMTT, p. 7.
5. MA, p. 129.
6. *Ibid.,* pp. 133–134.
7. Jerome Ch'en, *Mao and the Chinese Revolution* (London: Oxford University Press, 1965), p. 30; also see Siao-yü (Hsu-tung), *Mao Tse-tung and I Were Beggars,* historical commentary and notes by Robert C. North (Syracuse: Syracuse University Press, 1959), p. 229.

8. Mao Tse-tung, "Speech at the Ch'eng-tu Conference" (March 22, 1958), in JPRS, 90:47.

CHAPTER EIGHT

1. "Li-yun" [Evolution of Rites], *Li-chi* [Record of Rites], in *Ku-chu shih-san ching* [The Old Commentaries on the Thirteen Classics], Ssu-pu pei-yao edition (Taipei: Hsin-hsing shu-chü, 1959), 1.7:1–2.

2. Mao Tse-tung, "On the People's Democratic Dictatorship" (July 1, 1949), in SW, 4:412.

3. *Mencius*, III, 2.9:7–8, in James Legge, *The Four Books* (Taipei: Wen-hua shu-chü, 1960), pp. 676–677. Scholars have questioned which *Spring and Autumn* Mencius had in mind.

4. Adapted from "The Ch'un Ts'ew with the Tso Chuen," in James Legge, *The Chinese Classics* (Hong Kong: University of Hong Kong Press, 1970), V, 43.

5. *Ibid.*, p. 3.

6. *Ibid.*

7. Ch'en Li, *Kung-yang i-shu* [Commentary on the Meaning of the *Kung-yang*], Ssu-pu pei-yao edition (Taipei: Chung-hua shu-chü, 1966), 1.3:14.

8. Tung Chung-shu, *Ch'un-ch'iu fan-lu chu* [Luxuriant Gems of the *Spring and Autumn*, Annotated], Huang Ch'ing ching-chieh edition (Taipei: World Book), p. 7. Here and elsewhere where excerpts have been translated by them, I have checked my translations with those of Wing-tsit Chan, *A Source Book in Chinese Philosophy* (Princeton: Princeton University Press, 1963); Fung Yu-lan, *A History of Chinese Philosophy* (Princeton: Princeton University Press, 1953), vol. 2; Otto Franke, *Studien zur Geschichte des konfuzianischen Dogmas und der chinesischen Staatsreligion, Zweiter Teil: Tung Tschung-schu's Tsch'un-ts'iu fan lu* (Hamburg: Friedrichsen, 1920), pp. 89–308; and Kang Woo, *Les Trois théories politiques du Tch'ouen Ts'ieou, interprétées par Tong Tchong-chou d'après les principes de l'école de Kong-yang* (Paris: Presses Universitaires de France, 1932).

9. Legge, *The Chinese Classics*, 5:833.

10. *Chia yü* [Family Sayings (of Confucius)], cited in Legge, *The Chinese Classics*, 5:834.

11. Tung, *Ch'un-ch'iu fan-lu*, pp. 126–127.

12. Cited and translated in Fung Yu-lan, *Chinese Philosophy*, p. 129.

13. Tung, *Ch'un-ch'iu fan-lu*, p. 70.

14. Cited and translated in Fung Yu-lan, *Chinese Philosophy*, p. 83.

15. Jack Dull, "History and the Old Text–New Text Controversy in the Han" (Seattle: University of Washington, 1966), pp. 27–29.

16. Fei Mi, *Hung-tao shu* [Writings on the Vast Way], cited and translated in Mansfield Freeman, "The Philosophy of Tai Tung-yuan," *Journal of the North China Branch, Royal Asiatic Society*, 64:51.

17. Arthur Hummel, *Eminent Chinese of the Ch'ing Period, 1644–1912* (Washington, D.C.: U.S. Government Printing Office, 1943), pp. 908–910.

18. Liang Ch'i-ch'ao, *Intellectual Trends in the Ch'ing Period*, trans. Immanuel C. Y. Hsu (Cambridge: Harvard University Press, 1959), pp. 33–34.

19. Liu Feng-lu, *Liu Li-pu chi* [The Works of Liu Li-pu] (1829), 3:18–19; also see Hummel, *Eminent Chinese*, pp. 206–208, 518–520. The philological questions are examined carefully in Bernhard Karlgren, *On the Authenticity and Nature of the Tso Chuan* (Taipei: Ch'eng-wen Publishing Company, 1968). For a discussion of the possibility of the work being entirely forged by Liu Hsin, as well as a resume of the research of Liu Feng-lu, see Otto Franke, *Studien zur*

Geschichte des Confuzianischen Dogmas und der chinesischen Staatsreligion, Erster Teil, Das Problem des Tsch'un-ts'iu (Hamburg: Friedrichsen, 1920), especially pp. 34–36.

20. Hu Shih, "Tai Tung-yuan te che-hsueh" [The Philosophy of Tai Tung-yuan], *Kuo-hsueh chi-k'an* [Journal of Sinological Studies], 2:23.

21. Yun Ching, *Ta-yun-shan fang wen-kao* [Literary Drafts from the House on Ta-yun Mountain] (1884), 1.1:8a. Yun Ching founded the Yang-hu school of *ku-wen* prose.

22. *Ibid.*, 1.1:24a.

23. Ch'en Li, *Kung-yang*, 2.15:6–7.

24. This theme of the New Text school is explored with great sensitivity in Hellmut Wilhelm, "Chinese Confucianism on the Eve of the Great Encounter," in *Changing Japanese Attitudes toward Modernization*, ed. Marius Jansen (Princeton: Princeton University Press, 1967), pp. 283–310.

25. Ch'en Li, *Kung-yang*, 2.15:2a.

26. Wilhelm, "Chinese Confucianism," p. 299. The relationship between Wojen's antiforeignism and Ch'eng-Chu Confucianism is also suggested in Chang Hao, "The Anti-Foreignist Role of Wo-jen (1804–1871)," in *Papers on China*, ed. John K. Fairbank (Cambridge: Harvard East Asian Research Center, 1960), 14:1–29.

27. Kung Tzu-chen, *Ting-an wen-chi* [The Writings of (Kung) Ting-an] (Shanghai: Commercial Press, 1936), p. 63. For "equality" or "levelling," see p. 3.

28. *Ibid.*, p. 95. Like Li Chih, Kung argued that *kung* was only possible because of *ssu*. His rationalization was slightly different, though, and reflects the difference in times. Kung gave as an example the virtue of loyalty. Loyalty, he declared, was to one's *own* ruler, not to one of another country, and therefore reflected *ssu*: "First *ssu* and only later *kung*." See p. 94.

29. I have explored at somewhat greater length the relationship between Wei Yuan, Lin Tse-hsu, New Text learning, and the Opium War in an essay on that period written with John K. Fairbank for the as yet unpublished *Cambridge History of China* (vol. 5); also see Hummel, *Eminent Chinese*, pp. 431–434; and Frederic Wakeman, "The *Huang-ch'ao ching-shih wen-pien*," in *Ch'ing-shih wen-t'i*, 1.10:8–22. For a more knowledgeable account than mine of Wei Yuan's connections with the "statecraft" and *chin-wen* schools, see Peter Mitchell, "A Further Note on the HCCSWP," *Ch'ing-shih wen-t'i*, 2.3:40–46.

30. Hummel, *Eminent Chinese*, pp. 114–115, 535; Wilhelm, "Chinese Confucianism," p. 307; Wolfgang Franke, "Juan Yuan (1764–1849)," *Monumenta Serica*, 9:53–80; A. Vissière, "Biographie de Jouan Yuan: Homme d'état, lettré et mathématicien (1746–1849)," *T'oung Pao*, série II, 5:562–596. Franke's article includes a complete biography of Juan's works. The Vissière study is really no more than a translation of the official biography in *Kuo-ch'ao hsien-cheng shih-lüeh* [Historical Sketches of Deceased Worthies of the Present Dynasty].

31. Wing-tsit Chan, "K'ang Yu-wei and the Confucian Doctrine of Humanity (*Jen*)," in *K'ang Yu-wei, A Biography and a Symposium*, ed. Jung-pang Lo (Tucson: University of Arizona Press, 1967), p. 360.

CHAPTER NINE

1. K. C. Hsiao, "The Case for Constitutional Monarchy: K'ang Yu-wei's Plan for the Democratization of China," *Monumenta Serica*, 24:1–83.

2. K. C. Hsiao, "In and Out of Utopia: K'ang Yu-wei's Social Thought," pt. 1, in *Chung Chi Journal*, 7.1:1.

3. Joseph R. Levenson, *Confucian China and Its Modern Fate,* vol. 1 (Berkeley: University of California Press, 1958), pp. 79–83.

4. *Ibid.,* p. 81.

5. K'ang Yu-wei, *Chronological Autobiography of K'ang Yu-wei,* translated in Jung-pang Lo, *K'ang Yu-wei: A Biography and a Symposium* (Tucson: University of Arizona Press, 1967), p. 27.

6. *Ibid.,* p. 31.

7. *Ibid.,* pp. 33–34.

8. Here I have used Richard C. Howard's translation of the autobiography, which gives a more accurate sense of K'ang's vision of his own role; see Richard C. Howard, "K'ang Yu-wei (1858–1927): His Intellectual Background and Early Thought," in *Confucian Personalities,* eds. Arthur Wright and Denis Twitchett (Stanford: Stanford University Press, 1962), p. 302.

9. K'ang Yu-wei, *Chronological Autobiography,* p. 36.

10. *Ibid.,* p. 40.

11. Howard, "K'ang Yu-wei," pp. 306–313; Hsiao, "In and Out of Utopia," pt. 1, pp. 1–18.

12. Liang Ch'i-ch'ao, *Intellectual Trends in the Ch'ing Period,* trans. Immanuel C. Y. Hsu (Cambridge: Harvard University Press, 1959), p. 109.

13. K'ang, *Chronological Autobiography,* p. 41.

14. K'ang Yu-wei, *K'ang-tzu nei-wai p'ien* [Esoteric and Exoteric Essays of Master K'ang], translated in Hsiao, "In and Out of Utopia," pt. 1, p. 6.

15. Translated in Hsiao, "In and Out of Utopia," pt. 2, p. 103.

16. K'ang, *Chronological Autobiography,* p. 40.

17. K'ang, *K'ang-tzu,* translated in Hsiao, "In and Out of Utopia," pt. 1, pp. 6–7.

18. K'ang, *Chronological Autobiography,* p. 42.

19. *Ibid.*

20. K'ang Yu-wei, *shih-li kung-fa* [Substantial Truths and Universal principles], translated in Howard, "K'ang Yu-wei," p. 311.

21. *Ibid.,* p. 312.

22. K'ang Yu-wei, *Shih-li kung-fa,* translated in Hsiao, "In and Out of Utopia," pt. 1, p. 11.

23. Ch'eng I, *I Ch'eng chuan* [Ch'eng's Commentary on the *Changes*], 1:4; see K. C. Hsiao, "The Philosophical Thought of K'ang Yu-wei: An Attempt at a New Synthesis," *Monumenta Serica,* 21:136.

24. Tung Chung-shu, *Ch'un-ch'iu fan-lu chu* [Luxuriant Gems of the *Spring and Autumn,* Annotated], Huang Ch'ing ching-chieh edition (Taipei: World Book, n.d.), pp. 290–291.

25. K'ang Yu-wei, translated in Wing-tsit Chan, "K'ang Yu-wei and the Confucian Doctrine of Humanity (*Jen*)," in J. P. Lo, *K'ang Yu-wei,* p. 363.

26. *Ibid.*

27. K'ang Yu-wei, *Ta-t'ung shu* [Writings on the Great Harmony], pp. 64–65, translated in Hsiao, "In and Out of Utopia," pt. 2, p. 102.

28. Tan Ssu-t'ung, *Jen-hsueh* [A Study of Benevolence] (Taipei: Wen-hai ch'u-pan she, 1962), *shang,* pp. 1–2a.

29. K'ang, *Chronological Autobiography,* pp. 40–41.

30. *Ibid.,* p. 36.

31. *Ibid.,* p. 40.

32. *Ibid.,* p. 52.

33. Ch'ien Mu, *Chung-kuo chin san-pai nien hsueh-shu* [The Intellectual History of China during the Last Three Hundred Years] (Taipei: Commercial

Press, 1966), vol. 2, pp. 698–699; also see Hsiao, "In and Out of Utopia," pt. 2, p. 147.

34. K'ang Yu-wei, *Li-yun chu* [Annotation of the *Evolution of Rites*] (Chung-kuo t'u-shu kung-ssu, n.d.), 1 *ts'e*, 3 and 32 double leafs. The copy I have used, which is in the East Asian Library at Berkeley, is personally autographed by K'ang. This reference is to the preface, p. 1a.

35. *Ibid.*, pp. 1b–2a.

36. K'ang Yu-wei, *Ch'un-ch'iu pi-hsiao ta-i wei-yen k'ao* [An Examination of the Majestic Principles and Subtle Doctrines of the *Spring and Autumn*], 1:2. The edition which I have used is a hand copied set privately printed on Taiwan (no publisher, no date). It is also available in K'ang's *Wen-ch'ao* [Literary Jottings], *chüan* 5, but I have not had access to that edition. The work was evidently completed in 1901, when K'ang was in Penang, and published in 1913.

37. Translated in Fung Yu-lan, *A History of Chinese Philosophy* (Princeton: Princeton University Press, 1953), p. 675.

38. Translated in Hsiao, "In and Out of Utopia," pt. 2, p. 119.

39. *Ibid.*, p. 115.

40. *Ibid.*, p. 119.

41. Translated in Chan, "K'ang Yu-wei," p. 367.

42. John Fryer's *Tso-chih chu-yen* [Homely Words to Aid Governance], published by the Kiangnan Arsenal in 1885), is cited in Hsiao, "In and Out of Utopia," pt. 2, p. 134. K'ang mentioned Fryer in his *Chronological Autobiography*, p. 43. As Hsiao points out, Fryer's work probably led K'ang to believe that the *t'ien-hsia wei-kung* principle was universal for all humanity. The Russian historian, S. L. Tikvinsky, who has tried to stress the influence of Fourier on K'ang (a "Mr. Fu," Fu *hsien-sheng*, is mentioned in the *Ta-t'ung shu*), argues that Fryer's influence was more important. See S. L. Tikvinsky, *Dvizenia za reformy v Kitae v kontse XIX veka i Kan Iy-yei* [K'ang Yu-wei and the Late Nineteenth-Century Reform Movement in China] (Moscow, 1959), pp. 331–340. Adrian Arthur Bennett has also written a monograph on Fryer's influence during the nineteenth century, *John Fryer: The Introduction of Western Science and Technology into Nineteenth-century China* (Cambridge: Harvard East Asian Research Center, 1967).

43. Cited and translated in Hsiao, "In and Out of Utopia," pt. 2, p. 106.

44. Mao Tse-tung, "On the People's Democratic Dictatorship," in SW, 4:414.

CHAPTER TEN

1. K'ang Yu-wei, *Chronological Autobiography of K'ang Yu-wei*, translated in *K'ang Yu-wei: A Biography and a Symposium*, ed. Jung-pang Lo (Tucson: University of Arizona Press, 1967), p. 50.

2. *Ibid.*, p. 74.

3. K. C. Hsiao, "Weng T'ung-ho and the Reform Movement of 1898," *Tsing Hua Journal*, New Series, 1.2:158.

4. K'ang, *Chronological Autobiography*, p. 51.

5. K'ang, cited in K. C. Hsiao, "In and Out of Utopia," pt. 2, in *The Chung Chi Journal*, 7.2:115.

6. Although K'ang's chronological autobiography says that over 1200 scholars signed the 1895 petition to the emperor protesting the treaty with Japan, the compilers of the WHPF have only managed to find 603. See WHPF, 2:155–166.

7. The importance of the *hsueh-hui* to the reform movement is spelled out in an unpublished paper which Wang Erh-min delivered at the East-West Center in

1969. Chun-kao Poon has also studied this topic in an unpublished paper prepared for a graduate seminar at Berkeley in 1970.

8. Feng Kuei-fen, "Fu hsiang-chih i" [A Proposal to Restore Village Offices], in WHPF, 1:8. The feudalism/prefecturalism debate is carefully followed in Lien-sheng Yang, "Ming Local Administration," in *Chinese Government in Ming Times: Seven Studies*, ed. Charles Hucker (New York: Columbia University Press, 1969), pp. 1–22.

9. K'ang Yu-wei, "Shang Ch'ing-ti ti-i shu" [First Memorial to the Ch'ing Emperor, dated Kuang-hsu 14/9], in WHPF, 2:129. Parts of this are translated in K. C. Hsiao, "The Case for Constitutional Monarchy: K'ang Yu-wei's Plan for the Democratization of China," *Monumenta Serica*, 24:16.

10. K'ang Yu-wei, "Shang Ch'ing-ti ti-wu shu" [Fifth Memorial to the Ch'ing Emperor, dated Kuang-hsu 23/12], in WHPF, 2:194.

11. K'ang Yu-wei, "Shang Ch'ing-ti ti-liu shu" [Sixth Memorial to the Ch'ing Emperor, dated Kuang-hsu 24/1/8], in WHPF, 2:202.

12. K'ang Yu-wei, *K'ang Nan-hai kuan-chih i* [A Discussion of the Function of Officials by K'ang Nan-hai] (Shanghai: Kuang-chih shu-chü, 1906), 1:6, 2:1–3, 4:1–10. The original edition of the *Kuan-chih i* appeared in 1903.

13. *Ibid.*, 1:5, 7:3.

14. *Ibid.*, 7:2.

15. *Ibid.*, 7:1–2.

16. Liang Ch'i-ch'ao, *K'ang Yu-wei chuan* [A Biography of K'ang Yu-wei], in WHPF, 4:34; also see Hsia's use of this biography in "The Case for Constitutional Monarchy," pp. 18–19.

17. K'ang, *Kuan-chih i*, 1:1.

18. *Ibid.*

19. Hsiao, "The Case for Constitutional Monarchy," p. 3.

20. Translated in *Ibid.*, p. 12.

21. K'ang, *Chronological Autobiography*, p. 157.

22. *Ibid.*, p. 114.

23. K'ang Yu·wei, *Ch'un-ch'iu pi-hsiao ta-i wei-yen k'ao* [An Examination of the Majestic Principles and Subtle Doctrines of the *Spring and Autumn*], 5:1a; also translated in Hsiao, "The Case for Constitutional Monarchy," p. 8.

24. K'ang, *Chronological Autobiography*, p. 96.

25. K'ang, "Shang Ch'ing-ti ti-wu shu," in WHPF, 2:194.

26. K'ang, *Chronological Autobiography*, p. 100.

27. Translated in Hsiao, "The Case for Constitutional Monarchy," p. 21.

28. *Ibid.*, pp. 26–27.

29. K'ang, *Chronological Autobiography*, p. 105.

30. *Ibid.*, pp. 99–100.

31. Tung Chung-shu, *Ch'un-ch'iu fan-lu chu* [Luxuriant Gems of the *Spring and Autumn*, Annotated], Huang Ch'ing ching-chieh edition (Taipei: World Book, n.d.), pp. 240–241.

32. K'ang Yu-wei, *Meng-tzu wei* [Subtleties of Mencius] (1901), translated in K. C. Hsiao, "The Philosophical Thought of K'ang Yu-wei: An Attempt at a New Synthesis," *Monumenta Serica*, 21:159. The *Meng-tzu wei* was written in 1901.

33. K'ang Yu-wei, *Chung-yung chu* [Annotation of the *Doctrine of the Mean*], 46b, translated in Hsiao, "Philosophical Thought of K'ang Yu-wei," p. 173. Hsiao has also detailed K'ang's cosmic speculations written toward the end of his life; see K. C. Hsiao, "K'ang Yu-wei's Excursion into Science: *Lectures on the Heavens*," in J. P. Lo, *K'ang Yu-wei*, pp. 375–409. Between 1924 and 1926, K'ang's celestial interests inspired him to establish an astronomical academy.

34. K'ang, *Chronological Autobiography*, pp. 99, 111, 121.

35. This is reported by Liang Ch'i-ch'ao in his annotation to the emperor's edict of Kuang-hsu 24/3/23, in WHPF, 2:17.

36. Edict of Kuang-hsu 24/7/27, in WHPF, 2:85.

37. Here I am simply paraphrasing Wing-tsit Chan's excellent discussion in "K'ang Yu-wei and the Confucian Doctrine of Humanity (*Jen*)," in J. P. Lo, *K'ang Yu-wei*, pp. 359–362.

38. Cited in Hsiao, "In and Out of Utopia," pt. 2, p. 102.

39. *Ibid.*

40. This is expressed in *K'ang-tzu nei-wai p'ien* [The Inner and Outer Treatises of Master K'ang]. See Richard C. Howard, "K'ang Yu-wei (1858–1927): His Intellectual Background and Early Thought," in *Confucian Personalities*, eds. Arthur Wright and Denis Twitchett (Stanford: Stanford University Press, 1962), pp. 309–310.

41. Liang Ch'i-ch'ao, "Hsin-min shuo" [Discussing the New People], in *Hsin-min ts'ung-pao* [The New People Magazine], 11:1–14. The subsequent quotes by Liang are also drawn from this source.

42. MA, p. 133; LJMTT, p. 8; Siao Yü (Hsu-tung), *Mao Tse-tung and I Were Beggars*, historical commentary and notes by Robert C. North (Syracuse: Syracuse University Press, 1959), p. 226.

CHAPTER ELEVEN

1. MA, p. 141.

2. *Ibid.*, p. 143.

3. *Ibid.*, pp. 141–142.

4. LJMTT, p. 11.

5. Benjamin Schwartz, *In Search of Wealth and Power: Yen Fu and the West* (Cambridge: Harvard University Press, 1964), p. 117.

6. Thomas Henry Huxley, *Evolution and Ethics and Other Essays* (New York: 1925), p. 82, cited in Schwartz, *In Search of Wealth and Power*, pp. 103–110.

7. Schwartz, *In Search of Wealth and Power*, p. 158.

8. MA, p. 143.

9. Siao Yü (Hsu-tung), *Mao Tse-tung and I Were Beggars*, historical commentary and notes by Robert C. North (Syracuse: Syracuse University Press, 1959), pp. 38–41, 240–241; also Howard L. Boorman, *Biographical Dictionary of Republican China* (New York: Columbia University Press, 1971), 4:1–3.

10. Yang Ch'ang-chi, *Lun-yü lei-ch'ao* [Categorized Excerpts from the *Analects*], cited in LJMTT, p. 22.

11. *Analects*, IX, 25.

12. Cited in LJMTT, p. 23.

13. *Ibid.*, p. 23.

14. T'an Ssu-t'ung, *Jen-hsueh* [A Study of Benevolence] (Taipei: Wen-hai ch'u-pan she, 1962), *shang*, p. 14b.

15. Hannah Arendt, *The Human Condition* (New York: Doubleday Anchor, 1959), pp. 122–123.

16. Yang Ch'ang-chi, "Chih-sheng p'ien" [An Essay on Managing One's Life-work], in *Hsin Ch'ing-nien* [New Youth], pt. 1, 2.4:1–8, and pt. 2, 2.5:1–8.

17. *Ta hsueh* [The Great Learning], in *The Four Books*, trans. James Legge (Taipei: Wen-hua shu-chü, 1960), p. 37.

18. *Ibid.*, p. 7.

19. *Ibid.*, p. 2.

20. *Ibid.*, p. 6.

21. Mao Tse-tung, "Notebooks," cited in LJMTT, p. 39.
22. *Ibid.*
23. *Ibid.*
24. *Ibid.*
25. MA, pp. 147–148.
26. Ch'en Tu-hsiu, "Chin-jih chih chiao-yü fang-chen" [The Direction of To-day's Education], in *Ch'ing-nien tsa-chih* [Youth Magazine], 1.2:1–6.
27. *Ibid.*, p. 6.
28. MA, p. 144.
29. Mao Tse-tung, "Chairman Mao's Conversation with Comrades Ch'en Po-ta and K'ang Sheng" (1965), in JPRS, 90:26.

CHAPTER TWELVE

1. Christian Wolff, *Preliminary Discourse on Philosophy in General*, trans. Richard J. Blackwell (Indianapolis: Bobbs-Merrill, 1963), p. vii.
2. Edward, Lord Herbert of Cherbury, *De Veritate*, trans. Meyrick H. Carré (Bristol: Arrowsmith, 1937), pp. 77–81; Charles de Rémusat, *Lord Herbert de Cherbury, sa vie et ses oeuvres* (Paris: Didier, 1874), pp. 132–133.
3. Benson Mates, *Elementary Logic* (New York: Oxford University Press, 1965), p. 219.
4. Christian Wolff, *Preliminary Discourse*, p. 17.
5. W. H. Auden, "The Labyrinth," in *The Collected Poetry of W. H. Auden* (New York: Random House, 1945), p. 10.
6. George Berkeley, *The Principles of Human Knowledge*, ed. T. E. Jessop (London: A. Brown, 1937), pp. 120–122.
7. David Hume, *A Treatise on Human Nature* (Oxford: Clarendon Press, 1896), pp. 188–193.
8. Immanuel Kant, *Critique of Pure Reason*, trans. J. M. D. Meiklejohn (New York: Wiley, 1900), p. 7.
9. *Ibid.*, pp. 8–9.
10. *Ibid.*, p. 13.
11. *Ibid.*, pp. 21–22.
12. *Ibid.*, p. 25.
13. *Ibid.*, pp. 37–42.
14. *Ibid.*, p. 71.
15. *Ibid.*, p. 74.
16. *Ibid.*, p. 77.
17. *Ibid.*, p. 73.
18. Arnold Brecht, *Political Theory: The Foundation of Twentieth Century Political Thought* (Princeton: Princeton University Press, 1959), p. 75.
19. Kant, *Critique of Pure Reason*, p. 125.
20. *Ibid.*, p. 205.
21. *Ibid.*, p. 286.
22. *Ibid.*, p. 376.
23. Immanuel Kant, *Werke*, ed. Ernst Cassirer (Berlin, 1922), 4:133, translated in Nikolaus Lobkowicz, *Theory and Practice: History of a Concept from Aristotle to Marx* (Notre Dame, Ind.: University of Notre Dame Press, 1967), p. 133.
24. Immanuel Kant, *Kritik der praktischen Vernunft* (Leipzig: Felix Meiner, 1929), pp. 140–141.
25. Lobkowicz, *Theory and Practice*, p. 124.

26. Cited in Sidney Hook, *From Hegel to Marx: Studies in the Intellectual Development of Karl Marx* (New York: Humanities Press, 1950), p. 78.

27. Karl Marx, "Kant and Political Liberalism," translated in Hook, *From Hegel to Marx*, pp. 309–310.

28. *Ibid.*, p. 310.

29. Mao Tse-tung, "Chairman Mao's Conversation with Comrades Ch'en Po-ta and K'ang Sheng" (1965), in JPRS, 90:26. The italics are mine. In a talk before the Central Committee Cultural Revolutionary Group on January 9, 1967, Mao also said: "When we began making revolution, we did not come into contact with opportunism or Marxism–Leninism; when we were young, we never read the 'Communist Party Manifesto.'" Mao Tse-tung, "Talk before the Central Committee Cultural Revolutionary Group" (January 9, 1967), in JPRS, 90:39.

CHAPTER THIRTEEN

1. Otto Liebman, *Kant und die Epigonen: Eine kritische Abhandlung* (Stuttgart: Carl Schober, 1865), pp. 75–84.

2. Johann Gottlieb Fichte, "Letter to Jacobi" (August 30, 1795), in *The Popular Works of Johann Gottlieb Fichte*, trans. William Smith (London: Trubner, 1889), 1:66; also see the explanation in the memoir on pp. 63–64.

3. F. H. Bradley, *The Principles of Logic* (London: Kegan Paul, Trench, 1933), pp. 379–380.

4. Johann Gottlieb Fichte, "The Vocation of Man," in *The Popular Works of Johann Gottlieb Fichte*, 1:447.

5. G. W. F. Hegel, *The Phenomenology of Mind*, trans. J. B. Baillie (London: George Allen and Unwin, 1966), p. 794.

6. G. W. F. Hegel, *The Logic of Hegel*, trans. William Wallace (Oxford: Clarendon Press, 1874), p. 124.

7. *Ibid.*, p. 126.

8. *Ibid.*

9. *Ibid.*, p. 241.

10. *Ibid.*, p. 245.

11. Hegel, *The Phenomenology of Mind*, p. 558.

12. G. W. F. Hegel, *Science of Logic*, trans. W. H. Johnston and L. G. Struthers (London: George Allen and Unwin, 1929), 1:66.

13. W. A. Shenstone, *Justus von Liebig, His Life and Work (1803–1873)* (London: Cassell, 1901), pp. 31–34, 64–79; A. W. Hofmann, *The Life Work of Liebig in Experimental and Philosophic Chemistry; with Allusion to his Influence on the Development of the Collateral Sciences and the Useful Arts* (London: Macmillan, 1876), pp. 24–26, 71–79.

15. Theodor Schwann, *Microscopical Researches into the Accordance in the Structure and Growth of Animals and Plants*, trans. Henry Smith (London: Sydenham Society, 1847), pp. 36–40; Rembert Watermann, *Theodor Schwann: Leben und Werk* (Düsseldorf: L. Schwann, 1960), pp. 71–93, 157–162; Marcel Florkin, *Theodor Schwann et les débuts de la médecine scientifique* (Paris: University of Paris, 1956), pp. 13, 17–19.

16. Leon Königsberger, *Hermann von Helmholtz*, trans. Frances A. Welby (Oxford: Clarendon Press, 1906), pp. 38–50.

17. Frederick Albert Lange, *The History of Materialism*, trans. Ernest Chester Thomas (London: Kegan Paul, Trench, Trubner, 1925), 2:235–294, 3:111–161.

18. George Henry Lewes, *Problems of Life and Mind* (London: Trubner, 1874), 2:385.

19. *Ibid.*, 2:412.

20. *Ibid.,* 1:41.
21. *Ibid.,* 1:60.
22. *Ibid.,* 1:67.
23. Königsberger, *Hermann von Helmholtz,* p. 142.
24. E. E. Thomas, *Lotze's Theory of Reality* (London: Longman's, Green, 1921).
25. Cited in Königsberger, *Hermann von Helmholtz,* p. 236.
26. My understanding of Rickert and Windelband is based on Maurice Picard's excellent analysis of their thought in *Values Immediate and Contributory and Their Interrelation* (New York: New York University Press, 1920); and the resume given in Arnold Brecht, *Political Theory: The Foundation of Twentieth Century Political Thought* (Princeton: Princeton University Press, 1959), pp. 207–255.
27. For examples of the shift toward the science of culture in other Neo-Kantians, see Trude Weiss Rosmarin, *Religion of Reason: Hermann Cohen's System of Religious Philosophy* (New York: Block, 1936), p. 19; Paul Natorp, *Hermann Cohen als Mensch, Lehrer und Forscher* (Marburg: Braun, 1918), pp. 27–30; Paul Natorp, *Philosophie, ihr Problem und ihre Probleme* (Göttingen: Bandenhoed & Ruprecht, 1929), pp. 95–127; Paul Natorp, *Sozial-Idealismus, Neue richtlinien sozialer Erziehung* (Berlin: Julius Springer, 1920); Carl Siegel and Alois Riehl, *Ein Beitrag zur Geschichte des Neukantianismus* (Graz: Universität Graz, 1932), pp. 132–142.
28. Weber's article is cited in part in Brecht, *Political Theory,* p. 225. Brecht also explains Simmel's argument.
29. Marcel Foucault, *L'Illusion paradoxale et le seuil de Weber* (Montpellier: Coulet et fils, 1910), pp. 7–8.
30. Gustav Fechner, *Elements of Psychophysics,* trans. Helmut Adler (New York: Holt, Rinehart and Winston, 1966), 1:7.
31. Friedrich Paulsen, *An Autobiography,* trans. Theodor Lorenz (New York: Columbia University Press, 1938), pp. 351–352.
32. *Ibid.,* p. 232.
33. *Ibid.,* p. 351.
34. Friedrich Paulsen, *A System of Ethics,* trans. Frank Thilly (New York: Scribner's, 1908), pp. 6–7.

CHAPTER FOURTEEN

1. See especially Jerome Ch'en, *Mao and the Chinese Revolution* (London: Oxford University Press, 1965), pp. 44, 48.
2. Friedrich Paulsen, *A System of Ethics,* trans. Theodor Lorenz (New York: Scribner's, 1908), p. 11.
3. Cited in Stuart R. Schram, *The Political Thought of Mao Tse-tung* (New York: Praeger, 1963), p. 13.
4. Wang Fu-chih, *Ssu-wen lu* [A Record of Speculations], in *Ch'uan-shan i-shu* [The Bequeathed Writings of (Wang) Ch'uan-shan] (Shanghai: T'ai-p'ing yang shu-tien, 1933), *ts'e* 63, *nei-pien,* 2.
5. LJMTT, p. 42.
6. *Ibid.*
7. Paulsen, *System of Ethics,* p. 522.
8. *Ibid.,* p. 523, citing Lord Avebury (Sir John Lubbock), *Ants, Bees, and Wasps: A Record of Observations on the Habits of the Social Hymenoptera* (New York: Appleton, 1901), pp. 82–89.
9. Paulsen, *System of Ethics,* p. 525.

10. Wang Fu-chih, *Huang shu* [Yellow Book], in *Chung-hua min-kuo k'ai-kuo wu-shih nien wen-hsien* [Documents Commemorating the Fiftieth Anniversary of the Founding of the Republic of China], compiled by Tao Hsi-sheng, et al., vol. 1, no. 2, *Ko-ming yuan-yuan* [The Early Sources of the Revolution], p. 174.

11. Mao's note is cited in Ch'en, *Mao and the Chinese Revolution*, p. 44.

12. Mao Ze-dong, *Une Étude de l'éducation physique*, trans. Stuart R. Schram (Paris, La Haye: Mouton, 1962), p. 49.

13. Translated in Schram, *Political Thought*, p. 27.

14. Paulsen, *System of Ethics*, p. 9.

15. *Ibid.*

16. *Ibid.*, p. 15.

17. Cited in Ch'en, *Mao and the Chinese Revolution*, pp. 44–45.

18. *Ibid.*

19. *Ibid.*

20. These are also Mao's annotations to Paulsen, translated in Schram, *Political Thought*, p. 26.

21. Cited in LJMTT, p. 43.

22. *Ibid.*

23. *Ibid.*

24. JCMP, p. 47.

25. Mao Tse-tung, "On the Correct Handling of Contradictions among the People" (February 27, 1957), in SRMTT, p. 369.

26. MA, p. 138.

27. Howard L. Boorman, *Biographical Dictionary of Republican China* (New York: Columbia University Press, 1970), 1:338–344.

28. Chiang K'ang-hu (*nom de plume*, Hsü An-ch'eng), "Wu chia-t'ing chu-i" [Nonfamilism], in *Hsin shih-chi* [*Siècle nouveau*], 93:11–13.

29. Chiang K'ang-hu, "Tzu-yu ying-yeh kuan-chien" [My Humble Opinion of Free Enterprise], in *Hsin shih-chi*, 97:9–10.

30. Chiang K'ang-hu, "Wu chia-t'ing chu-i i-chien shu" [Writing on the idea of Nonfamilism] in Chinag K'ang-hu, *Hung-shui chi* [The Flood] (1913), p. 3a. I have used Chiang's personal copy, which is part of the collection of volumes he contributed to the East Asian Library of the University of California at Berkeley.

31. Chiang K'ang-hu, "She-hui chu-i yü nü-hsueh chih kuan-hsi" [Socialism and Its Relation to Female Education] (1911), in *Hung-shui chi*, p. 15a.

32. *Ibid.*, p. 16a.

33. Chiang K'ang-hu, "Hsi-yin kung-hui yen-shuo tz'u" [Text of Address at the Women's Progressive Society] (September 2, 1911), in *Hung-shui chi*, pp. 20b–22a.

34. Chiang K'ang-hu, "She-hui hsing fa-k'an t'zu" [Text of the Publication of the *Socialist Star*], in *Hung-shui chi*, p. 22a.

35. MA, p. 151.

36. Ch'en, *Mao and the Chinese Revolution*, p. 54.

37. Mao Tse-tung, "The Great Union of the Popular Masses" (July 21–August 4, 1919), trans. Stuart R. Schram, in *China Quarterly*, 49:76–87; also see Stuart R. Schram, "From the 'Great Union of the Popular Masses' to the 'Great Alliance,'" in *China Quarterly*, 49:88–105. The *Review* was published from July 14 to August 11, 1919, in five issues. One section of the second issue was discovered in a scrap paper mill in Ch'ang-sha. Later, a complete run of four issues was discovered in the Peking University library. See Fang Hui, "Chi hsin fa-hsien ti *Hsiang-chiang p'ing-lun*" [Noting the Newly Discovered *Hsiang River Review*], in *Li-shih yen-chiu* [Historical Research], 2:30 (1954).

38. Mao Tse-tung, "Great Union of the Popular Masses," p. 77.

39. MA, p. 155.

40. MA, pp. 155–156.

41. Ma-k'o-ssu (Marx), En-ko-ssu (Engels), *Kung-ch'an-tang hsuan-yen* [The Communist Manifesto] (Shanghai: Chieh-fang she, 1949), p. 17.

42. Karl Kautsky, *The Class Struggle (Erfurt Program)*, trans. William E. Bohn (Chicago: Charles H. Kerr, 1910), p. 15.

43. *Ibid.,* p. 28.

44. *Ibid.,* p. 38.

45. *Ibid.,* p. 40.

46. *Ibid.,* pp. 90–91.

47. *Ibid.,* pp. 140–141.

48. *Ibid.,* p. 119.

49. *Ibid.,* p. 120.

50. *Ibid.,* p. 120.

51. *Ibid.,* pp. 121–122.

52. *Ibid.,* p. 123.

53. Thomas Kirkup, *A History of Socialism* (London: Adam and Charles Black, 1913), p. 405.

54. *Ibid.*

55. *Ibid.,* p. 56.

56. See, for example, *ibid.,* p. 161 ff.

57. *Ibid.,* p. 23.

58. *Ibid.,* p. 414.

59. *Ibid.,* p. 415.

60. *Ibid.,* p. 419.

61. *Ibid.,* p. 422.

62. *Ibid.,* p. 148.

63. *Ibid.,* p. 159.

64. *Ibid.,* p. 56.

65. *Ibid.,* p. 268.

66. *Ibid.,* p. 65.

67. *Ibid.,* p. 426.

CHAPTER FIFTEEN

1. Mao Tse-tung, "Chairman Mao's Talk at the Reception for the Pakistan Liberation Organization Delegation" (March 1965), in JPRS, 90:2.

2. Mao Tse-tung, "Talk at the Hangchow Conference" (December 21, 1965), in JPRS, 90:2.

3. *Ibid.,* 90:3.

4. Mao Tse-tung, "Speech at the Ch'eng-tu Conference" (March 22, 1958), in JPRS, 90:48.

5. *Ibid.,* 90:49.

6. Mao Tse-tung, "Instructions Given at the Spring Festival Concerning Educational Work" (February 13, 1964), in CB, 891:42.

7. Mao Tse-tung, "Part-time Work and Part-time Study" (February 1958), in JCMP, p. 83; also see CB, 891:29; and *Issues and Studies,* 6.4:79.

8. Mao Tse-tung, "On Education—Conversation with the Nepalese Delegation of Educationists" (1964), in JCMP, pp. 22–23; also see CB, 891:46.

9. *Ibid.,* p. 22.

10. I am here simply summarizing Stuart Schram's introduction to *The Political Thought of Mao Tse-tung* (New York: Praeger, 1963).

11. *Ibid.*

12. The following information on Marxist debates during the period from 1936 to 1940 is largely drawn from O. Brière, "L'effort de la philosophie Marxiste en Chine," *Bulletin de l'Université de l'Aurore* (Shanghai), Série 3, 8.3:309–347.

13. Translated in René Ahlberg, "The Forgotten Philosopher: Abram Deborin," in *Revisionism: Essays on the History of Marxist Ideas*, ed. Leopold Labedz (New York: Praeger, 1962), p. 134.

14. Frederick Engels, *Dialectics of Nature* (New York: International Publishers, 1963), pp. 183–184.

15. Translated in Ahlberg, "The Forgotten Philosopher," p. 137.

16. *Ibid.*, pp. 140–141.

17. Howard L. Boorman, *Biographical Dictionary of Republican China* (New York: Columbia University Press, 1971), 2:216–219.

18. The above debate is summarized in Brière, "L'effort."

19. Mao Tse-tung, "Dialectical Materialism" (1938–1940?), trans. in Schram, *Political Thought*, p. 124.

20. Mao Tse-tung, "Talk at the Hangchow Conference" (December 21, 1965), in JPRS, 90:2.

21. Sakata Shiyouchi, "Kuan-yü hsin chi-pen li-tzu kuan ti tui-hua" [A Dialogue Concerning New Views of Elementary Particles], in *Hung-ch'i* [Red Flag], June 25, 1965.

22. Mao Tse-tung, "Summaries of the Second and Third Talks with Comrade Mao Yuan-hsin" (February 18, 1966), in JPRS, 90:29; also see Mao Tse-tung, "Chairman Mao's Conversation with Comrades Ch'en Po-ta and K'ang Sheng" (1965), in JPRS, 90:28. Mao had read an article by Sakata on elementary particles which appeared in *Tzu-jan pien-cheng-fa t'ung-hsun* [Natural Dialectics Communication].

23. Mao Tse-tung, "Reform in Learning," in *Mao's China: Party Reform Documents, 1942–1944,* ed. Boyd Compton (Seattle: University of Washington Press, 1952), p. 24.

24. I have used the edition of "On Practice" which is published in *Shih-chien lun hsueh-hsi wen-hsuan* [A Selection of Writings on the Study and Practice of "On Practice"] (Hankow: Chiang-nan jen-min ch'u-pan she, 1951), pp. 1–14. I have checked it against the version given in translation in the *Selected Works* (New York: International Publishers, 1954), 1:282–297. Because the essay is so well known, I have not bothered to give page references for any of the running quotes from it which follow. The English translations given here are in most cases *verbatim* from the International Publishers' edition.

25. Mao Tse-tung, "Where Do Correct Ideas Come From?" (May 1963), in SRMTT, pp. 405–406.

26. Vsevolod Holubnychy, "Mao Tse-tung's Materialistic Dialectics," *China Quarterly*, 19:7–9.

27. There is a summary of Lenin's position in Arthur A. Cohen, *The Communism of Mao Tse-tung* (Chicago: University of Chicago Press, 1964), pp. 9–10.

28. Translated in Schram, *Political Thought*, pp. 122–123.

29. Mao Tse-tung, "Hsin min-chu chu-i lun" [On New Democracy] (January 1940), in *Mao Tse-tung hsuan-chi* [Selected Works of Mao Tse-tung] (Peking, 1953), 2:657. Marx's words are from the preface to *A Contribution to the Critique of Political Economy*, in *Selected Works of Marx and Engels* (Moscow: Foreign Languages Publishing House, 1958), 1:363.

30. Marx to F. A. Sorge (October 19, 1877), in Karl Marx-Frederick Engels, *Selected Correspondence* (Moscow: Foreign Languages Publishing House, n.d.), p. 376.

31. Mao, *Shih-chien lun,* pp. 9–10.

32. *Ibid.,* p. 12.

33. *Ibid.*

34. Engels to J. Bloch (September 22, 1890), in Marx-Engels, *Correspondence,* p. 498.

35. Karl Marx, *The Poverty of Philosophy* (London: Martin Lawrence Ltd., n.d.), p. 93.

36. As described and analyzed by Schram in *Political Thought,* pp. 120–124.

37. Translated in *ibid.,* pp. 123–124.

38. Mao Tse-tung, "Our Strategy," in CLG, 2.1:6. This is a statement which was said to have been made by Mao in September of 1967. As it was reprinted in *I-chiu-liu-pa fei-ch'ing nien-pao* [1968 Yearbook on (Chinese Communist) Bandit Affairs] by the Institute for the Study of Chinese Communist Problems in Taipei, there has been some question of its authenticity. I have found no inconsistencies between the document and other recently acquired material from the Cultural Revolution period, and therefore agree with the editors of CLG as to its probable authenticity.

39. Mao Tse-tung, "Our Strategy," p. 10 (italics mine).

40. Mao Tse-tung, "Sixty Work Methods (Draft): The General Office of the Central Committee of the Communist Party of China" (February 19, 1958), CB, 892:6.

41. Marx to F. Lassalle (January 16, 1861), in Marx–Engels, *Correspondence,* p. 151.

42. Engels to P. L. Lavroy (November 12–17, 1875), in Marx-Engels, *Correspondence,* p. 267.

43. Mao Tse-tung, "Dialectical Materialism," translated in Schram, *Political Thought,* p. 124.

44. Holubnychy, "Materialistic Dialectics," p. 27.

CHAPTER SIXTEEN

1. Wang Yang-ming, *Instructions for Practical Living and Other Neo-Confucian Writings,* trans. Wing-tsit Chan (New York: Columbia University Press, 1963), p. 118.

2. *Ibid.*

3. *Ibid.,* p. 119.

4. *Ibid.*

5. *Ibid.,* p. 121.

6. *Ibid.,* pp. 122–123.

7. *Ibid.,* p. 124.

8. The following account of Wang Yang-ming's life is mainly drawn from Wing-tsit Chan's introduction to Wang, *Instructions,* pp. ix–xli; Carsun Chang, *Wang Yang-ming: Idealist Philosopher of Sixteenth-Century China* (Jamaica, New York: St. John's University Press, 1962), pp. 1–11; and Wang Tch'ang-tche, S.J., *La Philosophie morale de Wang Yang-ming* (Shanghai: T'ou-se-wei, 1936), pp. 2–37. An excellent study of Wang's life and thought is now being prepared for publication by Tu Wei-ming.

9. Wang Shou-jen (Yang-ming), *Wang Wen-ch'eng kung ch'üan-shu* [The Complete Works of Wang, Duke Wen-ch'eng] (Shanghai: Commercial Press, 1934), II.12:37.

10. *Ta hsueh* [The Great Learning], "Text of Confucius, 4," translated in James Legge, *The Four Books* (Taipei: Wen-hua shu-chü, 1960, pp. 4–6.

11. Chu Hsi, *Ssu-shu chi-chu* [Collected Glosses on *The Four Books*] (Taipei: I-wen, 1959), p. 5.

12. *Ta hsueh*, "Commentary of the Philosopher Tseng, 5," translated in Legge, *The Four Books*, pp. 16–17.

13. Lu Hsiang-shan, "Conversations," 35:287–8, translated in Huang Siu-chi, *Lu Hsiang-shan, a Twelfth Century Chinese Idealist Philosopher* (New Haven, Conn.: American Oriental Society, 1944), p. 31. I have altered the translation slightly.

14. Lu Hsiang-shan, "Letter to Chao Jan-tao," translated in Huang, *Lu Hsiang-shan*, p. 33. I have altered the translation slightly.

15. Wm. Theodore de Bary, "Introduction," in *Self and Society in Ming Thought*, ed. Wm. Theodore de Bary (New York: Columbia University Press, 1970), p. 20.

16. Wang Yang-ming, "Inquiry on *The Great Learning*," in Wang, *Instructions*, p. 275.

17. Wang, *Wang Wen-ch'eng kung ch'üan-shu*, II.12:32.

18. Wang Yang-ming, "Conversations recorded by Huang I-fang," in Wang, *Instructions*, p. 249.

19. Wang Yang-ming, "Letter in Reply to Ku Tung-ch'iao," in Wang, *Instructions*, p. 94.

20. Wang Yang-ming, "Letter in Reply to Vice-Minister Lo Cheng-an," in Wang, *Instructions*, p. 159.

21. Wang, *Instructions*, p. 86.

22. *Ibid.*, p. 15.

23. Wang, *Wang Wen-ch'eng kung ch'üan-shu*, I.4:37.

24. Wang, *Instructions*, p. 159.

25. Wang, *Wang Wen-ch'eng kung ch'üan-shu*, I.2:25–26.

26. Wang Yang-ming, "Inquiry on *The Great Learning*," in Wang, *Instructions*, p. 274.

27. Chu Hsi, *Ssu-shu chi-chu*, p. 1.

28. Wang Tch'ang-tche, *La Philosophie morale de Wang Yang-ming*, p. 78.

29. Wang Yang-ming, "Letter in Reply to Ku Tung-ch'iao," in Wang, *Instructions*, p. 104.

30. *Ibid.*

31. *Liang-chih* is frequently translated either as "innate knowledge" or "intuitive knowledge." I am here using T'ang Chün-i's phrase. Etymologically, *liang* means innate or original, as well as good. *Chih* means both knowledge and knowing. See T'ang Chün-i, "The Development of the Concept of Moral Mind from Wang Yang-ming to Wang Chi," in de Bary, *Self and Society*, p. 101.

32. Wang, *Wang Wen-ch'eng kung ch'üan-shu*, II.12:84.

33. Mencius, VII.1:15, translated in Legge, *The Four Books*, p. 943.

34. Wang Yang-ming, "Inquiry on *The Great Learning*," in Wang, *Instructions*, p. 278. The citations from *Mencius* can be found in II.1:6 and VI.1:6.

35. Wang, *Wang Wen-ch'eng kung ch'üan-shu*, I.3:42.

36. *Ibid.*, I.2:66.

37. *Ibid.*, I.3:4.

38. Wang Yang-ming, "Inquiry," p. 279.

39. Wang Tch'ang-tche, *La Philosophie morale de Wang Yang-ming*, p. 59.

40. T'ang Chün-i, "Moral Mind," p. 101.

41. Karl Jaspers, *Reason and Existenz: Five Lectures*, trans. William Earle (New York: Noonday, 1955), p. 63.

42. Wang, *Wang Wen-ch'eng kung ch'üan-shu*, I.3:80.

43. *Ibid.*, I.2:59.

44. *Ibid.*, I.3:24.
45. Wang Yang-ming, "Letter in Reply to Ku Tung-ch'iao," in Wang, *Instructions*, p. 99.
46. Wang Yang-ming, "Letter to Chou Tao-t'ung," in Wang, *Instructions*, p. 128. The quotation is from *Mencius*, II.1:2.
47. Wang, *Instructions*, p. 10.

CHAPTER SEVENTEEN

1. Li Hsin-chuang, *Ch'ung-pien Ming-ju hsueh-an* [Recompilation of the *Ming-ju hsueh-an* (of Huang Tsung-hsi)] (Taipei: Cheng-cheng shu-chü, 1955), 1:90.
2. *Ibid.*
3. *Ibid.*, 1:91.
4. *Ibid.*
5. *Ibid.*
6. *Ibid.*
7. *Ibid.*
8. *Ibid.*, 1:111.
9. Wang Shou-jen (Yang-ming), *Wang Wen-ch'eng kung ch'üan-shu* [The Complete Works of Wang, Duke Wen-ch'eng] (Shanghai: Commercial Press, 1934), II.12:21.
10. Ch'ien Te-hung, "The Doctrine in Four Axioms," in Wang Yang-ming, *Instructions for Practical Living and Other Writings*, trans. Wing-tsit Chan (New York: Columbia University Press, 1963), p. 244.
11. Cited in Wang Tch'ang-tche, S.J., *La Philosophie morale de Wang Yang-ming* (Shanghai: T'ou-se-wei, 1936), pp. 165–166.
12. Li Hsin-chuang, *Ch'ung-pien Ming-ju hsueh-an*, 1:107.
13. *Ibid.*, 1:103.
14. *Ibid.*, 1:104.
15. *Ibid.*, 1:145.
16. *Ibid.*
17. *Ibid.*
18. *Ibid.*, 1:162.
19. *Ibid.*, 1:162. Lo Hung-hsien's misgivings are detailed in Wang Tch'ang-tche, *La Philosophie morale de Wang Yang-ming*, pp. 148–153.
20. Translated in Takehiko Okada, "Wang Chi and the Rise of Existentialism," in *Self and Society in Ming Thought*, ed. Wm. Theodore de Bary (New York: Columbia University Press, 1970), p. 128.
21. *Ibid.*
22. Chou Tun-i, *T'ai-chi t'u shuo* [Explaining the Diagram of the Great Ultimate], in Chou Tun-i, *Chou Lien-hsi chi* [The Collected Writings of Chou Lien-hsi] (Shanghai: Commercial Press, 1936), 1:2; also see Wing-tsit Chan's translation in *A Source Book in Chinese Philosophy* (Princeton: Princeton University Press, 1963), p. 463.
23. Chou Tun-i, *T'ung shu* [Penetrating the Book (of Changes)], in Chou, *Chou Lien-hsi chi*, 2:87; also see Wing-tsit Chan's translation in *A Source Book*, p. 467.
24. Wang Fu-chih, annotator, *Chang-tzu Cheng-meng chu* [An Annotation of Master Chang's *Correcting Youthful Ignorance*] (Peking: Ku-chi, ch'u-pan she, 1956), pp. 3–4; also see Wing-tsit Chan's translation in *A Source Book*, p. 501.
25. Okada, "Wang Chi," p. 136.
26. *Ibid.* Another case for the existentialist cast of the Wang Yang-ming school

has been made by Hwa Yol Jung in "Wang Yang-ming and Existential Phenomenology," *International Philosophical Quarterly,* 5.4: 612–636.

27. Ch'eng Hao, *Ming-tao wen-chi* [Writings of (Ch'eng) Ming-tao], in *Ho-nan erh Ch'eng ch'üan-shu* [Complete Writings of the Two Ch'eng's of Honan] (Fryer Collection), 3.3:1b.

28. E. A. Burtt, *The Metaphysical Foundations of Modern Science* (Garden City, N.Y.: Doubleday Anchor, 1954), pp. 238–239.

29. Morohashi Tetsuji, *Dai Kan-wa jiten* [The Great Chinese-Japanese Dictionary] (Tokyo: Taishūkan shoten, 1957–1960), vol. 11, entry 10243. Donald J. Munro has analyzed the roots of *te* [virtue] in *The Concept of Man in Early China* (Stanford: Stanford University Press, 1969), pp. 185–197.

30. Wang, *Instructions,* p. 99.

31. Okada, "Wang Chi," p. 139.

32. Cited in Heinrich Busch, "The Tung-lin Academy and Its Political and Philosophical Significance," *Monumenta Serica,* 14:108.

33. Sidney Hook, *From Hegel to Marx: Studies in the Intellectual Development of Karl Marx* (New York: Humanities Press, 1950), pp. 274–283.

34. Karl Marx, "Theses on Feuerbach," in *The German Ideology,* pts. I and III, ed. R. Pascal (New York: International Publishers, 1947), p. 197.

35. Karl Marx, "Theses on Feuerbach," p. 197.

36. Hook, *From Hegel to Marx,* pp. 284–285.

CHAPTER EIGHTEEN

1. Yang Ch'ang, *Hsi-yang lun-li chu-i shu-p'ing* [A Critique of Western Ethical Theories] (Shanghai: Commercial Press, 1923).

2. *Ibid.,* pp. 27–28.

3. *Ibid.,* p. 33.

4. F. H. Bradley, *The Principles of Logic* (London: Kegan, Paul, Trench, 1933), p. vi.

5. Crane Brinton, *English Political Thought in the Nineteenth Century* (New York: Harper Torchbooks, 1962), p. 226. The brief summary of Green's political thought in the following paragraph is paraphrased from Brinton.

6. Herbert Marcuse, *Reason and Revolution: Hegel and the Rise of Social Theory* (New York: Humanities Press, 1954), p. 66.

7. Bradley, *Logic,* p. 10.

8. *Ibid.,* pp. 10–11.

9. *Ibid.,* p. 31.

10. *Ibid.,* p. 35.

11. *Ibid.,* p. 431.

12. *Ibid.,* p. 329.

13. *Ibid.,* p. 533.

14. *Ibid.,* p. 450.

15. *Ibid.,* p. 451.

16. F. H. Bradley, *Appearance and Reality: A Metaphysical Essay* (Oxford: Clarendon Press, 1930), p. 321.

17. *Ibid.,* p. 322.

18. *Ibid.,* p. 323.

19. B. Bosanquet, *The Principle of Individuality and Value* (London: Macmillan, 1927), pp. 44–46.

20. *Ibid.,* p. 37.

21. *Ibid.,* pp. 9–20.

22. *Ibid.,* p. 3.

23. *Ibid.,* p. 21.

24. *Ibid.*, p. 26.

25. *Ibid.*, p. 363.

26. *Ibid.*, p. 326.

27. *Ibid.*, p. 368.

28. See O. Brière, *Fifty Years of Chinese Philosophy* (New York: Praeger, 1965), pp. 53–56.

29. Cited in Harman Grisewood, ed., *Ideas and Beliefs of the Victorians: An Historic Revaluation of the Victorian Age* (New York: E. P. Dutton, 1966), pp. 178–179.

30. Ts'ai Yuan-p'ei, *Ts'ai Yuan-p'ei hsien-sheng ch'üan-chi* [The Complete Works of Mr. Ts'ai Yuan-p'ei], ed. Sun Ch'ang-wei (Taipei: Commercial Press, 1968), p. 140.

31. T. H. Green, *Prolegomena to Ethics* (Oxford: Clarendon Press, 1906), pp. 13–14, 47.

32. *Ibid.*, pp. 21–22.

33. *Ibid.*, p. 33.

34. *Ibid.*, pp. 37, 57–58.

35. *Ibid.*, pp. 76–78, 97–100.

36. *Ibid.*, pp. 172–173.

37. *Ibid.*, p. 173.

38. *Ibid.*, p. 216–217.

39. *Ibid.*, p. 229.

40. T. H. Green, *Lectures on the Principles of Political Obligation* (London: Longman's, 1941), p. xi.

41. *Ibid.*, pp. 10–11.

42. *Ibid.*, p. 5.

43. G. W. F. Hegel, *The Logic of Hegel*, trans. William Wallace (Oxford: Clarendon Press, 1874), p. 131.

44. Green, *Principles*, pp. 13–14.

45. *Ibid.*, p. 26.

46. *Ibid.*, p. 32.

47. *Ibid.*, p. 2.

48. *Ibid.*, pp. 143–144. His criticism of Rousseau can be found on pp. 80–92.

49. *Ibid.*, p. 244.

50. *Ibid.*, p. 6.

51. *Ibid.*, p. 245.

52. Yang, *Hsi-yang*, p. 34.

53. Engels to J. Bloch (September 22, 1890), in Karl Marx–Frederick Engels, *Selected Correspondence* (Moscow: Foreign Languages Publishing House, n.d.), p. 499.

54. Marx to P. V. Annenkov (December 28, 1846), in Marx–Engels, *Correspondence*, p. 42.

55. Cited in Sidney Hook, *From Hegel to Marx: Studies in the Intellectual Development of Karl Marx* (New York: Humanities Press, 1950), pp. 56–57.

CHAPTER NINETEEN

1. Mao Tse-tung, *Mao-tun lun* [On Contradiction], in *Mao Tse-tung hsuan-chi* [Selected Works of Mao Tse-tung] (Peking: Jen-min ch'u-pan she, 1969), 1:281. Although I occasionally change the translation, the English version cited in this chapter usually comes from Mao Tse-tung, *On Contradiction* (Peking: Foreign Languages Press, 1965). Hereafter, footnotes to *Mao-tun lun* will give the Chinese pagination first, followed by the English language one in parentheses.

2. Mao Tse-tung, "Comments on a Letter by Li Chung-yun" (July 26, 1959), in CLG, 1.4:51.

3. Mao Tse-tung, "Speech at the Eleventh Plenary Session of the Eighth CCP Central Committee" (August 1966), in JPRS, 90:8.

4. Mao Tse-tung, "Left, Center, Right" (April 27, 1968), in JCMP, p. 153. This is from a *Hung-ch'i* and JMJP commentary of April 27, 1968: "Class Analysis Should Be Made with Regard to Factionalism."

5. Quoted by Yao Wen-yuan ("The Working Class Must Exercise Leadership in Everything," in PR 39:9), who is cited by Gordon Bennett in "China's Continuing Revolution: Will It Be Permanent?" *Asian Survey*, 10.1:10.

6. Mao Tse-tung, "Chairman Mao's Important Instructions," in CLG, 1.4:23.

7. Mao Tse-tung, *Mao-tun lun*, p. 277 (4). Mao later said, "Dialectics can be made monistic, never pluralistic." See Mao Tse-tung, "Contradictions" (July 30, 1966), in JCMP, p. 115.

8. Mao, *Mao-tun lun*, p. 307 (45).

9. Vsevolod Holubnychy, "Mao Tse-tung's Materialistic Dialectics," *China Quarterly*, 19:31–34.

10. Mao, *Mao-tun lun*, p. 297 (33).

11. *Ibid.*, p. 304 (41).

12. *Ibid.*, p. 307 (46), 308 (47). According to the notes in *Mao-tun lun*, the aphorism goes back to Pan Ku of the Han dynasty. Lenin's phrase is from "On the Questions of Dialectics," *Collected Works* (Moscow, 1958), 38:358.

13. In Holubnychy, "Materialistic Dialectics," p. 30, he argues that Mao's imbalanced contradictions create motion along a one-way spiral route and therefore represent an advance from Engel's postulate that "motion is itself a contradiction and that spiral route of development is merely a law or an axiom."

14. Mao, *Mao-tun lun*, p. 279 (8).

15. *Ibid.*, p. 308 (47).

16. *Ibid.*, p. 293 (26).

17. *Ibid.*, p. 294 (28).

18. *Ibid.*, p. 282 (11).

19. *Ibid.*, p. 285 (15).

20. *Ibid.*, p. 306 (44).

21. Li Ch'i, *"Mao-tun lun" chien-shuo* [A Simple Explanation of "On Contradiction"] (Peking: Chung-kuo ch'ing-nien ch'u-pan-she, 1956), p. 104.

22. Mao, *Mao-tun lun*, p. 289 (21).

23. *Ibid.*, p. 296 (31).

24. *Ibid.*, pp. 300–301 (36–37); also see Mao's "Comment on the Second Group of Materials on the Hu Feng Anti-Party Clique" (1955), in JCMP, p. 52.

25. Mao, *Mao-tun lun*, p. 286 (16).

26. Mao, "Resolutions of the Eleventh Plenum" (August 1966), in JCMP, pp. 121–122.

27. Mao, *Mao-tun lun*, p. 287 (18).

28. Frederick Engels, *Herr Eugen Dühring's Revolution in Science (Anti-Dühring)*, trans. Emile Burns (New York: International Publishers, 1939), p. 41.

29. Mao, *Mao-tun lun*, p. 309 (38–39).

CHAPTER TWENTY

1. Mao Tse-tung, "Vice Chairman Lin's Instruction," in JPRS, 90:19.

2. Mao Tse-tung, "Speech at a Report Meeting" (October 24, 1966), in JPRS, 90:10.

3. Mao Tse-tung, "Speech at a Central Committee Work Conference" (October 25, 1966), in JPRS, 90:13.

4. Mao, "Speech at a Report Meeting," p. 10.

5. Mao, "Speech at a Central Committee Work Conference," p. 14.

6. Mao Tse-tung, "The Struggle in the Chingkang Mountains" (November 25, 1928), in SW, 1:91.

7. James R. Townsend, *Political Participation in Communist China* (Berkeley: University of California Press, 1969), p. 73.

8. Mao Tse-tung, "Speech to the First Plenary Session of the CCP's Ninth Central Committee" (April 28, 1969), in *Issues and Studies*, 6.2:97.

9. Mao Tse-tung, "Party Rectification" (October 16, 1968), in JCMP, p. 156.

10. Mao Tse-tung, "Circular of the Central Committee of the Chinese Communist Party" (May 16, 1966), in JCMP, p. 107; also see JMJP (May 17, 1967); and PR, 21:7.

11. Liu Lan-t'ao, "The Chinese Communist Party Is the Supreme Commander of the Chinese People in Building Socialism" (September 28, 1959), in John K. Fairbank and Robert R. Bowie, *Communist China: 1955–1959* (Cambridge: Harvard University Press, 1962), p. 572.

12. Mao Tse-tung, "Talk on the Question of Democratic Centralism" (January 30, 1962), in CB, 891:37.

13. *Ibid.*, 891:38.

14. Mao Tse-tung, "Notes on the Report of the Investigation of the Peking Teachers' Training College" (July 3, 1965), in JCMP, p. 102; also see CB, 891:50.

15. Mao Tse-tung, "Talks to Central Committee Leaders" (1966), in JPRS, 90:32.

16. Mao Tse-tung, "Party Rectification" (October 16, 1968), in JCMP, p. 156; also see SSPT, p. 326; and PR, 43:5.

17. Mao Tse-tung, "Emancipation of the Masses" (November 6, 1967); Mao Tse-tung, "Three-way Alliance" (November 6, 1967), in JCMP, p. 149. These are from a JMJP editorial of November 6, 1967: "Advance Along the Road Opened Up by the October Socialist Revolution."

18. Mao Tse-tung, "Speech at a Meeting of the Cultural Revolution Group under the Central Committee" (January 9, 1967), in CB, 892:47; also see JCMP, p. 46.

19. K. H. Fan, *The Chinese Cultural Revolution: Selected Documents* (New York: Grove Press, 1968), p. 138.

20. Mao Tse-tung, "Talk to the Leaders of the Center" (July 21, 1966), in JCMP, pp. 24–26; also see CB, 891:58–59.

21. Mao Tse-tung, "Reform in Learning" (1942), in Boyd Compton, *Mao's China: Party Reform Documents, 1942–1944* (Seattle: University of Washington Press, 1952), p. 23.

22. Mao Tse-tung, *The Historical Experience of the Dictatorship of the Proletariat* (Peking: Foreign Languages Press, 1969), p. 64.

23. Mao Tse-tung, "Speech at a Report Meeting," p. 12; also see Mao Tse-tung, "Talk at the Meeting of the Central Cultural Revolution Team," p. 38; and Mao Tse-tung, "Basic Contradictions of the Cultural Revolution" (September 24, 1966), in JCMP, p. 131; also see PR, 12.39:6.

24. Mao Tse-tung, "Bombard the Bourgeois Headquarters" (August 5, 1966), in PR, 33:5.

25. Mao Tse-tung, "Speech at a Report Meeting," p. 9.

26. Mao Tse-tung, "Speech at a Central Committee Work Conference," pp. 13–14.

27. Dai Siao-ai, cited in Ronald N. Montaperto, "The Origins of 'Generational Politics': Canton, 1966," *Current Scene*, 7.11:9. I am grateful to Gordon Bennett for allowing me to see a prepublication copy of Gordon A. Bennett and Ronald

N. Montaperto, *Red Guard: The Political Biography of Dai Siao-ai* (New York: Doubleday, 1971).

28. Mao Tse-tung, "Resolutions of the Eleventh Plenum" (August 1966), in JCMP, p. 122; also see PR, 33:7.

29. Dai Siao-ai, cited in Montaperto, "Generational Politics," p. 14.

30. Mao Tse-tung, "Talk at the Work Conference of the Center" (August 23, 1966), in JCMP, pp. 35–36; also see CB, 891:68.

31. Mao Tse-tung, "Anarchy" (March 1, 1968), in JCMP, p. 152.

32. Mao Tse-tung, "Resolutions of the Eleventh Plenum," pp. 123–124.

33. Karl Marx, *The Civil War in France,* in Karl Marx–Frederick Engels, *Selected Works* (Moscow, 1951), 2:521.

34. Engels to August Bebel (London, March 18–28, 1875), in Karl Marx, *Critique of the Gotha Programme* (New York: International Publishers, 1938), p. 31.

35. Nikolai Lenin, *The State in Revolution* (1916), appendix to Marx, *Gotha,* pp. 68–69.

36. Lenin, cited in Marx, *Gotha,* p. 49.

37. The editorial is quoted in John Bryan Starr, "Revolution in Retrospect: The Paris Commune through Chinese Eyes" (Paper delivered at the Conference on the Paris Commune, Kingston, Canada, October 1971), p. 16; also see Nakajima Mineo, "The Great Cultural Revolution and Mao's Conception of Commune," (Paper delivered at the Conference on Ideology and Politics in Contemporary China, Santa Fe, N.M., August 1971), pp. 18–25.

38. Starr, "Revolution in Retrospect"; also see Mao Tse-tung, "Chairman Mao's Speech at His Third Meeting with Chang Ch'un-ch'iao and Yao Wen-yuan" (February 6, 1967), in JPRS, 90:44.

39. Mao Tse-tung, "On Ten Major Relationships" (April 1956), in CB, 891:28.

40. This localism is demonstrated both in Ezra Vogel, *Canton under Communism: Programs and Politics in a Provincial Capital, 1949–1968* (Cambridge: Harvard University Press, 1969), and in Lynn White, III, "Shanghai's Polity in Cultural Revolution," (Hong Kong: University of Hong Kong, Center of Asian Studies, n.d.).

41. Mao Tse-tung, "Chairman Mao's Speech at His Third Meeting with Chang Ch'un-ch'iao and Yao Wen-yuan," p. 44.

42. Starr, "Revolution in Retrospect," p. 7.

43. "Long Live the Victory of the Dictatorship of the Proletariat" (joint editorial in JMJP, *Hung-ch'i* and *Liberation Army Daily,* March 17, 1971), *China Quarterly,* 46: 401–405.

44. *Ibid.*

45. Mao Tse-tung, "From Unity to Unity" (September 17, 1967), in JCMP, p. 146.

46. Mao Tse-tung, "The May Seventh Instruction" (May 7, 1966), in JCMP, pp. 103–104; also see CB, 891:56–57; and *Issues and Studies,* 6.4:86.

47. Philip Bridgham, "Mao's 'Cultural Revolution': Origin and Development, Part I," in Richard Baum and Louise Bennett, eds., *China in Ferment* (Englewood Cliffs, N.J.: Prentice-Hall, 1971), pp. 17–18.

48. The Proletarian Revolutionaries in the Offices of the Headquarters of the General Staff of the Chinese People's Liberation Army, "Basic Differences between the Proletarian and Bourgois Military Lines" (1967), PR, 10:48.

49. Mao Tse-tung, "Talk at the Enlarged Meeting of the Military Commission" (January 27, 1967), in JCMP, pp. 47–48; also see CB, 892:49.

50. "The masses, the army, and the cadres are the three pillars on which we rely," wrote Mao Tse-tung in his "Big Character Poster" (April–May, 1967), in

JCMP, p. 138. This statement was entitled "The People's Liberation Army and Schools," as it appeared in JMJP (March 7, 1967), p. 2. The army's role in "reopening schools, readjusting social organization, setting up leadership organizations of the three-way alliance, and carrying out struggle, criticism, and reform," is described in Mao Tse-tung, "People's Liberation Army" (March 8, 1967), in JCMP, p. 136; also see PR, 11.11:5, which quotes it as a directive from Mao dated March 7, 1968.

51. Provincial Chinese radio broadcast, cited in the *New York Times* (November 28, 1971).

52. Mao Tse-tung, "Comment on Comrade Ch'en Cheng-jen's Stay in a Primary Unity" (January 29, 1965), in JPRS, 90:23.

53. Mao Tse-tung, "Good Cadres—a Reaffirmation" (May 13, 1968), in JCMP, p. 154. Chen may have misdated this statement, since it appeared in a *Liberation Army Daily* and JMJP editorial of May 12, 1968, entitled: "Land of the Northeast Blossoms Red—Warmly Hailing the Establishment of the Liaoning Provincial Revolutionary Committee."

54. Mao Tse-tung, "Speech to First Plenary Session of the CCP's Ninth Central Committee," p. 98.

55. "Anniversary of the Founding of the Chinese Communist Party" (joint editorial in JMJP, *Hung-ch'i* and *Liberation Army Daily,* July 1, 1969), in *China Quarterly,* 40:170.

56. *Ibid.,* p. 169.

57. Report on Shanghai No. 17 State Cotton Mill, broadcast by Peking Radio (May 19, 1970), in "Quarterly Chronicle and Documentation," *China Quarterly* 43:173.

58. Mao Tse-tung, "On Ten Major Relationships," p. 29.

59. *Hung ch'i,* as quoted in the *New York Times,* November 6, 1971.

60. "National Day Editorial" (joint editorial in JMJP, *Hung-ch'i* and *Liberation Army Daily,* October 1, 1970), in *China Quarterly,* 45:195–197.

61. Georg Lukacs, *Lenin: A Study on the Unity of His Thought,* trans. Nicholas Jacobs (London: NLB, 1970), p. 36.

62. *Hung-ch'i* (November 17, 1970), in *China Quarterly,* 45:200–202.

63. Antonio Gramsci, *The Modern Prince and Other Writings* (New York: International Publishers, 1957), p. 140.

64. Franz Schurmann, *Ideology and Organization in Communist China* (Berkeley: University of California Press, 1968), pp. 71, 423–424, 522.

65. Gramsci, *Modern Prince,* p. 145.

66. Mao Tse-tung, "On the People's Democratic Dictatorship" (June 30, 1949), in SW, 4:411.

67. Mao, "On Ten Major Relationships," p. 29.

68. Mao Tse-tung, "Talk at the Hangchow Conference" (December 21, 1965), in JPRS, 90:2.

69. Mao Tse-tung, "Speech to the First Plenary Session of the CCP's Ninth Central Committee," p. 95.

70. "The Constitution of the Chinese Communist Party (adopted by the Ninth National Congress of the Communist Party of China on April 14, 1969)," PR, 18:36.

71. Mao Tse-tung, "Chairman Mao's Instructions," in JPRS, 90:21–22. This is undated but obviously comes from the Cultural Revolution period.

72. Mao Tse-tung, "Speech to the First Plenary Session of the CCP's Ninth Central Committee," p. 95.

73. Mao Tse-tung, "Speech at Supreme State Conference" (January 28, 1958), in CLG, 1.4:13.

74. Mao Tse-tung, "Comment on the Document Entitled, 'The Status of Tens of Mess Halls of Tao-chu Brigade, Tan-ling Commune, P'ing-chiang *hsien,* Hunan, which have been Dissolved and then Restored'" (August 5, 1959), in CLG, 1.4:64–65.

75. Mao Tse-tung, "Speech at a Central Committee Work Conference," p. 13.

76. G. W. F. Hegel, *The Logic of Hegel,* trans. William Wallace (Oxford: Clarendon Press, 1874), p. 243.

77. *Chung yung* [Doctrine of the Mean], in *The Four Books,* trans. James Legge (Taipei: Wen-hua shu-chü, 1960), p. 114.

78. Karl Marx, *Documente des Sozialismus,* III:215, translated in Sidney Hook, *From Hegel to Marx: Studies in the Intellectual Development of Karl Marx* (New York: Humanities Press, 1950), p. 53.

79. Chuang-tzu, *The Sayings of Chuang Chou,* trans. James Ware (New York: New American Library, 1963), p. 21. The presence of materialistic dialectics in Lao-tzu and Chuang-tzu was first pointed out by Hsiang Lin-ping's *Chung-kuo che-hsueh shih kang-yao* [Outline History of Chinese Philosophy] written in 1939. In 1940 Sung Wu explicitly urged that Marxist dialectical materialism be combined with Chinese philosophy. See Vselovod Holubnychy, "Mao Tse-tung's Materialistic Dialectics," *China Quarterly,* 19:15–16.

80. Mao Tse-tung, "Chairman Mao's Conversation with Comrades Ch'en Po-ta and K'ang Sheng" (1965), in JPRS, 90:28.

81. Mao Tse-tung, "Speech at the Tenth Plenary Session of the Eighth Central Committee" (September 24, 1962), in CLG, 1.4:87.

82. Mao Tse-tung, "On the People's Democratic Dictatorship" (1949), in SW, 4:422.

83. Mao Tse-tung, "Chingkangshan Revisited" (1965), translated in *Mao,* ed. Jerome Ch'en (Englewood Cliffs, N.J.: Prentice-Hall, 1969), p. 113.

84. Mao Tse-tung, *Mao-tun lun* [On Contradiction], in *Mao Tse-tung hsuan-chi* [Selected Works of Mao Tse-tung] Peking: Jen-min ch'u-pan she, 1969), I:302 (39).

85. I have argued on pp. 318–319 of this book that Ch'en Po-ta and Lin Piao fell from power because they identified themselves too closely with Mao's person. Documents which came to light while I was correcting proofs indicate that both men repeated the errors of their former opponents by once again transforming Mao into a *persona.* The documents, which detail Lin Piao's plot against Mao during the Second Plenary Session of the Ninth Central Committee (August–September, 1970), are summarized in the *New York Times,* December 17, 1972. According to knowledgeable American and Taiwanese sources, these are reasonable facsimiles of the originals. The documents, which argue that Lin Piao attempted to make Mao Tse-tung a mere "leader" of the People's Liberation Army (while Lin himself retained sole "command"), suggest that Mao was being cultified out of real power. This assertion is also substantiated by Mao's letter of July 8, 1966, to Chiang Ch'ing. The letter (published in *Chung-yang jih-pao,* T'ai-pei, November 4, 1972) is now being widely disseminated in China by way of showing that cultification was Lin's—not Mao's—idea. This would correspond with the personal "mass line" which I discuss on p. 319. In the letter, Mao frankly discusses his own fallibility, and adds that he had only agreed to allow the *Quotations* to be disseminated because his "friend," Lin Piao, had been so insistent. "This is the first time in my life that I have agreed with someone else while knowing in my heart that it was wrong," he said; and went on to intimate that such a degree of cutlification was a personal loss of power. If one is promoted to the "top of Mount Liang," then others might eventually call themselves "king."

Index